Love and Marriage in Globalizing China

As China globalizes, the number of marriages between Chinese people and foreigners is increasing. These Chinese–foreign marriages have profound implications for China's cultural identity. This book, based on extensive original research, outlines the different types of Chinese–foreign marriage and divorce, and the changing scale and changing patterns of such marriages and divorces, and examines how such marriages and divorces are portrayed in different kinds of media. It shows how those types of Chinese–foreign marriage where Chinese patriotism and Chinese values are preserved are depicted favourably, whereas other kinds of Chinese–foreign marriage, especially those where Chinese women marry foreign nationals, are disapproved of, male foreign nationals being seen as having a propensity to infidelity, deception, violence and taking advantage of Chinese women. The book contrasts the portrayal of Chinese–foreign marriage with the reality and with the depiction of Chinese–Chinese marriage where many of the same problems apply. Overall, the book sheds much light on changing social processes and on current imaginings of China's place in the world.

Wang Pan is a Postgraduate Researcher at University of Technology Sydney, Australia.

Asian Studies Association of Australia Women in Asia Series

Editor: Lenore Lyons (The University of Sydney)
Editorial Board:
Susan Blackburn (Monash University)
Hyaeweol Choi (The Australian National University)
Michele Ford (The University of Sydney)
Louise Edwards (University of Hong Kong)
Trude Jacobsen (Northern Illinois University)
Vera Mackie (University of Wollongong)
Anne McLaren (The University of Melbourne)
Mina Roces (University of New South Wales)
Dina Siddiqi (The City University of New York)
Andrea Whittaker (The University of Queensland)

Mukkuvar Women
Gender, hegemony and capitalist transformation in a South Indian Fishing Community
by Kalpana Ram 1991

A World of Difference
Islam and gender hierarchy in Turkey
by Julie Marcus 1992

Purity and Communal Boundaries
Women and social change in a Bangladeshi village
by Santi Rozario 1992

Madonnas and Martyrs
Militarism and violence in the Philippines
by Anne-Marie Hilsdon 1995

Masters and Managers
A study of gender relations in urban Java
by Norma Sullivan 1995

Matriliny and Modernity
Sexual politics and social change in rural Malaysia
by Maila Stivens 1995

Intimate Knowledge
Women and their health in north-east Thailand
by Andrea Whittaker 2000

Women in Asia
Tradition, modernity and globalisation
by Louise Edwards and Mina Roces (eds) 2000

Violence against Women in Asian Societies
Gender Inequality and Technologies of Violence
by Lenore Manderson and Linda Rae Bennett (eds) 2003

Women's Employment in Japan
The experience of part-time workers
by Kaye Broadbent 2003

Chinese Women Living and Working
by Anne McLaren (ed.) 2004

Abortion, Sin and the State in Thailand
by Andrea Whittaker 2004

Sexual Violence and the Law in Japan
by Catherine Burns 2004

Women, Islam and Modernity
Single women, sexuality and reproductive health in contemporary Indonesia
by Linda Rae Bennett 2005

The Women's Movement in Post-Colonial Indonesia
by Elizabeth Martyn 2005

Women and Work in Indonesia
by Michele Ford and Lyn Parker (eds) 2008

Women and Union Activism in Asia
by Kaye Broadbent and Michele Ford (eds) 2008

Gender, Islam and Democracy in Indonesia
by Kathryn Robinson 2008

Sex, Love and Feminism in the Asia Pacific
A cross-cultural study of young people's attitudes
by Chilla Bulbeck 2008

Gender, State and Social Power
Divorce in contemporary Indonesia
by Kate O'Shaughnessy 2008

Gender, Household and State in Post-Revolutionary Vietnam
by Jayne Werner 2008

Young Women in Japan
Transitions to adulthood
by Kaori Okano 2009

Women, Islam and Everyday Life
Renegotiating polygamy in Indonesia
by Nina Nurmila 2009

Feminist Movements in Contemporary Japan
by Laura Dales 2009

Gender and Labour in Korea and Japan
Sexing class
by Ruth Barraclough and Elyssa Faison (eds) 2009

Gender Diversity in Indonesia
Sexuality, Islam and queer selves
by Sharyn Graham Davies 2010

New Women in Colonial Korea
A sourcebook
by Hyaeweol Choi 2012

Women Writers in Postsocialist China
by Kay Schaffer and Xianlin Song 2013

Domestic Violence in Asia
Globalization, gender and Islam in the Maldives
by Emma Fulu 2014

Gender and Power in Indonesian Islam
Leaders, feminists, Sufis and *pesantren* selves
by Bianca J. Smith and Mark Woodward (eds) 2014

Practicing Feminism in South Korea
The women's movement against sexual violence
by Kyungja Jung 2014

The Korean Women's Movement and the State
Bargaining for change
by Seung-kyung Kim 2014

Gender, Nation and State in Modern Japan
edited by Andrea Germer, Vera Mackie and Ulrike Wöhr 2014

Women and Sex Work in Cambodia
Blood, sweat and tears
by Larissa Sandy 2015

Growing up Female in Multi-Ethnic Malaysia
by Cynthia Joseph 2015

Women, Sexual Violence and the Indonesian Killings of 1965–66
by Annie Pohlman

Love and Marriage in Globalizing China
by Wang Pan 2015

Love and Marriage in Globalizing China

Wang Pan

LONDON AND NEW YORK

First published 2015
by Routledge
2 Park Square, Milton Park, Abingdon, Oxon, OX14 4RN

and by Routledge
711 Third Avenue, New York, NY 10017

Routledge is an imprint of the Taylor & Francis Group, an informa business

© 2015 Wang Pan

The right of Wang Pan to be identified as author of this work has been asserted by her in accordance with the Copyright, Designs and Patents Act 1988.

All rights reserved. No part of this book may be reprinted or reproduced or utilised in any form or by any electronic, mechanical, or other means, now known or hereafter invented, including photocopying and recording, or in any information storage or retrieval system, without permission in writing from the publishers.

Trademark notice: Product or corporate names may be trademarks or registered trademarks and are used only for identification and explanation without intent to infringe.

British Library Cataloguing in Publication Data
A catalogue record for this book is available from the British Library

Library of Congress Cataloging in Publication Data
Pan, Wang (Researcher)
Love and marriage in globalizing China / Wang Pan.
pages cm. – (Asian Studies Association of Australia women in Asia series ; 7)
Includes bibliographical references and index.
1. Interracial marriage–China. 2. Marriage–China. 3. Divorce–China. I. Title.
HQ1031.P36 2015
306.810951–dc23
2014015077

ISBN: 978-1-138-02425-0 (hbk)
ISBN: 978-1-315-77589-0 (ebk)

Typeset in Times New Roman
by Fish Books Ltd.

Printed and bound in the United States of America by
Edwards Brothers Malloy on sustainably sourced paper.

Contents

List of illustrations	ix
Acknowledgements	x
Series editor's foreword	xi

1 Introduction: Chinese–foreign marriage   1
What are 'Chinese–foreign marriages'?   2
Researching intercultural marriage   6
Researching Chinese–foreign marriage in the PRC media   13
Chapter outline   17

2 Obstacles, statistics and regulations   21
Initial obstacles to Chinese–foreign marriage in the PRC   21
Statistics of Chinese–foreign marriage   24
Governing marriage in the reform era   35
Conclusion   41

3 Newspaper coverage of Chinese–foreign marriage   43
Changing numerical trends   43
Different countries of origin   49
Hypergamy   54
'Love' in the 2000s   58
Hypergamy revisited   61
Conclusion   64

4 Newspaper coverage of Chinese–foreign divorce   67
Chinese–foreign divorce: a rising trend   68
Deception, adultery, bigamy and divorce   71
Domestic violence and divorce   76
Marriage introduction services and divorce   83
Conclusion   88

5 Celebrity Chinese–foreign marriage   90
China's first celebrity Chinese–foreign marriage   91

viii Contents

Celebrity Chinese–foreign marriage in the 1990s 96
Celebrity Chinese–foreign marriage in the 2000s 102
Conclusion 108

6 Celebrity Chinese–foreign divorce 110
High rates of divorce 111
Speculation and hearsay 116
Amicable divorces and exemplary fatherhood 120
Female autonomy and exemplary motherhood 125
Conclusion 129

7 Documenting Chinese–foreign marriage 131
New documentary and Chinese–foreign marriage 132
Cross-Strait marriage 138
Cross-Strait marriage in the media 143
Rural Chinese and foreign nationals 149
Conclusion 155

8 Television talk shows and Chinese–foreign marriage 156
Television talk shows in the PRC 156
Foreign Chinese 161
Foreign spouses as country bumpkins 165
Making marital conflict 'fun' 169
Conclusion 174

9 Concluding comments 176
Defining and counting Chinese–foreign marriages 176
Media discussions of Chinese–foreign marriage 179
Potential avenues for further research 184

Appendix 1: Sources of statistical information on marriages
 and divorces registered in the PRC 186
Appendix 2: Documentary films on Chinese–foreign
 marriage (57 episodes) 191
Appendix 3: Television talk shows on Chinese–foreign
 marriage (20 episodes) 194
Appendix 4: Children in celebrity Chinese–foreign
 marriages (examples) 196

References 197
Index 233

List of illustrations

Figures

2.1	Chinese–foreign marriages	25
2.2	Chinese–foreign marriages: breakdown by category	27
2.3	Map of Chinese–foreign marriages	31
2.4	Marriages registered in Japan with spouses from China (1965–2011)	32
2.5	Marriages registered in Australia with spouses from Mainland China (1994–2011)	33
2.6	Chinese–foreign divorces	34
7.1	Taiwan spouses in cross-strait marriages registered in the PRC (1990–2011)	141

Tables

2.1	Gender composition of Chinese–foreign marriages registered in Mainland China (1979–2011)	28
2.2	Marital status of couples in Chinese–foreign marriages registered in the PRC (1987–1998)	29
3.1	Chinese–foreign marriages registered in the PRC: popular regions and foreign countries of origin	50
7.1	Number of marriages registered in Taiwan (1998–2011)	142

Acknowledgements

I would like to acknowledge my debt to the authors cited and to a great many others whose published work has contributed to the book's analysis and outcomes, as well as those who provided me with the inspirations and ideas for the production of the book.

First and foremost, I would like to express my utmost gratitude to Associate Professor Elaine Jeffreys for her intellectual stimulation and the time she invested in my work. Thanks are due to colleagues at the China Research Centre and Faculty of Arts and Social Sciences at the University of Technology Sydney (UTS) for providing a stimulating academic and professional culture. I would also like to thank Professors Louise Edwards and Richard Smith, Lauren Gorfinkel, Ivan Roberts, Susette Cooke, Terry Royce, Yang Jingqing, Lorrain Shannon, Jesica Kinya, Mehal Krayem, John Roberts and Sophie Wang, for various forms of assistance.

This book is dedicated to my mother Wang Ningsheng and uncle Yu Gongjie for their steady care and constant support for all of my endeavours in life.

Finally, the author and publisher would like to thank the following for granting permission to reproduce part of the material in this work: Elaine Jeffreys and Wang Pan (2013) 'The Rise of Chinese-Foreign Marriage in Mainland China (1979–2010)', *China Information*, 27, 3: 347–69 by kind permission of Sage Publications, http://cin.sagepub.com; and Wang Pan (2015) 'Media Presentations of Cross-Strait Marriage in Contemporary China' *China Media Research* (forthcoming).

Every effort has been made to contact copyright holders for their permission to reprint material in this book. The publishers would be grateful to hear from any copyright holder who is not here acknowledged and will undertake to rectify any errors or omissions in future editions of this book.

Series editor's foreword

The contributions of women to the social, political and economic transformations occurring in the Asian region are legion. Women have served as leaders of nations, communities, workplaces, activist groups and families. Asian women have joined with others to participate in fomenting change at micro and macro levels. They have been both agents and targets of national and international interventions in social policy. In the performance of these myriad roles women have forged new and modern gendered identities that are recognisably global and local. Their experiences are rich, diverse and instructive. The books in this series testify to the central role women play in creating the new Asia and re-creating Asian womanhood. Moreover, these books reveal the resilience and inventiveness of women around the Asian region in the face of entrenched and evolving patriarchal social norms.

Scholars publishing in this series demonstrate a commitment to promoting the productive conversation between Gender Studies and Asian Studies. The need to understand the diversity of experiences of femininity and womanhood around the world increases inexorably as globalization proceeds apace. Lessons from the experiences of Asian women present us with fresh opportunities for building new possibilities for women's progress the world over.

The Asian Studies Association of Australia (ASAA) sponsors this publication series as part of its on-going commitment to promoting knowledge about women in Asia. In particular, the ASAA Women's Forum provides the intellectual vigour and enthusiasm that maintains the Women in Asia Series (WIAS). The aim of the series, since its inception in 1990, is to promote knowledge about women in Asia to both academic and general audiences. To this end, WIAS books draw on a wide range of disciplines including anthropology, sociology, political science, cultural studies, media studies, literature and history. The series prides itself on being an outlet for cutting-edge research conducted by recent PhD graduates and post-doctoral fellows from throughout the region.

The series could not function without the generous professional advice provided by many anonymous readers. Moreover, the wise counsel provided by Peter Sowden at Routledge is invaluable. WIAS, its authors and the ASAA are very grateful to these people for their expert work.

Lenore Lyons (The University of Sydney)
Series Editor

1 Introduction
Chinese–foreign marriage

This book examines the phenomenon of Chinese–foreign marriage in the People's Republic of China (PRC) since 1979, and the nature of media discussions concerning this. From the founding of the PRC in 1949 until the early 1990s, intercultural marriage was an unusual occurrence in mainland China. Political differences between communist China and 'the rest of the world' severely limited the opportunities for such unions to develop in the first place. Restrictions on the capacity of foreign nationals to enter and reside in China, and on the ability of Chinese citizens to obtain passports and travel overseas further limited the opportunities for Chinese–foreign marriages (Lee 1997: 95–6; Quan Xiaoshu 2005; Liu Guofu 2009: 312–18).

However, following the decades of China's economic reform at the end of the 1970s, Chinese society has undergone dramatic social change. Improved diplomatic relations between mainland China and the outside world have resulted in rapid expansion of economic and business activities. This consequently encouraged the gradual loosening of government restrictions on population mobility and successive amendments to the legal frameworks. Along with the development of tourism, the Internet and commercialized matchmaking services and changing social attitudes towards marriage and the family, mainland Chinese citizens are gaining unprecedented opportunities to choose a spouse from societies beyond their own territory.

Statistics produced by the PRC's Ministry of Civil Affairs since the start of the reform period indicate that approximately 8,460 couples were registered as entering into a Chinese–foreign marriage in 1979. That figure climbed to a peak of almost 80,000 couples in 2001 and declined to less than 49,000 couples in 2011 (MCA, China Civil Affairs Statistical Yearbook 1979, 2002, 2012). An overwhelming majority of these marriages are between mainland Chinese women and foreign males. Correspondingly, around 80 Chinese–foreign couples filed for divorce in 1979, this figure jumped to more than 800 couples in 1992, before skyrocketing to nearly 9,500 couples in 2008. It then slowed down and reached about 5,700 couples in 2011 (MCA, China Civil Affairs Statistical Yearbook 1979, 1993, 2012).

The increased frequency and altered nature of intercultural marriages over the course of three decades reveal at least two aspects. First, they indicate a disruption of the conventional forms of marriage in China and a transformation of peoples' values in connection with marriage and family and perhaps a trend towards marital multiculturalism. Second, although the figures of Chinese–foreign marriage and divorce are insignificant both in comparison with domestic rates and the number of intercultural marriages in other countries, the potential social implications and consequences cannot be ignored. These include an unbalanced sex-ratio in local marriage markets and the social problems of bigamy, extra-marital affairs and domestic violence that are associated with the rising incidence of divorce.

The number of Chinese citizens who registered their marriages outside mainland China has also been growing substantially, and this trend has been made even more prominent by the fact that a rising number of mainland Chinese citizens are becoming the dominant group among all types of foreign spouses in the destination countries/regions. For example, from the late 1990s to the mid- 2000s, the majority of intercultural marriages registered in Taiwan and Hong Kong were between a local male and a female from mainland China (Ma Zhongdong *et al.* 2010: 93; Neizhengbu Huzhengsi 2011). Similarly, during the same period, China has become the main country of origin for international marriages registered in Japan and Korea, with the large majority of these marriages occurring between Chinese women and local men (Liaw *et al.* 2010: 62; Kim 2010: 135, 137).

These dynamics have caught the media's attention and created a notable amount of social discourse with reference to marriage and divorce registration, motivation, mobility, citizenship and social attitudes towards Chinese–foreign marriage in, and outside the PRC. For example, 'mainland wives' are a subject of negative media reportage in Hong Kong and Taiwan. They are often portrayed as the 'inferior other', poorly educated 'gold diggers' and the cause of social problems (e.g. Shih 1998: 287–319; Hsia 2007: 55–62; Tsai 2011: 245). Other socially concerned issues in the media include but are not limited to cultural differences, living habits, languages, education of children in a bicultural family and familial relationship in such kinds of marriages. Chinese–foreign marriage has consequently emerged as an important topic for public debate and discussion.

To date, there has been neither a major study of the phenomenon of intercultural marriage in China, nor an account of how that phenomenon has been constructed in different media formats in the PRC. The book aims to fill this gap by examining the evolution of Chinese–foreign marriage during reform-era China, in association with its socio-demographic characteristics and the amendment of legal frameworks that govern such marriages and divorces, as well as the various aspects of these as portrayed in print and online media and television programming in the PRC. In doing so, I map the architecture of Chinese–foreign marriage and divorce in the PRC and investigate how such a phenomenon has been presented and circulated for public consumption in China today.

What are 'Chinese–foreign marriages'?

Broadly speaking, the term 'Chinese–foreign marriage' is equivalent to the term 'intercultural marriage' and the two terms will be used interchangeably henceforth. An 'intercultural marriage' refers to 'a union of two people from diverse cultures as well as different countries' (Romano 1988: xii). Such a union may also, but not necessarily, indicate differences in race, ethnicity, religion and language (Romano 1988: xii; see also Breger and Hill 1998: 7). Chinese legal documents divide Chinese–foreign marriage into three categories according to the permanent residence and/or citizenship status of the non-mainland Chinese marrying party. These marriages are described below in a manner that facilitates a discussion of the translated terms rather than according to a hierarchal ranking. The first category of marriage involves a union between citizens of the PRC and foreign nationals (*waiguoren*, literally 'people from another country') – meaning people who are not citizens of mainland China, Hong Kong, Macau and Taiwan. In legal terms, this category includes Chinese nationals who have acquired a foreign passport, and hence ceded their right to Chinese citizenship. However, in colloquial Chinese, the term '*waiguoren*' refers to people with physical appearances that are distinctive from 'the Chinese' in terms of skin colour, cranial features and/or hair texture and who are viewed as members of a different ethnic grouping or race. For example, the term '*waiguoren*' is used to describe 'white' people or Caucasians with European ancestry, 'blacks' from different countries in Africa and 'south Asians' from Bangladesh, India and Pakistan and 'Asians' from countries such as Korea, Japan and Malaysia.

The second type of Chinese–foreign marriage is between citizens of the PRC and citizens of Hong Kong, Macau and Taiwan, i.e., territories that the PRC Government claims as part of a unified or 'greater' China. Hong Kong, Macau and Taiwan are territories of China distinguished by their histories as former colonies under foreign rule. Hong Kong was ceded to Great Britain from China following the first Opium War (1839–1842) and the signing of the Treaty of Nanjing on 29 August 1842 (Liu Shuyong 1996: 28). Hong Kong was occupied by Japan at the start of World War II and reclaimed by Britain in 1945, before its sovereignty was transferred to the PRC in 1997. Macau, a Portuguese colony since the sixteenth century, was placed under the PRC's sovereignty in 1999 (Deng Kaisong 1999: 5). Currently, both Hong Kong and Macau are Special Administrative Regions (SARs) and self-governing territories of the PRC that enjoy a high degree of autonomy, aside from their foreign policy and military defence powers, which are retained by the PRC Government. The Qing dynasty ceded Taiwan to the Empire of Japan in 1895 after the Sino-Japanese war. However, the island returned to Chinese sovereignty under the Republic of China (ROC) after Japan's defeat in World War II. Then the Civil War resumed in China between the CCP and the Nationalist Party (Guomindang). Following the victory of the CCP in 1949, the Guomindang retreated to Taiwan and the CCP founded the People's Republic of China on 1 October 1949 (Zhang Shanke 1988). The PRC and Taiwan have maintained strained relationships ever since, chiefly because the PRC Government continues to view Taiwan as a 'renegade province' that should transfer its sovereignty to China.

The third type of Chinese–foreign marriage is between citizens of the PRC (*Zhongguo gongmin*) residing in mainland China (*neidi jumin*) and 'overseas Chinese' (*huaqiao*). 'Overseas Chinese' are defined as citizens of the PRC who have settled abroad according to the 1990 Law of the People's Republic of China on the Protection of the Rights and Interests of Returned Overseas Chinese and the Family Members of Overseas Chinese (*Zhonghua Renmin Gongheguo guiqiao qiaojuan quanyi baohu fa* 1990). This group also includes 'returned overseas Chinese' (*guiqiao*) who have returned to the PRC, and made it their place of permanent residence.[1]

Unlike its clear legal definition, understandings of the term 'overseas Chinese' are contested in popular and academic discourses because the term 'overseas Chinese' can be rendered in the Chinese language as either '*huaqiao*' or '*huaren*'. Yow Cheun Hoe (2005: 560), for example, considers 'overseas Chinese' to be Chinese citizens who are residing outside China temporarily. Hoe defines 'overseas Chinese' as people who retain their citizenship of the PRC and their political loyalty to China, and have the ultimate intention of eventually returning to China. Tetsu Ichikawa (2006: 111) somewhat differently asserts that the terms '*huaqiao*' and '*huaren*' can be used to differentiate between groups of Chinese people residing outside China according to their different 'degrees of localization'. According to Ichikawa, the term '*huaqiao*' denotes people who maintain citizenship of the PRC while living abroad (comparable to Yow's definition), whereas '*huaren*' refers to those who have acquired local (foreign) citizenship, and do not intend to return to China. In the context of Chinese–foreign marriage, the term 'overseas Chinese' refers to '*huaqiao*', understood as PRC citizens who settled abroad but maintained PRC citizenship and who might or might not have returned to live in the PRC.

In short, a 'Chinese–foreign marriage', which seemingly refers to unions between citizens of mainland China and citizens of foreign countries, also encompasses marriages between citizens of the PRC who live in the PRC and citizens of the PRC who reside overseas and between citizens of the PRC and citizens of Hong Kong, Macau and Taiwan. This is primarily because of the distinct legal jurisdictions of marriages in mainland China and Hong Kong, Macau, Taiwan and in countries where people classified as overseas Chinese reside (Ding Jinhong *et al.* 2004: 66). In legal documents in the Chinese language, all three categories of Chinese–foreign marriages are referred to collectively as '*shewai hunyin*', which literally translates into English as a 'foreign-related marriage' or, as the *Shanghai Statistical Yearbook* puts it: a 'Chinese–foreign marriage' (Shanghai tongji nianjian 2007).[2]

However, the three-pronged legal categorization of Chinese–foreign marriages is not reflected in popular cultural discourses. Unlike marriages between citizens of the PRC and 'non-Chinese' foreign nationals (*waiguoren*), it is generally assumed that marriages between citizens of the PRC and citizens of Hong Kong, Macau and Taiwan and overseas Chinese are unions between two people who share a common culture or an overarching sense of 'Chineseness'. Hence, common terms for international and transnational marriages in the Chinese language, such as '*kuaguo hunyin*' and '*Zhongwai hunyin*', are not typically used to describe marriages between citizens of the PRC and overseas Chinese or marriages between citizens of the PRC and citizens of Hong Kong, Macau and Taiwan. They are only used to describe marriages between citizens of the PRC and citizens of foreign countries other than Hong Kong, Macau and Taiwan (Ding Jinhong *et al.* 2004: 66). The term used to describe marriages between citizens of the PRC and citizens of Hong Kong, Macau, Taiwan is '*she GangAoTai hunyin*', literally marriages involving people from Hong Kong, Macau and Taiwan. Another term used to describe marriages between citizens of the PRC and citizens of Taiwan is 'cross-Strait marriages' (*liang'an hunyin*), and the term used to describe marriages between citizens of the PRC and overseas Chinese is '*sheqiao hunyin*', literally marriages with overseas Chinese.

As I go on to explain, the term 'intercultural marriage' is used interchangeably with the term 'Chinese–foreign marriage' throughout this book because it offers a more accurate description of such marriages than other available Chinese and English terms. Some common and interchangeable terms for an intercultural marriage in the English language are 'international marriage', 'transnational marriage', 'interracial marriage', 'interethnic marriage', 'cross-border marriage', 'cross-cultural marriage' and 'mixed marriage' (Romano 1988: xii; Penny and Khoo 1996: 2; Breger and Hill 1998: 7; Ata 2005: 11). All of these terms imply the crossing of racial, ethnic, cultural, linguistic, religious and national backgrounds. However, they do not always capture the nuances of the Chinese situation.

For example, although terms such as 'interracial' and 'interethnic' marriage emphasize the different racial and ethnic backgrounds of citizens of the PRC and their non-ethnically Chinese marrying partners, they do not necessarily refer to marriages between citizens of mainland China and citizens of Hong Kong, Macau and Taiwan and marriages between citizens of the PRC and overseas Chinese. In some circumstances, the latter group of marriages may be viewed as marriages between members of the same ethnic and racial group, even though they fall under the legal heading of Chinese–foreign marriages. In any case, as Veda Khulpateea (2007: 16) and Monica Thiagarajan (2007: 3), explain, the terms 'interracial' and 'interethnic' are problematic because they may be used to divide people on a hierarchical and discriminatory basis according to social constructions of 'race' and 'ethnicity'. Likewise, 'international' and 'transnational' marriage may also exclude the category of marriages between mainland citizens and citizens of Hong Kong, Macau and Taiwan and marriages between PRC mainland citizens and overseas Chinese. The concepts of a 'cross-border' and 'mixed' marriage are too broad for an accurate analysis of the Chinese case. They may refer to both cross-ethnic/cultural or same-cultural marriages, for example, marriages between citizens from across various geographical borders within the PRC, and/or to the process of marrying outside one's ethnicity and culture (Lu 2007: 3). The term 'intercultural' refers to both the mutual interaction and differences between cultures whereas 'cross-cultural' emphasizes the differences between cultures.

At the same time, marriages between mainland Chinese citizens and citizens of Hong Kong, Macau and Taiwan are often constructed in China's media and public discourses as *intra*cultural (*wenhua jian*) rather than *inter*cultural (*kua wenhua*) for two reasons. First, the PRC lays claim to political sovereignty over the territories of Hong Kong, Macau and Taiwan as historical components of 'One China', even though the government in Taiwan disputes this claim (Harding 1993: 679; Kong Qingjing 2004: 92). Second, most citizens of Hong Kong, Macau and Taiwan are ethnic Chinese, perhaps even born in mainland China, thus sharing certain cultural similarities or affinities with mainland citizens of the PRC, at least when compared with people described as 'foreigners' (Harding 1993: 665). In fact, foreign nationals are often referred to in newspapers and popular discourses in the PRC as '*laowai*' – *lao* literately means 'old' and *wai* means foreign or alien, i.e., a person from outside 'China' (Pang Fan and Wen Huangwei 2005; Ni Yan and Xu Xiuyou 2006; Pan Meihong 2006; Shuai Yong and Jiang Yu 2007). The term '*laowai*' conveys a derogatory emphasis on the difference understood as inferiority of non-Chinese vis-à-vis Chinese as identified through ethnicity, cultural practices and languages. It therefore works to homogenize and affirm the sameness of 'Chineseness' as 'not foreign'.

Yet marriages between mainland Chinese citizens and citizens of Hong Kong, Macau and Taiwan may also be defined as *inter*cultural rather than *intra*cultural marriages for two reasons. First and as reflected in the legal use of the term 'Chinese–foreign marriage', Hong Kong, Macau and Taiwan have different economic and political systems from those that operate in mainland China. The historical status of Hong Kong, Macau and Taiwan as territories colonized by foreign states has generated obvious differences between the nature of everyday life in those territories and in mainland China, especially when compared with the nature of social and political life in the PRC during the Maoist or 'revolutionary' period (1949–1976). Second, despite the homogenizing rhetoric of notions of 'One China', not only are citizens of mainland China marked by multiple differences in terms of ethnicity, language and religion, so too are citizens of Hong Kong, Macau and Taiwan (Edmonds 1992: 169–89; Brown 2004: 2). For example, a marriage between a 30-year-old Uyghur and practising Muslim from the PRC's autonomous region of Xinjiang, to a non-practising Catholic and Cantonese speaker from Hong Kong, might be considered *intra*cultural from the point of view that the two marrying partners are citizens of the PRC. However, that same marriage may be defined as *inter*cultural when differences in ethnicity, religion and the languages used in their respective family homes are taken into consideration.

The terms 'Chinese–foreign marriage' and 'intercultural marriage' are therefore selected throughout this book to refer to marriages between citizens of the PRC and foreign nationals, as well as marriages between citizens of mainland China and citizens of Hong Kong, Macau and Taiwan and between citizens of mainland China and overseas Chinese. I now examine some of the available literature on intercultural marriage in general and intercultural marriage in the PRC, highlighting a main concern with the socio-economic mobility provided by marriages that occur between people from different cultures and the gendered nature of the practice of hypergamy or 'marrying up'.

Researching intercultural marriage

There is a considerable body of academic work on the subject of intercultural marriage in the context of western societies. The majority of this work focuses on the socio-economic mobility provided by marriages that occur between people from different races, especially in the context of black and white interracial relationships in the US (Davidson 1991: 14–19; Lewise *et al.* 1997: 60–78;

Romano 2003; Qian Zhenchao and Lichter 2007: 68–94). Taken as a whole, these studies are concerned with examining the motivations for marriages between people of a different race, religion, class and gender, and the implications of such marriages in terms of generating or disrupting familial harmony and national social cohesion. Some studies also examine mediated constructions of black and white interracial relationships. They commonly observe that despite an increasing number of positive presentations of intercultural relationships in the US media, black–white relationships continue to be stigmatized as 'unnatural' and/or 'dysfunctional', either explicitly or implicitly (Perry and Sutton 2006: 888–92; see also Hooks 1995: 113; Childs 2005: 45–6).

There is also a growing body of academic work on intercultural marriage in the Asian context. Such studies examine multiple issues and are often based on interviews and surveys with intercultural couples. Pertinent issues include the relationship between socio-economic development and the changing demographic features of intercultural marriage, marriage migration patterns, the gendered motivations of marrying partners and the social integration/exclusion of immigrant brides in destination communities (Piper 2003: 457–66; Constable 2005a; Sheu 2007: 179–96; Jones and Shen 2008: 9–25; Friedman 2010: 73–93; Yang and Lu (eds) 2010). An overarching concern is the gendered socio-economic motivations for intercultural marriages in the context of patterns of marital mobility between Asian societies, and between Asian and western societies (Piper 2003: 457–66; Chao 2005: 35–52; Constable 2005a; Thai 2005: 145–65; Lauser 2006: 321–37). These motivations are often discussed with reference to the concept of hypergamy or the practice of marrying someone from a higher socio-economic background. This is because marriage-related mobility commonly involves the movement of brides from remote and less developed locations to more developed and less isolated ones and from the poor and less developed global south to the comparatively wealthy and developed north.

Nicole Constable (2005b: 10) refers to these patterns of intercultural marriage mobility as 'global hypergamy'. Contemporary patterns of intercultural marriage mobility are 'global' in that they involve men and women from different regions of the world. They are 'hypergamous' in that they usually involve the marriage of a younger woman to an older man of a higher socio-economic grouping, with youth and other personal attributes being exchanged for improved economic status. However, reductive conceptions of hypergamy are complicated by the paradoxical and contradictory patterns of mobility in individual cases. For example, some women who appear to be 'marrying up' by moving from less developed geographical regions to a wealthier location may often actually be 'marrying down' to a man of lower class and educational levels (Constable 2003: 167; Freeman 2005: 95–100; Thai 2005: 148).

Discussions of global hypergamy have generated further research on the motivations for intercultural marriage and gendered geographies of power and desire. Early scholarship suggested that marriage-related mobility between Asian societies and between Asian and western societies entrenched established patterns of male privilege and this was especially reflected in the phenomenon of 'mail-order brides'. During the 1980s and 1990s, the term 'mail-order brides' was used in both academic literature and the popular press to describe the phenomenon of women from Asian countries who used a system of introductions provided by commercial institutions (marriage bureaus, friendship clubs and so forth) for the prime purpose of entering into a marriage with a foreign national (Del Rosario 1994: 2; Robinson 1996: 53–54). Such women were stigmatized as poor and desperate people who wanted 'passports', 'foreign citizenship' and 'money'; and, having entered into a commodified form of marriage, it was believed they would inevitably be treated as 'household slaves', and become victims of domestic violence, which indeed was sometimes the case (Glodava and Onizuka 1994; Narayan 1995: 107–8; Sheu 2007: 183–8; Shi Yanrong 2009: 89–91).

Recent scholarship has complicated early accounts of the motivations for and consequences of entering into an intercultural marriage by emphasizing the individual agency of Asian women and the diverse opportunities that intercultural marriage may provide them. They argue that women use marriage-related mobility as an opportunity to initiate their own marriage plans, facilitate their own migration and empower both themselves, and their families (Constable 2005a: 183; Oxfeld 2005: 18–33; Freeman 2005: 88–95). Entering into an intercultural marriage enables some women to escape from the constraints of local patriarchal marriages (Constable 2005b: 12), offering them improved standards of living and the acquisition of citizenship and associated rights in another country. Additionally, an intercultural marriage may include new opportunities for studying and working overseas, educating children, personal career advancement and other forms of personal fulfilment (Nakamatsu 2003: 187; Constable 2005a: 168; Constable 2005b: 12; Lauser 2006: 323).

Scholarship also draws attention to the fact that media reportage of 'Asian brides' in receiving countries often presents such women in terms of negative stereotypes, irrespective of whether such women are described as 'mail-order brides' or not. For example, women from the Philippines who married Australian men and subsequently moved to Australia between the late 1970s and 1990s were frequently described in the Australian media as 'oriental beauties with shady pasts' who used 'marriage to jump immigration queues' and whose marriage to an Australian national was therefore likely to end in divorce (Robinson 1996: 54, 56). Media reports in countries such as Japan, Taiwan and Hong Kong also often described 'brides' from other Asian countries as 'foreign workers disguised as brides', 'sex workers', and a source of 'social problems' (Piper 1997: 322–31; Nakamatsu 2003: 181; see also So 2003: 531; Hsia 2007: 58–62; Lu 2008: 161–71; Tsai 2011: 245). These examples show how media discussions of intercultural marriage may participate in the creation, dissemination and perpetuation of racial, gendered and sexualized stereotypes.

To date, the subject of intercultural marriage in reform-era China and its relation to broader patterns of gendered, socio-economic mobility, has attracted the attention of a limited number of researchers. This highlights a gap in the available literature given China's enhanced economic standing, and the recent growth in the numbers of intercultural marriages registered in China. Studies of marriage mobility in the PRC have largely focused on the opportunities created by China's economic reform, and the subsequent increased numbers of intra-provincial and interprovincial marriages flowing from the relaxation of Maoist-era constraints on population mobility (Fan and Huang Youqin 1998: 231–4; Davin 2005: 176–7; Fan and Li Ling 2002: 622–4). The sheer geographical size of the PRC, as well as the cultural diversity of its enormous population, has ensured that internal migration for work and/or marriage in the reform era has attracted considerable scholarly attention. Patterns of marriage mobility are usually discussed in the context of how young women from poor rural regions 'marry up' by marrying men living in developing urban areas (Fan and Huang Youqin 1998: 227; Davin 2005: 184–5). Some of these women, as with accounts of 'mail-order brides', meet their 'promised partners' through dishonest commercial introduction agencies, and end-up being trafficked and/or sold into prostitution as a result (Evans 1997: 170–1; Davin 2005: 184–5).

The few available studies of intercultural marriage in reform-era China focus on the growing phenomenon of Chinese–foreign marriage in the emerging 'cosmopolitan' cities of Shenzhen and Shanghai. Constance Clark (2001: 113–19) conducts interviews with marriage introduction agencies (*hunyin jieshaosuo*) and their female clients to show that some young rural migrants in Shenzhen seek foreign nationals as marriage partners, in order to enhance their opportunities for social mobility. Derided in local media as '"gold diggers" searching for foreign "airplane tickets"', Clark (2001: 106), notes that young rural migrant women often find it difficult to meet a domestic marriage partner in Shenzhen, especially when they do not have a Shenzhen resident permit. Yet many such women are accustomed to life in a large city, and wish to reside permanently there, and use marriage introduction services. Such businesses began to thrive in southern China in the 1980s and expanded rapidly in the 1990s, largely to service immigrant communities (Clark 2001: 111–12). In the late 1990s, some of these agencies provided urbanized migrant women with introductions to men from Japan, Singapore and other parts of Asia, via the medium of videos (Clark 2001: 114–15). In such videos, after some degree of coaching, these independent women presented themselves in stereotypical fashion as 'traditional Chinese women' – slender, attractive and demure homemakers, in order to attract a potential suitor (Clark 2001: 118–19). In other words, they actively performed 'traditionalism' to achieve their desired goal of an improved quality of life overseas. However, Clark (2001: 116, 119) concludes that female control over the opportunities associated with marriage mobility may be restricted once they relocate overseas because a failed marriage can compromise a woman's ability to stay in a receiving country.

Ding Jinhong *et al.* (2004: 66–70) and James Farrer (2008a: 7–29) provide different accounts of the growth of Chinese–foreign marriage in Shanghai. In a Chinese-language article entitled 'Characteristics and Trends of Cross-Nation Marriage in Modern Shanghai', Ding Jinhong *et al.* (2004), examine the demographic features of Chinese–foreign marriages registered in Shanghai between 1980 and 2002 using statistics compiled by the Shanghai Civil Affairs Bureau. They note that rapid economic growth has contributed to a significant growth in the number of Chinese–foreign marriages registered in Shanghai compared to other Chinese cities. Based on a comparison of the figures for 1996 and 2002, Ding Jinhong *et al.* (2004: 68), state that such marriages usually involve Shanghainese women and male foreign nationals, including citizens of Hong Kong, Macau, Taiwan and overseas Chinese. In 1996, a significant proportion of the Chinese–foreign marriages registered in Shanghai involved men from Hong Kong, Macau and Taiwan and those categorized as overseas Chinese. However, the number of marriages registered between Shanghai women and foreign men not categorized as overseas Chinese, or as citizens of Hong Kong, Macau and Taiwan, increased after 1996 and became the dominant type of Chinese–foreign marriage registered in Shanghai in 2002 (Ding Jinhong *et al.* 2004: 68). The number of female divorcees entering into Chinese–foreign marriages also increased from 1997, a factor which they suggest may relate to the fact that some of these women have had previous experience of travelling overseas or living overseas for work or study (Ding Jinhong *et al.* 2004: 68). Concluding with a brief comparison of domestic and Chinese–foreign marriages registered in Shanghai in 2002, Ding Jinhong *et al.* (2004: 69–70) note that couples in intercultural marriages are often older and have higher educational levels than couples in domestic marriages.

James Farrer (2008a: 7–29) focuses more specifically on marriages between mainland Chinese citizens and western expatriates residing in Shanghai. As Farrer (2008a: 9) explains, China's newspapers and popular magazines first began to report on Chinese–foreign marriages in the 1980s, typically in the form of cautionary tales. Such articles decried the perceived instrumentalist motivations of certain Chinese women in marrying foreign men to obtain a higher socio-economic position, echoing descriptions in colloquial Chinese of foreign marrying partners as 'airplane tickets' or 'passports'. They also centred on the 'problems' associated with Chinese–foreign marriages, such as dealing with parental opposition, facing adjustment problems when living abroad and the 'dangers' of illegal agencies promoting intercultural marriage for emigration purposes (Farrer 2008a: 9–10; see also Farrer 2010: 77). He adds that in literary works, such as Tang Ying's (1995) *Meiguo Laide Qizi* (My Wife from America), Shanghai women's strategies of emigration through international marriage were interpreted as a sign of a crisis of Chinese masculinity (Farrer 2008a: 10; Farrer 2010: 77). They highlighted the perceived failure of Chinese men to meet the desires and expectations of a new generation of Chinese women (see also Su Hongjun 2005: 232).

Farrer (2008a: 10) observes that these largely negative portrayals of Chinese–foreign marriages were replaced by more positive accounts in the late 1990s and early 2000s as growing confidence in China's economic development and increased frequency rates of intercultural marriage 'dampened social resistance to intermarriage'. Instead, China's media began to provide positive and romantic accounts of Chinese women's motives for dating foreigners, as well as positive stories of foreigners who had chosen to forsake their own countries of origin in order to live in Shanghai with their Chinese spouses. Such reports highlighted the newfound reliance of foreign men on their Chinese female partners and their partners' families to obtain the social, economic and cultural capital necessary to compete in emerging global cities such as Shanghai (Farrer 2008a: 10–11). Farrer concludes that this pattern demonstrates both a reverse trend of transnational marriage mobility, from 'north' to 'south' instead of vice versa and the growing attractiveness of China to foreign nationals, as opposed to the former 'abandonment' of China by citizens of the PRC, especially women. Adding to Farrer's arguments, I would conclude that this reversed pattern of marital migration reflects the changing motivations of some mainland Chinese citizens for entering into an intercultural marriage, which may be broadly characterized as a shift from 'global hypergamy' to 'romantic love'.

In *Chinese Women and the Cyberspace*, Liu Lihui and Liu Hong (2008: 254–61) note that the advent of the Internet has facilitated growing numbers of intercultural marriages in the PRC. The 'exponential growth of an internet-savvy population in China' is a cultural as well as a technological event (Roberts 2010: 229). Although the development of the Internet in the PRC only began in 1987, by late 1997, the PRC had 620,000 Internet users or netizens (*wangmin*) and by the end of June 2002 the PRC had 45.8 million Internet users (China Internet Network Information Centre (CNNIC) 1997; CNNIC 2002). By mid-2008, the PRC had 253 million Internet users, surpassing the United States and making China the world's largest online population (CNNIC 2008); and, by the end of 2011, the country had over 513 million netizens (CNNIC 2012). Chinese Internet users are predominately young men from urban centres, but the number of female and rural Internet users is increasing rapidly (Fallows 2007; CNNIC 2009; CNNIC 2012).

As a by-product of this growth, Liu and Liu (2008: 261) conclude that intercultural marriages stemming from Internet dating are increasing in the PRC. Online social networks enable people from across the PRC who are interested in establishing an intercultural marriage to meet, and communicate with people from overseas without the need to first meet in person or involve a mediator. Thus, people from parts of China other than the major cities of Beijing, Shanghai and Guangzhou, where overseas residents and visitors are more common, can now also meet and agree to marry someone from overseas without having to first physically meet that person (Liu Lihui and Liu Hong 2008: 254–5).

The implication in Liu and Liu's work is that the popularity and 'borderless' nature of dating on the Internet may reflect new motivations and desires for entering into an intercultural marriage on the part of different groups of people. Certainly, their work suggests that Chinese women who enter into intercultural marriages come from diverse socio-economic backgrounds and occupy a wide range of social positions. Chinese women who enter into intercultural marriages include: young women; older women; women with a limited education; women with a university education; women with professional and high-paying employment; women with low-paying jobs or no employment; divorcees; widows; women resident in towns; women from China's poor rural hinterland; and Chinese female celebrities (Liu Lihui and Liu Hong 2008: 252). However, Liu and Liu's (2008: 257–9) observations still refer to the standard motivations for intercultural marriages such as the desire to travel overseas, and improve one's socio-economic status and career advancement. Moreover, their brief discussion of the groups of Chinese women who entered into intercultural marriages from the mid-1990s to early 2000s paradoxically suggests that women from diverse groups in Chinese society entered into intercultural marriages without the added consideration of the Internet.

To date, there is limited information about the specific groups of male PRC nationals who enter into intercultural marriages, presumably because the low incidence of Chinese men in Chinese–foreign marriages makes it difficult to reach general conclusions about the nature of their socio-economic position and their motivations for marrying foreign women. The lower incidence of male citizens of the PRC marrying foreign women in the PRC context is usually explained in terms of different gendered expectations. Foreign women and especially women from developed western countries, reportedly often find Chinese men less physically attractive than western men and 'unattractive' because of their often lower socio-economic position (Constable 2005a: 185; Prasso 2005: 103; Zhang Qi 2010; 'Western wives' 2010). At the same time, the majority of Chinese men reportedly view western women as 'unattractive' and overly complicated as marriage partners because of their 'assertive/aggressive' character vis-à-vis traditional conceptions of ideal Chinese womanhood. Moreover, adherence to traditional Chinese family arrangements in the context of China's one-child family policy would require a male child and his wife to live and work in China in order to take care of his parents and siblings (Prasso 2005: 103; Zhang Qi 2010; 'Western wives' 2010). In short, mate selection preferences and decision-making relating to the location of family settlement and household finance management makes intercultural marriage a rarity for Chinese men.

Although there are no academic studies of the specific groups of male citizens of the PRC who enter into intercultural marriages, emerging anecdotal evidence suggests that such men come from diverse socio-economic backgrounds and occupy a wide range of social positions. Media reports indicate that male rural migrant workers and agricultural workers, for example, sometimes experience difficulties in finding a domestic marriage partner because they are poorly educated and have limited opportunities for economic advancement. As a result, some of these men marry women from poorer and less developed countries in Asia, such as Vietnam, Cambodia, the Philippines and Indonesia. Women from poor family backgrounds in such countries command less expensive dowries than their Chinese counterparts and have a reputation in the PRC for being more compliant and family-oriented than modern Chinese women (Zhang Yiye 2010; 'Asian Men Seek' 2010; 'Ximei: Zhongguo nanren' 2011). Consequently, some Chinese men living in major cities and having high levels of income, reportedly, now also marry women from Vietnam (Xu Shiwen *et al.* 2010). In addition, some men from the PRC marry foreign women while they are studying and/or working overseas ('Wo qu yangniu' 2009; 'Wuhan xiaohuo' 2009). For example, the number of Chinese men who marry African women has increased in recent years along with the number of Chinese investments and businesses in Africa (Zhao Lei *et al.* 2009; 'Zhongguo nan' 2011).

Conversely, recent reports in the PRC media suggest that women from developing Asian countries and from Hong Kong, Macau and Taiwan are marrying male citizens of the PRC because of China's comparative economic advantage in the region ('Gangnü qinglai Dalunan' 2007; Yuan Zhonghai and Sun Xianglan 2007; Ewing 2010; Zhang Yiye 2010; 'Liang'an hunyin xin xianxiang' 2011). Men from the PRC are also said to be attractive marriage partners for some women from Africa and Europe because they are viewed as caring for their families (*gujia*), honest (*zhencheng*), reliable and diligent (*qinfen kekao*), willing to do domestic chores (*gan jiawu*) and avoid excessive drinking of alcohol (*bu xunjiu*) ('Qu waiguo nüren' 2005; Zhao Lei *et al.* 2009; 'Zhongguo nanren' 2011). In addition, China's media sometimes suggest that a number of male citizens of the PRC who enter into intercultural marriages are entertainment or sports celebrities, because they have more opportunities to meet women outside the PRC, for example, through work and travelling and are less likely to be constrained by economic considerations and traditional Chinese values ('Jiang Wen Faguo' 2006; 'Liu Ye Yinglai' 2007; Bi Ran 2008; 'Western wives' 2010).

To summarize the preceding remarks, intercultural marriage in the PRC is a changing and largely unexplored phenomenon. Available studies have drawn on the insights presented in discussions of the altered patterns and motivations associated with marital mobility between Asian societies and between Asian and western societies in general. Most notably, they examine the relationship between socio-economic change and the changing demographics and motivations for Chinese–foreign marriage in 'global cities' such as Shenzhen and Shanghai. In addition, they examine how technological changes associated with the advent of the Internet have altered the possibilities and scope for intercultural marriage in the PRC. I now use the insights made available by the academic literature on intercultural marriage to introduce the theories and approaches adopted in this book for the analysis of media presentations of Chinese–foreign marriage in the PRC.

Researching Chinese–foreign marriage in the PRC media

The rising incidence of intercultural marriage in the PRC has attracted the attention of China's media, which has itself undergone a dramatic change in the reform period. From the founding of the PRC in 1949 until the early 1990s, China's print and communications media were funded by central or local governments and acted as the 'mouthpiece' of the Chinese Communist Party (CCP). The CCP promoted a system of 'Party journalism'. This system was based on the idea that the role of the media was to help the development of socialism in China by promoting the Party's guiding ideology and its concrete programmes and policies (Zhao Yuezhi 1998: 19). The effect of this was to engender a mass media that largely focused on propaganda, idolizing political leaders such as the PRC's founding leader Chairman Mao Zedong (1893–1976), and promoting public role models, in the form of idealized representations of socialist citizens, such as workers, farmers and soldiers (Jeffreys and Edwards 2010: 3).

The tightly controlled, propaganda-style media system of the Maoist era started to evolve towards a slightly more liberal framework following the introduction of broader economic reforms. Controls over China's media (particularly the non-official sectors) became more relaxed through the 1990s (Jeffreys and Edwards 2010: 4; see also Zhao Yuezhi 1998; Donald *et al.* 2002; Brady 2007; Keane *et al.* 2007). In 2003, the PRC Government instructed state-subsidized newspapers and magazines to earn at least half of their revenue from private subscriptions. To make China's television stations more competitive and independent, the government also introduced a series of regulations stimulating investment in new stations and the extension of broadcasting hours (Jeffreys and Edwards 2010: 4).

These reforms have had a significant impact on the business models adopted by China's media, which have been adjusted to increase audience numbers and advertising revenue, for example, by increasing the amount of 'light' news and entertainment, with a tabloid-style reporting of 'human interest' stories (Jeffreys and Edwards 2010: 4; see also Zhao Yuezhi 2002: 111–36; Hvistendahl 2005). This trend has been further accelerated by the expansion of the Internet, licensed and unlicensed cable networks and 'cross-investment by the Chinese media into other commercial enterprises, including joint ventures with international media giants' (Akhavan-Majid 2004: 1). The growth of commercially oriented media in China and the resulting emphasis on entertainment and advertising, has not only generated a broad interest in 'human interest' stories, but has also contributed to an increased focus on stories featuring intimate relationships and intercultural marriages in the PRC.

A brief glance at newspaper coverage of intercultural marriage in the PRC in the 1990s and 2000s reveals increased attention to the frequency rates of Chinese–foreign marriages and associated legal policies, as well as increasing attention on the different motivations for intercultural marriages, including individualized stories of romance and especially celebrity romances (Du Zhanfan 2001; Hu Shufeng and Xiong Yunbin 2007; 'Zhu Chen Muhanmude' 2009). Media coverage of intercultural marriage in the PRC in the 2000s also demonstrates a growing concern with issues of cultural difference, divorce, domestic violence and the activities of illegal marriage agencies both in China and abroad (Ni Yan and Xu Xiuyou 2006; Wang Fang 2006; Guo Yuandan 2007; Yang Min 2008; Wang Tianfu *et al.* 2009). In the 2000s, Shanghai Television's primetime programme *OK! Xintiandi* (OK! New World) covered stories about intercultural marriages in the PRC (Farrer 2008a: 10), as did talk shows such as *Guoji Shuangxingxian* (Common Ground) on Beijing TV-1 and *Feichang Fuqi* (Extraordinary Husband and Wife) on Beijing TV-3. Then, from 2006 to 2009, Channel Four of China Central Television (CCTV-4) broadcast a documentary series called *Yuanfen* (Predestined Love) on a weekly basis, which interviewed couples involved in Chinese–foreign marriages about how they met, fell in love and eventually married and about their married lives.

This media coverage on the phenomenon of Chinese–foreign marriage provides an important source of reference for the study of Chinese–foreign marriage in the PRC because newspapers, magazines, television, radio, billboards and the Internet, etc., offer a primary means of understanding the world we live in. Media texts typically attempt to depict, explain and propose solutions to selected aspects of everyday life, while simultaneously helping to create and give meaning to that which they claim to describe. In addition, an analysis of media coverage on Chinese–foreign marriage helps to enhance our understanding of how media shape public opinion on Chinese–foreign marriage by framing people and their activities in particular ways.

This book adopts media framing theory as its analytical framework. Media framing can be interpreted as journalists' cognitive process when they seek to organize, present and make sense of a given issue (Parsons and Xu Xiaoge 2001: 52; De Vreese 2005: 52). According to David Tewksbury and Dietram Scheufele's (2009: 17) analogy, how artists place the frame around a painting will influence the interpretation and reaction of reviewers. Similarly, the way journalists choose words and images may exert power that affects the evaluation and interpretation of the readers/audiences. The specific symbolic framing devices are comprised of but are not limited to quotes, soundbites, visual images, metaphors, exemplars, depictions and catchphrases (Gamson and Modigliani 1989: 3; Nelson *et al.* 1997: 568).

In *Making News: A Study in the Construction of Reality*, Tuchman (1978) was the first to apply the concept of frame analysis to the process of news reporting. She asserted that the news frame organizes everyday reality. Robert Entman suggests that framing involves selection and salience. To frame is to make certain ideas more noticeable, meaningful and memorable in a text. This can be achieved through replacement, repetition, or by associating the bits of information being described with culturally familiar symbols (Entman 1993: 52–3). He maintains that frames also 'define problems', 'diagnose causes', 'make moral judgments' and 'suggest remedies' (Entman 1993: 52). In addition, McCombs *et al.* (1997) conceptualize framing as an extension of agenda-setting. This model is concerned with how the news information influences recipients' perceptions of the importance of an issue and how such an issue can be understood by the recipients.

Nelson *et al.* (1997: 569) argue that media frames shape public opinion by underscoring 'specific values, facts and other considerations, endowing them with greater apparent relevance to the issue than they might appear to have under an alternative frame'. Akhavan-Majid and Ramaprasad (1998: 134) pinpoint the linkage between ideology and framing, and conclude that 'framing is an important mechanism by which ideology is transmitted through the news'. Scheufele (1999: 107–108) developed a typology that categorized media framing into two dimensions: 'frame building' and 'frame setting'. The former examines how journalists adopt different frames when reporting news while the latter deals with how audience perceptions are influenced by the media frames.

Within this framework, the book uses a mixture of quantitative and qualitative research methodologies to investigate the broad range of reports and stories across different genres that make up 'news' about intercultural marriage in China today. I examine statistics compiled by the PRC Government to provide a broad picture of the changing demographic features and characteristics of Chinese–foreign marriages in the reform period. Statistical data about Chinese–foreign marriage in the PRC is collated from relevant government archives, including statistical yearbooks, annual reports and national and local government websites. That information is analysed for subsequent discussions of media constructions of intercultural marriage in the PRC.

A discourse analysis is used as a qualitative research method to identify the organizing themes and concerns of media discussions of intercultural marriage in reform-era China. Examining media texts as products of social and discursive practices, which come together to constitute a particular form of reality, enables a 'rich description' of the particular 'social reality' generated from those themes and concerns (Zhang Yan and Wildemuth 2009: 318). I examine the multiple frames adopted by Chinese journalists, and how these frames create societal discourse in the coverage of Chinese–foreign marriages. I also examine the multiple meanings and political implications of media accounts of China's changing marriage and divorce rates, the altered composition of Chinese–foreign marriages in terms of gender and countries/places of origin, mobility, identity, as well as the rationales associated with those changes.

The samples for this study range across a wide range of mediums, including newspapers, magazines, television programming and the Internet. The key terms I used to obtain information on intercultural marriages in contemporary China included: '*shewai hunyin*' (Chinese–foreign marriage), '*guoji hunyin*' (international marriage); '*kuaguo hunyin*' (transnational marriage); '*Zhongwai hunyin*' (Sino-foreign marriage), '*kua wenhua hunyin*' (cross-cultural/intercultural marriage); '*kua zhongzu hunyin*' (interracial/interethnic marriage), '*she Gang Ao Tai hunyin*' (Hong Kong, Macau, Taiwan-related marriage) and '*liang'an hunyin*' (cross-Strait marriage).

I collected approximately 500 reports on Chinese–foreign marriages in the PRC from newspapers, magazines and the Internet. These reports were mainly obtained from the search engines Google and Baidu, which together account for approximately 97 per cent of the Chinese search engine market. Newspaper sources for the years prior to 2000, which are not always available on Google and Baidu were obtained from the *People's Daily* database (1946–2003) and *Xinhua News Agency* portals. Additional information was accessed from the China Core Newspapers Database (CCND), which covers over 700 newspapers published in mainland China since 2000. Newspaper reports were also obtained from the APABI full-image/full-text newspaper database. This database covers more than 80 per cent of China's newspapers from August 2007, with some content dating back to the 1990s. As a supplement to newspaper reports, magazine sources were collected from the China Journal Database (CJD), which covers over 8,200 magazines in mainland China since 1994. Both CCND and CJD are part of the China National Knowledge Infrastructure Databases (CNKI). The majority of the 500 reports I collected, focused on marriages between citizens of mainland China and foreign nationals rather than marriages between citizens of mainland China and overseas Chinese and citizens of mainland China and Hong Kong, Macau and Taiwan.

In terms of television programming, aside from relying on the search engines of Google and Baidu, I used different online video searching websites such as Sina.com, Tutou.com, Youku.com, Sohu.com and 56.com. I collected a total of 57 documentaries produced in the PRC on the subject of intercultural marriage (see Appendix 2). Of these, 36 episodes involved marriages between citizens of the PRC and citizens of Taiwan. These episodes were obtained from the official website of a television programme called *Yuanfen* (Predestined Love), which aired on CCTV-4. The 21 episodes involving marriages between citizens of the PRC and citizens of countries other than Taiwan were collected from a variety of websites, including Sina.com, Tudou.com and Sohu.com. I found no examples of documentary films that focused on marriages between citizens of mainland China and citizens of Hong Kong and Macau, or on marriages between citizens of mainland China and overseas Chinese.

I also collected a sample of 20 episodes of Chinese–foreign marriage talk shows that were broadcast in the PRC in the late 2000s (see Appendix 3). Ten of these episodes focus on 'ordinary' Chinese–foreign marriages and the other ten episodes focus on celebrity Chinese–foreign marriages. All of the 20 episodes in the sample focus on marriages between citizens of mainland China and non-ethnically Chinese foreign nationals rather than other types of Chinese–foreign marriage. The talk shows were obtained from various websites such as Sina.com, Tudou.com, Sohu.com *and* Youku.com and from the official websites of talk shows such as *Guoji Shuangxingxian* (Common Ground) on BTV-4 and *Feichang Fuqi* (Extraordinary Husband and Wife) on BTV-3.

Chapter outline

This chapter has defined the concept of Chinese–foreign marriage and synthesized the relevant scholarly literatures on the topic of intercultural marriage in the context of both western and eastern societies. It has also introduced the theoretical and methodological approaches to the study of media constructions of Chinese–foreign marriages in the PRC. The following chapters are organized as below.

Chapter 2 provides background information on the phenomenon of intercultural marriage in the PRC. It explains why Chinese–foreign marriage was an unusual occurrence in the PRC prior to 1979, and outlines some of the broader social and political changes that have contributed to the initial rise, and altered nature of intercultural marriage in post-1978 China. It then collates various numerical statistics to examine the major trends, and characteristics of Chinese–foreign marriages and divorces registered in and outside the PRC from 1979 to 2011. Finally, it examines the expansion of Chinese legal frameworks that regulate the increasing numbers of Chinese–foreign marriages and divorces. This provides the necessary background for subsequent discussions of how China's media frame the 'new' social phenomenon of intercultural marriage in the PRC.

Chapter 3 analyses newspaper coverage of Chinese–foreign marriage in the PRC since 1979, providing an overview of the broad trends and themes presented in media reports of intercultural marriage, as both a reflection of and influence on, wider social, economic and cultural changes in China. First, it examines how the PRC newspapers frame the growth of Chinese–foreign marriages as evidence of the PRC's wider social and economic achievements, and how the media highlight the symbolic meaning of Chinese–foreign marriages so as to conform to the political agenda of the PRC Government. The chapter then examines newspaper accounts of the motivations for mainland Chinese citizens entering into Chinese–foreign marriages and their perceived evolution from the criticized focus in the early reform period on hypergamy or 'marrying up' to today's emphasis on 'love'. Newspaper reportage in the PRC presents the evolution of these motivations as a straightforward sign of national advancement. However, a closer analysis of media representations across China's reform era reveals some inconsistencies that disrupt this linear narrative, pointing instead to a greater diversity of motivations and the altered circumstances of Chinese women.

Chapter 4 discusses newspaper coverage of the rising trend of Chinese–foreign divorce in twenty-first century China. It examines three areas associated with the increased incidence of Chinese–foreign divorce: deception, bigamy and adultery; domestic violence; and the role of illegal Chinese–foreign marriage introduction agencies in promoting fraudulent marriages resulting in divorce. I conclude that such reports constitute gendered cautionary tales with geographical dimensions. They warn Chinese women that if they marry a male foreign national, and live outside China, they are likely to become victims of adultery, and/or domestic violence and consequently will have to divorce. They may even attempt suicide or try to murder their spouses. Correspondingly, male foreign nationals are depicted as having a propensity to infidelity, deception, violence and taking advantage of Chinese women, with some men conspiring with 'evil' international marriage introduction agencies to exploit Chinese women. This implies, by default, that male citizens of the PRC are better husbands, even though the problems associated with domestic Chinese marriages and China's rising incidence of divorce are well documented. In doing so, Chinese newspaper reports provide their audiences with a dichotomous construction of bad foreign husbands and evil marriage introduction agencies and victimized Chinese women and good Chinese men.

Chapter 5 analyses print and online media coverage of celebrity intercultural marriages for the simple reason that 'celebrity news', including the 'drama' of celebrity romance, marriage and divorce, is an increasingly prominent feature of media reportage in China today. The analysis begins by looking at the case of Shen Danping, reportedly the first entertainment star in reform-era China to marry a foreigner in 1984. Shen's marriage is significant as the perceived 'starter' of the phenomenon of intercultural marriage within China's entertainment industry and related public debates over intercultural marriage in the PRC. The chapter then examines the newspaper accounts of celebrity intercultural marriage during the 1990s and 2000s. The 1990s reports feature a dichotomous construction of celebrity Chinese–foreign marriage. On the one hand, celebrities are celebrated as role models and successful professionals, exemplary wives and husbands in fairy-tale marriages. On the other hand, celebrities are portrayed as objects of derision and contempt for being unpatriotic. The 2000s reports underscore the altered pattern of both Chinese and foreign celebrities' transnational mobility as married couples choose to reside in the PRC or relocate from developed countries to live in the PRC, which echoes the portrayals of reversed patterns of migration by ordinary Chinese–foreign couples during the same period. The 2000s reports on contemporary celebrity Chinese–foreign marriage also introduce the notion that the inverted gender roles of foreign househusbands and career-oriented Chinese female celebrities are a key to a successful celebrity Chinese–foreign marriage. In such marriages, celebrity Chinese women share equal or higher socio-economic status than their foreign husbands. However, they simultaneously aspire to the role of being an 'ordinary' woman, mother and wife.

Chapter 6 analyses the various representations of celebrity Chinese–foreign divorces in China's print and online news media during the 2000s, a benchmark point which saw the public separation of many famous Chinese celebrities from their foreign spouses. Mediated accounts of individual celebrity intercultural divorces are often contradictory and speculative in nature. On the one hand, they are presented negatively as indicative of the problematic nature of celebrity intercultural marriages – a high divorce rate, irreconcilable cultural differences and complications such as long-term separation, extra-marital affairs and even sexual abuse. On the other hand, celebrity Chinese–foreign divorces are presented as more 'extraordinary' and differentiated from non-celebrity Chinese–foreign divorces as positive events associated with amicable separation, continuing friendship and exemplary parenthood. Celebrities themselves, while being the subjects of speculation and rumour, often stand to gain from these positive accounts of their divorce, emerging as the model caring father or modern liberated woman freed from the misery of a defective marriage. Such contradictory reportage, based on sensationalizing individual stories and capitalizing on the celebrity appeal of their protagonists, not only highlight both changing public attitudes towards marriage, divorce and spousal relationships, but also overarching market forces which dictate how particular stories and events are presented in the media.

Chapter 7 examines television documentaries featuring Chinese–foreign marriages broadcast in the PRC between the mid- and late 2000s. These documentaries focus on the 'true' life stories of 'ordinary people' as part of China's 'new documentary movement', and extend the analysis of Chinese–foreign marriage in the PRC to other forms of media. The 57 documentaries reviewed confirm the general characteristics of Chinese–foreign marriages observed in the print media. However, they also focus on two different forms of intercultural marriage – those between mainland Chinese citizens and Taiwan citizens ('cross-Strait') and those between rural citizens of the PRC and 'waiguoren' ('rural-foreign'). Both forms of marriages are depicted positively, describing how couples overcome initial miscommunication and the stigma of the 'mainland bride' in the first case and how foreigners are willing to 'marry down' to rural Chinese partners for love. In doing so, these documentaries suggest that stories about Chinese–foreign marriages often serve to reinforce the PRC Government's broader political agendas of promoting both closer cross-Strait ties, and the attractiveness and desirability of rural China and rural Chinese as part of a modern/urban China. Documentaries about cross-

Strait and rural-foreign marriages thus reflect not only changes in the nature of intercultural marriages in the PRC, but also changing political narratives about the nature of a future unified and urban modern China.

Chapter 8 examines television talk shows produced in the PRC about 'ordinary' and 'celebrity' Chinese–foreign marriages in the late 2000s. These talk shows are localized versions of a western television format that provide an entertainment-focused forum for the public discussion of how intercultural marriage may complicate or even challenge Chinese cultural norms and day-to-day habits. Stories of Sinicized foreign spouses internalizing and mastering traditional Chinese art forms and local languages and conversely, stories of 'foreign country bumpkins' who are unable to master the proper 'Chinese way of doing things', serve to affirm the assumed superiority of Chinese culture. At the same time, entertaining stories about the conflicts between foreign spouses and their Chinese counterparts highlight both the perceived universal aspects of intimate relationships, such as the importance of expressing love on a daily basis, the notion that absence makes the heart grow fonder, and the understanding that harsh words and deeds are often a sign of affection. In the process, they also highlight the progressively more open attitude of many Chinese people towards the public discussion of love, marriage and sex.

Chapter 9 summarizes the main findings of the book's examination of media presentations of Chinese–foreign marriage. It concludes by outlining the potential avenues for further research on the subject of Chinese–foreign marriage in the PRC.

Notes

1. See also Article 1 and 3 in Regulations on Defining Overseas Chinese, Chinese with Foreign Nationalities, Returned Overseas Chinese and Family Members of Overseas Chinese (*Guanyu jieding huaqiao waiji huaren guiqiao qiaojuan shenfen de guiding* 2009).
2. *Shanghai tongji nianjian* is compiled mainly by the Shanghai Municipal Statistics Bureau and contains comprehensive statistics of Shanghai's social and economic development in the reform period.

2 Obstacles, statistics and regulations

This chapter provides background information on the phenomenon of Chinese–foreign marriage in the PRC, and the nature of available studies dealing with this issue. It discusses the unusual nature of Chinese–foreign marriage in the PRC prior to 1979, and outlines some of the broader socio-political changes that have encouraged the growth of intercultural marriage following the adoption of market-based economic reforms and an Open Door Policy in December 1978. It then collates and examines the statistical data about Chinese–foreign marriages registered in the PRC between 1979 and 2011, and the altered characteristics of Chinese–foreign marriage in the late reform period. Finally, it details the expansion of Chinese legal frameworks to regulate the increasing numbers of Chinese–foreign marriages (and divorces) in the reform period.

Initial obstacles to Chinese–foreign marriage in the PRC

The 'closed' nature of Mao's China (1949–1976), meant that Chinese–foreign marriages were rare, and subject to structural and political constraints until after the introduction of economic reforms in 1979. During the Maoist era, the newly victorious Chinese Communist Party curtailed labour mobility, and rural–urban migration, in particular, to meet the requirements of socialist centralized planning. Centralized planning and the nationalization of industry replaced the monetary economy and labour mobility with a system wherein the Party-state allocated work, and distributed resources. Hence, the Party-state needed to know where its workers were and who they were (Jeffreys and Sigley 2009: 10).

From the late 1950s until the mid-1980s, the majority of urban Chinese spent their entire lives in the closed community of a socialist work unit (*danwei*). A work unit is 'an enterprise or institution that was meant to overcome the alienation of labour by merging life and work', and which 'provided all manner of welfare and services for its employees' (Jeffreys and Sigley 2009: 14; see also Bray 2005). At the same time, urban Chinese and rural agricultural producers became tied to their place of work, and/or birth following the implementation of a household registration system (*hukou*) in 1958. Household registration denied citizens of the PRC the right to move from one city to another, and from a rural area to an urban area, unless they had official permission to do so, which was extremely difficult to obtain. Such permission depended on a complicated system of employment quotas and associated education opportunities as specified in national and local economic plans (Whyte and Parish: 1984: 18; Chan 1992: 292; Lu Yilong 2002: 127).

Until the mid-1980s, the PRC Government also granted only a few citizens the permission and passport required to work, travel, study and/or live overseas (Rallu 2002: 6–7; Liu Guofu 2009: 316–17). In 1986, two laws were enacted that eased restrictions on the entry into and exit of people from the PRC. These were the Law of the People's Republic of China on Control of the Exit and Entry of Citizens (*Zhonghua Renmin Gongheguo gongmin chujing rujing guanli fa* 1986); and the Law of the People's Republic of China on Control of the Entry and Exit of Aliens (*Zhonghua Renmin Gongheguo waiguoren rujing chujing guanli fa* 1986). However, citizens of the PRC still required letters of invitation from organizations overseas, and written permission from their work unit and/or the authorization of local policing authorities to travel overseas (Liu Guofu 2009: 317). In fact, the PRC only adopted a 'passport-on-demand' policy after it joined the World Trade Organization in December 2001, in order to attract overseas talent to China and encourage citizens of the PRC to go overseas. Between 2002 and 2005, regulations requiring written permission from work units and letters of invitation from overseas were gradually phased out across the country as requirements for PRC passport applications and special channels at airports were established for citizens of mainland China (Rallu 2002: 7; Liu Guofu 2009: 318).

Restrictions on population mobility during the Maoist era, and at the start of the reform period meant that the place of residence of a PRC citizen became an important determinant of opportunities for socio-economic advancement and upward social mobility through marriage (Tu 2007: 34–5). China's rural citizens became second-class citizens, because of their more limited access to state welfare and services vis-à-vis urban citizens (Feng Xu 2009: 39–43). Young men with a rural household registration were sometimes able to alter their household registration status by entering the military or engaging in higher education (Fan and Huang Youqin 1998: 230). However, these kinds of opportunities were more limited for young women from rural areas who traditionally had fewer opportunities for social advancement in comparison to rural men. In this context, marriage to someone with a superior place of residence or urban residence became a means to achieve intra-provincial and inter-provincial geographic mobility and upward social mobility, especially for rural women (Fan and Huang Youqin 1998: 230–4; Tu 2007: 35; Fan 2008: 75). Such marriages often involved the marriage of a young, rural woman to a significantly older male with physical or mental challenges. However, his land and/or urban residence offered improved living conditions and employment opportunities for the young woman and ultimately her natal family (Fan and Huang Youqin 1998: 235; Huang Youqin 2001: 261).

Restrictions until the mid-1980s on population mobility obviously limited the aspirations and opportunities of citizens of the PRC with regard to intercultural marriage. The 'closed' nature of Chinese society during the Maoist era restricted the physical opportunities for citizens of mainland China and foreign nationals to meet and develop intimate relationships in the first place. The potential for intercultural romance was further limited by a corollary emphasis on the political supremacy of Chinese communism and the anti-communist attitude of developed nations, which encouraged both an ideology and a culture of cultural, racial and political separation. Adding to these obstacles, mainland Chinese citizens and foreign nationals were often marked by major differences in economic status. In 1985, the average annual income of a citizen of the PRC employed in a state-owned enterprise was only 1,213 yuan or USD 152 ('China income distribution' 2009).

Prior to the opening up of China's private property market in the early 2000s, intimate relationships between citizens of the PRC and foreign nationals were further limited by regulations restricting the physical space in which couples could meet and interact. Foreign nationals staying in the PRC were required to live in a small range of accommodation to which citizens of the PRC had restricted rights of entry. For example, diplomats residing on a long-term basis in the PRC lived in gated, foreign compounds with security guards. Foreign nationals in China on short-term visas were required to stay in state-owned 'four star' and 'five star' hotels and foreign students had to stay in university-controlled accommodation. Only men and women who were married and had certification to prove it were allowed to stay in the same room. Citizens of the PRC had to present their identity cards to security guards and register their details in order to enter such accommodation. They were also obliged to sign out when they departed, with entry times usually being restricted until after 8 a.m. and departure being required by 11 p.m. or earlier (Wu Fulong and Webber 2004: 203–6; 'Foreigners enjoy living, travelling in China' 2004; Zheng Na 2007). In addition, household registration regulations prohibited foreign nationals from staying overnight in the state-allocated homes of citizens of the PRC (*jumin jia*). Moreover, bars, clubs and other kinds of recreational enterprises only began to develop in China during the late 1980s, becoming more commonplace in the 1990s, with the venues patronized by foreign nationals being unaffordable for the majority of mainland Chinese citizens until the 2000s (Farrer 2008b: 6; Chew 2009: 3).

In short, the establishment of intimate relationships and marriages between citizens of the PRC and foreign nationals in early reform-era China was constrained by the structural and political legacies of the Maoist period. To offer an extreme example, in 1981, Li Shuang, a 24-year-old Chinese experimental artist, fell in love with a French diplomat, Emmanuel Bellefroid, who was working at the French Embassy in Beijing. The couple planned to marry and started living together in the French Embassy compound. In September of that year, Li was detained by members of China's public security forces and sentenced to the administrative punishment of two years 'reeducation through labour' (Earnshaw 1981).[1] She was accused of 'offending national decency' (*yousun guojia zunyan*) by cohabitating before marriage with a foreigner in a foreign compound (Zhang 2008). Although cohabitation before marriage was not prohibited by Chinese law, the reserved nature of early post-Maoist China meant that it was a society governed by strict moral codes and the practice was condemned (Liu 2007; 'Weihun tongju' 2009). Moreover, mainland Chinese officials and members of the public would likely have viewed the act of dating a foreigner, especially a diplomat, as both morally and politically suspect. After Li's detention, Bellefroid left China following accusations that he supported anti-government activities and returned to France where he lobbied the French government to intercede on their behalf (Stroud 1986; Yang Tian 2008). Li was eventually released from detention in July 1983 and permitted to travel to Paris, where the couple married and now live with their two sons (Earnshaw 1981; Zhang 2008).

Since the late 1980s, the number of marriages between citizens of the PRC and foreign citizens has increased significantly in keeping with the expansion of China's economic reforms. New business opportunities, labour mobility and the development of the PRC's tourist market and the Internet, have altered social behaviour and life-styles and contributed to a documented growth in Chinese–foreign marriages. This increase also stems from the relocation of Hong Kong and Macau to PRC sovereignty and improved political relations between the PRC and Taiwan. The following section draws on government statistics to examine the evolving trend and characteristics of Chinese–foreign marriages and divorces registered in the PRC during the reform era.

Statistics of Chinese–foreign marriage

Government statistics on the number of Chinese–foreign marriages registered in the PRC only became available in 1979 – that is, after the PRC shifted away from a centralized planned economy and a position of relative international isolation and adopted a policy of market-based economic reforms and opening up to the rest of the world in December 1978. Figure 2.1: 'Chinese–Foreign Marriages' offers a graphic illustration of the initial rise and more recent decline in the numbers of Chinese–foreign marriage registrations in the PRC from 1979 to 2011. It is based on statistics provided in the *China Civil Affairs Statistical Yearbook* (Zhongguo minzheng tongji nianjian) from 1979 to 2012. As Figure 2.1 shows, approximately 8,460 couples registered as entering into a Chinese–foreign marriage in 1979. That figure grew rapidly, climbing to a peak of 78,672 couples in 2001, before decreasing to 48,778 couples in 2011 (Zhonghua renmin gongheguo minzhengbu 1979, 2002, 2012, see Appendix 1).

These figures comprise a small proportion of the total number of registered marriages in the PRC as a whole. In 1979, the total number of marriages registered in the PRC, including Chinese–foreign marriages, was around 6.37 million couples. In 2001, the total number of registered marriages was about 8.05 million couples. In 2011, the corresponding figure reached around 13 million couples (Zhonghua renmin gongheguo minzhengbu 1979, 2002, 2012). Chinese–foreign marriages therefore accounted for approximately 0.1 per cent of the total number of registered marriages in the PRC in 1979, and 1 per cent of the total number of registered marriages in 2001, when the number of intercultural marriages in China reached a peak. This number has declined and constituted around 0.4 per cent of the overall registered marriages in the PRC in 2011. However, the documented figures of Chinese–foreign marriages are presumably conservative in that they refer to the

Obstacles, statistics and regulations 25

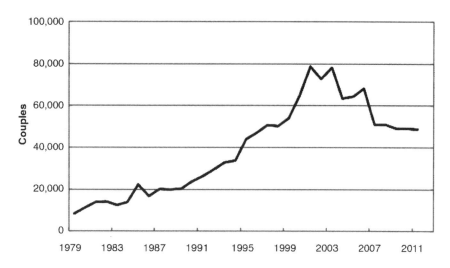

Figure 2.1 Chinese–foreign marriages
Source: *Zhongguo Minzheng Tongji Nianjian* (China Civil Affairs Statistical Yearbook).

total number of Chinese–foreign marriages registered in mainland China and do not include the growing number of Chinese–foreign couples who have married overseas.

Figure 2.2, 'Chinese–foreign marriages: breakdown by category', offers details of the types of 'foreign' parties in Chinese–foreign marriages registered in the PRC between 1979 and 2011. As Figure 2.2 indicates, the majority of Chinese–foreign marriages in the PRC both historically and in the present day occur between citizens of mainland China and citizens of Hong Kong, Macau and Taiwan, although the number of such marriages has been declining on average since 2003. Approximately 8,000 people from Hong Kong, Macau and Taiwan married citizens of mainland China in 1979. That figure peaked at slightly more than 48,000 people in 2003 and has since declined. Less than 18,000 people from Hong Kong, Macau and Taiwan married citizens of mainland China in 2011 (Zhonghua renmin gongheguo minzhengbu 1979, 2004, 2012). In other words, the type of intercultural marriage that accounts for the largest number of Chinese–foreign marriages registered in the PRC since 1979 has become less popular.

A breakdown of the figures of this type of marriage shows that between 1979 and 1989, citizens of Hong Kong, Macau and Taiwan were counted as one category of spouses registering Chinese–foreign marriages in mainland China, with at least 109,500 such marriages being registered in total (Zhonghua renmin gongheguo minzhengbu 1979 to 1990).[2] Between 1990 and 1998, citizens of Taiwan were treated as a separate category, with over 151,000 marriages being registered that involved a citizen of Hong Kong or Macau and over 54,000 that involved a citizen of Taiwan (Zhonghua renmin gongheguo minzhengbu 1991 to 1999). Since 1999, citizens of Hong Kong, Macau and Taiwan have been treated as three different groups of spouses registering a Chinese–foreign marriage in mainland China. Between 1999 and 2011 there were over 275,000 Chinese–foreign marriages registered in mainland China that involved a citizen of Taiwan, around 137,000 that involved a citizen of Hong Kong, and less than 18,000 that involved a citizen of Macau (Zhonghua renmin gongheguo minzhengbu 2000 to 2012). The data also show that the number of spouses from Taiwan increased steadily from 1999 to 2003 and then followed a downward trend till 2011. Conversely, the figure for Hong Kong spouses decreased from 1999 to 2003. It reached its highest level in 2006, before declining to the lowest level in 2011. In comparison, the number of spouses from Macau maintained a constantly lower level throughout the years, with a small peak occurring in 2006 (Zhonghua renmin gongheguo minzhengbu 2000 to 2012).

At the same time, marriages registered in Taiwan and Hong Kong that involved a mainland spouse revealed a different picture. From 1998 to 2011, more than 246,800 marriages were registered in Taiwan that involved a mainland spouse. The figure jumped rapidly from 1998 to 2003, it then suffered a sharp decline the very next year, but has since stabilized (Neizhengbu Huzhengsi 2011). Data from Hong Kong indicate that from 1986 to 2011, a total of 197,300 marriages registered in Hong Kong involved a spouse from mainland China. Although this number grew significantly from 1986 to 2006, it started to decline the very next year, before heading up again in 2010 (Xiang'gang tebie xingzhengqu, Zhengfu tongjichu (1987–2012)).

The second largest category of Chinese–foreign marriages registered in the PRC between 1979 and 2011 involved marriages between citizens of mainland China and '*Waiguoren*' or foreign nationals. Around 300 foreign nationals registered as entering into a Chinese–foreign marriage in the PRC in 1979 (Zhonghua renmin gongheguo minzhengbu 1979, see Appendix 1). That figure rose to reach a peak of over 26,000 people in 2001 and then started to fluctuate. It did not exceed the number of marriages between mainland Chinese citizens and citizens from Hong Kong, Macau and Taiwan until 2008. This figure then declined to approximately 25,000 people in 2011 (Zhonghua renmin gongheguo minzhengbu 2002, 2009, 2012, see Appendix 1). Hence, the number of registered marriages in the PRC that involve citizens of mainland China and foreign nationals has grown dramatically since 1979 and has remained relatively stable since the early 2000s.

There is no official statistical information available regarding the countries of origin of marriages registered in mainland China between PRC citizens and '*waiguoren*'. However, media reports and research conclusions suggest that during the early period, such marriages were often between mainland Chinese and people from the former Soviet Union and Eastern Europe, i.e., countries that once claimed a political affiliation as communist with the PRC (Gao Jiansheng 1995: 65; Li Sha 2009b). As China integrated further into the global economy, marriages now occur between PRC citizens and people from around the globe (Yuan Lanhua and Du Zhanfan 2005; Li Sha 2009b). The most popular countries of origin of foreign spouses of Chinese citizens are the developed countries, namely, Japan, the United

States, Canada, Western Europe (mostly Germany, France and the United Kingdom) and Australia (e.g., Ding Jinhong *et al.* 2004: 68; Wang Shengtian and Bao Wenfeng 2008; Pan Meihong 2006; Li Sha 2009b; Gao Ying *et al.* 2013: 31). In addition, due to geographical and cultural similarities, marriages between citizens living in the border areas of China and foreign nationals from the neighbouring countries are also prevalent. For instance, numerous ethnic Koreans residing in China's northeastern provinces of Jilin, Liaoning, Hei Longjiang and the Yanbian Korean Autonomous Prefecture have married people from Korea (Jiang Haishun 1999; Kim 2010: 134) and a great number of ethnic minorities from Guangxi and Yun'nan provinces in southwestern China have married people from Vietnam, Laos and Burma (Luo Wenqing 2006: 52; Li Juan and Long Yao 2008: 34; Gao Ying *et al.* 2013: 28).

Marriages between overseas Chinese and citizens of mainland China accounted for the smallest number of registered Chinese–foreign marriages in the PRC between 1979 and 2011. In 1979, less than 200 overseas Chinese married citizens of mainland China. That figure increased steadily, and arrived at a high of more than 7,500 people in 2005, declining to a figure of around 7,100 people in 2011, which means that the number of such marriages remained fairly constant since the late 1990s (Zhonghua renmin gongheguo minzhengbu 1979, 2006, 2012, see Appendix 1).

Table 2.1 provides a breakdown of the number and gendered composition of Chinese–foreign marriage registrations in the PRC from 1979 to 2011. It demonstrates that, over these three decades, the majority of mainland Chinese citizens registered as entering into intercultural marriages in the PRC are women. From 1979 to 1989, the average percentage of Chinese women in a Chinese–foreign marriage was 94.3 per cent and 5.7 per cent for Chinese males. The number of

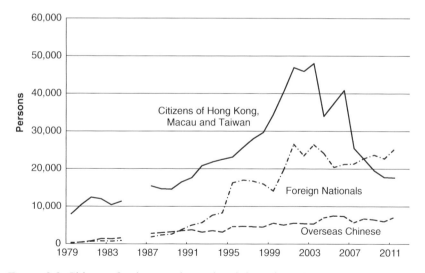

Figure 2.2 Chinese–foreign marriages: breakdown by category
Source: *Zhongguo Minzheng Tongji Nianjian* (China Civil Affairs Statistical Yearbook).
* Data for 1985 and 1986 are not available.

28 *Obstacles, statistics and regulations*

Chinese women reached its peak of 97.4 per cent in 1980 whereas the percentage of Chinese males stood for less than 3 per cent. Throughout the 1990s, the average percentage of Chinese women who entered into a Chinese–foreign marriage dropped to 90.6 per cent. Correspondingly, the average percentage of Chinese males increased to 9.4 per cent. From 2000 to 2011, the proportion of female PRC citizens marrying a foreign partner continued to decline, and reached an average of 81.6 per cent. Simultaneously, such figures for Chinese male citizens increased to 18.4 per cent. The percentage of Chinese male citizens who registered a

Table 2.1 Gender composition of Chinese–foreign marriages registered in mainland China (1979–2011)

Year	Total number of Chinese–foreign marriages (couples)	Citizens of mainland China				
		Total (persons)	Male Number	(%)	Female Number	(%)
1979	8,460	8,415	247	3.0	8,168	97.0
1980	11,317	11,287	295	2.6	10,992	97.4
1981	13,866	13,834	581	4.2	13,253	95.8
1982	14,193	14,166	613	4.3	13,553	95.7
1983	12,540	12,527	713	5.7	11,814	94.3
1984	13,921	13,895	776	5.6	13,119	94.4
1985	22,249	–	–	–	–	–
1986	16,851	16,820	1,219	7.2	15,601	92.8
1987	20,084	20,049	1,441	7.2	18,608	92.8
1988	20,021	19,980	1,885	9.4	18,095	90.6
1989	20,389	20,363	1,581	7.8	18,782	92.2
1990	23,762	23,700	2,030	8.6	21,670	91.4
1991	26,382	26,342	2,438	9.3	23,904	90.7
1992	29,589	29,467	3,518	11.9	25,979	88.1
1993	32,769	32,568	3,331	10.2	29,237	89.8
1994	33,829	33,760	2,660	7.9	31,100	92.1
1995	44,028	43,976	3,059	7.0	40,917	93.0
1996	47,227	47,104	4,138	8.8	42,966	91.2
1997	50,773	49,533	5,503	11.1	44,030	88.9
1998	50,320	50,373	4,431	8.8	45,942	91.2
1999	54,163	54,076	5,862	10.8	48,214	89.2
2000	64,881	64,569	9,038	14.0	55,531	86.0
2001	78,672	78,328	10,489	13.4	67,839	86.6
2002	72,778	70,730	8,529	12.1	62,201	87.9
2003	78,285	76,745	13,485	17.6	63,260	82.4
2004	63,544	61,973	7,972	13.0	54,001	87.0
2005	64,305	63,225	20,011	31.7	43,214	68.3
2006	68,183	66,881	16,158	24.2	50,723	75.8
2007	51,130	49,730	7,113	14.3	42,617	85.7
2008	50,995	49,815	7,701	15.5	42,114	84.5
2009	49,151	48,552	8,134	16.8	40,418	83.2
2010	49,036	51,573	11,682	22.7	39,891	77.3
2011	48,778	47,392	11,903	25.1	35,489	74.9

Sources: *Quanguo Minzheng Shiye Tongji Ziliao* (China Civil Affairs Statistical Yearbook, 1987–1988), *Zhongguo Minzheng Tongji Nianjian* (China Civil Affairs Statistical Yearbook, 1979–2012) and *Zhongguo Funü Tongji Ziliao* (Statistics on Chinese Women, 1949–1989).

Chinese–foreign marriage reached its climax of 31.7 per cent in 2005 while the figure for Chinese women decreased to its lowest level of 68.3 per cent in the same year. That is to say, although the vast majority of Chinese citizens who 'marry out' are PRC females, PRC males are catching up with this trend, and Chinese–foreign marriages were gradually becoming popular among this group during the 2000s.

China's Ministry of Civil Affairs provides information on the marital status of brides and grooms who registered a Chinese–foreign marriage in the PRC for the years between 1987 and 1998. Table 2.2 shows that the number of persons with different marital status who entered a Chinese–foreign marriage was on the rise throughout the decade. However, while the percentage of remarriages increased on an annual basis, the rate of first-time marriages declined. In 1987, around 37,500 persons registered a Chinese–foreign marriage for the first time. This constituted 93.3 per cent of the total number of persons who registered a Chinese–foreign marriage in that year. Although this figure almost doubled and reached 73,300 persons in 1998, its percentage declined by more than 20 per cent to 72.8 per cent (Zhonghua renmin gongheguo minzhengbu 1987, 1999). During the same period, around 2,600 persons with previous marital experience registered this type of marriage, which comprised only 6.7 per cent of the total in the earlier year. This figure maintained a strong momentum, increasing more than ten times, to over 27,300 persons in the final year, which accounted for 27.2 per cent of the total (Zhonghua renmin gongheguo minzhengbu 1987, 1999).

Although Table 2.2 only provides the picture of the marital status of couples in Chinese–foreign marriage for one decade from the late 1980s to late 1990s, the limited scholarly work available on intercultural marriages registered in China's major cities of Beijing, Shanghai and Fujian province from the mid-1990s to late 2000s suggests that the remarriage rate is much higher among Chinese–foreign couples than that of Chinese–Chinese couples (see Ye Wenzhen and Lin Qingguo 1996: 22, 29; Ding Jinhong *et al.* 2004: 68; Gao Ying *et al..* 2013: 32). Similarly, data on Chinese–Korean marriages registered in the Republic of Korea illustrates

Table 2.2 Marital status of couples in Chinese–foreign marriages registered in the PRC (1987–1998) (persons)

Year	Total persons	First marriage (%)		Remarriage (%)	
1987	40,168	37,496	(93.3%)	2,672	(6.7%)
1988	40,042	36,659	(91.6%)	3,383	(8.4%)
1989	40,778	36,884	(90.5%)	3,894	(9.5%)
1990	47,524	42,149	(88.7%)	5,375	(11.3%)
1991	52,764	45,345	(86%)	7,419	(14%)
1992	59,178	49,251	(83.2%)	9,927	(16.8%)
1993	65,538	50,489	(77%)	15,049	(23%)
1994	67,658	54,039	(80%)	13,619	(20%)
1995	88,056	68,903	(78.2%)	19,153	(21.8%)
1996	94,454	69,647	(73.7%)	24,807	(26.3%)
1997	96,398	72,278	(75%)	24,120	(25%)
1998	100,640	73,312	(72.8%)	27,328	(27.2%)

Source: *Zhongguo Minzheng Tongji Nianjian* (China Civil Affairs Statistical Yearbook, 1987–1999).

that both spouses of Chinese and Korean show high proportions of remarriage, especially since the beginning of the 2000s (Kim 2010: 139, 150). These figures indicate that in the last two decades, an increasing number of people in Chinese–foreign marriages, either Chinese or non-Chinese tend to marry a 'foreign spouse' after divorce.

Figure 2.3 shows that most of these marriages were registered in major cities such as Shanghai and provinces with an early history of economic development on China's eastern seaboard. The largest number of Chinese–foreign marriages registered in mainland China between 1979 and 2011 were in the provinces of Guangdong (with an annual average of 11,377 marriages), Fujian (with an annual average of 7,178 marriages) and Zhejiang (with an annual average of 1,846 marriages) and the city of Shanghai (with an annual average of 1,969 marriages) (Zhonghua renmin gongheguo minzhengbu 1979 to 2012). These areas are geographically close to Hong Kong, Macau and Taiwan and trade between mainland China and these regions has expanded since the 1990s and especially since the 2000s. By way of comparison, there was an average of 1,670 Chinese–foreign marriages registered in the northern province of Heilongjiang, 1,560 marriages in the northern province of Jilin and around 663 marriages in China's capital city of Beijing per year (Zhonghua renmin gongheguo minzhengbu 1979 to 2012). These areas are geographically close to Korea and Japan and trade between mainland China and these regions has also expanded since the 1990s and especially since the 2000s.

The number of Chinese–foreign marriages registered in provinces in the economically undeveloped areas of western China is insignificant statistically. Between 1979 and 2011, there was only an annual average of 66 Chinese–foreign marriages registered in the province of Gansu, 24 in Ningxia and 16 in Qinghai (Zhonghua renmin gongheguo minzhengbu 1979 to 2012). Less than the annual average of seven Chinese–foreign marriages were registered in the Tibet Autonomous Region during the same period (Zhonghua renmin gongheguo minzhengbu 1979 to 2012).

Unlike in Hong Kong and Taiwan, China's Ministry of Civil Affairs does not release data about the age, educational background and occupation of people registering a Chinese–foreign marriage, hence it is difficult to carry out a comprehensive evaluation of the socio-demographic character of such marriages registered in mainland China. However, a synthesis of scholars' research suggests that there are at least three common features of Chinese–foreign marriage registered in particular cities/regions in, and outside the PRC. First, marriages between younger PRC mainland women and older foreign males are a prominent phenomenon and the average age gap between couples varies from around seven years to over ten years. This is evidenced by the statistics of Chinese–foreign marriages registered in Beijing, Shanghai, Guangdong, Fujian, Hong Kong and Taiwan (Ye Wenzhen and Lin Qingguo 1996: 23; Zhang Guoxiong 1997: 37; Ding Jinhong *et al.* 2004: 69; Gao Ying *et al.* 2013: 33). In addition, the average age of couples in Chinese–foreign marriages is higher than couples in domestic marriages and this may be attributed to the high proportion of older first-time marriage couples and cases of remarriage in Chinese–foreign marriage (Ding Jinhong *et al.* 2004: 69). Second, the

Figure 2.3 Map of Chinese–foreign marriages

Note: Map adapted from www.freeworldmaps.net; areas with lines highlight the most popular cities and provinces for Chinese–foreign marriages registered in the PRC; Areas with dots highlight the least popular places for Chinese–foreign marriages registered in the PRC.

average educational level of Chinese–foreign couples is much higher than couples in domestic marriages in Beijing and Shanghai. In particular, a large percentage of foreign males have acquired a graduate diploma and bachelors' degree (Ding Jinhong *et al.* 2004: 69; Gao Ying *et al.* 2013: 32). In Japan, the educational level of female immigrants from China (as potential brides for Japanese males) is also documented as much higher in comparison with foreign brides from other countries, such as Brazil and the Philippines (Liaw *et al.* 2010: 63). Third, the figures in Shanghai and Fujian indicate that although intercultural marriages took place in earlier times were predominately between mainland Chinese and citizens from Hong Kong, Macau, Taiwan and overseas Chinese, these types of marriages have become less popular. Conversely, the number of mainland Chinese citizens marrying foreign nationals has become increasingly popular in the PRC (Ye Wenzhen and Lin Qingguo 1996: 22; Ding Jinhong *et al.* 2004: 68).

At the same time, the number of marriages between Chinese and foreign nationals registered outside the PRC has also been growing rapidly and such marriages were also predominantly between Chinese women and foreign males. For example, Figure 2.4 simply provides a reference of the number of marriages registered in Japan with spouses from China between 1965 and 2011 (Ministry of Health, Labour and Welfare, Japan). It shows the number of Chinese citizens registering marriages to Japanese citizens in Japan was under 1,000 persons prior to the 1980s. However, the figure rose from around 1,100 in 1980 to almost 6,000 in 1995, before arriving at its climax of nearly 15,000 persons in 2001 (Ministry of Health, Labour and Welfare, Japan). It is also documented that from 1995 to the early 2000s, the number of Chinese brides exceeded brides from other countries to become the main source of foreign brides in international marriages registered in Japan (Liaw *et al.* 2010: 62). Since 2001, the number of spouses from China has fluctuated, and by 2011 had decreased to less than 9,000 persons (Ministry of Health, Labour and Welfare, Japan).

Similarly, data from the Government of the Republic of Korea reveals that the number of marriages between Chinese and Koreans registered in the Korean peninsula has increased significantly since 1992 due to the establishment of bilateral diplomatic relations and rapid expansion of economic ties between the two countries (Kim 2010: 134). Doo-Sub Kim's study of cross-border marriage in Korea reveals that although the number of Chinese brides was less than 2,500 persons a year prior to the early 1990s, it grew rapidly and reached over 9,000 in 1996 and then increased to over 20,600 in 2005 (Kim 2010: 136). Correspondingly, the number of Chinese males maintained a much lower level of under 500 persons a year from the 1990s to the early 2000s. However, it continued to grow and exceeded that of the Japanese males to become the largest group of foreign husbands in 2004, before increasing to over 5,000 persons in 2005 (Kim 2010: 136–7). The statistics show that China has become the main country of origin for intercultural marriages registered in Korea by the mid-1990s.

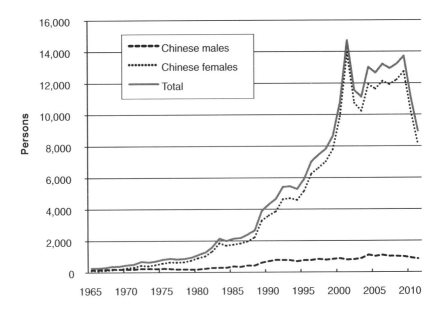

Figure 2.4 Marriages registered in Japan with spouses from China (1965–2011)
Source: Ministry of Health, Labour and Welfare, Japan. *Renkou dongtai tongji nianbao-hunyin.*

Obstacles, statistics and regulations 33

Figure 2.5 also demonstrates the rapidly increasing trend of marriages registered in Australia with spouses from China. The data record marriages between Chinese mainland citizens, and citizens either born in or outside Australia and marriages between two people both born in mainland China. As it reveals, the total number of marriages involving a Chinese spouse in Australia was under 2,000 each year from 1994 to 2002. The figure exceeded 2,200 in 2003 and more than doubled in 2009, before rocketing to more than 6,300 persons in 2011 (Australian Bureau of Statistics 1994 to 2011). A notable characteristic of such marriages is that approximately 60 per cent of marriages are between two people who were both born in mainland China. When viewed in conjunction with the high proportion of Chinese–foreign marriages registered in the PRC that involve citizens of Hong Kong, Macau and Taiwan, the figures suggest that many of the Chinese–foreign marriages in and outside the PRC may be 'intra-cultural' rather than 'inter-cultural' relationships at least when these terms are interpreted in a strict fashion.

Figure 2.6 shows the rising trend of Chinese–foreign divorce in the PRC from 1979 to 2011. At the beginning, only around 80 couples registered their divorces per year (Zhonghua renmin gongheguo minzhengbu 1979, see Appendix 1). With fluctuations, the figure increased considerably and reached more than 800 couples

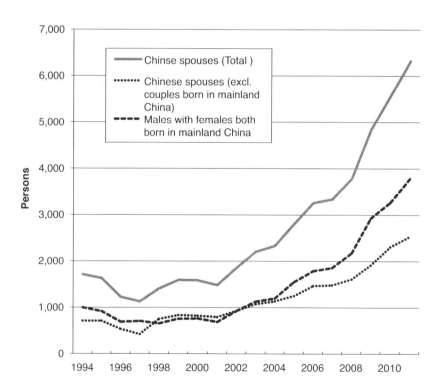

Figure 2.5 Marriages registered in Australia with spouses from mainland China (1994–2011)

Source: 'Country of Birth of Parties' (Australian Bureau of Statistics, 1994–2011).

34 Obstacles, statistics and regulations

in 1992, which was ten times higher than that in 1979 (Zhonghua renmin gongheguo minzhengbu 1993, see Appendix 1). The figure accelerated and increased to over 3,300 in 2003, before skyrocketing to nearly 9,500 couples in 2008. It then dropped to approximately 5,700 couples in 2011 (Zhonghua renmin gongheguo minzhengbu 2004, 2009, 2012 see Appendix 1). This illustrates the highly unstable nature of Chinese–foreign divorce, as it increased over a hundred times within the three decades. In comparison, the overall registered number of divorces in the PRC barely increased seven times from nearly 320,000 couples in 1979 to approximately 2.3 million in 2008 (Zhonghua renmin gongheguo minzhengbu 1979, 2009). The reason for the soaring rate of divorces in China correlates with revisions to the PRC's marriage laws and regulations, which clarified the meaning of the breakdown of mutual affection as a ground for divorce in 2001 and simplified the procedure for divorce by removing the requirement of supporting letters for divorce applications from work units in 2003 (Article 32, Zhongguo renmin gongheguo hunyinfa 2001; Article 11, Hunyin dengji tiaoli 2003).

The PRC's Ministry of Civil Affairs began to disaggregate Chinese–foreign divorce statistics in 2005, by including separate figures for those involving '*waiguoren*'. The figure shows that in 2005, out of the 8,267 couples who registered a Chinese–foreign divorce in the PRC, 556 were foreign nationals. The number increased over three times, reaching 2,315 in 2007, before stabilizing at around 2,200 from 2009 to 2011 (Zhonghua renmin gongheguo minzhengbu 2006, 2008–2012 see Appendix 1). Such a trend indicates that the number of divorced foreign nationals grew in proportion to their rising number in Chinese–foreign marriages registered in the same period. Unsurprisingly, given the higher proportion of other categories of Chinese–foreign marriage until recently, most divorces

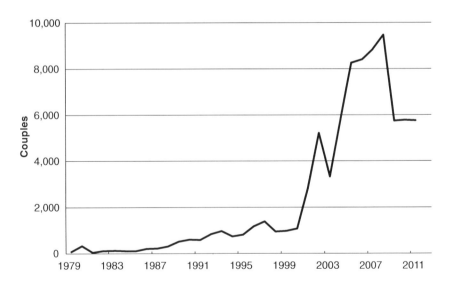

Figure 2.6 Chinese–foreign divorces

Source: *Zhongguo Minzheng Tongji Nianjian* (China Civil Affairs Statistical Yearbook).

relate to the 'Chinese' categories of Chinese–foreign marriage and the divorce rate is recorded as being proportionately higher in the coastal provinces of Guangdong, Fujian, Zhejiang and Shanghai city where most Chinese–foreign marriages are registered.

In short, Chinese–foreign marriage is a reform-era phenomenon. It accounts for a small proportion of total registered marriages in the PRC. However, the growth rate of such marriage and divorce is astonishing as both largely exceed the increasing number of overall registered marriages and divorces in the PRC during the same period. Similarly, the number of marriages that were registered outside mainland China and involved a Chinese spouse increased significantly from the 1990s to the present, especially with Chinese gradually becoming the dominant group among all types of foreign spouses in certain countries, such as Japan and the Republic of Korea. New features of Chinese–foreign marriage in the 2000s show that the number of foreign nationals overtook that of citizens from Hong Kong, Macau and Taiwan to become the most popular group of foreign spouses in Chinese–foreign marriages registered in mainland China after 2008. Although Chinese women dominate the number of PRC citizens in Chinese–foreign marriages, this proportion gradually decreased as a rapidly growing number of PRC males started to 'marry out' after the 2000s. These statistics imply that Chinese–foreign marriage has become an increasingly popular social phenomenon, and has started to disrupt the traditional forms of marriage and families in the PRC. The following section looks beyond the statistics by investigating the changing nature of PRC legal regulations governing marital and familial relations in the reform period.

Governing marriage in the reform era

Marriage and family relations in China are regulated by the Marriage Law of the People's Republic of China (*Zhonghua renmin gongheguo hunyin fa*), first promulgated in 1950 and revised in 1980 and 2001. The 1950 Marriage Law abolished polygamy, along with arranged and mercenary marriages and established a new marriage and family system based on the free choice of (heterosexual) partners, monogamy and equality between the sexes. A revised version of that law was approved in 1980, which contained several amendments designed to promote the PRC's one-child family policy of 1979 (*Zhonghua renmin gongheguo hunyin fa* 1980). The 1980 Marriage Law raised the legal age of marriage from 18 to 20 years for women, and from 20 to 22 years for men (Article 5) and it enjoined couples to practise 'family planning' (Article 12). It also stipulated for the first time that the People's Courts would grant a divorce in cases where couples had experienced a 'break down in mutual affections', and attempts at mediation had failed (Article 25). The 2001 Marriage Law contains various amendments and further clarifies the conditions for obtaining a divorce (*Zhonghua renmin gongheguo hunyin fa* 2001). Article 3 prohibits domestic violence, bigamy and the cohabitation of a married person with any third party; and Article 32 states that an individual may file a suit for divorce with the People's Courts and that a divorce shall be granted in cases involving the alienation of mutual affection.

The Marriage Law is supplemented by a national marriage registration system – a marriage is legal in the PRC only when it is registered with an appropriate department of civil affairs. This system has been revised numerous times since 1980, in order to accommodate the changing nature of social institutions and social behaviour and growing numbers of Chinese–foreign marriages. In November 1980, the 1980 Marriage Registration Procedures came into effect, replacing the procedures from 1955 ('Hunyin dengji banfa' 1980, 1955). The 1980 Marriage Registration Procedures referred only to marriages between PRC citizens, presumably because Chinese–foreign marriages were rare before the 1980s. In March 1986, they were superseded by revised procedures, which included the category of Chinese–foreign marriage for the first time ('Hunyin dengji banfa' 1986). Article 14 of the 1986 Marriage Registration Procedures stipulated that marriages between citizens of mainland China (*guonei gongmin*) and overseas Chinese (*huaqiao*), or between citizens of mainland China and their 'compatriots' (*tongbao*) from Hong Kong and Macau, should be administered according to the Rules on Marriage Registration between Chinese Citizens and Overseas Chinese and Hong Kong and Macau Compatriots (*Huaqiao tong guonei gongmin, Gang Ao tongbao tong neidi gongmin zhijian banli jiehun dengji de jixiang guiding* 1983) (hereafter the March 1983 Rules). It further stipulated that marriages between citizens of mainland China and foreign nationals (*waiguoren*) should be managed according to the Rules on Marriage Registration between Chinese Citizens and Foreigners (*Zhongguo gongmin tong waiguoren banli jiehun dengji de jixiang guiding* 1983) (hereafter the August 1983 Rules) (Article 14, 'Hunyin dengji banfa' 1986).

The 1986 procedures were replaced in 1994 by the Marriage Registration Management Regulations – the first of the PRC's marriage regulations to mention marriages between citizens of the PRC and Taiwan ('Hunyin dengji guanli tiaoli' 1994). Article 2 stipulated that marriages between citizens of mainland China and foreigners, or overseas Chinese, or residents from Hong Kong, Macau and Taiwan (*Xianggang, Aomen, Taiwan diqu de jumin*), should be managed according to the relevant procedures, i.e., the March 1983 and August 1983 Rules. The first document outlining the specific procedures relating to marriages between citizens of mainland China and people from Taiwan was the 1988 Notice on Issues Relating to Marriage Registration between Taiwan Compatriots and Mainland Citizens (*Guanyu Taiwan tongbao yu Dalu gongmin zhijian banli jiehun dengji youguan wenti de tongzhi* 1988) (hereafter the 1988 Notice), which was replaced in 1998 by the Interim Measures for Managing the Registration of Marriages between Mainland Residents and Taiwan Residents (*Dalu jumin yu Taiwan jumin hunyin dengji guanli zanxing banfa* 1998) (hereafter the 1998 Measures).

All of these different marriage registration procedures require parties applying for marriage registration to appear in person before the marriage registration authorities in order to verify their identity and confirm that they are single and entering into a marriage of their own free will. Prior to 1994, PRC applicants had to produce two types of documentation: a certificate of household registration or a resident identity card (*shenfenzheng*); and a certificate issued by their work unit, indicating the applicant's name, sex, date of birth, marital status and other identity-related details. From 1994 and until 2003, PRC citizens had to produce four types of documentation: a certificate of household registration; a residence identity card; a certificate issued by the applicant's work unit or local neighbourhood committee verifying their marital status; and a pre-marital health check-up report issued by a hospital designated by the marriage registration department ('Hunyin dengji guanli tiaoli' 1994). Mandatory pre-marital health check-ups aimed to protect the health of the marrying parties and their future children.

Chinese–foreign marriage registrations were and are still subject to somewhat different procedures because the identity of the foreign marrying party is verified based on proof of nationality/permanent residence. The Nationality Law of the PRC (1980) stipulates that 'any person born in China whose parents are both Chinese nationals or one of whose parents is a Chinese national shall have Chinese nationality' (Article 4) and 'any person born abroad whose parents are both Chinese nationals or one of whose parents is a Chinese national shall have Chinese nationality' (Articles 5). It further states that the PRC does not recognize dual nationality for any Chinese national, which means that citizens of the PRC who acquire foreign nationality are defined as 'Chinese with foreign nationalities (*waiji huaren*)' or a 'foreign national (*waiguoren*)' (Articles 3, 5 and 9). In the 1980s and 1990s, heightened claims by the PRC to sovereignty over Hong Kong and Macau meant that concepts of Chinese nationality were extended to include people from Hong Kong and Macau who were defined as Chinese 'compatriots' living in greater or non-mainland China. This understanding appears in the March 1983 and August 1983 Rules and was later given formal expression in the Basic Law of the Hong Kong Special Administrative Region of the PRC (1997) and the Basic Law of the Macau Special Administrative Region of the PRC (1999), which define people from Hong Kong and Macau of Chinese descent who were born in Chinese territory, including Hong Kong and Macau, as Chinese nationals (*Zhongguo gongmin*), irrespective of the particular passports they may hold.

The March 1983 and August 1983 Rules divide foreign applicants for marriage registration into three different categories: overseas Chinese, Hong Kong and Macau compatriots and foreigners per se. According to Article 2 of the March 1983 Rules, applicants categorized as overseas Chinese must produce four types of documentation: 1) a valid passport; 2) evidence of their single status issued by a notary office and confirmed by the Chinese embassy or consulate in the country of residence; 3) a work certificate or proof of a reliable source of income issued in the country of residence; and 4) a pre-marital health check-up report issued by a designated hospital in the PRC (*Huaqiao tong guonei gongmin, Gang Ao tongbao tong neidi gongmin zhijian banli jiehun dengji de jixiang guiding* 1983). People categorized as Hong Kong and Macau compatriots were required to produce similar documentation, with their Hong Kong or Macau identity card rather than an overseas passport. A document entitled 'Reply from the Ministry of Civil Affairs to [the Shanghai Civil Affairs Bureau] on Issues Related to Foreign Applicants for Marriage Registration' in 1983 suggests that the 'work certificate/proof of reliable income' requirement for overseas Chinese and Hong Kong and Macau compatriots, aimed to protect mainland Chinese citizens from fraud (*shou qipian*) and to ensure that their intended spouse was capable of supporting them financially once they relocated to regions other than mainland China ('Minzhengbu guanyu banli hunyin dengji zhong jige shewai wenti chuli yijian de pifu' 1983).

Marriage registration applicants categorized as foreigners – people with foreign nationality/passports, including Chinese people with foreign citizenship – had to produce four types of certification according to the August 1983 Rules. First, they had to produce a passport or another appropriate document proving their identity and citizenship. Second, they had to produce a residence permit for Foreigners (*waiguoren juliuzheng*), issued by a public security department, an identification certificate issued by a foreign affairs department, or an entry permit and residence permit for foreign nationals staying in China on a short-term basis. Third, they needed to produce a certificate confirming their single status issued by a notary in their country of origin and confirmed by the Chinese embassy or consulate in that country, or by their embassy or consulate in China. In cases where the foreign marrying partner had become a permanent resident of China, they had to obtain appropriate certification as per PRC citizens from government departments and work units. Finally, all foreign marrying partners had to present a pre-marital health check-up report issued in the PRC (Article 3, 'Zhongguo gongmin tong waiguoren banli jiehun dengji de jixiang guiding' 1983).

Unlike the March 1983 Rules, the August 1983 Rules precluded foreign nationals from marrying certain groups of Chinese citizens for reasons relating to national security and reputation. These included members of the army on active service, diplomatic personnel, public security personnel; state personnel in charge of confidential work or 'state secrets' and persons serving a criminal sentence or receiving re-education through labour (Article 4, 'Zhongguo gongmin tong waiguoren banli jiehun dengji de jixiang guiding' 1983). Also unlike overseas Chinese and Hong Kong and Macau compatriots, marriage registration applicants categorized as foreigners were not required to demonstrate a reliable source of income, perhaps because visa and permanent residence requirements for foreigners entering into China at that time required proof of work and income.

Additional regulations were introduced in 1988 to clarify local government departmental procedures regarding the registration of marriages between PRC citizens, and people defined as 'Taiwan compatriots' (*Taiwan tongbao*) (*Guanyu Taiwan tongbao yu Dalu gongmin zhijian banli jiehun dengji youguan wenti de tongzhi* 1988). The 1988 Notice divides Taiwan compatriots into different categories and outlines different marriage registration procedures for each type. Article 1 stipulates that Taiwan compatriots with permanent residence status in the PRC should be handled according to the 1986 Marriage Registration Procedures, with the additional requirement that they provide a certificate verifying their single status before registering a marriage in mainland China. Article 2 states that Taiwan compatriots visiting mainland China temporarily for the purposes of seeing family, or for travel and business purposes, should be dissuaded politely from registering a marriage (*wanyan quanzu*). However, if such persuasion failed, they had to produce five documents: 1) a valid travel certificate for Taiwan compatriots or a travel certificate for the PRC with the term 'Taiwan compatriots', or a PRC passport; 2) a temporary residence permit for the PRC issued by the public security department; 3) a personal identity card from Taiwan; 4) a certificate verifying their single status and 5) a pre-marital health check-up report issued in the PRC. Article 4 stipulates that Taiwan compatriots with foreign nationalities should be handled according to the August 1983 Rules; and Article 5 states that Taiwan compatriots with permanent residence status in Hong Kong, Macau, or an overseas country, should be treated according to the March 1983 Rules.

The 1988 Notice was replaced in 1998 by the Interim Measures for Managing the Registration of Marriages between Mainland Residents and Taiwan Residents, replacing the term 'Taiwan compatriot' with the expression 'Taiwan resident', defined as 'Chinese citizens residing in the Chinese region of Taiwan' (*juzhu zai Zhongguo Taiwan diqu de Zhongguo gongmin*) (Article 2, *Dalu jumin yu Taiwan jumin hunyin dengji guanli zanxing banfa* 1998). The 1998 Measures also omit references to discouraging marriage between certain types of Taiwan compatriots and residents of mainland China. Instead, they outline the procedures required to register both a marriage and a divorce between (Chinese) 'residents' of mainland China and Taiwan, describing them as a legal framework designed to protect the rights and interests of couples in such marriages (Article 1). Taiwan residents with permanent residence status in the PRC applying to register a marriage with a citizen of mainland China had to provide documents similar to those outlined in the 1994 Marriage Registration Management Regulations and undergo a pre-marital health check. For the purpose of verifying their identity and marital status, they had to provide a Taiwan residence identity card, a valid exit-entry permit and a certificate verifying their single status issued by a notary in Taiwan and a certified copy, valid for three months, of their permanent residence identification (Article 16). Other Taiwan residents applying to register a marriage with a PRC citizen had to produce the following four types of documentation: 1) a mainland travel permit for Taiwan residents or another valid travel pass; 2) a Taiwan residence identity card and a valid exit-entry permit; 3) a certificate verifying their single status issued by a notary in Taiwan and a certified copy, valid for three months, of their permanent residence identification; and 4), a pre-marital health check-up report issued in the PRC (Article 4).

In 2003, the 1994 Marriage Registration Management Regulations and all supplementary regulations governing the procedures for registering a Chinese–foreign marriage in the PRC were replaced by the current Marriage Registration Regulations ('Hunyin dengji tiaoli' 2003). In the 2003 regulations, the procedures for registering a domestic marriage have been simplified by the removal of the requirements for marital status certificates issued by work units, and abolishing mandatory pre-marital health check-ups. Domestic applicants for marriage registration are now required to produce a certificate of household registration, a residence identity card and a signed declaration stating that they are single and not a close blood relative of their intended spouse (Article 5), marriages between two people of direct lineal descent or collateral consanguinity within three generations being viewed from a medical standpoint as increasing the possibility of congenital disorders in children.

The 2003 regulations have simplified the registration procedures for applicants from all three categories of Chinese–foreign marriages. Applicants are no longer required to undergo a pre-marital health check-up; applicants categorized as overseas Chinese and residents of Hong Kong and Macau no longer have to provide evidence of a reliable source of income; and applicants from Taiwan are no longer required to present a certified copy of their Taiwanese permanent residence book. Applicants from Hong Kong, Macau and Taiwan now need to provide a valid exit-entry permit for the PRC, a residence identity card and a declaration issued by a notary in their place of domicile indicating that they are single and not a close blood relative of their intended spouse (Article 5, 'Hunyin dengji tiaoli' 2003). Overseas Chinese applicants must provide a valid passport and documentation proving that they are eligible to marry and are not a close blood relative of their intended spouse, issued by a notary in their country of residence and certified by the consulate of the PRC in that country. Foreign nationals need to provide a valid passport and documentation verifying their single status, issued by a notary and certified by the consulate of the PRC in their country of residence (Article 5). Unlike applicants categorized as overseas Chinese and residents of Hong Kong, Macau and Taiwan, foreign nationals do not have to prove that they are not a close blood relative of their intended spouse.

The 2003 Marriage Registration Regulations have also simplified the procedures for registering a divorce. Article 13 stipulates that a 'divorce certificate shall be issued at once when a divorce is desired by both parties and agreements have been reached regarding child care, property and outstanding debts' (Article 13, 'Hunyin dengji tiaoli' 2003). The 1994 regulations stated that the marriage registration department would process divorce applications within one month. However, only those persons who met the criteria for divorce would be issued a divorce certificate (Article 16, 'Hunyin dengji guanli tiaoli' 1994). Citizens of mainland China had to provide a letter supporting their divorce application from their work unit or an equivalent authority (Article 14), which was extremely difficult to obtain in practice because of an emphasis on mediation rather than the dissolution of troubled marriages.

Taken as a whole, these changes reflect an increasingly supportive governmental approach towards intimate and broader intercultural relations. This shift is underscored by the PRC Government's effort in facilitating travel for people from Hong Kong, Macau and Taiwan to the mainland. For example, China's Ministry of Public Security started researching and updating the old (1999) version of the 'Home Return Permit' (Mainland Travel Permit for Hong Kong and Macau Residents) (Gang Ao jumin laiwang neidi tongxingzheng) in 2010 for the convenience of people from Hong Kong and Macau to travel and reside in the mainland (Zhao Yang 2012). In doing so, it has granted a permanent ID number to permit holders and extended the validity period for holders under 18 years of age from three years to five years (Zouwei and Fuqing 2012).

At the same time, the PRC Government has taken consistent measures to facilitate citizens of Taiwan to travel, work, study and reside in mainland China. It has simplified the administrative procedures for Taiwan citizens to travel and stay in mainland China ('Zhong Tai ban' 2005). It has authorized a number of local government bodies including the municipalities of Shanghai, Beijing, Tianjin and the provinces of Jiangsu, Fujian Chongqing and Zhejiang to issue 'Taiwan Compatriot Certificates' (Mainland Travel Permit to Taiwan Residents) to allow Taiwanese travellers to stay on the mainland for up to five years ('Geren yewu' 2005; 'Chinese Mainland Issues New Policies to Ease Cross-Strait Travel' 2008). In addition, the PRC Government is planning to further simplify the procedures for Taiwanese to travel to the mainland by digitalizing their 'Taiwan Compatriot Certificates' ('Mainland Entry Permits More Accessible to Taiwanese' 2013).

This shift was also enhanced by the introduction in August 2004 of the Measures for the Administration of Examination and Approval of Aliens' Permanent Residence in China (2004) (hereafter the 2004 Measures). The 2004 Measures standardize the system of permanent residence for foreigners in China, making it easier for people who have made outstanding contributions to China, or who have an established record of successful investment in the PRC, or who hold key academic, professional and senior business management posts, to obtain permanent residence in China, along with their spouses and children under 18 years of age. Foreign spouses of PRC citizens, or foreign spouses of foreigners with permanent residence in the PRC, are entitled to permanent resident status, when they have been married for at least five years and have lived in the PRC for at least nine months of each year of those five years and have a stable source of income and residence (Article 6). In addition, the 2004 Measures contain provisions allowing the children and elderly parents of foreigners with permanent residence in the PRC to apply for permanent resident status. According to China's Ministry of Public Security, by the end of 2011, 4,752 foreigners had obtained a permanent residence card in China, of which 1,735 were elite professionals and their family members and 3,017 were applicants who came to China for family reunification ('Gonganbu' 2012). Additional regulations issued by the Ministry of Public Security in June 2010 also make it easier for the spouses, children and elderly parents of PRC citizens, foreigners with permanent resident status in the PRC and Chinese with foreign nationality, to obtain long-term resident status in the PRC, chiefly for the purposes of (re)uniting families.

Conclusion

This chapter has provided the background necessary for the discussions of media presentations of Chinese–foreign marriage in the PRC, which are the subjects of the following chapters. It has explained why Chinese–foreign marriage in the PRC was in many respects a reform-era phenomenon by outlining the kinds of obstacles that existed for intercultural marriages during the Maoist period. It has also outlined the numerical trend of both Chinese–foreign marriages and divorces, various types of foreign spouses in Chinese–foreign marriages, as well as the socio-demographic characters of Chinese–foreign marriages that are registered both in and outside mainland China from the 1980s to 2011. Finally, it has detailed some of the social and legal changes that have facilitated the growth of Chinese–foreign marriage in the PRC since the early reform period. The next chapter begins my analysis of the source materials I collected, focusing on newspaper coverage of the fluctuations of Chinese–foreign marriage in the PRC both prior to and after the 2000s.

Notes

1 'Reeducation through labour' (*laodong jiaoyang*) refers to a system of administrative punishments implemented by the State Council of the People's Republic of China in 1957. This system was used in theory to punish people who had committed 'minor' offences, for example, petty theft, fraud, assault and 'anti-Communist behaviours' and whose outlook on life could be transformed through education and the 'consciousness-raising' act of engaging in productive labour. Re-education through labour was normally imposed for a period of between one and three years (Bureau of Reeducation-through-Labor Administration 1979; Wang Zhaihua 2001: 58; Huang 2003a: 304). The system has attracted critical attention over the past decades for being politically motivated, encouraging human rights abuses and running counter to China's proclaimed adoption of a 'rule of law' (Huang 2003b: 37; Fu Hualing 2005: 812; Wing Lam and Zenobia Lai 2005: 31; Wang Lin 2010).

2 Figures for 1985 and 1986 are not available from the government archive.

3 Newspaper coverage of Chinese–foreign marriage

This chapter analyses newspaper coverage of Chinese–foreign marriage in the PRC since 1979, providing insight into how the media present, reflect and manipulate social, economic and cultural change in China via their reportage. First, the chapter discusses the newspaper portrayal of the numerical trends and countries/regions involved in Chinese–foreign marriages registered in reform-era China. It shows that the media interpret the 'new' social phenomenon of intercultural marriage as evidence of China's wider social, political and economic achievements stemming from the successful implementation of the opening-up and economic reform policy in late 1978. The chapter then examines newspaper accounts of Chinese citizens' motivations for entering into Chinese–foreign marriages and their evolution – from the criticized focus in the early reform period on hypergamy or 'marrying up' to today's emphasis on 'love'. Although newspaper reportage frames the evolution of these motivations as a straightforward sign of national advancement, an analysis of media representations across China's reform era reveals some inconsistencies that disrupt this image, particularly in the apparent rise of twenty-first-century manifestations of hypergamy.

Changing numerical trends

Newspaper discussions of the phenomenon of Chinese–foreign marriage in the PRC prior to the 2000s chiefly address the increasing number of intercultural marriages in the developing eastern seaboard regions of China, such as the cities of Haikou, Shanghai and Hangzhou. Haikou is a major port city and the capital of Hainan Province in the south of China's eastern seaboard. Shanghai is a major port city located on China's central eastern seaboard near the mouth of the Yangtze River Delta. Hangzhou is another core city of the Yangtze River Delta area and the capital city of Zhejiang Province in southeast China. These cities were among the first of China's cities to open to foreign trade in the 1980s, and soon became relatively affluent when compared to many other cities in the PRC (Chang Jian 2008; Zhou Huimin 2009; 'Zai gaige kaifang' 2011). Haikou was declared an open coastal city in 1983 and became the capital city of Hainan Province in 1988. Shanghai was among the first 14 of the PRC's coastal cities that were opened to foreign trade in 1984. Hangzhou was opened to foreign trade in 1988.

Newspaper discussions of the phenomenon of Chinese–foreign marriage in the PRC prior to the 2000s list the registered annual figures of intercultural marriages in each of these developing cities, and suggest that they indicate an ascending numerical trend. For example, several articles were published in the 1990s on the growth of intercultural marriage in Hainan Province after its establishment as a Special Economic Zone (SEZ) in 1988 ('Hainan shewai hunyin' 1993; Liu Gong and Wang Tingfeng 1999). 'Open coastal cities' and 'Special Economic Zones' are places or regions where the PRC Government adopted preferential economic policies and mechanisms that differed from those operating in the rest of mainland China in order to promote export-oriented business activity and investment, following the introduction of market-based economic reforms and the Open Door Policy in December 1978 (Yang Xiaobing 1988). In the early 1980s, the PRC Government established four SEZs in the cities of Shenzhen, Zhuhai and Shantou in China's southern coastal province of Guangdong and Xiamen in China's southeastern coastal province of Fujian, i.e., areas that are in close geographical proximity to the global trading hubs of Hong Kong and Taiwan ('Jingji tequ' 2002). Hainan Province, which is also near Hong Kong and Taiwan, was proclaimed the fifth and largest SEZ in China in 1988.

A 1999 report in the *Hainan Ribao* (Hainan Daily), entitled 'Chinese–Foreign Marriages Increase in Haikou' (*Haikou shewai hunyin rizeng*) indicates that the number of Chinese–foreign marriages registered in the city began to grow after Hainan Province became a SEZ in 1988. Haikou municipal authorities first began registering the number of Chinese–foreign marriages in the city in 1975 and only three couples registered an intercultural marriage in the city that year (Liu Gong and Wang Tingfeng 1999). During the 13-year period between 1975 and 1987, the total number of Chinese–foreign marriages registered in Haikou City comprised only 497 couples. However, in 1992, 385 couples registered an intercultural marriage in Haikou City. This figure grew to 512 couples in 1997 and 585 couples in 1998 ('Hainan shewai hunyin' 1993; Liu Gong and Wang Tingfeng 1999).

Other articles sketch the growing trend of intercultural marriage in Shanghai after the city was opened to foreign trade in 1984, as demonstrated by figures collected by the Shanghai Marriage Registration Office (Shanghai renmin zhengfu hunyin dengjichu), which was established on 1 July 1985 ('Shanghai shewai hunyin jianwen' 1988). A 1988 report in the *Shanghai Fazhibao* (hereafter Shanghai Legal Daily), entitled 'Chinese–Foreign Marriage in Shanghai', details the number of registered Chinese–foreign marriages in Shanghai between 1985 and 1987 ('Shanghai shewai hunyin jianwen' 1988). According to this report, 394 couples registered a Chinese–foreign marriage in Shanghai between 1 July and December 1985, whereas 574 couples registered a Chinese–foreign marriage in Shanghai between 1 January and 5 October 1987. A 1993 report in the *Renmin Ribao* (hereafter People's Daily) further indicates that over 800 couples entered into a Chinese–foreign marriage in Shanghai in 1989. That figure climbed to over 1,800 couples in 1991, and exceeded 2,500 couples in 1992 (Deng Huajuan 1993).

A number of other reports suggest an ascending trend in intercultural marriage in Hangzhou City after the opening of the city to foreign trade in 1988. Hangzhou municipal authorities first began registering the number of Chinese–foreign marriages in the city on 1 January 1986. Those figures show that 65 couples registered a Chinese–foreign marriage in Hangzhou City in 1986. This figure increased to 78 couples in 1987 and 86 couples in 1988 ('Heping, Youyi, Xingfu' 1989). However, the number of couples registering a Chinese–foreign marriage in Hangzhou City increased to 249 couples in 1991 (Ling Zaiming 1992).

Some of these reports indicate that the majority of such marriages were marriages between female citizens of mainland China and male citizens of Hong Kong and Macau. For example, the aforementioned 1988 report in the *Shanghai Legal Daily* categorizes the number of Chinese–foreign marriages registered in the city of Shanghai in 1986 in terms of nationality and gender ('Shanghai shewai hunyin jianwen' 1988). It notes that the number of Chinese–foreign marriages in Shanghai totalled 794 couples in 1986. This included 440 citizens from Hong Kong and Macau, 109 Chinese with foreign nationalities and 89 (non-ethnic Chinese) foreign nationals, with no explanation offered to account for the missing figures. It also indicates that out of the combined figure of 198 intercultural marriages involving citizens of the PRC and Chinese with foreign nationalities and foreign nationals, only 16 women with foreign nationality married male citizens of the PRC in Shanghai in 1986 ('Shanghai shewai hunyin jianwen' 1988). In other words, the article suggests that the majority of Chinese–foreign marriages that were registered in Shanghai in 1986 were marriages between citizens of the PRC and citizens of Hong Kong and Macau and between citizens of the PRC and Hong Kong, in particular.

The aforementioned 1999 report in the *Hainan Daily* similarly suggests that over 80 per cent of the Chinese–foreign marriages registered in Haikou City between 1975 and the mid-1990s were marriages between citizens of mainland China and Hong Kong (Liu Gong and Wang Tingfeng 1999). Municipal authorities in Haikou began to collect statistics on the number of Chinese–foreign marriages registered in the city in 1975. However, the same report indicates that marriages between citizens of the PRC and Taiwanese citizens were becoming more popular in Haikou City than marriages between citizens of mainland China and citizens of Hong Kong in the late 1990s. Of the 585 couples who registered a Chinese–foreign marriage in Haikou City in 1998, 457 marriages were marriages between citizens of the PRC and citizens of Taiwan.

Apart from brief descriptions of the figures, the early reports offer no specific discussions on the rapid growth of marriages between mainland Chinese citizens and citizens from Hong Kong, Macau and Taiwan. Yet scholarly works suggest that the growing popularity of marriages in eastern coastal areas of China in the 1980s and 1990s between mainland Chinese women and men of Chinese ethnicity from Hong Kong and Macau stemmed from the altered political environment of reform-era China and the consequent introduction of legislation facilitating business and private exchanges. Following the establishment of the PRC in 1949, the border between the British colony of Hong Kong and the PRC was heavily policed to protect the different political/ideological interests of both countries and to control the flow of political refugees and (illegal) economic migrants from mainland China to Hong Kong (Shen Jianfa 2003: 3). Similarly, the inhabitants of the former Portuguese colony of Macau had little communication with people from mainland China (Zhao Yajuan *et al.* 1999: 42; Shen Jianfa 2003: 5). This meant that opportunities for marriages between citizens of the PRC and citizens of Hong Kong and Macau were extremely limited until the early 1980s. In 1983, the PRC Government granted permission for mainland Chinese citizens living in Guangdong Province to visit friends and relatives in Hong Kong as part of organized tours. This was followed by the granting of similar permission for mainland Chinese citizens to visit friends and relatives in Macau in 1984 (Qu Hailin and Lam 1997: 594; Zhang Guangrui 2003: 15; Zhang *et al.* 2005: 67).

Along with rapid economic development in the PRC and the return of Hong Kong and Macau to the PRC in 1997 and 1999, business and private exchanges between the three legal jurisdictions has increased dramatically. Initially, such exchanges involved the flow of people from the wealthier countries of Hong Kong and Macau[1] to the PRC in order to visit family and/or conduct business (Qu Hailin and Lam 1997: 593–4; Wen and Tisdell 2001: 130). The inferior economic position of the PRC vis-à-vis Hong Kong was reflected in the new phenomenon of male entrepreneurs and managers from Hong Kong keeping mistresses or 'second wives' (*bao er'nai*) during their periods of work in China. Their 'mainland wives' typically were young migrant factory workers in the developing cities of southern China who sought upward social mobility (Lang and Smart 2002: 546–69; So 2003: 521–2). At the same time, single men from Hong Kong, especially men working in low-paid employment as lorry drivers, manual labourers and construction workers, began to marry women from mainland China, reportedly viewing them as both more 'affordable' and 'less picky' than Hong Kong women (So 2003: 525). Some single men with menial forms of employment and who had fled mainland China for Hong Kong in the 1960s and 1970s, also sought to marry women from mainland China, reportedly viewing them as both 'less choosy' and more culturally compatible than Hong Kong women (So 2003: 521–5).

Similarly, the easing of political tensions between the PRC and Taiwan in the late 1980s, and subsequent permission for individuals to travel across the Taiwan Strait for the purposes of family reunification, led to a growing number of marriages between citizens of mainland China and citizens of Taiwan. The first group of Taiwan nationals to enter the PRC consisted predominantly of elderly veterans of the Nationalist Party who had retreated to Taiwan with the Nationalist army in 1949 and wished to visit their place of birth. These were also the first cohort to engage in cross-Strait marriage as they brought younger spouses from their native homes back to Taiwan with them (Friedman 2010: 76; Tsai 2011: 244). This first cohort of 'mainland brides' was comprised largely of divorced and widowed women between 30 and 50 years of age (Friedman 2010: 76). In the late 1990s and early 2000s, the number of marriages between citizens of mainland China and citizens of Taiwan increased dramatically along with increased social, economic and political interaction between the PRC and Taiwan (Lu 2008: 192; Friedman 2010: 76–7).

Although discussions of intercultural marriage in China's newspapers in the 2000s continue to emphasize the popularity of Chinese–foreign marriage, they also highlight a new and descending numerical trend. Newspaper reports from eastern coastal cities such as Shanghai, Weihai and Wenzhou, as well as other eastern cities such as Jinhua and Nanjing, began to comment on this changing situation as early as 2004. Wenzhou is a sea port city located in southeastern Zhejiang Province and Weihai is a major sea port city located at the eastern end of Shandong Province in eastern China (Weihai Provincial Government 2004; Wenzhou Provincial Government 2010). Nanjing, the capital city of China's eastern coastal province of Jiangsu, is situated in the lower Yangtze River (Changjiang) Drainage Basin and Yangze River Delta economic zone. It is a major political, economic, transport and cultural centre ('Map of Nanjing City' 2010). Jinhua city is located in the central part of China's eastern coastal province of Zhejiang and is connected to the three port cities of Hangzhou and Shanghai in the north and Ningbo in the east (Zhejiang Provincial Government 2006).

A report entitled 'Chinese–Foreign Marriage Encounters "Seven-Year-Itch"' (*Shewai hunyin zaoyu 7 nian zhiyang*) in the *Wenhui Bao* (hereafter Wenhui News) notes that the number of intercultural marriages registered in Shanghai rose between the mid-1990s and 2001, but has since started to slow down (Shao Zhen and Liang Hongying 2004). The *Weihai Ribao* (hereafter Weihai Daily) covered a similar story in September 2005 called 'Why Is Chinese–Foreign Marriage Decreasing Yearly?' (*Shewai hunyin yuanhe zhunian jiangwen*). As it points out, prior to 2003, approximately 100 couples registered as entering into a Chinese–foreign marriage in Weihai city on an annual basis. That figure fell to 80 couples in 2004, and decreased to only 50 couples in 2005 (Zhang Keguo 2005).

Newspaper reports about intercultural marriage in the sea port city of Wenzhou further point to a decreasing trend in the number of Chinese–foreign marriages in the PRC during the mid- to late 2000s. The *Taizhou Wanbao* (hereafter Taizhou Evening News) published an article in 2007 called 'Records of Chinese–Foreign Marriage Lowest in Four Years: Cross-Cultural Love Is No Longer Favoured by Wenzhounese' (*Shewai hunyin dengji shuliang wei jin 4 nian zuidi, kuaguo hunyin buzai shou Wenzhouren qinglai*). It states that statistics released by the local department of Civil Affairs show that over 200 Chinese–foreign couples registered their marriage in Wenzhou in 1991. That figure rose to over 500 couples in 2000, reaching 1,200 couples in 2003. However, only 1,000 Chinese–foreign couples registered their marriage in Wenzhou in 2006 and that figure decreased to 600 couples between January and August 2007, demonstrating a continued decreasing trend ('Shewai hunyin dengji' 2007).

In a similar vein, a 2006 report in the *Nanjing Ribao* (hereafter Nanjing Daily) notes that the number of intercultural marriages registered in Nanjing in 2005 was 1,378 couples, which constitutes a decrease from 2004 (Ni Yan and Xu Xiuyou 2006). Likewise, the *Jinhua Ribao* (Jinhua Daily) featured a story in 2007 entitled 'Intercultural Marriage Decreases in Our City' (*Woshi shewai hunyin shuliang yousuo xiajiang*) (Jiang Zhongyi 2007). As the title suggests, the number of intercultural marriages in Jinhua city had previously reached a constant figure of around 130 couples per annum. However, that figure had decreased by more than ten couples in 2007 when compared with the same period in 2006 (Jiang Zhongyi 2007).

By 2009, national newspapers were covering stories that suggested a descending trend in the number of Chinese–foreign marriages across the PRC as a whole. Both the *Zhongguo Funü bao* (hereafter China Women's News), and the *Fazhi Wanbao* (hereafter Legal Evening News) featured articles indicating that the total number of intercultural marriages registered in the PRC had remained constant in 2007 and 2008 at around 51,000 couples (Gao Li 2009; Li Sha 2009a). However, as both articles concluded, those figures were lower than the number of Chinese–foreign marriages registered in previous years (Gao Li 2009; Li Sha 2009a).

Newspaper coverage of changing trends in the number of intercultural marriages in the PRC reflects an obvious interest in new social phenomena, while also aiming to demonstrate the success of China's post-1978 economic reforms and Open Door Policy (Zhong Qing 1989; 'Difang "guoji"' 1992; 'Hainan shewai hunyin' 1993). For example, the *People's Daily* noted in 1989 that Chinese–foreign marriage began to increase on a gradual basis after China opened its door to the outside world (Zhong Qing 1989). Other reports similarly emphasize a causal relationship between China's adoption of market-based economic reforms, and the increased numbers of Chinese–foreign marriages in the PRC prior to the mid-2000s. Such presentations repeatedly remind the reader of the importance of China's Open Door Policy and economic reform as historical evidence of the CCP's success. Simultaneously, such frames use Chinese–foreign intimacy as evidence to underscore the ongoing integration of China and the rest of the world ('Difang guoji' 1992; Du Zhanfan 2001; Wu Xiaoyan 2008; Gao Li 2009).

Reports on decreasing rates of intercultural marriage in the PRC newspapers in the 2000s are used in a somewhat different way to explain both China's ongoing socio-economic development and perceived positive changes in the 'mindset' of Chinese citizens. The term 'rational' (*lizhi, lixing*) is frequently used to describe the recent decrease in the number of intercultural marriages in the PRC (Zhang keguo 2005; 'Shewai hunyin dengji' 2007; Jiang Zhongyi 2007). For instance, the *Weihai Daily* states that intercultural marriage in Weihai city has been decreasing in recent years, mainly because people of a marriageable age in Weihai city have become more 'rational' about their marital choices, flowing from improved local standards of living and expanded communications between Weihai and the outside world (Zhang Keguo 2005). By presenting Chinese citizens' 'rationality' as a reason for the decreasing trend of Chinese–foreign marriages, the media divert the readers' attention from the negative causes which might have led to such change, such as social, individual or institutional factors. A 2007 report in the *Taizhou Evening News* similarly asserts that economic development in the city of Wenzhou has reduced the gap between the standards of living of its citizens, and those of people from overseas, resulting in fewer intercultural marriages ('Shewai hunyin dengji' 2007). A similar style of framing in both reports suggests that Chinese citizens are no longer entering into an intercultural marriage for reasons of socio-economic advancement or hypergamy, but rather are now marrying on the more 'rational' basis of love, as reportedly evidenced by the narrowing age gap, education level and economic circumstances, between Chinese marrying parties and their foreign spouses (Jiang Zhongyi 2007; Tan Lujie 2009).

In sum, both increased and decreased rates of intercultural marriage are framed in PRC newspaper reports as a sign of China's national progress, modernization and integration into the world. The next section of this chapter examines newspaper coverage of the various places and countries of origin of non-PRC citizens entering into Chinese–foreign marriages in mainland China, before moving on to a discussion of the perceived motivations for intercultural marriages in the PRC.

Different countries of origin

Along with changing rates of intercultural marriage, newspaper discussions of Chinese–foreign marriage in the PRC demonstrate that non-PRC marriage partners come from a broadening range of countries and regions. Newspaper articles from the 1980s and early 1990s suggest that Chinese–foreign marriages predominantly took place between PRC citizens and people from the neighbouring regions of Hong Kong, Macau and Taiwan and to a lesser extent between PRC citizens and overseas Chinese (*huaqiao*) and between PRC citizens and foreign nationals, which include Chinese with foreign nationality (*waiji huaren*). The rising incidence of marriages between PRC citizens and Chinese with foreign nationality is indicated by the use of terms such as 'Chinese with American nationality' (*Meiji huaren*), 'Chinese with foreign nationality' and 'Chinese–American marriage introduction agency' (*Zhong Mei hunyin jieshaosuo*) ('Shanghai shewai hunyin jianwen' 1988; 'Lianyungang kaiban shewai hunyin jieshaosuo' 1992; Deng Huajuan 1993). Early newspaper reports also refer to Chinese–foreign marriages as involving marriages between PRC citizens and non-ethnic Chinese citizens of Denmark, France, Germany, Japan, Singapore, the United Kingdom and the United States of America ('Shanghai shewai hunyin jianwen' 1988; 'Hainan shewai hunyin' 1993; Min Zheng 1994).

More recent reports indicate that intercultural marriages in the PRC now include citizens of Australia, Canada, South Korea, Denmark, France, Germany, Holland, India, Indonesia, Japan, Malaysia, New Zealand, Singapore, Spain, South Korea, the UK, the USA and African countries such as Ethiopia and Tanzania (Meng Xiaoyun 2001; Chen Liyu 2003; Yuan Lanhua and Du Zhanfan 2005; Pan Meihong 2006). Although there are no comprehensive statistics available regarding the non-Chinese or 'foreign' countries of origin for intercultural marriages in China, media reports and statistics from local governments in the PRC suggest that this figure amounted to 60 countries by 2009 and perhaps more in advanced coastal cities like Shanghai. For example, a 2003 report in the *People's Daily*, entitled 'Shanghai Foreign Marriage Maintains Healthy Growth: Love Links all Continents' (*Hu shewai hunyin jiankang fazhan, wanli yinyuan qianshou ge dazhou*) asserts that Chinese–foreign marriages in the city of Shanghai alone now include partners from all the continents in the world other than Antarctica (Chen Liyu 2003).

Table 3.1 below provides a reference for the most popular foreign countries of origin for people involved in Chinese–foreign marriages across several major cities and regions in the PRC, based on a summary of foreign countries of origin as provided in Chinese newspaper reports from the 1980s to 2000s, excluding Hong Kong, Macau and Taiwan. According to these reports, the most popular foreign countries of origin for people registered as entering into a Chinese–foreign marriage in the PRC are Australia, Canada, European countries, Japan, South Korea and the USA. These countries are ranked in order of popularity in the case of the following four cities – Shanghai, Dalian, Qingdao and Tianjin (Chen Liyu 2003; Pan Meihong 2006; Wang Shengtian and Bao Wenfeng 2008; Yu Xiaoyang and Du Zhanfan 2008). However, such rankings are not definitive as they have been reported in an inconsistent manner and on an irregular basis. In fact, inconsistent reporting makes it impossible to rank the most popular foreign countries of origin for intercultural marriages in the regions of Hainan, Shantou, Ningxia and Xiamen. Hence, Table 3.1 simply provides at best an indication of the most popular foreign countries of origin for intercultural marriages across several major cities and regions in China, as represented in newspaper reports in the PRC ('Hainan shewai hunyin'1993; Zhao Yuanyuan 2007; Lin Guifen 2008; Zhou Min 2009).

Newspaper discussions of Chinese–foreign marriage in the PRC between the 1980s and 1990s highlight the rising number of countries of origin for such marriages to remind the readers of the successful nature of China's economic reforms and Open Door Policy and the perceived benefits of those reforms for both PRC citizens and non-PRC citizens. A 1988 article in the *Shanghai Legal Daily*

Table 3.1 Chinese–foreign marriages registered in the PRC (popular regions and foreign countries of origin)

Cities/provinces in China	Foreign country of origin
Shanghai*	Japan, USA, Australia, European countries, Canada
Dalian*	Japan, USA, Australia, Canada
Qingdao*	Japan, South Korea, USA, Canada, Australia
Tianjin*	USA, European countries, South Korea, Japan, Australia, Southeast Asian countries (Indonesia, Thailand, the Phillippines and Singapore)
Hainan**	Denmark, France, Germany, Japan, Singapore, UK, USA
Shantou**	Australia, Canada, Japan, South Korea, UK
Ningxia**	Bangladesh, Canada, India, Japan, Kyrgyzstan, South Korea, USA
Xiamen**	Canada, Italy, Japan, Malaysia, Phillippines, Singapore, South Korea, Switzerland, Thailand, UK, USA

* Ranked according to popularity as documented in source (see Chen Liyu 2003; Pan Meihong 2006; Wang Shengtian and Bao Wenfeng 2008; Yu Xiaoyang and Du Zhanfan 2008).
** Not ranked (alphabetical order used as default). 'Hainan shewai hunyin 1993; Zhao Yuanyuan 2007; Lin Guifen 2008; Zhou Min 2009.

notes that Chinese–foreign marriages in Shanghai involved partners from 23 different foreign countries of origin ('Shanghai shewai hunyin jianwan' 1988). It then offers a personalized story of a marriage between a German woman and a male citizen of the PRC, stating that the German woman studied Chinese at university and finds China enormously attractive. The report implies that China's opening-up has generated benefits for foreign citizens in that they can now marry and live in China. Conversely, a 1993 article in the *Hangzhou Ribao* (Hangzhou Daily) details a growth in the foreign countries of origin for intercultural marriage in Hainan, concluding that economic reform has benefited Chinese women by providing them with a new freedom to migrate and marry outside the PRC ('Hainan shewai hunyin' 1993).

In the 2000s, newspaper discussions of intercultural marriage in the PRC highlight the expansion of foreign countries of origin for intercultural marriages in order to demonstrate the impact of modernization on societal values and behaviours in China. In this context, Chinese–foreign marriage is framed as evidence of the social development and internationalization of cities. For example, a 2002 article in the *Wenhui News* refers to the increased number of countries of origin for Chinese–foreign marriages in Shanghai, stating that 'the opening-up of the city has enabled women from Shanghai to 'walk with confidence' (*chongman zixin de zou*) to different parts of the world (Liang Hongying 2002). The article concludes that these changes indirectly reflect the social progress (*cong yige cemian fanying le shehui de jinbu*), and renewed values (*guan'nian de gengxin*) of Shanghai people (Liang Hongying 2002). In using phrases such as 'walk with confidence', 'social progress' and 'renewed values', the article basically tells the readers that Shanghai's economic development has empowered its (female) residents to interact with people from other countries and has also given them the freedom to act in a similar fashion to the people of western and Asian cosmopolitan cities such as London, New York and Tokyo.

Other reports, such as 'Love Connects the World – Intercultural Marriage in Qingdao (Qianshou shijie de yinyuan – Daocheng shewai hunyin pandian)' by the *Zhongguo Shehuibao* (hereafter China Society News) in 2005, explain that enhanced communication and business cooperation between Qingdao and overseas countries has increased the number of Chinese–foreign marriages in China's eastern coastal city of Qingdao (Yuan Lanhua and Du Zhanfan 2005). As the *China Society News* article continues, changes in the countries of origin of intercultural marriage correlate with the openness of the now global city of Qingdao and with the 'gradually broadening horizons' (*riyi kaikuo de yanjie*) and 'mature values' (*riyi chengshu de shijieguan he jiazhiguan*) of its people (Yuan Lanhua and Du Zhanfan 2005). Although the report does not specify exactly what is meant by the use of expressions such as 'broad horizons' and 'mature values', it nevertheless suggests that enhanced interaction between Chinese citizens and non-ethnic Chinese citizens of overseas countries has resulted in positive changes in the mindset and behaviours of PRC citizens. In other words, such framing implies that economic development has led to significant changes in the city of Qingdao and in the mentality of its people.

At the same time, recent newspaper discussions of intercultural marriage in the PRC also aim to show that China's economic development has had an impact on the migration patterns and values of the 'foreign' partners in Chinese–foreign marriages. This situation is illustrated with reference to the fact that many 'foreign partners' are now willing to marry and live in the PRC rather than returning to their countries of origin. In framing such issues, the PRC newspapers tend to attach and/or elevate the meaning of Chinese–foreign marriages so as to affirm and seek support of the PRC Government's efforts in promoting the construction of Socialist Spiritual Civilization in China.[2] For example, the *China Society News* featured a 2001 article, entitled 'Standardizing and Institutionalizing Chinese–Foreign Marriage Services' (*Tuijin shewai hunyin fuwu zhiduhua guifanhua jianshe*), which states that a changing feature of intercultural marriages in Qingdao is that more Chinese–foreign couples now chose to live in Qingdao after they marry (Du Zhanfan 2001). After outlining other new dynamics of Chinese–foreign marriages in Qingdao, the article states that Chinese–foreign marriage (registration service), as 'a window of the construction of spiritual civilization' (*jingshen wenming jianshe de chuangkou*), mirrors the values and conceptions of the Chinese people. Hence it plays a significant role in accelerating social progress and the development of civil society. In conclusion, it notes that as a window for 'international communication' and a reflection of the 'quality of Chinese citizens' (*guomin suzhi xingxiang*), Chinese–foreign marriage registration bureaus should provide efficient services so as to show the good spirit and ideological level of the Chinese people.

Likewise, a 2007 article in the *People's Daily* states that along with rising numbers of intercultural marriages in China's open coastal regions and large and medium-sized cities, an increasing number of 'foreign sons and daughters-in-law' (*yang nüxu, yang xifu*) are becoming part of Chinese family structures (Wu Xuemei and He Xin 2007a). In its following paragraph, the article quotes the widely cited opinion of Li Yinhe, an academic director of China's Academy of Social Sciences. In Li's view, Chinese–foreign marriage is like a 'catalyst' (*runhuaji*), which binds people of different national and ethnic backgrounds. Mutual understanding of each other's cultures, religions and languages will contribute to the communication between countries and maintain social stability (Wu Xuemei and He Xin 2007a). Finally, a 2009 story in the *China Women's News* notes that an increasing number of 'Loving Chinese–Foreign Couples' (*yiguo yuanyang*) are now living and working in the PRC (Gao Li 2009). It then concludes that with the development of China's economic reform and expanding cooperation and communication with the outside world, Chinese–foreign marriages will gradually manifest Chinese people's generosity (*xiongjin*) and tolerance (*baorong*), as well as the boundless nature of love (*ai wu guojie*).

The construction of these new dynamics exposes a recent and under-studied pattern of Chinese–foreign marriage migration. Studies of migration patterns in relation to intercultural marriage chiefly focus on the emigration strategies of women from less developed countries, such as the Philippines, Vietnam and the Chinese hinterland, to developed countries, such as the USA, Canada, Japan and parts of Europe (Constable 2005b: 10; Chao 2005: 34–52; Schein 2005: 53–79). The reasons behind this outward pattern of transnational mobility are complex but usually described in terms of social and economic advancement, studying overseas and/or for possible career advancement (Romano 1997: 194; Constable 2005b: 10; Chao 2005: 34–52; Schein 2005: 53–79; Liu Lihui and Liu Hong 2008: 258).

As Nicole Constable (2005a: 168, 183) explains in *Cross-Border Marriages: Gender and Mobility in Transnational Asia*, Chinese women and Filipino women often seek American spouses because marriage to an American empowers their blood families by providing them with economic assistance and offers family members, including children, an opportunity to emigrate to the developed West. Emily Chao (2005: 34–52) somewhat differently observes that some women from the rural area of Lijiang, in the Naxi Autonomous Prefecture in China's Yunnan Province, seek to marry people from overseas in order to escape from the constrains of local systems of patriarchal marriages and to achieve residence in more desirable and modern areas. Liu Lihui and Liu Hong (2008: 258), in *Chinese Women and the Cyberspace*, argue that intercultural marriage is used as a tool by some Chinese people to enter the USA for the purposes of advancing their education, in part by enabling them to apply for scholarships in their new, host country. They further contend that some PRC citizens marry people from overseas in order to expand their business operations to a different country.

In contrast to this focus on outward patterns of transnational migration, newspaper discussions of intercultural marriage in the PRC during the mid- to late-2000s highlight a different and reverse trend. They point to the marriage-related movement of people from wealthy industrial countries to the economically dynamic but still relatively poor new 'global cities' of the developing world. Such cities include China's increasingly cosmopolitan cities of Shanghai and Beijing, the perhaps less well-known but self-proclaimed 'global city' of Qingdao in Shandong Province, northeastern China and the rapidly developing municipalities of Tianjin and Chongqing in northeastern and southwestern China respectively (Li Demin 2004; Yuan Lanhua and Du Zhanfan 2005; Wu Xuemei and He Xin 2007a; Zhao Junhui 2007; Ma Xin 2009).

James Farrer (2008a: 7–29) discusses the emergence of this new pattern of intercultural marriage migration in Shanghai in the late 1990s. According to Farrer (2008a: 8), a survey conducted by the PRC's Ministry of Civil Affairs in 1997 revealed that an increasing number of couples who registered a Chinese–foreign marriage in Shanghai were choosing to live in that city rather than moving abroad as previously. Based on a combination of media analysis and ethnographic research, Farrer (2008a: 10) notes that people in their respective work units or universities treated many Chinese women who dated foreigners in the 1990s in a negative manner. This acted as a social discouragement to Chinese women entering into an intercultural marriage, although it did not necessarily stop Shanghainese women from marrying foreign citizens. Farrer (2008a: 10) concludes that the ascending trend of intercultural marriage in the PRC between 1995 and 2005, combined with growing confidence in China's continued economic development, has dampened social resistance to intercultural marriage in the PRC.

As this new pattern of intercultural marriage migration is linked to perceived changes in the motivations for people entering into Chinese–foreign marriages, I will now turn to an examination of how the motivations of Chinese citizens entering into an intercultural marriage are described in newspaper reports in the PRC from the 1980s to the late 2000s. These motivations are typically portrayed in terms of a shift from hypergamic motivations – which were much criticized by China's media throughout the 1980s to 1990s – to the more acceptable, and celebrated focus on love in the 2000s. This narrative overlooks the complexity and altered nature of hypergamic motivations in their twenty-first century manifestations.

Hypergamy

Of the few articles published in the 1990s that address the issue of motivation in relation to Chinese–foreign marriage in the PRC, the practice of hypergamy is singled out for special attention as a gendered phenomenon that often results in either personal disappointment or tragic consequences ('Difang guoji' 1992; 'You nü Yu yuanjia' 1993; Ji Zhe 1996; Liu Gong and Wang Tingfeng 1999). Hypergamy refers in this instance to the practice of women from mainland China marrying foreign men from 'Western' countries as a means to improve their social or financial circumstances. Such women are typically framed as being in their late twenties and early thirties, marrying foreign men who are considerably older than them. This phenomenon is described in the Chinese language as the 'old husband–young wife' (*laofu shaoqi*) phenomenon. The Chinese female marrying partner is usually 10 to 15 years younger than her foreign spouse, although in some cases the age gap is greater than 40 years ('Shanghai shewai hunyin jianwen' 1988; Liu Xiaoxiao 2005; Pan Meihong 2006; Liang Ying and Peng Xuemei 2008; Gao Li 2009). These Chinese women reportedly marry older foreign men to go abroad, obtain a 'green card', to become rich and/or to change their life circumstances (Liu Xiaoxiao 2005; Pan Meihong 2006; 'Shewai hunyin dengji' 2007; Wu Xiaoyan 2008). In other words, they allegedly view intercultural marriage as a 'springboard' (*tiaoban*) to improve their socio-economic circumstances.

Newspaper reports of Chinese–foreign marriages based on hypergamous motivations in the PRC are frequently presented in the form of cautionary tales of tragedy and personal disappointment that warn young women not to enter into a Chinese–foreign marriage solely for the purposes of social advancement. A 1996 report in the *Zhejiang Ribao* (hereafter Zhejiang Daily) entitled 'Dream Ends in Baghdad' (*Meng duan Bageda*), offers an early and dramatic example of this style of reportage (Ji Zhe 1996). As it explains, in the early 1990s, a young, beautiful and talented Chinese woman named 'Wang Jiali' met an Iraqi man named 'Ba' who claimed to be a millionaire. The couple met through an introduction by the woman's friend – that friend being Ba's 'girlfriend' at the time. Envious of her friend and desiring to live overseas and become a 'rich wife' (*fupo*), Wang began dating and eventually married Ba in China. However, upon arriving in Baghdad, she discovered that he was already married with a son, and was definitely not rich. Instead of living in comfort, Wang was treated like a house servant by Ba and his wife. Moreover, Ba and his local male cohorts sexually abused her. Ba allegedly ensured Wang's compliance by placing drugs in her food, resulting in a tragic drug addiction. After Wang managed to 'escape' and return to China, she wound-up murdering her father, who worked in a hospital, when he refused to procure and inject her with the drug 'Dolantin' (Ji Zhe 1996), a narcotic analgesic used for pain relief that leads to dependence with prolonged use.

Another report entitled 'Striking at the Heart of Chinese–Foreign Marriages' (*Zhiji Zhongguo kuaguo hunyin mingmen*) by the *Fazhi Zaobao* (Legal Morning Post) in 2005 narrates two stories which reportedly happened in 1989 and early 2000 respectively. The 1989 story is about a Chinese woman in her early twenties who had been offered a local government job in Beijing after graduating from university. Dissatisfied with the 'mundane' and 'ordinary' nature of her life in China, she started visiting places where foreigners gathered in Beijing in the hope of meeting a potential marriage partner and starting a new life abroad (Liu Xiaoxiao 2005). Eventually, she met 'Tom', an American citizen who was 15 years older than she was. Despite the objections of family and friends, she separated from her long-term Chinese boyfriend and married and moved to the USA. However, not long after they arrived in the USA, she discovered that Tom was a violent alcoholic, who often beat and even raped her when they quarrelled. The early 2000 story is about a 29-year-old Chinese woman from Shanghai who, also longing for a wealthy life abroad, married a Japanese man who was 15 years older than she was (Liu Xiaoxiao 2005). Contrary to her dreams of social advancement, married life in Japan proved to be one of daily household and farm-work drudgery and constant beatings when she did not perform those 'duties' to her husband's satisfaction.

The depiction of Chinese women's 'hypergamous' behaviours closely links their upward social mobility to subsequent tragic consequences. It functions to warn its potential readers, young Chinese women in particular, that intercultural marriage is not a straightforward 'bridge to heaven' (*tongwang tiantang de qiaoliang*). It suggests, albeit in melodramatic form, that Chinese women in the early reform period often were unaware of the potential marital difficulties associated with cultural differences. Moreover, they were unaware of the social and day-to-day realities of life in a foreign country. Such reportage of Chinese–foreign marriages somehow generalizes Chinese women's motivation as hypergamous in nature. It simultaneously simplifies the complexities of their motivation to the level of anecdotal evidence.

Certainly, several articles relate tales of disappointment flowing from intercultural marriages based on a combination of hypergamous motivations of going abroad and the 'blind worship of everything foreign' (*chongyang meiwai*), or the reported practice of 'idolizing' and 'fawning on' foreign people and cultures in the 1980s and 1990s ('Ruci hunlian 1990; Shu Enyu 1996; Liu Xiaoxiao 2005; see also Wang Tao 1987: 181; Xu Zhensheng 2002: 118). In keeping with the deepening of China's economic reforms and the gradual removal of former restrictions placed on the capacity of PRC citizens to travel abroad, a 'craze for going abroad' (*chuguore*) occurred in Chinese society at that time (Feng Junyu and Su Xiaohuan 2001: 88; Fang Ning *et al.* 2002: 14–15). The majority of PRC citizens who travelled abroad in the 1980s and 1990s did so in order to conduct undergraduate and postgraduate study with the intention of returning to China to reap the benefits of an overseas education (Zhao Dingxin 1996). However, the PRC Government observed a marked trend in 'brain-drain' during the late 1980s and especially in the early 1990s following the 1989 Tiananmen Square incidents (Zweig and Rosen 2003). China's media in the 1980s was in the throes of a national campaign against what were viewed as negative western influences, including campaigns against 'spiritual pollution' and 'bourgeois liberalization'. In the early 1990s, this included negative media responses to what was described as the 'western' strategy of 'peaceful evolution (*heping yanbian*)'[3] vis-à-vis China, which was perceived to have encouraged the 1989 pro-democracy movement (Hong Junhao 2002; Yang Lijun and Lim 2010: 471). In this context, a popular view was that Chinese people who left China and went overseas were 'insufficiently patriotic' and 'blindly idolized everything foreign' (Fang Ning *et al.* 2002: 14–15; Brady 2003: 28). This is despite the fact that a 1993 survey by USA researchers found that 30 per cent of non-returners were concerned about political instability, while another 30 per cent were concerned about professional problems in China – such as low salaries, poor research facilities and difficulties changing employment (Zweig and Rosen 2003). Hence, although newspaper accounts in the PRC of some Chinese women marrying foreigners and going abroad because they 'idolized all things foreign' had some basis in fact; the description of their motivation as a form of moral corruption served to reinforce existing political ideologies, rather than to report the complexities of the phenomenon.

In addition, newspaper reports of Chinese–foreign marriage in the PRC intimated that Chinese women who lacked the necessary educational requirements to obtain the right to long-term residence or overseas citizenship were simply using intercultural marriage as an easier and faster way to fulfil their ill thought-out dreams of going overseas and living overseas (Ji Zhe 1996; Pang Fan and Wen Huangwei 2005; Liu Xiaoxiao 2005). For example, a 2004 report in the *Wenhui News* notes that a young Chinese woman married a German man in 1996, believing that life in a foreign country was preferable to life in China. However, after only one week in Germany, she returned to Shanghai (Shao Zhen and Liang Hongying 2004). Drawing on 'expert commentary' from a marriage lawyer named Jia Mingjun, the article states that Chinese women should be wary of treating intercultural marriage as a 'springboard' to change their lives as they will wind up regretting that decision. As this, and other newspaper reports conclude, intercultural marriage in 1980s and 1990s China was utilitarian and limited in nature. This is because the majority of Chinese people who married foreigners were allegedly motivated not by considerations of love, but rather by hypergamous motivations and a naïve conception of life abroad (Ye Huiyuan 2004; Liu Xiaoxiao 2005; Pan Meihong 2006; Wu Xuemei and He Xin 2007b).

Recent newspaper reports focus in more detail on the hypergamous motivations for early intercultural marriages in the PRC, but suggest that such motivations are historical, and no longer common in China today. As they argue, the phenomenon of young Chinese women marrying older foreign men for the purposes of socio-economic advancement was common in 1980s and 1990s China. However, that pattern is changing as China modernizes and its economy develops (Shao Zhen and Liang Hongying 2004; Ye Huiyuan 2004; Liu Xiaoxiao 2005; Wu Xiaoyan 2008). Mainland Chinese marrying partners reportedly now enter into intercultural marriages for the more 'healthy' reason of 'love'. This development is illustrated with reference to decreased gaps in the age, education level, occupation, social class and financial background of mainland Chinese women and foreign men entering into a Chinese–foreign marriage (Li Demin 2004; Liu Xiaoxiao 2005; Ye Huiyuan 2004; Pan Meihong 2006; Wu Xiaoyan 2008). It is further underscored with reference to the fact that an increasing number of men from mainland China are entering into Chinese–foreign marriages (Li Demin 2004; Liu Xiaoxiao 2005; Wu Xuemei and He Xin 2007a).

A number of reports underscore these changes to claim that rapid economic growth and the changing values of Chinese citizens have created a new emphasis on love as the basis for intercultural marriage (Du Zhanfan 2001; Li Demin 2004; Liu Xiaoxiao 2005; Wu Xuemei and He Xin 2007b). Some reports emphasize this change by arguing that the age gap between couples entering into an intercultural marriage in Shanghai has narrowed from a previous high of over 40 years to a gap of only five years in the 2000s (Liang Hongying 2002; 'Shanghai shewai hunyin' 2002; Li Demin 2004; 'Tianjinshi' 2006). They further argue that intercultural marriages are becoming 'normal' marriages, which are increasingly based on a 'match' between the 'character of a person' (*renpin*), 'educational level' (*xueshi*) and 'personalities' (*xingge*) of certain PRC and foreign citizens (Liang Hongying 2002; 'Shanghai shewai hunyin' 2002; Li Demin 2004; Yuan Lanhua and Du Zhanfan 2005; 'Tianjin shi' 2006).

Other reports underscore this perceived new emphasis on love as a determinant of intercultural marriage by highlighting the increased equality in educational, occupational and financial status of Chinese women and foreign men entering into an intercultural marriage. Many such Chinese women reportedly are now university graduates in white-collar employment with solid incomes (Liang Hongying 2002; 'Shanghai shewai hunyin' 2002; Yuan Lanhua and Du Zhanfan 2005). At the same time, several cities in China have reported an increased number of Chinese men entering into Chinese–foreign marriages in recent years when compared with previous years (Du Zhanfan 2001; Li Demin 2004; Liu Xiaoxiao 2005). Yet other articles add that growing numbers of foreign visitors and residents in cities such as Shanghai, Wenzhou and Tianjin, combined with increased levels of English-language literacy in China, have removed former barriers of communication between Chinese citizens and foreign visitors, thereby paving the way for the 'healthy' development of intercultural marriages based on love ('Shanghai shewai hunyin' 2002; Chen Liyu 2003; Ye Huiyuan 2004; Pan Meihong 2006; 'Tianjinshi' 2006; 'Shewai hunyin dengji shuliang' 2007). As a 2004 report in the *Wenzhou Dushibao* (Wenzhou Metropolitan News) proclaims, '270 Wenzhou Men Married Foreign Women Last Year – Experts Point Out that Intercultural Marriage Has Changed From Being "Green Card-Oriented" to the Pursuit of Love' (Ye Huiyuan 2004).

'Love' in the 2000s

Newspaper discussions of Chinese–foreign marriage in the PRC in the late 2000s increasingly emphasize that love is now the primary motivation for intercultural marriage, offering lengthy descriptions of individual love stories, narrating how people met and fell in love. In doing so, these kind of reports commonly use multiple framing devices such as adjectives, metaphors, quotations and catchphrases to highlight elements of love and romance in the depiction of Chinese–foreign marriages. A 2007 article in the *Anqing Wanbao* (Anqing Evening News), entitled 'An American Guy Finds Love in Anqing City' (*Yiwei Meiguo xiaohuo zai Anqing de aiqing*), relates the story of love between a female citizen of the PRC and her American spouse (Li Hui 2007). It starts with an account of the couple's traditional Chinese wedding ceremony and then explains how they met, fell in love and finally married. The report uses four subtitles to underscore the happy trajectory of their intercultural union. These may be roughly translated as: 'They fell in love in the ancient city of Anqing', 'Love blossoms with parental support', 'I am your bride today' and 'Marital bliss' (Li Hui 2007). The emphasis on love is further underscored by the use of phrases to describe their relationship such as 'they felt like old friends at their first meeting' (*yijian rugu*), 'pure and genuine love' (*chunjie zhencheng de aiqing*) and 'sweet and romantic' (*tianmi er langman*). The article concludes by congratulating and offering good wishes to the couple: 'Destiny Brings the Lovers Together! Best Wishes to Them' (*Youqingren zhongcheng juanshu! Zhufu tamen!*) (Li Hui 2007). The article's conclusion reads more like a personal letter than a newspaper article. The repeated use of exclamation marks in one short sentence strongly affirms the significance of love in this case of Chinese–foreign marriage.

Other articles similarly narrate tales of love conquering the geographical and cultural distance between Chinese women and American and British men, and between Chinese men and Russian and Vietnamese women (Chen Daoqiang 2008; Yang Ying 2008; Wang Tianfu *et al.* 2009). A 2008 report by the *Wujin Ribao* (Wujin Daily) starts by describing the wedding ceremony in China between a man from Henan Province and a Russian airline steward ('Eguo kongjie' 2008). As the title suggests, 'Russian Airhostess Chases after Chinese Man for Thousands of Miles' (*Eguo kongjie wanli chizhui Zhongguo xiaohuo*), this article narrates the melodramatic story of a couple who overcome enormous difficulties in order to enter into an intercultural marriage. The Chinese man in question reportedly came from a poor family, worked for an architectural company in Henan Province and then travelled to Russia to work on a building project in 2005. While in Russia, he risked his life to save a Russian woman kidnapped by a group of gangsters. The couple subsequently fell in love. However, believing that she deserved a better marriage partner than him, being beautiful and from a good family, the man returned to China when the building project was finished. Unhappy with this state of affairs, the woman followed him temporarily to China before returning to Russia. When they lost contact, she resigned her job and travelled throughout China in search of him, and eventually they married. Phrases such as 'infinite love' (*wuxian aiyi*), 'could hardly eat or sleep' (*qinshi nan'an*) and 'love lasts till the end' (*jiang aiqing jinxing daodi*), are used in this tale or quest to underscore that the couple married despite their perceived differences in status and class because they were deeply in love.

In these kinds of stories, it is usually the foreign marrying partner rather than the PRC citizen who is portrayed as overcoming difficulties and 'chasing love across the miles' to enter into an intercultural marriage (Zhu Minghong and Che Shijun 2003; 'Zhongguo liyi' 2007; 'Xiao shancun' 2007; 'Eguo kongjie' 2008; Bi Ran 2008; Yang Ying 2008). The absent framing about Chinese citizens behaving in a similar manner achieves two things. First, it suggests that foreign citizens now find contemporary China and citizens of the PRC attractive, reversing the former emphasis on the attraction of Chinese citizens for 'all things foreign' in early discussions of hypergamy in relation to intercultural marriage. Second and in doing so, it erases the issue of PRC citizens entering intercultural marriage for hypergamous purposes and highlights 'love' as the dominant motivation for contemporary Chinese–foreign marriages.

Newspaper discussions of Chinese–foreign marriage in the PRC in the 2000s also emphasize the comparative independence and modernization of Chinese women today to suggest that they now enter into intercultural marriages for reasons of 'love' rather than hypergamy, as demonstrated by their improved social and educational status vis-à-vis foreign men. Such women are described as educated or having a similar occupational status to their foreign spouses. They are modern 'white-collar' workers, university graduates and doctoral students with competent levels of English literacy ('Shanghai shewai hunyin' 2002; Chen Liyu 2003; Li Hui 2007; Xin Kai and Ye Xiaochuan 2008).

Conversely, newspaper reporters utilize the continued 'big gap' in the educational levels, social status and financial circumstances of many Chinese women and foreign men to provide 'Chinese Cinderella' stories that underscore the new importance of 'love' as a determinant of intercultural marriage. In such accounts, the 'Cinderella' is a woman from a poor and remote area of China, often working as a migrant, second-class citizen in an urban area, whereas the 'prince' is a man from the developed global 'north' or someone with a wealthy family background (Gao Ying 2005; Yang Ying 2008; Wang Yingxia 2009). For example, a 2005 article in the *Dahe Bao* (hereafter Dahe News), called 'Henan Girl Marries Polish Presidential Candidate, She Will Bring Him to Her Native Home' (*Henan meizi jiagei Bolan zhun zongtong, yiding hui daizhe zhangfu hui niangjia*), presents a classic story of love and intercultural marriage transcending the usually formidable boundaries between the rich and the poor and people from different racial, social and political backgrounds (Gao Ying 2005).

Newspaper discussions of Chinese–foreign marriage in the PRC in the late 2000s also emphasize the new importance of love as a motivating factor with reference to notions of mate selection. On the one hand, they highlight the physical and cultural rather than financial attractiveness of foreign men for some Chinese women. Such women are described as being attracted to certain foreign men because they are 'handsome' (*yingjun de*), 'physically strong' (*kuiwu de*), 'talented' (*youcaineng de*), 'educated' (*youwenhua, shouguo lianghao jiaoyu de*), 'considerate' (*titiede*) and a 'China expert' (*Zhongguotong*), i.e., someone who speaks Mandarin and/or is familiar with the intricacies of Chinese culture (Li Hui 2007; Chen Daoqiang 2008; Xin Kai and Ye Xiaochuan 2008; Zhao Lei *et al.* 2009). On the other hand, they highlight the cultural attractiveness of certain Chinese men for some foreign/non-PRC women, describing such men as 'diligent' (*qinfen de*), 'honest' (*zhonghou laoshi de*), 'reliable' (*kekao de*), 'considerate' (*titie de*), 'caring for the family' (*gujia*) and 'knowledgeable' (*you fengfu zhishi de*) and therefore are good candidates for husbands (*lixiang de zhangfu renxuan*) ('Eguo kongjie' 2008; Wang Tianfu, *et al.* 2009; Tan Lujie 2009; Zhao Lei, Tao Duanfang and Cui Xiangsheng 2009). Several reports indicate that the cultural attractiveness of certain Chinese men for some foreign/non-PRC women stems from China's strengthening economic capacity, simultaneously implying that some Asian and African women, in particular, are marrying Chinese men for socio-economic advancement (hypergamy) (Yuan Zhonghai and Sun Xianglan 2007; Tan Lujie 2009; Zhao Lei *et al.* 2009; 'Taiwan nü jia Dalu nan' 2010).

In turn, some foreign/non-PRC men are portrayed as preferring the 'the oriental beauty' (*dongfangmei*) of mainland Chinese women, who are described as 'slim, small and tender' (*jiaoxiao wenwan*); 'mild and virtuous' (*xianliang shude*) and 'beautiful and gentle' (*meili wenrou*) (Li Hui 2007; 'Zhongguo liyi' 2007; Yang Ying 2008; Xin Kai and Ye Xiaochuan 2008; Chen Daoqiang 2008; 'Xun'ai 10 nian' 2009; Yang Jie 2010). At the same time, Chinese men are said to prefer foreign women who display similar characteristics to those associated with traditional Chinese women, such as being 'diligent' (*qinfen*), 'gentle' (*wenrou*) and 'mild and virtuous' (*wenshu xianhui*) (Hu Shufeng and Xiong Yunbin 2007; 'Eguo kongjie' 2008; Zhao Lei *et al.* 2009). This focus on biologically informed notions of mate selection suggests that the intrinsic traits of 'Chinese womanhood' are what attract both foreign and Chinese men into entering into a Chinese–foreign marriage, as opposed to the previous emphasis on the hypergamous motivations of Chinese women.

Last, but not least, 'love of China' is presented as an important factor in newspaper discussions of intercultural marriages based on love. Such accounts underscore the attachment of certain foreigners to Chinese culture, and their willingness to integrate themselves into Chinese society ('Shanghai shewai hunyin jianwen' 1988; Meng Xiaoyun 2001; 'Xiao Shancun' 2007; Xin Kai and Ye Xiaochuan 2008; Wang Tianfu *et al.* 2009). For example, a 2001 report in the *People's Daily* introduces three Chinese–foreign marriages, the first between a Chinese woman and a British man, the second between a Chinese woman and a Swedish man and the third between a Chinese man and a Canadian woman (Meng Xiaoyun 2001). The first two marriages are described as being based on a love of Chinese culture, the poems of the famous Tang Dynasty poet, Du Fu (712–70), in the first instance, in an assorted collection of memorabilia relating to the PRC's revolutionary leader, Chairman Mao Zedong (1893–1976), in the second instance. In the case of the third marriage, the Canadian woman's 'love of China' is demonstrated by her willingness to bring up their son in China so that he can learn to speak Mandarin and appreciate Chinese culture, thereby enabling him to do well in the future (Meng Xiaoyun 2001). Other newspaper articles similarly suggest that Chinese–foreign marriages are now marriages of love because foreign marrying partners increasingly are willing to learn the Chinese language, appreciate Chinese food and are passionate about the Chinese city they reside in (Liang Hongying 2002; Yu Xiaoyang and Du Zhanfan 2008; Gao Li 2009; Xu Xianzhong 2007). This emphasis on love as opposed to hypergamy serves to suggest that intercultural marriage in the PRC, as with China's social and economic modernization, has advanced from a stage of 'infancy' to 'adulthood', marked in this instance by an appreciation of the value of pure sentiment as opposed to socio-economic advancement. These 'love' frames also serve as manifestations of the previously discussed fruitful results of China's national progress, either in terms of economic achievement or the construction of Socialist Spiritual Civilization of the PRC.

Hypergamy revisited

To the extent that hypergamous motivations feature in newspaper discussions of Chinese–foreign marriage in the PRC in the late 2000s, these articles focus on what they portray as a new phenomenon – this is the practice of middle-aged and divorced Chinese women, rather than young and single women, seeking a foreign husband (Pang Fan and Wen Huangwei 2005; Hu Yongmou 2007; 'Bei youhuo' 2008; 'Nüzi wanglian' 2008). China's economic restructuring from a planned to a market economy has clearly disadvantaged certain groups of Chinese women, even though it has provided new opportunities for others (Jing Lin 2003: 88; Lu Aiguo 2002; Gustafsson and Shi 2000). In contrast to the pre-reform period where state employment was guaranteed, many women aged from their mid-thirties to fifties have been laid-off from their former employment in state-owned enterprises (SOEs) and forced to compete for work in an increasingly competitive job market (Rosenthal 1998; Jing Lin 2003: 88; China Labour Bulletin 2004; Li Jing 2010: 55). Also in contrast to the pre-reform era, a growing number of these laid-off women (some are divorced) need to shoulder the burden of child-rearing and take care of elderly family members (China Labor Bulletin 2004; Li Jing 2010: 55). These women often constitute a marginalized group of women with a low economic position and stigmatized social status who face reduced opportunities for future employment and remarriage. In this context, some newspaper reports in the PRC state that older, unemployed and divorced Chinese women are looking to find a non-ethnic Chinese foreign spouse, not because they 'prefer western men', but because intercultural marriage offers 'the only choice out of no choice (*meiyou xuanze de xuanze*)' ('Zhongguo liyi' 2007). A Chinese–foreign marriage may offer such women opportunities not only for socio-economic advancement, but also romance, given that Chinese men are viewed as preferring to marry young women and being reluctant to support children from a woman's previous marriage.

A 2005 report in the *Shidai Xinbao* (hereafter Times News) called 'Middle-Aged Women in Pursuit of Intercultural Marriage Study Hard at English to Please Foreigners' (*Zhongnian funü kaishi zhuiqiu shewaihunyin wei bo huanyan kuxue yingyu*), draws attention to this new phenomenon, and its potentially negative consequences (Pang Fan and Wen Huangwei 2005). As it explains, a group of middle-aged, divorced Chinese women in Chongqing Municipality were learning English, computer skills and 'American humour' (*meishi youmo*), in the hope of 'catching' a foreign spouse. The article offers a detailed account of a 50-year-old woman who was allegedly disillusioned with Chinese men after the failure of her marriage. Determined to marry a foreign man and move abroad, she had reportedly already sold the house in which she and her son lived and was in the process of studying English while searching online and in real life for a foreign partner (Pang Fan and Wen Huangwei 2005). Although the woman in question is cited as pursuing an intercultural marriage in order to find a 'perfect and romantic love' (*wanmei langman de aiqing*), the report implies that her motivations and those of other women in her position are more hypergamous in nature. Divorced and with lower levels of education, such women have limited opportunities for remarriage and social advancement in present-day China.

A 2007 report in the *Chutian Dushibao* (Chutian Metropolian News) summarizes the stories of seven poor, divorced and middle-aged Chinese women who used their meagre wages or unemployment benefits to learn English and search for a foreign partner as a pathway to go abroad and start a new life (Hu Yongmou 2007). All of these women allegedly paid introduction fees to a 'friend-of-a-friend' in order to meet foreign men with no success. The report focuses on the story of a 43-year-old, divorced Chinese woman named 'Jia Yun'. To realize her goal of finding a foreign marriage partner, Jia started learning English at a local English-language school on a weekly basis, she also paid an introduction fee of over 24,000 yuan (US$3,000) to meet a potential husband from Australia, a man named 'Peter'. Believing that their relationship was genuine, she accepted Peter's claim that he was unable to use his credit card in China. Consequently, she not only paid for their wedding-related expenses in the PRC, but also lent him money to return to Australia. Peter then disappeared, and Jia was unable to establish contact with him thereafter (Hu Yongmou 2007).

As the preceding examples suggest, newspaper reports typically frame such women as 'victims' who experience financial loss and emotional grief at the hands of disreputable marriage agencies and potential foreign partners, rather than women who are maximizing their resources and achieving their dreams (Pang Fan and Wen Huangwei 2005; Hu Yongmou 2007; 'Bei youhuo' 2008; 'Nüzi wanglian' 2008). They are described as unemployed, middle-aged women who do not speak English and who date foreigners with the aid of translation software or with the assistance of intercultural matchmaking agencies. While acknowledging that many such women view intercultural marriage as a means to escape their unenviable position in Chinese society, newspaper reports in the PRC tend to conclude that the promise of intercultural marriage is a dangerous trap with disastrous consequences.

The media construction of hypergamy as a motivation for intercultural marriage in the PRC since 1979 is thus gendered in that it focuses exclusively on the phenomenon of Chinese women adopting intercultural marriage as a means to go abroad, and improve their financial and social circumstances, or to escape from a 'sad city' and start a new life. The defined problem reinforces the gendered stereotype that women are the 'social climbers' in Chinese–foreign marriages by failing to explore reasons other than love for which Chinese men enter into intercultural marriages. Although this omission partly reflects the dominance of Chinese women in Chinese–foreign marriage statistics, it frames young Chinese women as 'gold-digging passport hunters' and older Chinese women as 'sad' and 'desperate'. It also suggests that such women are predominantly naïve and lack understanding of the social and day-to-day realities of life in other countries.

The characteristics attributed to this 'new' form of hypergamy reflect those reported in China's newspapers in the 1980s and 1990s – namely, of women blindly following an idealized rich life in the developed world and being unprepared for the potentially harsh realities of life outside the PRC. In both versions, it is the perceived economic prowess of western men and not love that plays the motivating factor. However, while dismissed in effect as 'fantasy', the rationales provided by older Chinese women and foreign men for entering into an intercultural marriage emphasize the importance of personal satisfaction rather than strictly economic concerns. For example, a 50-year-old Chinese woman is quoted as stating that, unlike Chinese men, 'foreign men are romantic, gentle and humorous'; if he loves you, he says so (Pang Fan and Wen Huangwei 2005). In addition, some foreign men who are married to divorced, middle-aged Chinese women with children describe their partners as 'hard-found treasures' (*dazhe denglong nanzhao de baobei*), whose maturity (*chengshu*), kind-heartedness (*you aixin*) and mental strength (*jianqiang*), have contributed to a happy and stable marriage ('Zhongguo liyi' 2007).

Newspaper reports typically characterize this group of women as being disillusioned with Chinese men because of their failed marriages and seeking a foreign partner who will 'change their destiny' (*gaibian mingyun*). Their reported motivations are that a foreign husband comprises a 'good' marriage option for the following reasons. He will take the woman away from her home and 'sad city' (*shangcheng*), potentially turn her into a 'rich wife' (*fupo*) and provide her child with the opportunity to study abroad for a better future ('Bei youhuo' 2008; 'Nüzi wanglian' 2008; 'Gei hunyin' 2008; Shang Bin 2008; Wei Minghui 2009). This indicates the changing cultural values of 'marrying up' that both reinforces and alters the motivations that women hold when seeking intercultural marriages during China's early reform era. Whereas women in the earlier post-reform era married 'up' based on better economic conditions and a 'decadent' western lifestyle, this newer form of hypergamy sees women marrying western men because of the perceived – and perhaps stereotypical – cultural superiority of western men as romantic, gentle and genuine spousal partners compared to domestic Chinese men.

The depiction in China's media of divorced women seeking foreign men, as 'victims' or 'losers' is not only biased but reinforces traditional values that present women who seek to 'marry up' as distasteful. While the hypergamic marriages depicted in newspaper reports in the PRC in the 1980s and 1990s describe the spectacular failure of marital unions between younger Chinese women and older foreign men, reports in the 2000s depict older Chinese women as being too foolish to even attract foreign partners. Instead, they are framed as falling prey to conmen and disreputable organizations. Although such women have attempted to empower themselves by taking up English, learning how to use new technologies and demonstrating a capacity to make their own financial decisions, China's print media has rarely focused on positive outcomes resulting in successful intercultural marriages between middle-aged Chinese divorcees and foreign men. The downplaying of successful marriages is surprising given that foreign men have been depicted in Chinese newspaper reports as desiring these women as 'treasures' ('Zhongguo liyi' 2007). Moreover, it is unlikely that the bulk of the marriage introductions and actual marriages between older Chinese women and foreign men have ended in the kind of disaster depicted above.

The hypergamic motivations for intercultural marriage in China today as represented in newspaper reports in the PRC may be interpreted in at least two different ways. On the one hand, the emergence and increase of older divorced women seeking to 'marry up' reinforces the traditional naïve belief that foreign men, being more financially, emotionally or culturally superior, are better marriage material and constitute an 'escape route' from the harsh realities of life in China. On the other hand, the framing focus on the efforts rather than outcomes of older, divorced women to obtain intercultural marriage can be interpreted as evidence of women empowering themselves to realize their objectives. It is also notable that unlike earlier depictions of hypergamy, these women often cite romantic notions of 'love' and the ideal 'dream partner' as their motivations for seeking a foreign partner.

Thus, on closer analysis, a comprehensive reading of newspaper coverage of Chinese–foreign marriage suggests that intercultural marriages are no longer either experienced or perceived in China as a purely black-and-white issue based on hypergamic motivations and/or the desire for (ideologically and spiritually corrupt) western lifestyles. Instead, Chinese society is framed as adopting 'modern' and 'rational' ideas about 'love', which, in turn, have become the motivation for intercultural marriage. This shift in emphasis suggests that individual women in China today are motivated to enter into an intercultural marriage via a process of consciously selecting and negotiating the factors that are most important to them, be it money, spousal support and understanding, or love.

Conclusion

This chapter has examined the interplay between three features of Chinese–foreign marriage as presented in newspaper coverage in the PRC from 1979 up to the present day. It has discussed the rise and more recent fall of numbers of Chinese–foreign marriages registered in mainland China. It outlined the broadening nature of intercultural marriages in terms of the expanding number of the countries of origin of marital partners. It then analysed the different motivations attributed to Chinese people entering into an intercultural marriage, and their portrayal as an indication of the changing values of a particular group of Chinese women seeking marriage and of the PRC's national development.

Such an examination demonstrates that newspaper discussions of intercultural marriage in the PRC in the late 2000s tend to emphasize the importance of love, as opposed to socio-economic advancement, as the primary motivator for contemporary Chinese–foreign marriages. In contrast to the focus of early reports featuring young Chinese women 'exporting' themselves from mainland China to the developed world, recent reports highlight the changing demographics and patterns of intercultural marriage in the PRC today to convey the following three messages to their readership. First, China is culturally, politically and economically attractive to people from other parts of the world. Second, it is not only Chinese people who are interacting with people from other parts of the world, but also an increasing number of non-Chinese people and foreign nationals are interacting with Chinese society and culture. Finally and in doing so, they suggest that China and Chinese citizens in the late reform period have shifted away from a position of national and cultural isolation and adopted an increasingly internationalized and cosmopolitan identity. Viewed in this context, the phenomenon of intercultural marriage is framed in newspaper reports as positive evidence of the fruitful results achieved by China's national progress during the reform era.

However, reports of divorced or older Chinese women motivated to marry for reasons of hypergamy or love present a somewhat different picture. Although reports of modern-day Chinese–foreign marriages in China's print media serve to promote an idealized view of the PRC's national and cultural advancement, stories of victimized and naïve Chinese women losing out in their pursuit of 'marrying up' to a foreigner reveal that intercultural marriage has not evolved in a straightforward or 'clean' fashion. The desire for Chinese women to enter into an intercultural marriage remains a complex and contestable phenomenon, exhibiting elements of new social values, but also entrenched traditional values with respect to the kinds of gendered and hierarchical relationships that exist between women and men, as well as between the 'east' and the 'west'.

Notes

1 Hong Kong and Macau counted as foreign territories during the 1980s being returned to PRC sovereignty in 1997 and 1999 respectively. Today, both Hong Kong and Macau are Special Administrative Regions (SARs) of the People's Republic of China. This means in effect that apart from considerations of foreign policy and national defence, the two SARs of Hong Kong and Macau are able to exercise a high degree of autonomy, a separate political system from mainland China and a capitalist economy, under the principle of the 'one country, two systems' policy, which was proposed by China's former political leader, Deng Xiaoping in 1982 (He Jingru 2006).
2 In 1979, the concept of the 'construction of socialist spiritual civilization (*shehui zhuyi jingshen wenming jianshe*)' was first raised in the Fourth Plenary Session of the Eleventh Central Committee of the Chinese Communist Party. In 1986, the Sixth Plenary meeting of the Twelfth Central Committee passed the Resolution Concerning Guiding Policies for the Construction of a Socialist Spiritual Civilization (*Zhonggong zhongyang guanyu shehui zhuyi jingsheng wenming jieshe zhidao fangzhen de jueyi*). It further clarified the strategic position, the fundamental task and the guiding principles of the construction of socialist spiritual civilization (*shehui zhuyi jingshen wenming*

2003). According to the Resolution, socialist spiritual civilization guided by Marxism constitutes an important component of socialism with Chinese characteristics. Construction of socialist spiritual civilization is a requirement for solving the main conflict of socialist society and achieving the goal of socialism. The fundamental task of the construction of Socialist Spiritual Civilization is to meet the demand of socialist modernization, to cultivate citizens with ideals, morals, culture and discipline and to strengthen the moral, scientific and cultural qualities of the entire nation ('shehui zhuyi jingshen wenming' 2003).

3 The Chinese phrase *heping yanbian* (peaceful evolution) refers to what is viewed negatively in China as a non-military strategy by the West to transform the PRC's political system by promoting private ownership, free-markets, human rights and liberal democracy, leading to the erosion of Marxism-Leninist ideology and Communist Party rule (Ong 2007: 22–3).

4 Newspaper coverage of Chinese–foreign divorce

Divorce in the context of Chinese–foreign marriages was not a prominent feature of newspaper reportage in 1980s and 1990s China. A 1988 article in the *Shanghai Legal Daily* briefly mentions that the incidence of divorce in intercultural marriages was increasing on a gradual basis in the city of Shanghai ('Shanghai shewai hunyin jianwen' 1988). The article concludes by noting that there are many happy Chinese–foreign marriages, but some end in tragedy. Five couples in Chinese–foreign marriages had filed for divorce based on mutual agreement in Shanghai in 1985. That number increased to 17 couples in 1986 and 23 in 1987 and many more contested cases were pending in the divorce courts. In the 1990s, a small number of articles were published that focused on the subject of Chinese–foreign marriage and divorce in relation to issues such as deception, family violence and bigamy and the activities of illegal marriage introduction agencies ('Difang guoji' 1992; Deng Huajuan 1993; Ji Zhe 1996). The limited nature of such reportage demonstrates that divorce in the context of Chinese–foreign marriages was not a feature of newspaper reportage in 1980s and 1990s China, chiefly because the incidence of divorce was small when compared to the rapid growth in numbers of Chinese–foreign marriages at that time.

However, by the 2000s, divorce in the context of Chinese–foreign marriages had become a major feature of newspaper coverage on the phenomenon of intercultural marriage in the PRC. Instead of divorce being mentioned only briefly, if at all, the headlines of relevant newspaper articles began to highlight a rising trend of failed intercultural marriages and to offer detailed discussions, along with individual stories and expert commentary of the reasons why they had failed. Such reports explained the rising trend of divorce in the context of Chinese–foreign marriages with reference to deception, adultery, bigamy and domestic violence and associated legal issues.

This chapter first discusses the rising trend of Chinese–foreign divorce in contemporary China, which is commonly associated in newspaper coverage with five issues – the introduction of regulations simplifying the procedures for marriage and divorce; cultural differences; long-term separation of couples; deception, infidelity and domestic violence; and the activities of unscrupulous matchmaking agencies. The chapter then examines in more detail three key areas that are associated with the increased incidence of Chinese–foreign divorce in twenty-first-century China: deception; adultery, bigamy and domestic violence; and the role of illegal Chinese–foreign marriage introduction agencies in promoting fraudulent marriages. I conclude by summarizing the prominent features of the social problems associated with Chinese–foreign marriage and divorce as documented in the PRC's print media, which presents stereotypical depictions of bad foreign husbands, victimized Chinese women and good Chinese men.

Chinese–foreign divorce: a rising trend

As with discussions of growing numbers of intercultural marriages in the 1980s, newspaper coverage of Chinese–foreign divorces in the 2000s began with reports of a rising trend of divorce in the eastern coastal areas of China, especially in the southeastern cities of Shanghai and Wenzhou and in Jiangsu Province. The majority of these reports focus on the ascending divorce rates, before mentioning strong marriage rates, in order to attract the attention of their readers. For example, a 2004 report in the *Wenhui News* and a 2005 report in the *Zhejiang Daily* both adopt the same headline, 'Chinese–Foreign Marriage Encounters "Seven-Year-Itch"' (*Shewai hunyin zaoyu '7 nian zhiyang'*) (Shao Zhen and Liang Hongying 2004; Ye Huiyuan 2005). The reference to a 'seven-year-itch' is used metaphorically to highlight a slowdown in Chinese–foreign marriage registrations in Shanghai and Wenzhou and a rise in the number of Chinese–foreign divorces. As the article in the *Wenhui News* notes in its opening paragraph, 120 Chinese–foreign couples filed for divorce in Shanghai between January and June 2004, which exceeded the total number of divorces filed by couples in intercultural marriages in Shanghai in 2002 (Shao Zhen and Liang Hongying 2004, see also Li Hongguang 2006; Zhou Qijun 2007). The *Zhejiang Daily*'s report similarly explains that 104 Chinese–foreign marriages 'collapsed' in Wenzhou in 2004, which roughly equalled the total number of Chinese–foreign divorces between 1999 and 2002 in that city (Ye Huiyuan 2005).

Two reports in the *Nanjing Daily* in 2005 and 2006 also use strong headlines to highlight the rising number of Chinese–foreign marriages in Jiangsu Province that had ended in divorce (Ni Yan 2005; Ni Yan and Xu Xiuyou 2006). A 2005 report, entitled 'Chinese–foreign Divorces Increase 57 Per Cent Yearly' (*Shewai hunyin lihun renshu nianzeng 57%*) opens by stating that the number of Chinese–foreign marriages registered at the Jiangsu Provincial Civil Affairs Department in 2004 had increased by 10 per cent when compared to 2003. However, the incidence of divorce had increased by 57 per cent during the same period (Ni Yan 2005). It further notes that the number of Chinese–foreign marriages in Jiangsu Province that ended in divorce had increased 88 per cent from 32 couples in 2002 to 60 couples in 2003, following the implementation of new Marriage Registration Regulations which simplified the procedures for obtaining a divorce (*Hunyin dengji tiaoli* 2003). Likewise, a 2006 report, entitled 'Hundreds of Chinese– Foreign Marriages Ended in Divorce Last Year in Jiangsu Province' (*Qunian Jiangsu baiyu dui shewai hunyin polie*), states that 1,378 couples registered an intercultural marriage in 2005, which constituted a decrease when compared to the number of intercultural marriages registered in 2004 (Ni Yan and Xu Xiuyou

2006). At the same time, the number of those marriages that had ended in divorce totalled 118 couples in 2005, which constituted an increase of 26 per cent when compared to the figures for 2004.

As with the ascending trend of Chinese–foreign marriage, newspaper reports in the PRC relate the growing number of Chinese–foreign marriages that end in divorce to China's economic progress and rapid integration into the world (Chen Liyu 2003; Ye Xiaonan 2006; 'Taiduo gongli' 2008). A 2008 report in the *Yangcheng Wanbao* (Yangcheng Evening News) cites an anonymous lawyer who claims that the number of Chinese–foreign divorce cases is rising yearly (*shewai lihun anjian zhunian cheng shangsheng qushi*) ('Taiduo gongli' 2008). On the one hand, this reflects China's growing familiarity with the outside world, including practices that were formerly associated with developed, western countries, such as divorce. On the other hand, it indicates that some Chinese–foreign marriages were based on impulse and couples failed to consider the pragmatic issues that may arise during life after marriage, or lacked 'genuine motives' when registering a marriage ('Taiduo gongli' 2008).

Although there would be multiple reasons leading to each individual case of divorce, newspaper reports in the PRC offer five main reasons for the increased number of failed Chinese–foreign marriages. First, the processes of registering an intercultural marriage and obtaining a divorce have been simplified by legal changes, most notably, by the introduction of the 2003 Regulations on Marriage Registration (*Hunyin dengji tiaoli* 2003), which replaced the 1994 Regulations on Marriage Registration Management (*Hunyin dengji guanli tiaoli* 1994). Following the implementation of the new regulations, couples who want to file for divorce no longer required references from their work units or evidence of premarital health examinations to do so. In theory, local departments of civil affairs can issue a certificate of divorce on the same day that a couple file for divorce. A certificate can be issued if the relevant couple have reached consensus on child custody, property distribution and debts, produced the original marriage certificate and proof of identity and paid an administration fee of ten yuan (approximately US$1.25) (*Hunyin dengji guanli tiaoli* 1994; *Hunyin dengji tiaoli* 2003; see also Shao Zhen and Liang Hongying 2004; Ni Yan 2005).

While indicating that legal changes have simplified the procedures for registering and terminating a Chinese–foreign marriage, journalists caution that mainland Chinese citizens in a failed intercultural marriage are likely to experience problems when initiating divorce proceedings because of the lack of financial, legal and other supporting services, in both the PRC and overseas. Newspaper coverage of Chinese–foreign divorce cases in the 2000s suggest that they may take over a year to organize because couples have lost contact with each other and/or live in different places across the globe (Li Hongguang 2006; Wu Hui 2008b; Bi Ran 2008). Contested divorces may also be protracted in nature because of different legal procedures in different countries and the varying costs of filing for divorce which involves property disputes and child custody battles (Li Hongguang 2006; Zhang Guannian 2007; Luo Bin 2008; Wu Hui 2008b; Bi Ran 2008).

Second, the rising trend of Chinese–foreign divorce cases in the PRC is framed with reference to the complications arising from different cultural values and practices and living outside China. Many reports conclude that differences in cultural values, living habits, languages and religious beliefs, are 'killers' in intercultural marriages, hence Chinese–foreign marriages are more 'high risk' (*gao fengxian*) and 'insecure' (*bu wending*) than Chinese–Chinese marriages (Shao Zhen and Liang Hongying 2004; Liu Xiaoxiao 2005; Li Hongguang 2006; Zhou Qijun 2007). For example, an article in the *Jiating Zhoumo Bao* (Family Weekly) relates the story of a Chinese woman who married a Japanese national and moved with him to Japan (Miao Hui 2006). However, the man's unwillingness to let his wife find employment in the public sphere as is normal practice for the majority of women in China, along with other marital conflicts, led to divorce. Another report by the *Shanghai Morning Post* in 2007 begins by recounting the story of a Chinese woman who divorced her American spouse because of different lifestyles, including his preference for salads and sandwiches, rather than Chinese-style cooking. It concludes that many intercultural marriages involving Shanghai women end badly, with a Shanghai-based company that handles divorces (*lihun gongsi*) receiving numerous 'tearful' phone calls from Chinese 'wives' who live overseas (Chen Liyu 2007).

Newspaper reports in the PRC cite a rising trend in divorce in the context of Chinese–foreign marriages, along with stories of individual divorce cases, to indicate that Chinese–foreign couples who live abroad are likely to experience additional hardships because of cultural differences (Shao Zhen and Liang Hongying 2004; Liu Xiaoxiao 2005; Ni Yan and Xu Xiuyou 2006; Miao Hui 2006). Female citizens of the PRC, in particular, are presented as suffering more from marriage failure as a result of living overseas rather than in the PRC (Shao Zhen and Liang Hongying 2004; Liu Xiaoxiao 2005; Ni Yan 2006; Miao Hui 2006; Chen Liyu 2007). A 2005 report in the *Fazhi Zaobao* (Legal Morning Post), entitled 'Striking at the Heart of Chinese–Foreign Marriages' (*Zhiji Zhongguo kuaguo hunyin mingmen*), relates the stories of five Chinese women who had divorced after marrying foreign nationals and living abroad in Japan, the UK and the USA. All of these women explained their desire to return to China as flowing from a lack of social integration and ability to adapt culturally in foreign countries (Liu Xiaoxiao 2005). They further indicated that their unwillingness to live abroad again had led them to prefer domestic Chinese men as new marriage partners (Liu Xiaoxiao 2005).

Apart from implying that the incidence of Chinese–foreign divorce is much higher than the domestic divorce rate, newspaper reports in the PRC conclude that marriages between Chinese citizens and foreign nationals are even more likely to end in divorce when couples reside overseas, as opposed to when they live in China. Such reports often begin with the phrase 'what concerns people is … (*lingren danxin de shi…*)' and conclude by noting that people are concerned by the growing phenomenon of Chinese–foreign divorces. They then emphasize that the incidence of divorce increases when the couple are culturally and geographically distant from China. For example, a 2005 report in the *Times News* concludes that approximately 30 per cent of marriages, registered in either the PRC or Japan, between Chinese women and Japanese men where the couple ultimately lived in Japan had ended in divorce by 1997. Conversely, 35 per cent of marriages, registered in either the PRC or Japan, between Chinese men and Japanese women where the couple ultimately lived in Japan had ended in divorce by 1997. In addition, approximately 60 per cent of marriages, registered in either the PRC or Canada, between Chinese and Canadian citizens where the couple ultimately resided in Canada had ended in divorce by the early 2000s (Pang Fan and Wen Huangwei 2005; see also Chen Bao 2003; Chen Liyu 2003; Sun Yuan'er 2003; Shao Zhen and Liang Hongying 2004).

Third, the failure of many Chinese–foreign marriages registered in the PRC is attributed in newspaper coverage to the long-term separation of couples (Ye Huiyuan 2005; Li Hongguang 2006; Zhou Qijun 2007). Many couples in intercultural marriages reportedly live apart for substantial periods of time and often in different countries due to career development, business ventures, difficulties in processing visa applications, or simply feelings of homesickness. As a result, some couples grow apart emotionally and this problem is particularly the case in situations where couples have insufficient finances to reunite on a regular basis.

Fourth and as I discuss below, the rising trend of divorce in Chinese–foreign marriages is attributed to problems associated with the foreign male marrying partner, especially men who are non-ethnically Chinese. These problems reportedly include a propensity to infidelity, violence and deception (Liu Xiaoxiao 2005; Ye Xiaonan 2006; Zhang Guannian 2007; Wang Jianwei 2008; Feng Manlou 2008).

Finally and as I also discuss below, growing divorce rates are linked to deception through new institutional structures flowing from commercial advancement and technological development. International marriage introduction agencies, including those that offer online matchmaking services, offer a pertinent case in point (Liu Xiaoxiao 2005; Miao Hui 2006; 'Shewai hunjie' 2008; Wei Minghui 2009; Luo Ronghua 2009).

Deception, adultery, bigamy and divorce

The issue of divorce in Chinese–foreign marriage stemming from deception received little attention in newspaper reports in the PRC prior to the 2000s. A *People's Daily* report in 1993, called 'Be On Guard Against An Unusual Phenomenon in Intercultural Marriage' (*Jingti shewai hunyin zhong buzhengchang xianxiang*), alerts its readers to the potential dangers of entering into a Chinese–foreign marriage (Deng Huajuan 1993). It relates the stories of three women from Shanghai who were deceived by Chinese men with American nationality. Two of these men had registered and cancelled a marriage with a Shanghainese woman within the space of one week and then promptly proceeded to register another marriage with a different Chinese woman. The third man had falsely declared that he was single in an unsuccessful attempt to register several marriages with Chinese women living in different parts of China during the space of one month (Deng Huajuan 1993).

As mentioned in the previous chapter, a 1996 report in the *Zhejiang Daily*, entitled 'Dream Ends in Baghdad' (*Meng duan Bageda*), relates a cautionary tale of deception resulting in sexual slavery. According to this article, an Iraqi man named 'Ba' married a young Chinese woman claiming that he was a millionaire with luxury villas and a luxurious lifestyle in Iraq (Ji Zhe 1996). However, after marrying and moving overseas, the woman discovered that 'Ba' was an average suburban resident, who also was married with a six-year-old child (Ji Zhe 1996). Citing an alleged letter from the Chinese woman to her mother, the article states: '[Ba] cheated me and treats me as a tool to vent his anger... he uses me as a maid, I cook for his family every morning, then milk the cow and whenever I try to rest his wife abuses me'. Apart from verbally and physically abusing his Chinese partner, the article indicates that 'Ba' sexually abused her and bound her so that the 'local barbarian men' (*ye nanren*) could also rape her (Ji Zhe 1996). The use of autobiographical anecdotal evidence and strong imagery in this report creates sympathy for the Chinese woman as a tragic victim of her own hypergamous motivations for entering into a Chinese–foreign marriage, while generating hatred of the foreign marrying partner as both fraudulent and 'bestial' (*shouxing de*) (Ji Zhe 1996).

Since the 2000s, newspaper accounts in the PRC of divorce stemming from deception in Chinese–foreign marriages have become more frequent and complex (Wei Minghui 2009). Chinese men with foreign nationality continue to be presented as the primary perpetrators of bigamy. A 2005 report in the *Nanjing Daily* and a 2009 report in the *Chongqing Evening News* on the rising trend of divorce in intercultural marriages both highlight the phenomenon of Chinese men with foreign nationality falsely claiming that they are single in order to register a marriage with a Chinese woman in the PRC (Ni Yan 2005; Luo Bin 2009). Indeed, the *Nanjing Daily* report goes so far as to suggest that Chinese men with foreign nationality represent a kind of 'club', wherein it is common for such men to ask each other at social gatherings whether they have found themselves a 'Chinese wife', i.e., a 'second wife' (Ni Yan 2005).

Some newspaper reports in the PRC address the issue of men from Japan or the USA, who marry mainland Chinese women for 'sex and/or money' and then 'disappear' (*renjian zhengfa*) once they have achieved their duplicitous goals. Such men are portrayed as 'swindlers' (Ni Yan 2005; Miao Hui 2006; Shuai Yong and Jiang Yu 2007; 'Nüzi wanglian' 2008; Wang Jianwei 2008; Shang Bin 2008; Wu Changhua 2008; Wu Hui 2008b; 'Weizhuang haiwai' 2009). They reportedly live in China on a temporary basis and register marriages with local and usually younger Chinese women. Sometime after registering a Chinese–foreign marriage in the PRC, they leave China and their new bride to go overseas, citing reasons such as work commitments, difficulties with visas, or the need to explain their new marital arrangements to family members. In many such cases, the female partner in China waits for an indefinite period of time for her husband to return before realizing that the relationship was never a genuine one (Ni Yan 2005; Miao Hui 2006; Zhang Guannian 2007; Wang Jianwei 2008; Wu Hui 2008b).

Other reports relate cautionary tales of Chinese women being divorced by men from Australia and the USA who married them simply to exploit their money and resources while holidaying in China (Hu Yongmou 2007; Wang Si 2008; 'Cong Xuenaiyin'an' 2009). These men are portrayed as lacking financial and other resources, but are attractive to some women because of their promise to take their potential Chinese partners back to their home countries after registering a marriage in China. During their stay in the PRC, they rely financially on their Chinese partners and 'borrow' money from them to support the cost of travelling and living. As soon as they have finished with their stay in China, they then either ask for a divorce or 'disappear', leaving the Chinese partner with no option other than to file for divorce through the courts (Hu Yongmou 2007; Zhang Zhiqiang 2008b; Wang Si 2008; 'Cong Xuenaiyin'an' 2009).

Yet other reports portray foreign men as manipulating the hypergamous desires of some Chinese women for a 'better life as a rich wife abroad' (*guo fupo shenghuo*) by pretending to be wealthy or successful businesspersons ('Nüzi wanglian' 2008; 'Weizhuang haiwai' 2009). Such men reportedly 'hook' a Chinese bride by providing false information about their wealth and status to marriage agencies, or by telling similarly fraudulent stories to the individual women they meet. Once a relationship is established, the men 'borrow' money from these women on the pretext of 'doing business' in China, but that money is never returned ('Nüzi wanglian' 2008; 'Weizhuang haiwai' 2009). The 'victims' are framed as more than willing to pay high introduction fees to marriage agencies in order to meet a potential foreign husband who can provide them a better lifestyle overseas. They are further portrayed as being overly willing to accommodate the financial and physical needs of foreign men from the 'developed north' being easily duped by their perceived physical beauty and 'sweet' yet false words.

Another phenomenon associated with the rising trend of Chinese–foreign divorce cases in the PRC is post-marital betrayal in the form of extra-marital affairs on the part of the (male) foreign marrying partners (Ye Xiaonan 2006; Fu Guiming 2007; Xu Xianzhong 2007; 'Zhongguo xin'niang' 2008). In such reports, young and innocent Chinese women fall in love with physically attractive but older men (40 years and over) from Japan and the USA (Ye Xiaonan 2006; Xu Xianzhong 2007; Zhongguo xin'niang' 2008). However, after their marriage, they discover based on information from friends that their spouses are adulterers, being involved in numerous sexual relationships with other Chinese women. Faced with betrayal, some of these women reportedly attempt suicide or physically attack their foreign partners, resulting in divorce (Ye Xiaonan 2006; 'Zhongguo xin'niang' 2008).

Newspaper discussions in the PRC of deception, bigamy and adultery in Chinese–foreign marriages both prior to and after the 2000s focus on the activities of male foreign nationals, but rarely discuss the issue of deception, bigamy and adultery in relation to Chinese–foreign marriages involving men from Hong Kong, Macau and Taiwan. Yet, there is a considerable body of academic literature on the 'second wife' phenomenon in this context (Chang 1999: 75; Lang and Smart 2002; So 2003: 520–24; Ming 2005: 38–9; 'Hong Kong Man' 2006; Shen 2008: 58–61). These discussions refer to the practice wherein married men from Hong Kong, Macau and Taiwan keep 'mistresses' (*bao ernai*) in mainland China, which may result in marriage or the establishment of family arrangements akin to marriage but without the formal legal sanction. For example, in 'Migration and the Second Wife in south China: Toward Cross-Border Polygyny', Graeme Lang and Josephine Smart (2002: 546–69), note that rapid industrialization in southern China since the 1980s had resulted in many married Hong Kong and Taiwanese men sojourning for long periods in the provinces of Guangdong and Fujian for business purposes. Many such men engage in extra-marital sexual relationships with young female migrant workers from the Chinese hinterland who seek work and upward mobility in these cities, with some entering into short-term extra-marital relationships in a serial fashion or long-term extra-marital relationships akin to marriage. In 'The First Taiwanese Wives and the Chinese Mistresses: The International Division of Labour in Familial and Intimate Relations across the Taiwan Strait', Hsiu-hua Shen (2005: 426), similarly notes that the phenomenon of male entrepreneurs from Taiwan engaging in extra-marital affairs with mainland Chinese women had become commonplace by the late 1990s. These kinds of relationships and the growth in extra-marital sexual relationships between Hong Kong men and mainland female sex workers in Hong Kong, are creating documented problems for married women and their families in Hong Kong and Taiwan (Ming 2005: 39; Emerton *et al.* 2007: 65; Lee 2008: 101). In the PRC, women who have become the 'second wives' of men from Hong Kong and Taiwan are discussed as part of a continuum of prostitution (Zhao Baosheng 2000b; 'Guanyu aizibing' 2002; 'Gang Tai zai neidi' 2003; 'Zhongguo maiyin' 2009).

Although mainland Chinese women who have become the 'second wives' of men from Hong Kong and Taiwan are a focus of academic and media debate, the related issues of deception and bigamy are not often discussed in media reports about failed intercultural marriages in the PRC. In Hong Kong and Taiwan, mainland Chinese women who have become the 'second wives' of men from Hong Kong and Taiwan are often vilified in sensationalist media reports as 'seducers', 'family wreckers', 'husband-snatchers' and 'money seekers' who threaten the family system and moral order of Hong Kong and Taiwanese society (Shih 1998: 301–4; Lee 2008: 103). Such condemnation is sensationalist and gendered because some mainland 'second wives' are unaware of their partners' existing relationships in Hong Kong or Taiwan, i.e., they may be victims of deception rather than active or willing accomplices in bigamy or adultery. The relationship between deception/bigamy/adultery and marriage dissolution is downplayed in the context of media discussions about failed Chinese–foreign marriages in the PRC that involve men from Hong Kong, Macau and Taiwan. However, issues of deception and bigamy are a prominent feature of media discussions of failed Chinese–foreign marriages in the PRC that involve men from other parts of the world.

In short, the majority of the reports in newspaper discussions in the PRC of deception in the context of Chinese–foreign marriage are cautionary tales that frame PRC women as victims of duplicitous and adulterous foreign men, understood as men with foreign nationality. This point is emphasized by citing the complaints and sorrows of the alleged victims. For example, a 2009 report in the *Fushun Wanbao* (Fushun Evening News) entitled 'These 32 Women Were Truly Cheated' (*Zhe 32 ge nüde bei huyou le*) begins by quoting the words of four women who paid exorbitant fees to a marriage introduction agency after meeting a foreign national and potential spouse named 'Carl' (Wei Minghui 2009). In their words, 'Carl is a swindler' (*Carl jiushi ge pianzi*), 'We were cheated' (*Women doubei huyou le*), 'We were so stupid, we cannot blame others' (*Women tai hutu, yuanbude bieren a*) (Wei Minghui 2009). As it turned out, 'Carl' was a 'marriage trap' (*huntuo*), i.e., the 'front-man' for an illegal marriage introduction agency whose job was to convince the women he met to pay introduction fees based on the false assumption that he was an attractive marriage partner who would take them abroad. The deception came to light when three members of the agency discovered that they were dating the same person, a man named 'Carl' and complained to the agency's manager. The owner of the agency promptly disappeared with fees amounting to 1.8 million yuan (US$225,000), leaving behind a total of 32 female members who had registered and paid fees with the agency, none of whom had met a successful match after being on the agency's books for nearly two years.

Some of these newspaper discussions of deception both caution and instruct Chinese women who are considering entering into an intercultural marriage to truly 'know' their foreign partners before marriage. Such women are advised to study the cultures, living habits, educational background and ways of thinking, of their potential spouses. They are further enjoined to study and prepare for the extra effort required to integrate into a foreign society when married and living overseas (Ni Yan 2005; Zhang Guannian 2007; 'Bei youhuo' 2008; 'Cong Xuenaiyin'an kan' 2009).

In doing so, newspaper discussions in the PRC on deception in intercultural marriage tend to stereotype PRC women as a 'vulnerable group' in contemporary Chinese society who are prone to being hurt and cheated. This remains the case even though some reports intimate that young Chinese women who marry foreign men for hypergamous motivations are in a sense also 'deceiving' and therefore are bound to 'be deceived' by their spouses (Zhang Guannian 2007; Wu Changhua 2008; Wei Minghui 2009). This focus engenders bigamy and infidelity, albeit by default, as 'male'. It therefore replicates popular gendered stereotypes of women as loyal, faithful caretakers of the men in their lives and men as people with uncontrollable urges and an absence of values such as loyalty and fidelity (see Brand *et al.* 2007: 101–9).

Certainly, the author has found no newspaper reports in the PRC to date of men from mainland China deceiving their foreign wives. This omission partly reflects the fact that over 85 per cent of intercultural marriages registered in the PRC between 1979 and 2011 involve a foreign male and a female citizen of the PRC. However, the absence of such reports implies that foreign men victimize Chinese women in the context of intercultural marriages, and that Chinese men in intercultural marriages with foreign women are loyal and faithful partners. When viewed in conjunction with positive reports of intercultural marriage suggesting that foreign women are attracted to Chinese men because of their considerate and faithful nature vis-à-vis foreign men, it is implied that Chinese men are ideal marriage partners (see 'Eguo kongjie' 2008; Zhao Lei *et al.* 2009; Li Sha 2009a).

The default representation of male citizens of the PRC as sexually faithful is somewhat at odds with current social practice. Mainland Chinese men from all walks of life are also implicated in bigamy, adultery and the practice of keeping mistresses (Lü Guojiang 2002: 22; Jeffreys 2006: 160). Some academic and literary works suggest that the PRC's rising rate of divorce stems from the tendency of wealthy Chinese men, in particular, to either cheat on their 'middle-aged' wives or else to abandon them for younger and prettier women (Jeffreys 2006: 172; 'Understanding the attraction' 2007; 'One in five marriages' 2010). Indeed, while some authors suggest that extra-marital relationships and polygamy were tolerated by many Chinese women prior to the establishment of the communist regime in 1949, others note that the increasing emphasis on love as a determinant of marriage in mainland China has made such practices unacceptable, resulting in increased rates of divorce and second marriages (Liao and Heaton 1992: 413; Fan and Lui 2004: 443; Pan Suiming 2006: 31–2).

Whether intentional or not, this default representation of male citizens of the PRC as more loyal marriage partners than foreign men may encourage some Chinese women to be wary of entering an intercultural marriage, while helping to erase the stereotypically negative description of Chinese men as physically undesirable to foreign women. It may also help to erase the so-called 'failure' of Chinese masculinity as described in literature such as Tang Ying's (1995), *Meiguo Laide Qizi* (My Wife from America). These works comment on the perceived failure of Chinese men to dominate or satisfy the desires of Chinese women, who are obliged by default to enter into intercultural marriages and move overseas (Tang Ying 1995; see also Davin 2007: 88; Farrer 2008a: 10). As China's currently unbalanced sex ratios indicate that there may be over 23.5 million more men of marriageable age than women by 2020 (Poston and Glover 2005: 13; Davin 2007: 88), this implied revaluing of Chinese men may serve to encourage more Chinese women to look for a domestic rather than foreign spouse.

In summary, newspaper reports in the PRC discuss the issue of deception in Chinese–foreign marriages chiefly in terms of foreign men victimizing Chinese women. There is limited coverage of Chinese women cheating foreign males and no accounts of Chinese men deceiving foreign females (Fu Guiming 2007; Bi Ran 2008). The selected framing thus functions to normalize foreign males as a group prone to fraud and marital infidelity, whereas mainland Chinese citizens and especially Chinese men are constructed as loyal and good marriage partners, at least in the context of intercultural marriages.

The practice of deception, bigamy and adultery in the context of Chinese–foreign marriages and on the part of foreign males is not only associated in newspaper reports in the PRC with marital disruption and dissolution, but also with domestic violence, attempted suicide, and even murder. Hence, the next section moves on to discuss the issue of domestic violence in print media presentation of Chinese–foreign marriage.

Domestic violence and divorce

The PRC media did not cover the issue of domestic violence in a consistent fashion until 1993, when publicity of domestic violence became part of the preparatory work for the United Nation's Fourth World Conference on Women held in Beijing in 1995 ('Fourth World Conference on Women' 1995; Liu Meng and Chan 1999: 1470; Liu Meng and Chan 2000: 79).[1] Although the scope of the term is contested, UNICEF (2000: 1–2) defines 'domestic violence' as an under-recorded and under-reported crime that reflects the historically unequal power relations between women and men and that involves 'violence by an intimate partner and by other family members', wherever it takes place and in whatever form. Domestic violence includes: physical abuse (beating, burning, choking and kicking and threatening physical abuse or murder with an object or weapon; sexual abuse (coerced sex, forcing unwanted sexual acts or forcing sex with others; psychological abuse (verbal aggression, constant humiliation, threats of abandonment, confinement to the home and threats to withdraw custody of the children); and economic abuse (denial of funds, food and basic needs and controlling access to health care and employment) (UNICEF 2000: 2). This definition matches the broad nature of discussions of domestic violence in China's media.

Initial media coverage of domestic violence in the PRC, which is literally translated as household or family violence in Chinese (*jiating baoli*), aimed to raise international concerns about the issue so that Chinese participants at the 1995 Women's Conference could better engage with overseas participants and speakers (Huang Qizao 1994; Liu Meng and Chan 2000: 79). After the conference, public debate on domestic violence as a social problem in China began to increase (Liu Meng and Chan 2000: 74; Jin Mei 2009: 56). This debate was enhanced by revisions to the PRC's *Marriage Law* in 2001, which introduced the term 'domestic violence' to Chinese law and stipulated that domestic violence is both prohibited, and grounds for divorce (Articles 3 and 32, *Zhonghua renmin gongheguo hunyinfa* 2001). The All-China Women's Federation (*Zhonghua quanguo funü lianhehui*) and the Network Research Centre for Combating Domestic Violence of the China Law Society (*Zhongguo faxuehui fan jiabao wangluo*) drafted two versions of the Law on Domestic Violence Prevention and Control (*Jiating baoli fangzhi fa*); and in the 2000s, they presented the completed drafts of that law for discussion to China's top legislature, the Standing Committee of the National People's Congress on numerous occasions. A draft law was finally tabled for endorsement and legislation by the Standing Committee in August 2011 ('Miandui jiabao' 2011).

By the early 2000s, the issue of domestic violence was widely reported in China's media as a problem that affected around 30 per cent of Chinese–Chinese marriages, with an estimated 90 per cent of the abusers being male and their victims being women and children ('Family violence becomes public evil in China' 2003). Lately, the *Report on Major Results of the Third Wave Survey on the Social Status of Women in China* issued by the All-China Women's Federation and the National Bureau of Statistics revealed that 24.7 per cent of Chinese women have suffered various forms of domestic violence from their spouses, such as verbal and physical abuse, restriction of personal freedom, economic control, as well as rape within marriage. Among these, 5.5 per cent of women claimed that they had experienced physical violence, with 3.1 per cent in the urban area, and 7.8 per cent in the rural area (*Di sanqi Zhongguo funü shehui diwei diaocha zhuyao shuju baogao* 2011).

From the late 2000s, China's media started to cite domestic violence as a major reason for the nation's growing incidence of divorce ('China domestic violence complaints soar 70%' 2007; 'Domestic violence increases in China' 2009; 'lihun'an jin sicheng' 2010).

Reflecting on the relative newness of discussions of domestic violence in the PRC in general, the significance of domestic violence as a factor contributing to the rising trend of Chinese–foreign divorce cases was not addressed in China's newspapers until the mid-2000s (see Liu Xiaoxiao 2005; Shuai Yong and Jiang Yu 2007; Feng Manlou 2008; 'Cong Xuenaiyin'an kan' 2009). The first reports to broach the topic of domestic violence as a cause of failed intercultural marriages replicated the conventional wisdom that domestic violence is typically perpetrated by (physically stronger) men against (physically weaker) women, in order to dominate or control the weaker (female) partner. They also tended to sensationalize the subject by giving it a geographical location, implying that it was a problem for women in Chinese–foreign marriages who lived overseas rather than in the PRC.

Reports on domestic violence in the context of Chinese–foreign marriage underscore the perceived links between hypergamy and male dominance. While sympathizing with the desires of certain Chinese women to improve their socio-economic prospects by entering into an intercultural marriage and living overseas, such reports depict these women as vulnerable to abuse or even destined to be beaten, i.e., as victims of their (over)willingness to enter into a Chinese–foreign marriage. Conversely, they frame foreign men, especially those who are non-ethnic Chinese, as perpetrators of domestic violence, and as brutal barbarians (Liu Xiaoxiao 2005; Zhang Guannian 2007; Shuai Yong and Jiang Yu 2007).

In such newspaper reports, Chinese women are presented as being abused by their foreign spouses for failing to fulfil the gendered expectation that they will act as compliant and unquestioning 'housewives' (Liu Xiaoxiao 2005; Shuai Yong and Jiang Yu 2007; Zhang Guannian 2007). Several reports cite horrific stories of Chinese women living abroad who are beaten by their foreign spouses, resulting in injuries ranging from bruises to fractures, with some requiring hospitalization (Liu Xiaoxiao 2005; Shuai Yong and Jiang Yu 2007; Cong Xuenaiyin'an kan' 2009). Other reports narrate stories of Chinese women being insulted and spat upon by their foreign husbands, for example, being forced to bark like a dog (Liu Xiaoxiao 2005). Yet other reports relate stories of Chinese women being subjected to constant rape and abuse from their foreign spouses (Liu Xiaoxiao 2005; 'Cong Xuenaiyin'an kan' 2009).

For example, a 2007 report in the *Nanning Ribao* (hereafter Nanning Morning Post), entitled 'Intercultural Marriage: "I Love You" Easier Said Than Done' (*Haiwai 'weicheng': xiang shuo ai ni bu rongyi*), relates the story of a Chinese woman who wanted to go abroad through marriage, and was subsequently abused (Zhang Guannian 2007). After marrying a Japanese man, she moved from the PRC to Japan, where she had to engage in heavy farm work and housework and was abused verbally and physically by her husband on a regular basis. She returned to the PRC, but unable to survive economically on her own, she went back to Japan, only to face increasingly brutal treatment from her husband, and her husband's family. Finally, the woman returned to her hometown in the PRC. The story ends with expressions of her regret and self-condemnation for being so 'vain' (*xurong de*) and 'stupid' (*wuzhi de*) as to expect an easier life overseas.

In a somewhat different vein, a 2008 report in the *China Women's News* narrates the story of a Chinese woman named Li, who was introduced to a wealthy Japanese man in exchange for a large payment to cover her mother's hospital treatment. After marrying in Japan, Li was not allowed to work outside. Her husband 'Xiao Ye' told her that he needed her to provide sexual services and domestic work. When Li told her husband that she had twice been raped by his cousin, Xiao made no response and kept silent. In conclusion, the report notes that Li wanted to talk to her 'sisters' (Chinese women) who intend to 'marry out' through the media – 'Real happiness solely belongs to those who sincerely love each other and those who marry for wealth or 'face' will be destined to suffer' (*zhenzheng de xingfu zhi shuyu zhenxin xiang'ai de ren, chanza le xurong chengfen, jiajie zai caifu he mianzi shang de shewai hunyin zhineng shouhuo kuguo*) ('Zhongguo xin'niang' 2008).

Such reports, which include either self-condemnatory or advisory quotations, effectively normalize female vulnerability to and acceptance of, domestic violence by suggesting they are in some sense blameworthy. In China, as elsewhere, media reports of domestic violence often turn on implied notions of victim precipitation, and associated connotations of victim blaming. In such instances, women become vulnerable to domestic violence because of their failure to accept their circumstances in China and their 'romanticized' desire for a better life overseas. Such reports underscore the links between violence, domination and masculinity, by suggesting that Chinese women who marry for hypergamous purposes and who live overseas and are financially dependent on their foreign partners, will inevitably be 'disciplined' by the man they have 'married-up to'.

Several reports cite professional commentary from lawyers and other experts to augment the suggestion that domestic violence is a particular problem for couples in Chinese–foreign marriages who live overseas, flowing from cultural differences and lack of support. On the one hand, domestic violence is described as an outcome of differences in languages, cultures and living habits, which inevitably disadvantage those Chinese women who have married and live abroad, especially those who were unaware of the significance of such differences to begin with (Liu Xiaoxiao 2005; Zhang Guannian 2007; 'Cong Xuenaiyin'an kan' 2009). This overlaps with and reinforces the previously discussed frames on the rising incidence of divorce caused by Chinese women's inability to adapt to foreign cultures when residing overseas. This also accentuates the commonly perceived notion that Chinese–foreign marriages have a higher divorce rate than Chinese–Chinese marriages. On the other hand, domestic violence is framed in association with the inherent violent nature of certain foreign men, with these tendencies being discovered 'too late' by Chinese women in intercultural marriages who are living overseas and hence living without the protections afforded by friends and family in China (Liu Xiaoxiao 2005; Zhang Guannian 2007; 'Cong Xuenaiyin'an kan' 2009).

The emphasis on domestic violence in Chinese–foreign marriages where couples live outside the PRC indicates that geographical (re)location is a significant determinant of domestic violence. In short, it suggests that the incidence of domestic violence largely depends on where the couples live in a Chinese–foreign marriage. This conclusion echoes Lucy Williams and Yu Mei-Kuei's (2006: 62) assertion that 'migration is intrinsically a risk factor for domestic violence and intimate abuse', for reasons discussed below. Conversely, it indicates that Chinese nationals in Chinese–foreign marriage where the couple continue to live in the PRC are less likely to experience domestic violence because they have access to greater support and resources in their home country (Perilla 1999: 119).

Research on domestic violence and migrant women in general suggests that women who migrate because of marriage are vulnerable to abuse for four reasons. First, domestic violence is viewed in many cultural contexts as a private or family matter that should not be discussed in public and as part of the 'normal' dynamics of a marital relationship (Perilla 1999: 124; Liu Meng and Chan 2000: 75–6; Raj and Silverman 2002: 384; Xu Xiao *et al.* 2005: 78). Second, migrant women, especially women with lower educational levels and language barriers, seldom seek assistance and support from domestic violence services because they believe that such services are inaccessible or culturally irrelevant to them (Perry *et al.* 1998: 129; Perilla 1999: 124; Raj and Silverman 2002: 386). Third, migrant women are often unwilling to disclose their experiences of abuse for fear of shaming their husbands and families and/or generating criticism of their culture or country of origin (Bauer *et al.* 2000: 38; Raj and Silverman 2002: 384). Finally, when migrant women seek help and guidance from local community and religious groups, they often do not receive help, but rather are encouraged to keep silent for the sake of saving their marriages (Perry *et al.* 1998: 129; Liu Meng and Chan 2000: 76; Raj and Silverman 2002: 384).

These arguments have some substance in the Chinese context. Although relevant authorities in the PRC have taken steps to publicize and condemn the practice of domestic violence in recent years, traditional Chinese aphorisms point to a historical culture of acceptance based on the concept of woman as man's private property. These sayings include: 'The horse I buy and the wife I own are mine to beat' (*taolaide laopo malaide ma, renwo qilai renwo da*); 'a beating shows intimacy, a scolding shows love' (*da shi qin, ma shi ai*); and 'don't wash your domestic problems (dirty linen) in public' (*jiachou buke waiyang*) (Liu Meng and Chan 1999: 1472; Rong Weiyi 2004; Xu Xiao *et al.* 2005; Jin Mei 2009: 57).

Hence, many Chinese women in intercultural marriages who migrate overseas and experience domestic violence allegedly hide their abuse from family and friends in China, claiming instead that they are living a good life (Liu Xiaoxiao 2005; 'Cong Xuenaiyin'an kan' 2009). They may tolerate domestic violence rather than face social stigmatization, or lose their economic security and children in custody battles (Bui and Morash 1999: 790; Bauer *et al.* 2000: 38, 41; Raj and Silverman 2002: 385). In addition, they may fail to seek help from relevant local institutions and the Chinese consulate, or not know how to access those institutions (Liu Xiaoxiao 2005; Feng Manlou 2008; 'Cong Xuenaiyin'an kan' 2009).

Newspaper reports in the PRC further suggest that many women choose to tolerate domestic violence rather than 'lose face' (*diu lian*) by divorcing and returning to China (Liu Xiaoxiao 2005; 'Cong Xuenaiyin'an kan' 2009). This tendency stems from the fact that discrimination against divorced women is prevalent in the PRC and divorced women often end up occupying an inferior socio-economic position. Traditional cultural values place a high emphasis on virginity, even though that value is increasingly at odds with actual social practice. This means that divorced women are viewed as 'used items' and unattractive marriage partners by Chinese men (Chan *et al.* 2005: 148). Many women in China consequently find divorce unacceptable and subscribe to the belief that marriage is for life (Chan *et al.* 2005: 157), even when the marriage is violent. Thus, in many newspaper discussions of Chinese–foreign divorce cases, Chinese women are framed as sad, tearful and highly unwilling to divorce (Liu Xiaoxiao 2005; Miao Hui 2006; Chen Liyu 2007; 'Cong Xuenaiyin'an kan' 2009).

Other newspaper reports in the PRC of domestic violence in the context of failed intercultural marriages frame Chinese women as victims of abuse who may also in turn become involved in criminality or excess. These women are typically both physically and mentally abused by their partners and resort to 'fighting violence with violence', with some cases resulting in homicide ('Family violence becomes public evil in China' 2003; Liu Xiaoxiao 2005; 'Zhongguo xin'niang' 2008). A small number of reports portray Chinese women in intercultural marriages with Japanese men, as physically attacking their spouses with knives or sharp weapons, with an intent to kill (Liu Xiaoxiao 2005; 'Zhongguo xin'niang' 2008). The noted causes of such violence vary from frustration over trivial matters to anger about sexual infidelity (Liu Xiaoxiao 2005; 'Zhongguo xin'niang' 2008).

For example, a 2005 report in the *Fazhi Chenbao* (Legal Morning Post) cites two cases of Chinese women who married Japanese men, relocated to Japan and subsequently murdered their husbands (Liu Xiaoxiao 2005). The first woman reportedly quarrelled with her husband over domestic matters. She lost her temper and grabbed a board and hit her husband. In the second case, a Chinese woman murdered her Japanese husband by stabbing him to death with a kitchen knife on the second night after their marriage. The report indicates that this case might have been related to the practice of 'mercenary marriage' (*maimai hunyin*), wherein 'families purchase women as wives or daughters-in-law from traffickers in women' (Zhang Weiguo 2000: 60). Although the PRC's revised *Marriage Law* of 2001 forbids mercenary marriages and the exaction of money and/or gifts in connection with marriage (Article 3, *Zhonghua renmin gongheguo hunyinfa* 2001), mercenary marriages still occur, especially in poor agricultural communities that retain patrilocal residence customs, and therefore expect newly married couples to take up residence in the groom's family household. In such areas, women may wish to marry elsewhere, and daughters may be viewed as a commodity that attracts a 'bride price'. Moreover, a family may purchase a bride for a son who is experiencing difficulties finding a wife locally because the area is an unattractive place to live or he is physically challenged (Zhang Weiguo 2000: 60; 'Guanyu dui' 2010; 'Hunyin' 2010).

Likewise, a 2008 report in the *China Women's News* entitled 'Chinese Brides Suffer in Chinese–Japanese Marriages' (*Zhongguo xin'niang zai ha Ri hunyin li tongku jian'ao*), relates the story of an educated Shanghainese woman called Zhao Xuejiao, who married a Japanese professor whom she met through a mutual friend named Mi Li. The husband later informed Zhao that he was having an affair with Mi Li. When Zhao heard this, she grabbed a fruit knife next to her, and stabbed him ('Zhongguo xin'niang' 2008).

Although domestic violence is predominantly associated with male abusers and female victims, a review of newspaper reports in the PRC show that men in Chinese–Chinese and Chinese–foreign marriages also occasionally experience domestic violence and/or psychological abuse from their Chinese wives ('Family violence becomes public evil in China' 2003; Liu Xiaoxiao 2005; 'Zhongguo xin'niang' 2008; 'Qizi changqi jiating baoli' 2010). Such women reportedly suspect their husbands of infidelity and vent their anger in various ways. They may physically beat their husbands and constrain their partner's freedom of movement by stalking him or locking him in a room at home. Some even abuse and murder their male children in order to deprive their husbands of an ancestral line ('Family violence becomes public evil in China' 2003; 'Qizi changqi jiating baoli' 2010).

There is limited newspaper coverage available in the PRC of instances of male citizens of the PRC abusing their foreign partners. One report concerns a male citizen of the PRC abusing his wife, a woman from Vietnam (Wu Hui 2008a). The couple reportedly had been married for over ten years and had two children – a son and a daughter. However, the Chinese man was disabled, blind and bad-tempered and frequently beat his wife following arguments over everyday matters. Thus, the woman eventually filed for divorce (Wu Hui 2008a).

A second and more recent case of domestic violence involves Li Yang, a famous English-language teacher in the PRC and founder of the Crazy English franchise (*Fengkuang yingyu*), a method of language learning based on shouting. Kim Lee, Li's American wife of 12 years and mother of their three daughters, accused Li of domestic violence and posted photographs on a microblog in August 2011 of her bruised face and legs after he had responded to a domestic quarrel by smashing her head on the floor. Lee eventually filed for divorce in December 2011. The case attracted widespread media publicity because of Li Yang's status as a public figure in the PRC, generating both condemnation of Li's actions and renewed concern about domestic violence in the PRC in general (Zhuanfang Li Yang Jiabao 2011; Lu Man 2011; 'Li Yang lihun'an' 2011; Zhang Lei 2011).

There are no reports in the PRC media of female foreign nationals abusing their Chinese husbands either inside or outside the PRC. This omission presumably reflects the fact that only a limited number of male citizens of the PRC enter into an intercultural marriage in the first place. Moreover, such men allegedly marry women who display traditional Chinese female characteristics, such as being 'diligent' (*qinfen*) and 'mild and virtuous' (*wenshu xianhui*) (Hu Shufeng and Xiong Yunbin 2007; 'Eguo kongjie' 2008; Zhao Lei *et al.* 2009). They also tend to reside in the PRC after marriage either for the purposes of work and/or to care for aged parents (Hu Shufeng and Xiong Yunbin 2007; 'Eguo kongjie' 2008; Gao Baoliang 2009). The limited number of such marriages, combined with the lack of detailed information available about the countries of origin and socio-economic background of the women involved in such marriages, means it is not possible to speculate whether domestic violence is a problem in such marriages or not. Although domestic violence is a documented problem in present-day China, the subject does not feature in newspaper reports in the PRC as a reason for divorce in the context of marriages involving female foreign nationals and male citizens of the PRC who live in mainland China.

In summary, along with deception and adultery, newspaper reports in the PRC cite domestic violence as a major reason for the growing rate of Chinese–foreign marriages ending in divorce. Media coverage of domestic violence in this context is marked by gendered ethnic and geographical imbalances. The perpetrators of violence are predominantly foreign men and the victims of that violence are Chinese women who live overseas rather than in the PRC. There is limited coverage of Chinese nationals in intercultural marriage as perpetrators of domestic violence other than the case of Li Yang and there are no reports of foreign women abusing their Chinese husbands. This way of framing reinforces the implicit juxtaposition of 'bad foreign husbands' and 'good Chinese husbands' in the context of intercultural marriage.

Marriage introduction services and divorce

Many newspaper reports in the PRC about divorce in Chinese–foreign marriages, especially since the mid-2000s, focus on the problems created by 'international marriage introduction agencies' (*shewai hunyin jieshao*). This term refers to Chinese–foreign marriages arranged through the medium of an individual matchmaker or an organization that provides international matchmaking services. The existence of such agencies became the focus of prohibitory governmental regulations in 1994 and 1995.

Marriage introduction services became available and institutionalized in the PRC in the early 1980s ('Hunyin jieshao' 2008). For example, a marriage introduction agency was established in Shenyang City in 1980 to help older, divorced and widowed people meet potential partners. Such services were generally run as a community service for Chinese people and were run by organizations affiliated with the Chinese Communist Party, such as the Communist Youth League of China, the All-China Women's Federation, the All-China Federation of Trade Unions and local residents' committees ('Hunyin jieshao' 2008).

In the 1990s, marriage introduction agencies began to operate as businesses and those that offered international matchmaking services, in particular, became associated with profiteering through deception ('Hunyin jieshao' 2008). Such agencies are described by journalists in disreputable terms as shady, sinister and/or greedy, profit-driven go-betweens (*hei zhongjie*) that are responsible for many of the problems associated with Chinese–foreign marriages, especially deception and consequently divorce (Miao Hui 2006; Fu Guiming 2007; Hu Yongmou 2007; Wang Si 2008; Luo Ronghua 2009; 'Cong Xuenaiyin'an' 2009).

In December 1994, China's Ministry of Civil Affairs expressed concern about increasing reports of international marriage introduction agencies colluding with foreign nationals to take money from Chinese women under the pretence of offering matchmaking services. The Ministry reported to the State Council that these institutions were causing harm to their victims and damaging China's national reputation and requested that it take action to remedy the situation. The State Council responded by issuing the Notice on 'Strengthening the Management of International Marriage Introduction Agencies (*Guowuyuan bangongting guanyu jiaqiang shewai hunyin jieshao guanli de tongzhi* 1994, hereafter the 1994 Notice), in order to protect women's legal rights and interests.

The 1994 Notice prohibited the establishment and advertisement of international marriage introduction agencies by enterprises, institutions and individuals and granted local bureaus of civil affairs, public security and industry and commerce, the power to investigate, identify and punish any individuals and organizations that disobeyed that ban. Shortly after, key municipalities and provinces such as Jiangsu, Fujian, Shanxi, Gansu, Guangxi, Zhejiang, Anhui, Qinghai, Shanghai, Guangzhou, Harbin, Nanjing, Chengdu, Shenyang, Xi'an, Chongqing and Dalian, established management plans to regulate domestic matchmaking agencies and ban those that provided international matchmaking services ('Hunyin jieshao' 2008). However, problems associated with the practical definition of 'international marriage introduction agencies', and the absence of a national ruling on how to regulate the matchmaking industry in practice, meant that the number of agencies providing such services continued to expand.

On 24 May 1995, the General Office of the PRC's Ministry of Civil Affairs issued the Notice on Issues Concerning the Rigorous Implementation of the State Council's 1994 Notice on Strengthening the Management of International Marriage Introduction Agencies (Minzhengbu bangongting guanyu renzhen guanche *guowuyuan bangongting guanyu jiaqiang shewai hunyin jieshao guanli de tongzhi* youguan wenti de tongzhi 1995). This Notice reiterated the importance of enhancing the management of domestic marriage introduction agencies in the PRC and closing down those agencies that provided international marriage introduction services and urged local governments to cooperate in 'tidying up' or rectifying (*qingli zhengdun*) the matchmaking industry. As a result, different municipal governments and local departments of civil affairs in Jiangsu, Fujian, Dalian, Shenyang and Shanghai initiated measures to check domestic marriage introduction agencies and to ensure that such agencies were registered with relevant government departments and did not provide international marriage introduction services ('Hunyin jieshao' 2008).

However, agencies that provide introduction services for Chinese–foreign marriages have continued to proliferate throughout the PRC for three main reasons. First, there is clearly a demand for the services of such agencies from PRC women seeking a foreign spouse ('Zhongguo liyi' 2007; 'Yujing lüshi' 2010). Second, the provision of such services is a profitable business (Pan Meihong 2006; Fu Guiming 2007; 'Yujing lüshi' 2010). Third, the 1994 and 1995 Notices offer guidelines rather than a national legal framework and consequently have been interpreted and implemented in different ways at the local level ('Hunyin jieshao' 2008; 'Yujing lüshi' 2010). As a result, some providers of international marriage introduction services have either ignored the Notices or found various ways to run their business in disguised forms.

Newspaper reports in the PRC indicate that individuals and businesses flout governmental rulings against the establishment of international marriage introduction agencies in various ways. Individuals may provide matchmaking services for a fee in the form of introductions provided through groups of acquaintances and friends, thereby evading detection by policing or other authorities (Hu Yongmou 2007; 'Jiadao Riben' 2007; 'Yujing lüshi' 2010). In a similar vein, small agencies may solicit business by circulating street flyers (Wei Minghui 2009; 'Yujing lüshi' 2010), or by disguising their operations as a translation service or as a Chinese–foreign marriage consultation company (*shewai hunyin zixun gongsi*) ('Hunyin jieshao' 2008; Luo Ronghua 2009; Wang Na 2009; 'Yujing lüshi' 2010). A Chinese–foreign marriage consultation company is a non-profit institution that may legally provide intercultural marriage consultation services after meeting relevant criteria and obtaining a business licence from the local department of civil affairs ('Shanghai shi shewai hunyin guanli zanxing banfa' 2000; 'Yujing lüshi' 2010). Other businesses avoid detection from governmental authorities by operating under the guise of domestic marriage agencies offering introductions to citizens of the PRC (Pan Meihong 2006; 'Yujing lüshi' 2010) and yet others conduct their business online (Miao Hui 2006; Luo Ronghua 2009).

Newspaper reports in the PRC reiterate and underscore the illegal nature of international marriage introduction agencies by citing the two bans issued by the PRC government in 1994 and 1995 respectively (Li Zijun 2005; Hu Yongmou 2007; Qi Xinxin 2008; Wei Minghui 2009). Many reports also feature titles that emphasize the illegal nature of such agencies and highlight the newspapers' implicit opposition to their existence. These headlines include statements such as: 'International Marriage Introduction Agencies Are Illegal' (*shewai hunjie shu feifa*) ('Shewai hunjie' 2008); 'International Marriage Introduction Agencies – They Are Illegal!' (*jieshao shewai hunyin, weigui!*) (Hu Yongmou 2007); and 'International Marriage Introduction Agencies Operate in a Black-Box Environment' (*kuaguo hunjie jinqu nei anxiang caozuo*) (Gu Hui 2007). Such frames draw a clear line between who is right (the government) and who is wrong (Chinese–foreign marriage agency). Hence they serve to affirm the authoritative power of the PRC Government by turning into a weapon against Chinese–foreign marriage agencies, which the PRC regulations have failed to control.

Newspaper reports in the PRC routinely condemn international marriage introduction agencies by relating stories concerning the large number of fraudulent and violent marriages and subsequent divorces, that are associated with them (Miao Hui 2006; Fu Guiming 2007; Hu Yongmou 2007; Wang Si 2008; Zhang Lisha 2008). In terms of deception, the standard cautionary tale is about Chinese women paying large sums of money to international marriage introduction agencies in order to meet their potential foreign husbands with the aim of going abroad. Having paid the requisite fees and entered into a 'whirlwind' romance and marriage, none of these women realizes their dreams of living overseas. They quickly discover that they are victims of deception on the part of the marriage introduction agencies and their partners/spouses. They also soon discover that they are unable to obtain a visa to travel abroad and lose contact with the man they married who has returned to his home country and not remained in contact. As a result, such women are left with no option other than to divorce, and often experience difficulties in doing so because of the lack of appropriate supporting documentation about their spouse, etc.

For example, a 2006 report entitled 'Blind Spots of Chinese–Foreign Marriage' (*Shewai hunyin "sanbuqu" bubu you mangdian*) in the *Jiating Zhoumobao* (Family Weekly) tells the story of a Chinese woman called Liu Jing, who subscribed to and subsequently paid an online marriage agency the sum of 12,000 yuan (US$1,500) to meet an American man named Jack (Miao Hui 2006). Liu and Jack married shortly after they met; and she gave Jack a large sum of money, 150,000 yuan (US$18,750), which he said was required to apply via an immigration company for a visa for her to travel to the USA as a spouse. However, the visa never appeared and Jack disappeared. Liu then filed for a divorce but this took over 18 months to finalize because she had lost contact with Jack. Liu also attempted to get the marriage introduction agency to return the fees she had paid to meet Jack in the first place, but was unable to obtain a refund because of technicalities associated with her receipts and the contract she had signed. In conclusion, the report cites expert commentary from lawyers to suggest that international marriage introduction agencies flourish despite their illegality because many brokers operate via the Internet, which makes it difficult for relevant authorities to track them down and hence to close them down (Miao Hui 2006).

Newspaper reports in the PRC also offer investigative accounts of Chinese–foreign marriage introduction agencies, explaining the types of people who run them and work for them, the kind of people who form their client base and the type of services they provide and at what financial and social cost (Gu Hui 2007; Cao Guangyu 2008; Luo Ronghua 2009). A 2009 report in the *Nanguo Jinbao* (Southern China News) offers an example of this kind of investigative report (Luo Ronghua 2009). The report, entitled 'Many Women Seeking Foreign Husbands Fall Into A Trap – Insiders Reveal the "Rules" of Chinese–Foreign Marriage Matchmaking Services' (*Wei jia yanglaogong bushao nüzi zhong heizhao – yenei renshi baoguang shewai hunyin qian guize*), cites an industry insider to suggest that greedy people with no social conscience (*zhuan meixinqian de ren*) run international marriage introduction agencies. Their employees are often college graduates with a major in English, their clients are typically divorced women aged between 35 and 50 years, although some clients are younger women who have been made redundant from work, as well as rural migrant labourers. It reveals that one privately operated agency charged around 2,000 yuan (US$250) for putting clients' information on an international matchmaking website. However, if that information led to a successful introduction and encouraged a foreign client to come to China in order to meet the Chinese client, then, the agency would charge the woman another 5,000 yuan (US$625). The agency would also claim 20 per cent of monies expected to be given to the Chinese woman by the foreign male national as a gift upon their first meeting, a sum of around 20,000 yuan (US$2,500). If they married, the matchmaker would claim another 10,000 yuan (US$1,250) in fees from the couple. Hence, the cost of a single successful introduction may reach a total of 50,000 yuan (US$6,250) and a successful marriage broker may earn around 100,000 yuan (US$12,500) per year (Luo Ronghua 2009).

Other Chinese–foreign marriage introduction agencies reportedly charge up to 200,000 yuan (US$25,000) for an introduction, and charge additional, often exorbitant fees, for services such as administration, advertising and assisting with communication, translation and visa applications (Cao Guangyu 2008). Yet other agencies allegedly use various deceptive methods to evade police detection and/or obtain extra fees from their clients. Fees for 'introductions' are presented on receipts as fees for 'translation services'; clients are charged fees but given no service; clients are provided with false information about potential partners; and clients receive false or exaggerated letters from potential partners in order to encourage the payment of further fees ('Shewai hunjie' 2008; 'Fanyi gongsi' 2009; 'Weizhuang haiwai' 2009). Metaphors such as the 'The lion opens its maw' (*shizi dazhang kou*) and 'lambs to the slaughter' (*daizai de gaoyang*) are further used to underscore the unscrupulous practices of such agencies (Cao Guangyu 2008; Luo Ronghua 2009). These agencies are basically described as manipulating 'desperate women' who, if the agency actually facilitates a face-to-face introduction, will meet foreign men who happen to be 'old' (*lao*), 'poor' (*qiong*), unemployed, 'repeat divorcees' (*duoci lihun*) and/or 'marriage-related swindlers' (*huntuo*) ('Bei youhuo' 2008; Shang Bin 2008; Wang Si 2008; 'Fanyi gongsi' 2009; Wei Minghui 2009).

Other newspaper reports in the PRC focus on the closure of illegal Chinese–foreign marriage introduction agencies to demonstrate both policing successes and the futility of running such an illegal business enterprise despite their evident popularity and profitability (Qi Xinxin 2008; Wu Xiuyun 2008; Zhang Zhiqiang 2008a; 'Shewai hunjie' 2008; Wang Na 2009). A case in point is the story of the company, Yi Guanglian, established by Qi Yaomin in Guangzhou in 2004. Although Qi registered the company as providing marriage consultation and translation services, it was essentially an international marriage introduction agency (Zhang Zhiqiang 2008a). Qi's business was so successful that he opened subsidiary branches in approximately 20 major cities across the PRC, subsequently, attracting the attention of Fortune Time (*Caifu Rensheng*), a popular business programme on China's Central Television Station. One episode of the programme told of how a divorced migrant worker in Shenzhen called Zhang Xiaoying met her 'Prince Charming' from the USA, with the help of Qi's matchmaking services, thereby advertising the business ('International Marriage Broker' 2008). However, the Department of Industry and Commerce in Guangzhou closed the company down in 2008 following consumer complaints (Qi Xinxin 2008; Zhang Zhiqiang 2008a).

A large number of complaints relating to fraudulent business practices were laid against the Yi Guanglian international matchmaking agency. One woman reportedly had paid for membership and later discovered that her photograph and personal information had been posted on the Internet, making her the subject of workplace gossip ('International Marriage Broker' 2008). Another woman complained that the company had demanded an extra fee of 20,000 yuan (US$2,500) for her Australian date to come to China to visit her. One woman who did get a visit from a potential foreign spouse found him sleeping with another woman in a hotel the morning after he arrived. Other women claimed that they had received identical letters from supposedly different 'foreign boyfriends'. While some women complained, many others kept silent for fear of public humiliation. Those who complained were informed that the company had a non-refund policy written into the contract, and some were warned that if they complained to the police or other authorities they would be 'blacklisted' and hence would never get the opportunity to go abroad ('International marriage broker' 2008).

Qi Yaomin was arrested on 12 March 2008 and subsequent investigations revealed that his agency had made a total of 15.11 million yuan (US$1.9 million) from the provision of international marriage introduction services. The court ruled that Qi was not guilty of fraud, because he had fulfilled his matchmaking responsibilities by posting the women's information on overseas 'personals' websites. However, Qi was sentenced to ten years in jail was for running an illegal business for more than five years ('International marriage broker' 2008; Wu Xiuyun 2008).

In short, newspaper presentations of Chinese–foreign matchmakers warn (female) readers to 'stay away' from these introduction agencies, unless they want to become the next victims of fraudulent business practices that may result in 'fake' marriages and ultimately divorce. There are no reports of male citizens of the PRC using intercultural marriage agencies to seek a foreign wife. Nor are there any reports that feature stories of foreign nationals looking for Chinese partners through the medium of Chinese–foreign marriage agencies in the PRC. These omissions reflect the fact that citizens of the PRC who seek foreign partners are overwhelmingly female. However, they also reinforce the notion that Chinese women who seek a foreign spouse for hypergamous reasons are destined to become the victims of those who seek to exploit those desires. This style of reportage effectively commercializes and demonizes the modes of matchmaking that are associated with Chinese–foreign marriages. Such coverage may also exert great social power at the discursive level by strengthening public support for government policies in tackling this issue. In other words, any other positive framing of Chinese–foreign marriage matchmakers by different media outlets may be marginalized and risk being perceived as lacking credibility, or going against the mainstream political orientation of the 'gate keepers' of the PRC. However, to some degree, this reportage constrains the choices available to citizens of the PRC who wish to enter an intercultural marriage, especially those who have limited resources and social networks. Arguably, a better alternative would be to remove existing bans on Chinese–foreign marriage introduction agencies and professionalize both the international and domestic matchmaking industries in the PRC.

Conclusion

In summary, the rising incidence of Chinese–foreign divorce in twenty-first century China as documented in newspaper reports in the PRC is associated with deception, bigamy, adultery, domestic violence and the activities of exploitative Chinese–

foreign marriage introduction agencies. Such reports are gendered cautionary tales with geographical dimensions. They effectively warn Chinese women that if they marry a foreign national and live outside China, then, they are likely to become victims of adultery and/or domestic violence and consequently will have to divorce. They may even attempt suicide or try to murder their spouses. Correspondingly, male foreign nationals, especially those who are non-ethnic Chinese, are depicted as having a propensity to infidelity, deception, violence and taking advantage of Chinese women, with some men conspiring with 'evil' international marriage introduction agencies to exploit Chinese women. This implies, by default, that male citizens of the PRC are better husbands, despite the problems associated with domestic Chinese marriages and China's well documented rise in the incidence of divorce. In doing so, newspaper reports in the PRC provide their audiences with a dualistic construction of bad foreign husbands and evil marriage introduction agencies and victimized Chinese women and good Chinese men.

A closer look at this construction also suggests that frames on different topics (e.g. bigamy, deception, extra-marital affairs, domestic violence, illegal marriage agencies in relation to Chinese–foreign divorces) with similar selected elements (bad foreign males) can reinforce each other and make the problems being discussed more prominent than they actually appear to be. In addition, the PRC newspapers have to some extent attributed responsibility for these social problems to foreign male partners in Chinese–foreign marriages. In doing so, they have simultaneously shifted the responsibility of the problems associated with Chinese–foreign marriages from the government to individuals.

Note

1   Violence in the context of marriage was a topic under discussion among the Chinese Communist Party's early marriage reform campaigns of the 1940s and 1950s as well. See Susan Glosser (2003) *Chinese Visions of Family and State, 1919–1953* and Gail Hershatter (2011) *The Gender of Memory: Rural Women and China's Collective Past*.

5 Celebrity Chinese–foreign marriage

This chapter examines print and online media coverage in the PRC of celebrity Chinese–foreign marriages in the reform period. Since the mid-1990s, the growth of large-scale entertainment industries and commercial advertising in the PRC has facilitated the emergence of a celebrity culture and both national and international celebrity stories have become a staple feature of China's media (Jeffreys and Edwards 2010: 1–3). Media coverage of Chinese entertainment and sports stars prior to the mid-1990s tended to focus on their professional accomplishments. However, recent media coverage of such famous individuals is also concerned with the nature of their private or 'real' lives, including details of their romances, marriages and divorces.

Graeme Turner (2004: 8) argues that: 'we can map the precise moment a public figure becomes a celebrity. It occurs at the point at which media interest in their activities is transferred from reporting on their public role to investigating the details of their private lives'. In this sense, many of China's public figures are now actively celebrities in that they work with media representatives to augment their fame and attract the interest and curiosity of not only their fans, but also broader audiences, by providing intimate and entertaining details about their personal lives. Chinese celebrities and journalists alike are increasingly exploiting the spaces between the different personas of the star-as-entertainer and the star-as-real-person, with a corresponding growth in celebrity-related news, information and advertising.

As media reports on celebrity Chinese–foreign marriages are both widely disseminated and growing in number when compared to reports of 'ordinary' Chinese–foreign marriages, they offer a useful point of comparison for examining popular constructions of the phenomenon of intercultural marriage in China today. Media discussions of celebrity Chinese–foreign marriages in the PRC focus mainly on marriages between foreign nationals and mainland entertainment and sports celebrities. Some of these reports refer to both celebrities from mainland China and celebrities from Hong Kong, Macau and Taiwan. However, celebrities from Hong Kong, Macau and Taiwan are not differentiated from mainland Chinese celebrities or made a separate focus of analysis in such reports – they are treated as a generic group of celebrity Chinese citizens who have entered into a Chinese–foreign marriage (e.g. 'Mingren mingxing' 2007; 'Lihunlü gao!' 2007; 'Pilu: shezu yiguo lian' 2008; Mingxingmen' 2009). Consequently, the chapter focuses on media reports of Chinese–foreign marriages involving foreign nationals and celebrities from mainland China.

This chapter proceeds as follows. It first looks at the case of Shen Danping, reportedly the first entertainment star in reform-era China to marry a foreigner in 1984. Retrospective media reports indicate that Shen's decision to marry a German citizen was not only opposed by her family and work unit in the early 1980s, but also generated significant public gossip, with many people speculating that she wanted to marry an older foreign man because of a hypergamous desire to live abroad. It then takes a closer look at other media reports of celebrity Chinese–foreign marriage in the 1990s, showing how they simultaneously deride female celebrities who marry and move overseas as unpatriotic and celebrate them as extraordinary women with modern careers and fairy-tale romances and marriages. Finally, it examines celebrity Chinese–foreign marriages in the 2000s, revealing that these marriages are portrayed in terms of a reversed migration trend, wherein celebrities and their foreign partners relocate from abroad back to China and in terms of inverted gender roles. In contrast to media accounts of 'ordinary' Chinese–foreign marriages, Chinese female celebrities in intercultural marriages are frequently constructed as 'breadwinners', rather than as dependent and victimized women, while they simultaneously aspire to the role of an ordinary wife and mother. Foreign husbands are constructed as 'good housekeepers' rather than as violent and abusive men. Through these reports, China's media instruct consuming audiences on the nature of exemplary intercultural marriages and reconfigure conventional understandings of gender roles within marriage.

China's first celebrity Chinese–foreign marriage

Retrospective media reports claim that actress Shen Danping was the first (female) entertainment star to enter into an intercultural marriage in reform-era China, with 'intercultural marriage' being defined in this context as 'international marriage' (*kuaguo hunyin*) (Lü Suozhi 2005; Fang Hai 2008; 'Huangruo geshi' 2008). In July 1984, she married Uwe Kraeuter (Wu Wei in Chinese), a German anti-Vietnam war activist working as an editor at the Foreign Languages Press in Beijing. At that time, Shen was a student with the Beijing Film Academy.

Shen Danping became famous not long after her marriage because of her starring role in the feature film *Bei Aiqing Yiwang de Jiaoluo* (hereafter *A Love-Forsaken Corner*, dir. Li Yalin and Zhang Qi 1981), which was released in 1986 (Lü Suozhi 2005; Fang Hai 2008; Yan Jin 2009). The film is a melodrama about the pursuit of true love and the rejection of arranged marriage. It is set in the context of the early 1980s political and social rejection of the Cultural Revolution and the late Maoist period as 'ten years of disaster' (1966–1976). The Cultural Revolution is said to have only truly ended with the arrest of its purported leaders (the Gang of Four)[1] in 1976 and the subsequent adoption of Deng Xiaoping's economic reforms and Open Door Policy at the Third Plenary Session of the Eleventh Central Committee of the Communist Party of China in December 1978 ('Shiyi jie sanzhong quanhui' 2008; Marxists Internet Archive 2009; Yan Jin 2009).

In *A Love-Forsaken Corner*, Shen Danping plays the part of a young peasant woman called 'Shen Huangmei' whose experience of love and life mirrors the vicissitudes of the Chinese revolution. The melodrama relates the love and marriage stories of several peasant women, via a series of flashbacks starting in the early 1950s and ending in the late 1970s. Following the CCP's assumption of national political power in October 1949, Shen Huangmei's mother, Ling Hua, refuses to go through with an arranged marriage and marries instead the man she loves. This action reiterates for Chinese audiences the understanding that the CCP liberated Chinese women by introducing the 1950 Marriage Law, which banned the 'feudal' practice of arranged marriages, and upheld the principle of free choice and love in marriage (*Zhonghua renmin gongheguo hunyin fa* 1950). The film then jumps forward to the Cultural Revolution period, where the Gang of Four are portrayed as being in power and Shen Huangmei's family are living in dire poverty. Shen's father has been expelled from the Communist Party and also discharged from his position as head of an agricultural cooperative society for committing political 'errors' and the family has gone into debt. Ling Hua organizes an arranged marriage for her daughter in order to pay that debt. Shen initially resists but eventually agrees to sacrifice herself for the sake of the family by agreeing to enter into an arranged marriage.

The film concludes in the late 1970s, when the Gang of Four have been tried and sentenced to life imprisonment for attempting to overthrow the government and for 'crimes against the people' ('Sirenbang fandang' 1992). In keeping with the rejection of late Maoist politics, Shen Huangmei's father in the film is rehabilitated, he has been reinstated as a Communist Party member and regains his work position. With her father earning money once again, Shen is able to decline the arranged marriage and look forward to a future marriage based on love. In addition, Shen Huangmei and her family, along with the rest of the Chinese people, can look forward to increased economic prosperity and a brighter and less politicized future.

Following her success in *A Love-Forsaken Corner*, Shen Danping went on to star in numerous movies and television dramas. In *Ye Shanghai* (Night in Shanghai, dir. Hu Xiaofeng 1982), Shen plays the role of Zhou Xuan, a famous singer in China and Southeast Asia during the 1930s. In *Zhanzheng Ziwuxian* (The Meridian of War, dir. Feng Xiaoning 1990), she plays a young nurse and survivor of a group of 13 unarmed youths attacked by the Japanese army along the Great Wall in the 1940s. *Liucun Chakan* (Probation Within the Village 1994, dir. Lei Xianhe, Wang Xingdong, Luo Liang and Du Cailing) tells the story of a village teacher who falls in love with a disgraced government official who redeems himself by eliminating poverty in a formerly impoverished village. In *Sanba Xian shang de Nübing* (Female Soldiers on the Thirty-Eighth Parallel 2000, dir. Wang Xiaomin), Shen plays one of the five female soldiers who volunteered to fight, and died, in the Korean War (1950–1953). *Butian* (Stitching the Sky 2002, dir. Ma Shuchao) tells the story of a primary school teacher who brings love, knowledge and joy to a village in rural China. Shen Danping has also starred in a number of television series. For example, she starred in *Zhiyao Ni Guode Bi Wo Hao* (Wishing You a Better Life Than Me 1994), *Yi Nian You Yi Nian* (Year after Year 1998); *Mingyun de Chengnue* (The Promise of Life 2001); and *Yi Aiqing de Mingyi* (In the Name of Love 2007).

Although Shen Danping's celebrity is associated with her acting career, she has also attracted public attention because of her 'love marriage' in 1984 to a German national, Uwe Kraeuter. Shen met Kraeuter in 1983 at a party organized by mutual friends in Beijing. The couple reportedly fell in love at first sight. However, contrary to the portrayal of reform-era China in *A Love-Forsaken Corner* as a depoliticized country where romantic love could finally thrive unhindered, their courtship was conducted in secret for fear of negative reactions to their relationship by the public, work unit and family.

Retrospective media reports indicate that both Shen's family and work unit initially opposed her decision to marry Kraeuter. Her parents allegedly felt shamed (*diuren*) by her desire to marry a 'foreigner' (*guizi*) ('Huangruo geshi' 2008). They even asked her to stay away from the family home during the Chinese Lunar New Year holidays, traditionally a period when family members spend time with each other. In keeping with general suspicion of foreigners in China at the time, when Shen's parents met Kraeuter they apparently treated him as someone who planned to marry her and then traffic her overseas ('Huangruo geshi' 2008; Fang Hai 2008). Shen's work unit also initially refused to issue supportive documents for their marriage registration (Fang Hai 2008). When Shen and Kraeuter finally obtained the documentation required to register their marriage in Beijing on 21 July 1984, Shen's parents declined to celebrate the event. Only a small number of friends attended their wedding celebration (Chen Zikun 1993: 38–9; 'Huangruo geshi' 2008). Despite these difficulties, Shen and Kraeuter are still married, have two daughters and have resided in Beijing for nearly 30 years ('German jumps cultural wall' 2004; Lü Suozhi 2005; Fang Hai 2008).[2]

As China's first reform-era entertainment star to marry a foreigner, Shen Danping has been celebrated in media reports in the 2000s for her bravery in daring to marry a foreigner for 'love' in the face of 'unfair' criticisms of her actions from family members and other members of the Chinese public (Xie Xiao and Shen Yangwen 2001; 'Huangruo geshi' 2008; Mu Xuan 2009). She is praised as courageous for being the first entertainment star from the PRC mainland to marry a foreigner in reform-era China and thus 'daring to eat the crab' [of intercultural marriage] (*Zhongguo gan chi pangxie de diyi ren*). Her marriage is also cited as starting the phenomenon of intercultural marriage within China's entertainment industry (Xie Xiao and Shen Yangwen 2001; Mu Xuan 2009).

According to media reports published in the 2000s, Shen's marriage to Kraeuter in 1984 not only attracted initial opposition from her family and work unit, but also generated significant public gossip, with many people speculating about the negative motivations behind her marriage, understood in terms of hypergamy and a desire to live abroad. For example, a 2004 report in the *China Daily*, an English-language subsidiary of the *People's Daily*, which is the official voice of the Chinese Communist Party, cites Kraeuter as saying: 'At the beginning, many people said Shen Danping married me to get a chance to go abroad' ('German Jumps Cultural Wall' 2004). The fact that Shen is 14 years younger than Kraeuter was viewed as confirming the perceived hypergamous nature of her motivations for marrying a foreigner (Chen Zikun 1993: 38–9; Liu Jun 1994: 28; Fang Hai 2008; 'Huangruo geshi' 2008).

While encountering obstacles, Shen Danping's intercultural marriage attracted media coverage chiefly because of her standing as a professional movie star, rather than because the details of her marriage were viewed as 'national news' in their own right. Unlike the widely reported case of Li Shuang in 1981, an experimental artist who was detained and sentenced to two years 're-education through labour' for 'offending national decency' by cohabiting with her boyfriend Emmanuel Bellefroid, a French diplomat, in the French Embassy Compound (Earnshaw 1981; Zhang 2008, see Chapter 1), Shen did not live with her partner before marriage. Moreover, her courtship and marriage did not involve any 'politically sensitive' issues.

In fact, newspaper reports about Shen Danping in the 1990s focus mainly on her professional career development rather than her marriage to a foreigner, suggesting limited media interest at the time in the private lives of entertainment stars. They typically detail Shen's starring roles in popular films and television series, then briefly relate the story of her love for and marriage to, Kraeuter and conclude with a discussion of her latest professional achievements (Wu Wei 1994; Du Pin 1995; Zhao Xin 1998). For example, a 1994 report in the *Hangzhou Ribao* (Hangzhou Daily) briefly introduces her completed role in the television series *Zhiyao Ni Guode Bi Wo Hao* (Wishing You a Better Life Than Me) and her cooperation with her husband on a forthcoming television programme called *Yige Shaonü he Liangge Nanhai* (A Girl and Two Boys) (Wu Wei 1994). The report concludes with Shen's plans to produce a new film, *Hunxue Haizi de Shijie* (World of the Mixed Blood Children) by the end of that year, a plan which does not appear to have been completed and her preparation of a then forthcoming biography, *Yang'guangxia de Piaobo: Wo de Yishu yu Hunlian* (Life in the Sun: My Art, Love and Marriage, 1995).

However, magazines as a medium, started to develop in China during the 1980s and some of these ran feature articles about Shen's intercultural marriage in the 1990s. Examples of such magazines include: *Zhongguo Jiankang Yuekan* (China Health Monthly), which was established in 1982; *Renmin Tiaojie* (People's Mediators), which was founded in 1985; and *Dangdai Dianshi* (hereafter Modern Television), which was established in 1986. These magazines featured articles about Shen Danping that were longer in length, and more detailed than contemporaneous newspaper stories about her. Moreover, apart from introducing Shen's career achievements and recent activities, they contained more personalized and detailed information about her husband and their courtship, marriage and family life (see Liu Jun 1994: 27–9; Yuan Ye 1995: 24–5; Zeng Yang 1998: 14–15).

To offer a specific example, *Modern Television* featured an article entitled 'Shen Danping in the Nest of Love' (*Aichao zhong de Shen Danping*) in 1994 (Liu Jun 1994: 27–9). The article talks about Shen's cooperation with her husband on film production, how they fell in 'love at first sight', what obstacles were presented to their marriage by family and friends, the nature of their married life and their relationships with their daughter. It concludes by revealing the couples' plan to travel to the USA in that year (Liu Jun 1994: 27–9).

In the late 1980s and throughout the 1990s, Shen Danping's marital circumstances ceased to be unusual as an increasing number of Chinese mainland celebrities from the fields of entertainment and sports and especially female celebrities, entered into intercultural marriages. In 1986, Siqin Gaowa (film actress) married Chen Liangsheng, an overseas Chinese man with Swiss nationality ('Siqin Gaowa: Ruishi' 2006). In 1988, Li Donghua, a former Chinese gymnastics champion married a Swiss woman named Friedli Esperanza (Shi Ping 1999; 'Kuaguo hunyin pinchuan' 2008). In 1989, He Zhili, a table tennis champion known under the name of Xiaoshan Zhili, married a Japanese table tennis player Xiaoshan Yingzhi ('Kuaguo hunyin pinchuan' 2008). Also in 1989, Jiao Zhimin, formerly a table tennis champion and currently an entrepreneur, married a South Korean table tennis player, Ahn Jae-hyung, whom she met while participating in the 1984 Asian Table Tennis Championships in Pakistan (Xu Baokang 1993). In 1992, Chen Chong (film actress also known by the name of Joan Cheng) married her second Chinese–American husband, cardiologist Peter Hui after her marriage with Jimmy Lau ended in 1990 ('Liangci hunyin' 2007). In 1994, Wei Wei (Mandopop singer) married a famous American composer Michael Joseph Smith in Sweden (Li Jun 1994a). In 1997, Jiang Wen (film actor) married Sandrine Chenivisse, a French actress ('He Faguo qizi' 2007); and Li Lingyu (singer and actress) married 'Jerry', a Canadian entrepreneur in 1999 ('Zhongguo mingren' 2006).

As in the case of Shen Danping, newspaper reports about celebrity Chinese–foreign marriages in the 1990s focus predominantly on the professional achievements of the stars in question, rather than their marital arrangements and domestic life. The majority of images attached to these early reports are also still shots from movies and television programmes in which a given celebrity has performed (Cang Lide and Mu Ya 1993; Du Pin 1995; Wei Jiang 1997; Wang Linchang 1999). Such images do not generally include glimpses of the perceived real person behind the celebrity image, whether the celebrity-at-home with family and children, or the kind of 'off-guard', 'unkempt' and 'unready' photographs that are captured by paparazzi and circulated by contemporary media for the enjoyment of multiple audiences (Holmes 2005: 24).

However, some reports in newspapers and especially articles in the then relatively new but flourishing popular magazines do focus on the personalized and perceived extraordinary details of celebrity intercultural marriages in the 1990s. On the one hand, a minority of Chinese celebrities who entered into intercultural marriages in the 1990s are presented as objects of derision and contempt for marrying a foreigner and leaving the PRC to live overseas. They are criticized as being unpatriotic and undeserving of the love given to them by their Chinese audiences. On the other hand, the majority of celebrities in Chinese–foreign marriages are framed as being in fairy-tale marriages characterized by a surfeit of love and romance and removed from the mundane day-to-day problems that are associated with marriages of 'ordinary people'. Celebrities as 'extraordinary people' are framed as successful professionals, and exemplary wives, mothers, husbands and sons-in-law, through media narratives that claim to investigate and reveal the 'secrets' behind the success of extraordinary Chinese–foreign marriages,

Celebrity Chinese–foreign marriage in the 1990s

As with media discussions of the phenomenon of intercultural marriage in general, media accounts of celebrity Chinese–foreign marriage in the PRC since 1979 indicate that the phenomenon is gendered. The majority of Chinese celebrities who entered into intercultural marriages in the 1980s and 1990s are women. These women subsequently migrated to Europe, the USA, or other parts of Asia, to be with their husbands who were either non-ethnic Chinese foreign nationals or Chinese with foreign nationality (Cai Lide and Mu Ya 1993; Li Jun 1994b: 73–4; A Hen 1996: 38; Wang Linchang 1999).

There are a small number of media reports about marriages between male celebrities from mainland China and foreign women in the 1980s and 1990s. One of the few examples is Li Donghua, a former PRC gymnastics champion who married a Swiss woman, Esperanza Friedli, in 1988 (Kuaguo hunyin pinchuan' 2008). Actor Zhang Tielin, who is famous for his performance as an 'emperor' in a popular television series, *Huanzhu Gege* (Princess Pearl) in the PRC, married 'Marissa', a Polish woman and resident of the UK in 1990 (Bai Lu 2009); and Jiang Wen, a film actor in the PRC, married a French woman, Sandrine Chenivisse, in 1997 ('Mingxing men' 2009).

There are also only a small number of reports about marriages between foreign male celebrities and 'ordinary' Chinese women in both the 1990s and 2000s. In 1993, Canadian performer and television host Mark Roswell (Da Shan) married a female citizen of the PRC named Gan Lin (Li Yan 2008); and, American actor Jonathan Kos-Read (Cao Cao) married a Beijing woman, Li Zhiyin, in 2002 ('Yang Cao Cao' 2010). The author found no reports of marriages between foreign female celebrities and ordinary Chinese men in the 1990s and only one recent report of such a marriage. In the late 2000s, some newspapers retrospectively covered the story of the marriage in 1995 between a Beijing taxi driver named Wang Hongye and a German comic actor Esther Haubensack (Hao Lianlu), as Haubensack's work has started to become popular in China (Chen Zhonghe 2007).

The association of celebrity Chinese–foreign marriage in the 1980s and 1990s with female entertainment and sports stars leaving the PRC to marry and live overseas has attracted negative commentary, usually in the form of noting the celebrity's perceived lack of patriotic attachment to China and their rejection of both their Chinese fans and Chinese men. This style of commentary draws on the concerns noted in the preceding chapter regarding the 'uninformed love' of certain Chinese people for 'everything foreign'. It also draws on concerns regarding the flow of 'talented people' away from China to overseas countries in search of better economic and social opportunities.

As the headline of a 1994 article in the *Chuangyezhe* (hereafter Entrepreneur) magazine puts it: 'Female [Chinese] Stars: Can Foreigners Love You?'

(*Nümingxing, yangrenmen hui chong ni ma?*) (Feng Xinzi 1994: 34). Noting that a number of female mainland Chinese celebrities have moved overseas and expressed no plans to return to the PRC, the article offers two reasons for this phenomenon. First, although the celebrities in question told their fans in China that they went overseas to take up new opportunities, they have unrealistic expectations of life abroad and their careers are actually in decline. Second, their move overseas was motivated by the failure of their marriages to Chinese men (Feng Xinzi 1994: 34). The article concludes by raising a set of questions that reveal concerns about female celebrities as representatives of both China and China's position in the world. Why do so many Chinese celebrities think that they have to go overseas to 'advance' (*jinxiu*) their careers? Why have we seen not a single celebrity from overseas coming to China to advance their careers? Why do Chinese female celebrities effectively reject Chinese men by preferring to marry foreigners? Are foreigners capable of giving Chinese celebrities who go abroad the love that they receive from people in China?

In answering these questions, the *Entrepeneur*'s contributor concludes that 'foreigners' cannot 'love' the female celebrities in question like their Chinese audiences do, while implying that they may be unworthy of the love of their fans because they are unpatriotic and have rejected Chinese men (Feng Xinzi 1994: 34). The author notes that nearly all of China's female stars who went abroad for career development in the 1990s failed in their efforts and ended up living an isolated life overseas. Like the 'failed dreams' of ordinary Chinese women in intercultural marriages, this is attributed to their unrealistic expectations of life overseas compared to life in the PRC. The author claims, for instance, that one celebrity went to the USA with the professed aim of advancing their language skills and caustically concludes that: 'In the eyes of these celebrities, not only is American English better than Chinese, their Chinese is even better than that of the Chinese people'. The author further claims that some female celebrities complained publicly about their failed marriages in China in order to attract the attention of foreign people. Moreover, they have such a high opinion of themselves that they consider no mainland Chinese man would be a suitable marriage candidate for them (Feng Xinzi 1994: 34).

Other reports imply that the exodus of Chinese stars from the PRC in the context of intercultural marriage creates problems not only for female celebrities, but also for China's developing international film industry. A 1997 report in the *Dianying Pingjie* (hereafter Movie Comments) talks about actress Ning Jing's marriage to American actor Paul Kersey, whom she met in 1996 during the shooting of *Honghe Gu* (Red River Valley, dir. Feng Xiaoning 1996) (Shi Qing 1997: 18–19). After marrying, Ning moved to the USA, and had a child there, before returning to the PRC to continue a film career in 1998 (Pu Liu 2002). Published before her return to China, the report notes that Ning Jing's marriage and move abroad probably signifies the end of a promising career. It further suggests that this is a tragic situation because of the noted 'brain drain', a loss of talent from China to overseas that is associated with the PRC's creative industries, the difficulties Chinese celebrities face in developing a career overseas, and the fragile nature of intercultural marriages (Shi Qing 1997: 18). The report concludes with a cautionary gendered tale about an unspecified and extremely beautiful Chinese actress who moved to the USA after marriage only to be deserted by her husband shortly after and who wound up being a hostess in a bar and then the 'second wife' of an already married but wealthy Taiwanese entrepreneur (Shi Qing 1997: 19). This cautionary tale suggests that, just like ordinary Chinese women, extraordinary and talented Chinese women who marry a foreigner and live overseas may also encounter difficulties and become victims of duplicitous husbands via their hypergamous desire for further socio-economic and career advancement.

Media reports that censure Chinese entertainment and sports celebrities who marry foreign nationals and live overseas do so because the professional achievements of such celebrities as Chinese make them a source of national pride and, conversely, inadequacy. The story of Li Donghua, formerly a national gymnastic champion with the China National team, offers a different case in point. A 1998 article in the *Huanqiu Shibao* (hereafter Global Times) expresses annoyance at Li's decision to marry a Swiss backpacker, Esperanza Friedli, whom he met in Tiananmen Square in 1988 (Wang Dazhao 1998). Li's coach reportedly gave him one of two choices; he could either stay in the Chinese team or leave the team to get married. Li chose the latter option and emigrated to Switzerland where he acquired Swiss citizenship after waiting five years and then won a gold medal competing for Switzerland in the 1996 Atlanta Summer Olympics. The article indicates that, quite apart from Li Donghua's regrettable lack of patriotism, the extraordinary efforts undertaken by a Chinese man and national hero to gain acceptance in a foreign country show that intercultural marriage would not be a good option for ordinary people (Wang Dazhao 1998).

The commentaries by contributors in popular magazines indicate that Chinese celebrities are considered to be the property of the PRC. Hence they are not supposed to 'marry out'. Such frames provide moral judgements by building up a causal relation between 'marrying out' and 'unpatriotic' and 'bad consequences'. They share similarities with the PRC newspapers' portrayal of the likelihood of divorce for couples residing overseas in Chinese–foreign marriages. This consequently underscores the significance of geographical location in such marriages. Although some of the views do not necessarily represent the media's perspective, publishing personal opinions on celebrity Chinese–foreign marriages serves to promote Chinese nationalism by inviting readers to join a public debate on this topic.

In contrast, other media reports from the 1990s idealize celebrity Chinese–foreign marriages as extraordinary, fairy-tale stories of romance. This style of reporting implies that celebrities in Chinese–foreign marriages are extraordinary people who can be distinguished from ordinary people not only because they are accomplished, but also because some of them are 'trend-setting' pioneers who married foreigners for 'love', and not for hypergamous reasons. Such reports augment the fame of a given Chinese celebrity and also 'celebritize' their foreign partner by introducing them to Chinese readers and generating interest, curiosity and potential debate among readers about why such persons deserve to be married to their favourite stars. In the process, positive media reports of celebrity Chinese–foreign marriages act as a kind of manual for revealing the secrets of and therefore achieving 'true love' in marriage, understood as recognizing the importance of loyalty and respecting cultural diversity.

Such reports portray celebrity intercultural marriages as marriages of love between extraordinary people who consequently are not constrained by the problems that affect 'ordinary' Chinese–foreign marriages, such as socio-economic insecurity, infidelity and insurmountable cultural differences. Photographs of smiling, happy couples are accompanied by descriptive prose containing multiple metaphors and adjectives associated with romance. For example, a 1994 article called 'Wei Wei: A Journey to Love and Happiness' (*Wei Wei: xingfu yougui*) by *Yinyue Tiandi* (hereafter Music World) cites pop singer Wei Wei as saying: 'I need love, therefore I chose my husband Michael' (Li Jun 1994a). The article explains how Wei Wei met the American composer and pianist Michael Joseph Smith, how they began to collaborate on musical ventures, and why Wei Wei travelled to Sweden where Smith resides. In the style of true romance stories, it tells the reader that Wei Wei and Smith were walking along the seashore one morning at dawn, listening to and watching the crashing sea waves and the seagulls calling and circling above their heads, when Smith gently held Wei Wei's arm and whispered 'I love you'. The report concludes that the two hearts had finally found one another (Li Jun 1994a).

Media reports similarly describe Shen Danping's marriage to Uwe Kraeuter in fairy-tale terms. A 1995 report in the *Zhongguo Fushi Bao* (China Fashion Weekly), called 'Shen Danping: The Little Match-Girl' (*Shen Danping: mai huochai de xiao nühai*) notes that: 'She says she loves him because he is good and stirs her heart; He says he loves her because she is as pure as the early morning breeze' (Du Pin 1995). Shen also tells the interviewing journalist and hence those who are interested in her biography that Kraeuter is a good husband. He fulfilled her childhood dreams of having a beautiful home and beautiful children and of travelling to Paris to visit the Louvre and Notre Dame. He also gave her the self-confidence to grow from a shy girl into a mature woman filled with love and happiness (Du Pin 1995). The journalist concludes that Shen's marriage was 'destined to be beautiful'. Ten years have passed, as if it were one day, and the relationship will continue in the same way for their entire life (*meihao de yinyuan, shinian ru yiri, yisheng ru yiri*) (Du Pin 1995).

The fairy-tale romances and subsequent marriages of certain Chinese female celebrities are portrayed as relating to the professional accomplishments and traditional female virtues of the celebrities in question. Shen Danping is described as a great actress and talented author, who is also beautiful, possesses irresistible charm (*nanyi kangju de meili*), is a good cook and keeps a clean home (Liu Jun 1994; Yuan Ye 1995; Zhao Xin 1998). Siqin Gaowa reportedly possesses excellent stage performance techniques, a generous attitude and a pair of bright eyes and waterfall-like black hair. She also enjoys housework and encouraging her children to develop their potential according to their attributes and interests (Li Erwei 1994: 32; Li Ranran 1999: 62). Wei Wei is depicted as a woman with a wild, natural beauty (*ziyou, yexing de mei*), who is not only loved by everybody, but is also a good mother and patriotic daughter of China (*hao mama, zuguo de hao er'nü*). She apparently never forgets that she is Chinese and that China is her motherland when she sings English songs. She teaches her children to speak Chinese and study Chinese culture. She also returned to the PRC from overseas in 1998 to perform at a fundraising event for flood-related disaster relief (Li Jun 1994b: 73; Mu Zi 1999: 44).

These reports suggest that news frames are constructed in the cultural context of Chinese society wherein the traditional role of a woman, being a good housewife and mother, is celebrated as both a virtue and a 'bonus' for the well-accomplished woman in contemporary China. However, a closer look at these portrayals shows that the PRC media is constructing and promoting the notion of 'contemporary ideal Chinese womanhood' through Chinese female celebrities in Chinese–foreign marriages, in which they are assigned hybrid roles by conforming to such values. These women need to demonstrate professional achievement in the first place. They need to acquire traditional Chinese female virtues – having physical beauty, fulfilling the role of child-rearing and ensuring smooth domestic operations. They are also expected to be heartily committed to Chinese society and culture and exert social influence beyond their professional working spheres for China.

Chinese female celebrities frequently further reify the ideal of romantic love and monogamous heterosexual marriage in interviews with media representatives by praising their foreign spouses as model husbands with model careers. This focus stands in marked contrast to the media focus on the 'abusive' and 'cheating' nature of the foreign husbands of ordinary Chinese women in intercultural marriages, as noted in the preceding chapter. For example, in a 1993 interview with the *Global Times*, actress Chen Chong speaks of her husband Peter Hui (Xu Yimin) with pride as an outstanding cardiologist (Cang Lide and Mu Ya 1993). In a 1994 report in the *Modern Television* magazine, Shen Danping states that her husband is a solicitous man who takes great care of his wife (*titie ruwei guanxin beizhi*) (Liu Jun 1994). These descriptions indicate that celebrities can use the media to promote their own marriages and spouses. Meanwhile, their positive rhetoric works to cover up negative tales of their marriages, which might also be explored by journalists.

Taken as a whole, positive accounts of celebrity Chinese–foreign marriages read as a kind of manual on how to achieve a successful marriage and demonstrate respect for cultural diversity. A report in *Modern Television* says: 'Chen Chong [film actress]: The Key to a Successful Marriage is Loyalty' (*Chen Chong: weixi hunyin de mijue shi zhongcheng*) (Juan Zi 1996). A journalist from the *Global Times* implores Jiao Zhimin, an Olympic medallist for China in table tennis at the 1988 Seoul Olympic Games, to reveal the 'magic' behind her marriage to Ahn Jae-hyung, a South Korean table tennis player, in 1989 (Xu Baokang 1993). Noting that Jiao has a happy family and a successful career, the journalist asks: 'what is your secret?' 'How did you deal with career advancement and the arrival of the 'god of love' (*aiqing zhishen*)? (Xu Baokang 1993). Jiao responds that she did not like South Korean food at first, but she and her husband now enjoy both Chinese and South Korean food and alcohol, and their home is decorated with artifacts from both cultures (Xu Baokang 1993). Jiao also claims to have a good relationship with her Korean mother-in-law: 'My mother-in-law and I have a very good relationship ... She is a good, sensible mother-in-law ... whenever she visits us in Seoul, she does everything and understands us well. I am very proud to have such a good mother-in-law' (Xu Baokang 1993).

Unlike stories of 'ordinary' Chinese women in intercultural marriages being treated as domestic property and denied the opportunity to work (Ji Zhe 1996; Miao Hui 2006; Zhang Guannian 2007), a 1999 article further stresses that Jiao Zhimin has an active social and professional life in South Korea (Wang Linchang 1999). She works as a television host and runs a business in China and South Korea involving paper-product manufacturing and sales of western-style clothes and agricultural products. Although Jiao tries to modify her behaviour to be more like a South Korean woman, she also claims to have turned Ahn Jae-hyung into a 'half' Chinese man because whenever they encounter a problem they talk it over with each other and do so with respect, tolerance and understanding (Wang Linchang 1999).

Foreign men who are famous in China and who live in China with their Chinese wives are also depicted as having harmonious relationships with their new Chinese families. Canadian Mark Roswell, better known in China by the name Da Shan, is a case in point. Although relatively unknown in the West, Roswell has worked as a performer, television host and cultural ambassador in the PRC for over 20 years and is arguably the country's 'most famous foreigner' (Dashan wangzhai 2010). In 1993, Roswell married Gan Lin, a Chinese citizen whose family comes from the southwestern city of Chongqing and they now have two children and two homes, one in Canada and one in Beijing.

Contrary to descriptions of intercultural marriage as a source of family tensions (Chen Zikun 1993; Du Pin 1995), a 1999 report in the *Hainan Ribao* (Hainan Daily) entitled 'Da Shan: Happy Chinese Son-in-law' (*Da Shan: xingfu de Zhongguo nüxu*) describes Roswell's relationship with his father-in-law as one of unbounded happiness (*wengxu zhijian qilerongrong*) (He Ying 1999). According to Roswell, unlike the formal Canadian custom of referring to one's parents-in-law as 'Sir' or 'Madam', he calls his Chinese in-laws 'mum' and 'dad'. He also often jokes with his Chinese father about their different drinking habits (He Ying 1999).

The predominance of positive framing of celebrity Chinese–foreign marriage in the 1990s relates to at least four considerations. First, it reflects an obvious and market-based concern to cater to the admiring audiences of such celebrities and to promote a positive image of Chinese public figures. Second, it reflects the fact that celebrities who are willing to talk about their marriages to journalists prefer to tell positive stories in order to protect themselves and their families from public gossip about their private lives. Although scandal about the private lives of celebrities is a well-known means of promoting celebrity in western societies, sexual and marital scandals have not been part of the celebrity-making machinery in China until quite recently. Third, many female celebrities in Chinese–foreign marriages who lived overseas would not have been easily contactable by Chinese media representatives because of the cost of travel, and other difficulties associated with communications in the PRC at the time, such as a costly and often ineffective telecommunications system. Finally, there are no reports of celebrity Chinese–foreign divorces prior to the 2000s and hence no accounts of the more mundane problems associated with failed celebrity intercultural marriages. Consequently, media coverage of celebrity Chinese–foreign marriages, especially in popular magazines, reflects the general preoccupation in 1990s China with positive understandings of 'romantic love' in the context of youth culture (see also Farrer 2010: 71).

In summary, although some media reports in the PRC of celebrity intercultural marriages in the 1990s are antagonistic and nationalistic in tone, many celebrity Chinese–foreign marriages are framed as exemplary marriages based on 'true love'. Reports that are negative in tone express concern about celebrities as the 'pride of China' marrying foreigners and then migrating with their partners and talents to live abroad. This focus reflects broader concerns about China's uncertain position in the world in the 1990s following negative reactions to the brutal government suppression of student and worker demonstrations in Tiananmen Square in June 1989. It also reflects broader fears in China during the 1990s of a 'brain and talent drain' and more longstanding beliefs regarding the incompatibility between foreign values and lifestyles and Chinese values and lifestyles. Such reports suggest that mainland Chinese celebrities who gave up their privileged life in China were naïve in thinking that marrying and living abroad would help them to develop their careers and have a better life. Simultaneously, such reports affirm for certain audiences a sense of pride in China and provide entertainment in the sense that they may deride the choices of certain celebrities and the nature of celebrity culture in general.

However, the couples in celebrity Chinese–foreign marriages are typically framed as positive models for public emulation because they have successful professional careers and fairy-tale romances followed by perfect marriages. These idealized accounts of celebrity intercultural marriages cater to audience expectations of the 'glamorous' celebrity lifestyle. They also condition audiences to expect the 'perfect marriage' to be characterized by romantic love, loyalty and respect for cultural diversity. At the same time and in doing so, they reinforce the notion of a hierarchical division between the lives of extraordinary Chinese celebrities and ordinary Chinese people. Celebrities live the dream life and that life will remain a dream for the average Chinese person.

Celebrity Chinese–foreign marriage in the 2000s

Media coverage of celebrity Chinese–foreign marriage in the PRC has expanded since the turn of the new millennium and especially since the mid-2000s. Such reports discuss new marriages and provide up-to-date accounts of established ones. They also offer increased details about the private lives of Chinese celebrities in intercultural marriages compared with reports from the 1990s. Like earlier reports, media coverage of celebrity Chinese–foreign marriage in the 2000s turns on idealized constructions of fairy-tale romances resulting in perfect marriages, with celebrities and their partners being presented as exemplary wives, mothers, husbands and fathers. However, recent media coverage of celebrities and intercultural marriage in the PRC display an altered concern with issues such as transnational mobility and the national and gendered identity of the celebrity persona.

Recent media reports typically point to a reversed trend of transnational migration, while simultaneously underscoring the patriotic identity of certain celebrities as Chinese, by noting that many famous Chinese people who married foreign nationals, migrated abroad and acquired foreign citizenship in the 1980s and 1990s are now living and working in the PRC. In contrast to the general craze for going overseas (*chuguore*) that characterized 1980s and 1990s China, entertainment stars such as Siqin Gaowa, Zhang Tielin and Ning Jing, have returned to the PRC and re-established successful careers in China.

A 2006 report about Siqin Gaowa illustrates the perceived inevitability of this reversed trend of migration given China's emergence as a global superpower in economic and cultural terms ('Siqin Gaowa: Ruishi' 2006). Translated into English, the title of this report reads: 'Siqin Gaowa: Switzerland is Not My Home' (*Siqin Gaowa: Ruishi bushi wo de jia*). Siqin Gaowa married Chen Liangsheng, a Chinese orchestral conductor with Swiss nationality in 1986 and acquired Swiss nationality that same year. However, she reportedly never felt at home while living in Geneva and wanted to return to live and star in movies in Beijing ('Siqin Gaowa: Ruishi' 2006; see also Xin Li 2005: 13). An online article in 2009 further claims that Siqin Gaowa always wanted to return to China. However her husband only realized this after he found her crying in bed in their home in Switzerland (Zhen Xing 2009). Such presentation works effectively to create an emotional response in readers. It highlights Gaowa's strong attachment to China and implies that her change of nationality does not represent an alteration of her national feeling and sense of belonging.

The career of actor Zhang Tielin as narrated in media reports offers another example of a Chinese celebrity who moved overseas in the 1980s, acquired foreign citizenship and who has since returned to China. After graduating from the Beijing Film Academy in 1982, Zhang starred in three Chinese movies in 1984, before leaving China to study at the British Film Institute between 1987 and 1990 ('Zhang Tielin chuyan' 2010). While living in England, Zhang met and married a Polish woman. He subsequently moved to Hong Kong, where he worked as a television host at *Phoenix TV* and acquired British citizenship in 1997 (Nan Chen 2007). Along with the expansion of mainland Chinese television broadcasting in the 1990s ('China's TV industry' 2006), he returned to the PRC in the mid-1990s to star in a number of television drama series ('Zhang Tielin jieshi' 2008; 'Zhang Tielin Bolan' 2009). A 2008 report in the *Dongfang Zaobao* (Oriental Morning Post) carries a title with patriotic connotations: 'Zhang Tielin Explains Why He Acquired British Nationality: To Make the World Better Understand China' (*Zhang Tielin jieshi weihe jiaru Yingguo guoji: rang shijie liaojie Zhongguo*). As the title explains, Zhang Tielin allegedly acquired British citizenship so that he would have more opportunities to become a better and exemplary Chinese person by helping the world to understand China better (*wo weide shi zhengqu gengduo de jihui, rang shijie liangjie Zhongguo, zuo genghao de Zhongguoren*) ('Zhang Tielin jieshi'

2008). Zhang's claim strongly asserts that his change of nationality was not for self-convenience but patriotism to China. This, however, can stimulate readers' critical acuity and generate public debate on patriotism with respect to the phenomenon of Chinese celebrities' acquisition of foreign citizenship.

Likewise, Chinese actress Ning Jing resided in the USA for two years after her marriage to the American actor Paul Kersey in 1997. Although she now flies back and forth between the USA and China, Ning claims that she prefers to live in the PRC because that is where her fans are located (Xie Rong and Ding Li 2000: 67–8; Pu Liu 2002). Ning Jing also claims to have happily relinquished the opportunity presented by her marriage to acquire American citizenship because she prefers to work in China. Two reports in 2008 – one in the *Wuhan Ribao* (Wuhan Daily) and another in the *Dangdai Shenghuo Bao* (Modern Life) – both cite her self-identification as a 'stubborn Chinese' (*wangu de Zhongguoren*) who wants to remain Chinese ('Wo weishenme' 2008; Qing Bao 2008).

Chinese celebrities who entered into intercultural marriages in the 2000s, such as Shi Ke (film actress), Chen Lu (China's first Olympic medallist in figure skating in 1994) and Zhang Shan (Olympic skeet-shooting champion in 1992), are also portrayed as preferring to live in the PRC rather than abroad. Shi Ke, a renowned film and television actress in 1990s China, left the PRC to live in Switzerland between 2001 and 2003 after marrying her second husband Christian Könitzer in 2000, but did not acquire Swiss nationality. Prior to moving to Switzerland, Shi Ke was the star of films such as *Shashou Qing* (Killer's Love, dir. Yan Xueshu 1988) and *Yaogun Qingnian* (Rock Kids, dir. Tian Zhuangzhuang 1988) and television series such as *Guo Ba Yin* (Have a Good Time 1993). Shi and Könitzer relocated to China in 2003, where they established the Shi Ke Drama Studio in Beijing and Shi went on to star in a number of drama films ('Mingxing Shi Ke' 2009).

Chen Lu, a champion figure skater from Jilin Province who is known in China as the 'ice butterfly' (*bingshang hudie*), married Denis Alekseyevich Petrov, a Russian figure skater, and 1992 Olympic silver medallist in 2005 ('Chen Lu, Dan Nisi' 2009). Before their marriage, both of them lived and worked in the USA. However, after their marriage, they moved to China and settled in the booming city of Shenzhen in Guangdong Province where Chen managed the World Ice Arena. They have since had two children ('Chen Lu, Dan Nisi' 2009).

The perceived trend of reverse migration in the 2000s also extends to examples of foreign men who are celebrities in China and who have married Chinese women and chosen to reside and work in the PRC, such as Canadian performer and television host Mark Roswell and American actor Jonathan Kos-Read. After graduating from the University of Toronto with a major in Chinese studies in 1988, Roswell studied advanced Chinese language at Beijing University and later met Gan Lin, whom he married in 1993 ('Jianadaren' 2008). Roswell has since become a household name in China for his roles as a television host and his performance of *Xiangsheng*, a traditional form of comedy dialogue. While maintaining a home in both Canada and Beijing, Roswell is described as spending so much time in Beijing that he has literally become a 'Beijinger' (*yijing suanshi yige Beijingren le*) (Qiu Ying 2007).

A 2008 report in the *Chongqing Wanbao* (hereafter the Chongqing Evening News) suggests that the marriage between Roswell and Gan Lin is successful because he wants in effect to be Chinese and hence people from different regions of China are willing to claim him as their 'own'. The report, entitled 'Da Shan: I am a Chongqing Son-in-law (*Da Shan: woshi Chongqing nüxu*)', explains that Roswell feels like he belongs in Chongqing and even loves the famous hot and spicy food (Li Yan 2008). Another report in the *Chongqing Chenbao* (Chongqing Morning Post) cites Roswell as saying that he has visited Chongqing many times and has a better Chongqing dialect than his wife, who was born in Beijing, but whose household residence and hence family ancestry is located in Chongqing (Li Ping 2008). A 2008 report entitled 'Canadian Da Shan – A Foreign National But Not an Outsider' (*Jianadaren Da Shan: shi waiguoren que bushi wairen*), in the *Wenhui News* similarly suggests that Roswell is like a local, because he takes care of his family just like men from Shanghai ('Jianadaren' 2008).

In a similar vein, after graduating in the USA in 1996 with a major in film studies and Chinese language, Jonathan Kos-Read went to China where he worked as an English-language tutor before starring in a number of Chinese soap operas in 1999. In 2002, Kos-Read married a Beijing woman, Li Zhiyin, whom he met on a blind date ('Yang Cao Cao' 2010). The couple have continued to live in Beijing and now have a daughter. Kos-Read is described in media reports as speaking fluent Chinese with a heavy Beijing accent (*jiang yikou liuli de Jing pianzi*) and self-identifying as a typical Chinese man (*hen su de Zhongguo nanren*) ('Yang Cao Cao' 2010).

Recent media reports further highlight the self-identified 'Chineseness' of male foreign celebrities in Chinese–foreign marriages by describing them in celebratory terms as 'Chinese sons-in-law' (*Zhongguo nüxu*), 'Chinese men' (*Zhongguo nanren*) and 'patriotic sons of China' (*re'ai Zhongguo de erzi*) (Cao Wei 2000: 46; Li Yan 2008; 'Yang Cao Cao' 2010). Michael Joseph Smith, husband to Chinese pop singer Wei Wei, is similarly reported as saying that China has not lost a good daughter because of their marriage. Rather, China has gained a [patriotic] son who loves China' (*Zhongguo bing meiyou yinwei wo he Wei Wei de jiehe shaole yige youxiu de nüer, xiangfan daoshi duole yige re'ai Zhongguo de erzi*) (Cao Wei 2000: 46).

The documented flow of celebrities in Chinese–foreign marriages away from the PRC to developed countries in the 1980s and 1990s and from developed countries back to the PRC in 2000s echoes the presentation of the reversed trend in the migration pattern of ordinary Chinese–foreign couples during the same period. The altered pattern of celebrities' transnational mobility suggests that China's economic development has had an impact on the migration patterns of both PRC citizens and their foreign partners. It also weakens previous understandings of China as a locus for the export of Chinese to the West and other sites in the Asia Pacific (Erwin 1999: 253), by portraying the PRC as a magnetic, global center that is attractive to foreigners and overseas Chinese.

At the same time, these reports effectively build a connection with the reader by augmenting the 'Chinese component' of these high achieving foreign males in celebrity Chinese–foreign marriages. On the one hand, they help the foreign elites (and the media themselves) to gain popularity and acceptance among a broader audience in the Chinese market. On the other hand, these frames convey to the readers a sense of pride in China from the foreigners' perspective, implying that celebrity Chinese–foreign couples live a happy life in the PRC whereas this might not be the case if they resided overseas.

The media focus on celebrity Chinese–foreign marriage in terms of renewed patriotism and reversed migration patterns also inverts traditional gender roles: the foreign husbands of Chinese female celebrities are framed as willing to 'sacrifice' their own careers for love (*wei ai xisheng*) and relocate to China in order to support the careers and well-being of their wives. The story of Zhang Shan, an Olympic skeet-shooting medallist for China offers a pertinent example here. Zhang married Dexter Barnes, an Australian shooting referee in 2004. Barnes reportedly gave up a successful career in Australia in order to move to China and run a shooting club with his wife (Xu Xuelian 2005; see also Deng Hong 2005). Similarly, Christian Könitzer, Swiss finance analyst and 'billionaire', moved with actress Shi Ke to Beijing two years after their marriage in Switzerland to establish the Shi Ke Drama Studio (Li Yan 2005; 'Mingxing Shi Ke' 2009). Denis Petrov also gave up his job as a figure skating coach in the USA after his marriage to Chen Lu in 2005 and moved to Shenzhen where Chen manages the World Ice Arena ('Chen Lu, Dan Nisi' 2009).

This particular group of men is feminized by being portrayed in terms of 'the husband follows the wife' (*fu chang fu sui*), reversing the popular Chinese idiom, 'the wife follows the husband' (*fu chang fu sui*). They are also portrayed as 'staying behind the scenes' (*tuiju muhou*) to take care of domestic chores and children for their working wives ('Zhongguo mingren' 2006; 'Pilu: shezu yiguo lian' 2008; 'Chen Lu, Dan Nisi' 2009). Könitzer reportedly is a 'househusband' (*jiating zhunan*), who cooks Chinese cuisine and applauds his wife Shi Ke for her acting and philanthropic activities while watching her on the home television ('Mingxing Shi Ke' 2009). Michael Smith devotes himself to children and domestic life so that singer Wei Wei can continue with her career (Qu Yinghua 2004). Media descriptions of foreign husbands as househusbands and/or followers of their celebrity wives implicitly present this particular group of Chinese women as modern, career-orientated individuals who are active in the public rather than private domain.

These descriptions of inverted gender roles are reinforced with visual images. For example, a 2003 report in the *Chongqing Evening News* includes a photograph of the Chinese chess grandmaster Zhu Chen, and her Qatari husband Mohammed Ahmed Al-Modiahki, whom she married in 1999, at home. Al-Modiahki is towards the front of the photograph holding a tray full of tea cups, while Zhu Chen is behind him smiling at the photograph's viewers. Contrary to the stereotypical portrayal of Muslim men as unwilling to assist with household chores, it suggests that Al-Modiahki is happy to do 'what a wife does' and/or shares an equal status with Zhu Chen at home ('Meiman de' 2003; see also 'Shiwei jiagei' 2008). Similarly, a 2005 report in the *Dahe News* presents a photograph of the 2005 Polish presidential candidate Stanislaw Tyminski and Wu Mulan (pseudonym), a woman from Henan Province whom he married in 2004, in the kitchen and smiling as they wear aprons and cook together (Gao Ying 2005).

Media accounts of celebrity intercultural marriages that are based on interviews and photographs of the couple 'at home' are staged, but nevertheless reconfigure stereotypical understandings of gender roles within marriage. The personalized stories and visual imagery of celebrity couples in intercultural marriages take on the characteristics of a staged performance (Lee 2004: 218), because they are published both with the consent of the celebrity in question, and in the spirit of cooperation, in order to improve the public visibility or 'well-knowness' of a given celebrity (Turner 2004: 36). However, such way of framing injects new meanings of masculinity and femininity into the context of Chinese–foreign marriage through the suggestion that Chinese female celebrities in intercultural marriages have an equal or higher status than their foreign husbands.

This inversion of traditional gender roles is clearly an effect of the media focus on the Chinese female celebrity rather than the individuals involved in an intercultural marriage, with foreign husbands being used as a foil to reflect the importance of the Chinese celebrity to Chinese audiences. Nevertheless, it implies that many Chinese female celebrities have an equal if not higher socio-economic position than their foreign husbands. This focus functions, in turn, to erase the issue of hypergamy. It implies that China's celebrities are powerful women with financial independence and the ability to dominate foreign men, unlike ordinary women in Chinese–foreign marriages who are stereotypically framed as 'social climbers' who 'marry up' to foreigners for economic security and consequently occupy an inferior position in the relationship with associated problems.

While ascribing Chinese female celebrities with masculine attributes vis-à-vis their (feminized) foreign partners, media reports of female celebrities in Chinese–foreign marriages also emphasize that the celebrities in question want to be like 'ordinary (Chinese) women'. A 2005 report in the *Legal Evening News* states that Zhang Shan's marriage to Australian man Dexter Barnes has enabled Zhang to realize her dream of being not only a world champion in sports, but also of being 'a good (dutiful) wife, and a good (loving) mother' (*xianqi liangmu*) (Xu Xuelian 2005). In Chinese, this phrase epitomizes the traditional and gendered division of roles within the public and private spheres. Men are assumed to be in charge of outside affairs or matters in the public domain, whereas women are assumed to be responsible for affairs within the family and to have no or little responsibility for affairs outside the family and in the public domain (Zhang Xiaohong 2003: 214).

In a 2004 interview with the magazine *Beijing Jishi* (Beijing Documentary), actress Shen Danping says that marriage to Uwe Kraeuter has enabled her to become a real woman as being a good wife and the mother of two children (Hao Xiaohui 2004: 20). As Shen puts it:

> I am thankful to him … I am so lucky that I can live the same kind of life as ordinary people do' (*wo feichang qingxing guoshang pingchang ren de shenghuo*). He encourages me to be a woman, a mother and a wife … after I finish my work I come back home, wait for him and cook for my kids, words cannot describe my happiness …
>
> (Hao Xiaohui 2004: 20)

Likewise, a 2008 article entitled 'Zhu Chen: Breast Feeding and Nappy Changing Are Great Too! (*Zhu Chen: weinai, huan niaobu ye shi hen xingfu de shi!*)' in the *Baoding Wanbao* (Baoding Evening News) suggests that Zhu Chen is so happy in the role of wife and mother that she may even retire from her professional career as a chess grandmaster ('Zhu Chen: Weinai' 2008). The use of exclamation marks in the report title emphasizes that Zhu Chen puts family before her career and hence is a good Chinese woman.

Media coverage of the family life of Wendi Deng, a woman from Jiangsu Province who married Rupert Murdoch, media magnate and executive chairperson of News Corporation, in 1999, offers another example of this focus on Chinese female celebrities as 'wannabe ordinary women' ('Chuanqi nüren' 2008; 'Deng Wendi' 2009). Although marriage to Rupert Murdoch has made Deng rich and famous, a 2008 online article entitled 'The Married Life of Legendary Woman, Wendi Deng' (*Chuanqi nüren Deng Wendi de hunyin shenghuo*) claims that she values marriage and being a wife more than wealth and celebrity. Deng is cited as saying that she is first and foremost a woman and, if there is anything to add, she is 'Murdoch's woman', a woman who loves Murdoch and is loved by him ('Chuanqi nüren' 2008). The report later uses the subtitle 'I just want to be an ordinary woman' (*wo zhixiang zuoge pingfan de nüren*) to detail the story of the couple's romance and marriage and underscore Deng's desire to have an ordinary life with her husband (*xiangqin xiang'ai, guo pingfan de rizi*) ('Chuanqi nüren' 2008).

Such frames appear to invert the assumed relationship between the celebrity and their audiences, while simultaneously reinforcing the distinction between the celebrity as an extraordinary individual and the audience/reader as an average person. Instead of the audience/reader desiring a celebrity lifestyle, this style of reporting presents the Chinese female celebrity as desiring the everyday life of a typical Chinese woman. In doing so, it encourages audience identification with and sympathy for the celebrity in question as someone who is 'just like them'. However, while encouraging the audience/reader to 'feel good about themselves', it reinforces the distinction between the celebrity and the average person by reminding them that an ordinary life is beyond the reach of a celebrity. It therefore augments the celebrity as a branded commodity by reminding the audience/reader of their glamorous attributes and lifestyle.

Conclusion

Media presentations of celebrity Chinese–foreign marriage in reform-era China produce four concerns. First, in some media reports, Chinese celebrities who entered into Chinese–foreign marriages and moved overseas in the 1980s and 1990s are accused of being 'unpatriotic'; and, as with accounts of 'ordinary' Chinese–foreign marriages in general, these marriages are presented as being hypergamous in nature. These reports, albeit nationalistic in tone, serve to promote Chinese nationalism by encouraging public debate and discussion on Chinese–foreign marriages. However, most media accounts of celebrity Chinese–foreign marriages in the 1990s and especially in the 2000s present such marriages as marked by romantic love, with the emphasis being placed on fairy-tale romances followed by exemplary marriages. These reports indicate that celebrities are able to use the media to promote their own interests. Simultaneously, the media can rely on celebrity-style romance to expand their domestic readership. Second, these reports document a reversed trend in migration patterns and highlight China's growing global significance as Chinese–foreign couples choose to live in the PRC rather than abroad or are relocating from overseas back to China after marriage. Third, unlike Chinese–foreign marriages in general, media reports of celebrity intercultural marriages emphasize the renewed patriotism of mainland Chinese female celebrities in particular. This, again, propels the topic of patriotism to public prominence through the reportage of Chinese–foreign marriage. Finally, the media reports portray celebrity Chinese–foreign marriages in terms of inverted gender roles, wherein the foreign husbands of Chinese female celebrities are feminized as househusbands and the female celebrities themselves are masculinized as modern, career-orientated individuals who are active in the public rather than private domain. Such constructions signify celebrity Chinese women as having equal or even higher socio-economic status than their foreign husbands. Celebrity Chinese women's social and financial power thus plays an important role in shifting the conventional division of labour in Chinese–foreign marriages. However, these women are also framed as aspiring to the 'ordinary' role of being a woman, wife and mother. This paradoxically enhances the hierarchical relationship between the 'extraordinary' and the 'ordinary'.

Notes

1 The 'Gang of Four' was a leftist political faction composed of four Chinese Communist Party officials: Jiang Qing, wife of Chairman Mao Zedong; Zhang Chunqiao; Yao Wenyuan; and Wang Hongwen (Brugger 1980: 21; 'Fensui sirenbang' 2009).
2 Many celebrity couples in Chinese–foreign marriages have at least one child, with some having up to three children (see Appendix 4). According to the PRC birth control regulations, Chinese citizens who marry foreign nationals, or citizens from Hong Kong, Macau and Taiwan, or overseas Chinese and give birth to children in mainland China, shall adhere to the birth control policy in the local areas, where the Chinese citizens' households are registered. In marriages between mainland citizens and foreign nationals and citizens from Hong Kong, Macau and Taiwan, the numbers of children from the non-PRC partners' previous marriage(s) and the children of Chinese–foreign couples who do not reside in mainland China are not counted. In marriages between mainland citizens and overseas Chinese and where their children reside overseas, these couples are allowed to have children in mainland China in accordance with the birth control policy in the PRC (see *Guanyu neidi jumin she Gang shengyu wenti de guiding* 1998; *Guanyu Zhongguo neidi jumin shewai shengyu wenti de guiding* 1998; *Guanyu sheqiao jihua shengyu zhengce de ruogan yijian* 2009).

6 Celebrity Chinese–foreign divorce

Divorce in the context of celebrity Chinese–foreign marriages first became a focus of media coverage in the PRC in the 2000s as many entertainment and sports celebrities who entered into intercultural marriages in the late 1980s or during the 1990s ended their marriages and the increasingly commercialized media began to cover more celebrity news. For example, Xiaoshan Zhili, a table tennis player and coach, married a Japanese man in 1989 and divorced him in 2000 and gymnast Li Donghua married in 1988 and obtained a divorce from his Swiss wife Esperanza Friedli in 2004 ('Xiaoshan Zhili lihun hou' 2007; 'Li Donghua ren' 2008). Chinese pop star Wei Wei married Michael Joseph Smith, an American composer, in 1994 and they divorced in 2004. Similarly, Chinese singer Li Lingyu, known as the 'Sweet Song Queen' (*tiange huanghou*) married a Canadian CEO in 1999 and divorced him in 2005 (Liu Zhonghua and Zhang Xuejun 2004; 'Tiange huanghou' 2008).

As in western societies, China's media present celebrity gossip as a site for discussing and evaluating the drama of everyday life, including stories of failed marriages and divorces. Such reporting is usually brief and limited in content and tends to sensationalize and celebrate the phenomenon of divorce in relation to celebrities and intercultural marriage. On the one hand and contrary to the framing of fairy-tale celebrity intercultural marriage discussed in the previous chapter, divorce is constructed as the predictable and inevitable consequence of entering into a Chinese–foreign marriage and celebrity intercultural marriages are portrayed as more likely to fail than other types of marriages. However, there are no statistics provided to support such a conclusion and associated discussions of the problems that lead to celebrity divorces are usually limited in nature. On the other hand and contrary to standard depictions of failed marriages as having tragic consequences for women and children in China (Liu Xiaoxiao 2005; Ye Xiaonan 2006; Zhang Guannian 2007), celebrity Chinese–foreign divorces are typically portrayed as concluding amicably, and marked by ongoing personal relations.

This chapter examines media constructions of failed celebrity intercultural marriages in the PRC in four stages. First, it discusses negative constructions of celebrity intercultural marriage as marked by a high incidence of divorce. The perceived likelihood of divorce is associated with problems such as the ill-advised preference of Chinese female celebrities for foreign as opposed to Chinese men, entrenched cultural differences, long-term separation of couples, extra-marital affairs and sexual abuse. Second, it looks at media speculation surrounding failed celebrity intercultural marriages, helping to explain the fascination of media, celebrities and readers alike. The media is able to capitalize on sensationalist news to increase profits, driven by demand from readers for 'info-tainment' stories and the opportunity to indulge in narratives in which celebrities lose their godly status and become 'ordinary' persons dealing with the earthly problems of divorce and relationship breakdown. However, for celebrities, even negative media attention increases their public profile – the lifeblood to maintaining celebrity status. Third, it analyses positive constructions of celebrity Chinese–foreign divorce, revealing that they are framed as characterized by the amicable severance of marital relations and ongoing displays of exemplary parenting. Finally, it shows that positive constructions of celebrity Chinese–foreign divorce often turn on notions of (Chinese) female autonomy and empowerment.

These different and often contradictory accounts of celebrity Chinese–foreign divorce highlight the commercial interests of China's news media in responding to market demands with respect to celebrity intercultural marriage. This mediation of intercultural celebrity relationships reflects a plurality of forces within Chinese society, be it changing perspectives and values on marriage, divorce, family and gender roles, increased reader fascination with celebrity 'news', the media's commercial profit-driven imperatives, or celebrities encouraging and refuting media reports on their relationship breakdown as a tactic to remain in the 'fame game'.

High rates of divorce

Media reports in the PRC from the late 2000s often suggest that celebrity intercultural marriages, as with Chinese–foreign marriages in general, are likely to end in divorce. Emotive headlines reinforce this conclusion. Examples of such headlines are 'High Divorce Rate! Why do Chinese Female Celebrities Prefer to Marry Foreigners?' (*Lihunlü gao! Zhongguo nümingxing yuanhe dou leyi jiagei waiguoren?*), 'Bitterness after Sweetness: Many Celebrity Chinese–Foreign Marriages End in Divorce' (*Mingxingmen kuaguo hunlian nancheng zhengguo, xiantian houku lihun duo*) and 'Intercultural Marriages Keep Ending in Divorce' (*Kuaguo hunyin pinchuan lihun shouchang*) ('Lihunlü gao!' 2007; Yang Min 2008; 'Mingxingmen' 2009). These titles highlight a perceived growing rate of divorce in relation to celebrity Chinese–foreign marriages and express concern about it.

Many reports emphasize the perceived high divorce rate in celebrity Chinese–foreign marriage by using the Chinese adjective 'duo' (literally 'many', 'most', 'lots') in a repetitive fashion (Mu Xuan 2009). For example, a brief account in the *Daqing Ribao* (Daqing Daily) in 2009 entitled 'Why Do the Intercultural Marriages of Most Stars End in Divorce?' (*Mingxing kuaguo hunlian weisha lihun duo*) repeats the same question in its first paragraph but expresses it in a slightly different way, 'Why Do Most Celebrity Chinese–Foreign Marriages End in Divorce?' (*Daodi shi shenme zaocheng le Zhongguo mingxing de shewai hunyin duoyi shibai *shouchang ne?*). After a second paragraph providing cases of failed celebrity intercultural marriages, the report uses the term 'many' (*duo*) on four occasions to underscore the writer's conclusion that many of such marriages will inevitably end in divorce.

Relevant media reports also cite numerous cases of celebrity Chinese–foreign divorce through parallelism – the use of similar words, phrases, or clauses in a list or series, in structuring sentences and through repetitive paragraph structures. These cases are either listed in a chronological order or structured according to the professional backgrounds of the celebrities in question. For example, in the realm of sports, a 2008 article in the *Guangzhou Ribao* (Guangzhou Daily) informs the readers that gymnast Li Donghua divorced his Swiss wife Esperanza Friedli after 16 years of marriage for unspecified reasons; table tennis player Xiaoshan Zhili divorced her Japanese husband Xiaoshan Yingzhi after 12 years because of his infidelity; and table tennis player Guo Fangfang divorced her South Korean husband Kim Seung-hwan after nearly three years of marriage because of personality differences and financial disputes (Yang Min 2008). The repetitive listing of each celebrity Chinese–foreign divorce and the type of celebrities involved underscores the notion that such marriages are problematic and likely to fail (see also 'Zhongguo titan' 2008; Mu Xuan 2009).

Similarly, a 2009 report in the *Shenzhen Wanbao* (Shenzhen Evening News) titled 'Looking for Love Overseas – The Tragicomedy of Celebrity Intercultural Relationships' (*Yuandu chongyang qu zhao ai – mingxing kuaguo lian de beixi ju*) lists the 'failed' and 'successful' intercultural relationships of Chinese celebrities from the entertainment field ('Yuandu chongyang' 2009). Female celebrities are divided into those who have 'successful marriages' (*chenggongzhe*), those who have 'failed marriages' (*shibaizhe*), those who are involved 'in an intercultural relationship but not yet married' (*dai guancha zhe*) and those whose relationship status is 'unclear' (*qingkuang buming zhe*). The article cites four cases of failed celebrity intercultural relationships along with a brief statement for each case [in brackets]: the divorces of actress Ning Jing [Long-term separation–destined to part], pop singer Wei Wei [Not as good as it looks] and singer and writer Yang Erche Namu ['7-year-itch' inescapable] and the failed relationship between singer Zhang Mi and her American boyfriend 'Dan Ni' [Destined to separate] ('Yuandu chongyang' 2009). The brief comments on these cases are pessimistic in tone, conveying to the reader through such a frame that celebrity Chinese–foreign marriages are fragile in nature, and are destined to fail.

Some media reports even categorize celebrity marriage and divorce into different types. A 2007 report in the *Jinri Wanbao* (Today Evening News) called 'The Reasons for Divorce' (*Gei lihun zhaoge liyou*) categorizes Chinese celebrity divorces in general, including examples of failed celebrity Chinese–foreign marriages, into six categories: economic disputes (*wei qian er fendao yangbiao*); unsettled marriage (*bu anyu pingjing de hunyin shenghuo*); long-term separation (*hunhou de liangren jushao liduo*); failed relationships flowing from the pressure of public opinion (*yulun de yali daozhi fenshou*); extra-marital affairs (*di sanzhe de jieru*); and differences in age and personality (*xing'ge yu nianling de chaju*)

('Gei lihun' 2007). Another 2007 report in the *Nanguo Dushibao* (south China Metropolitan Daily), entitled 'Celebrity Chinese–foreign Marriage – Who Cares?' (*Mingren mingxing shewai hunlian beixi guan shuiqing*), offers three categories. It states that actress Ning Jing and her American husband Paul Kersey divorced because of their conflicting personalities (*zai reqing yu lengjing zhijian*), film actor and director Jiang Wen and his French wife Sandrine Chenivisse divorced because of their different and opposing mindsets (*jiqing yu lixing de pingheng*) and actress and singer Yang Erche Namu and her Norwegian 'husband' divorced because their 'de facto marriage' hit the 'seven-year-itch' (*shou buzhu '7 nian zhiyang'*) ('Mingren mingxing' 2007). The use of categories presents a purported comparison among different celebrity divorces and builds the impression that each individual case of divorce is representative of a larger number of divorces in the context of celebrity Chinese–foreign marriages in general.

Taken as a whole, media reports of failed celebrity intercultural marriages suggest that they are likely to end in divorce for five reasons. The most commonly cited reasons for the failure of such marriages are: 1) the perceived 'unhealthy' infatuation of some Chinese female celebrities with foreign men vis-à-vis Chinese men; 2) irreconcilable cultural differences; 3) long-term separation; 4) extra-marital affairs, typically on the part of the foreign husband; and 5) sexual abuse.

First, divorce is framed as a natural consequence of the 'rash' (*caoshuai de*) decision of certain Chinese female celebrities in the early 1980s and 1990s to marry foreign men and therefore to leave China and live abroad ('Lihunlü gao!' 2007; 'Yang Erche Namu de' 2007; 'Mingxingmen' 2009). A 2007 online article entitled 'High Divorce Rate! Why Do Chinese female Celebrities Prefer to Marry Foreigners' begins by asking: 'Why do so many Chinese female celebrities worship foreigners when it comes to love [and marriage]?' (*Weihe bushao Zhongguo nümingxing zai ganqing shang chongwai*?) ('Lihunlü gao!' 2007). In response, the article states that many Chinese female celebrities worship foreigners blindly, concluding that they are destined for divorce because of this preference and their unwillingness to marry ordinary (Chinese) men whom they allegedly look down on. Such reports reiterate the negative suggestion, as discussed in the preceding chapter, that Chinese female celebrities who reject Chinese men and prefer instead to marry foreign men and live abroad, are doomed to live an unhappy and isolated life overseas.

Second, celebrity intercultural marriages are framed as likely to end in divorce because of 'cultural differences' (*wenhua chayi*). For example, pop singer Wei Wei reportedly divorced her American husband, Michael Joseph Smith in 2004 because of daily problems flowing from different practices and values, although the precise nature of those practices and values are not specified (Liu Zhonghua and Zhang Xuejun 2004;'Lihunlü gao' 2007). To use Wei Wei's words: 'our divorce is not the result of mutual suspicion or extra-marital affairs. We divorced because of the cultural differences between us, which meant I could not feel happy in the marriage' ('Lihunlü gao' 2007; 'Pandian mingxing' 2009). Chinese actress Ning Jing is similarly described as divorcing her American husband, Paul Kersey, because of cultural differences, as did actor Jiang Wen and his French wife, actress Sandrine Chenivisse ('Jiang Wen Faguo' 2006; 'Gaodiao jia' 2010).

114 *Celebrity Chinese–foreign divorce*

The notion of 'cultural differences' thus plays a dual function in media framing of intercultural marriages in China. In accounts of fairy-tale celebrity romance and marriage, celebrities in Chinese–foreign marriages are portrayed as being able to overcome cultural differences, thereby highlighting the aura of romance and love associated with media depictions of successful intercultural marriages (Xu Baokang 1993; He Ying 1999; 'Meiman de' 2003; Li Yan 2008). In accounts of celebrity divorces, the notion of 'cultural difference' is put forward as an unspecified but inevitable factor contributing to the perceived failure of a large number of celebrity intercultural marriages.

The third factor reportedly contributing to high rates of celebrity Chinese–foreign marriages that end in divorce is long-term separation between couples (*jushao liduo*), usually as a result of an individual celebrity pursuing their career. For example, actress Ning Jing claimed to have spent more time away from her American husband than with him because of filming at different locations ('Mingren mingxing' 2007). Conversely, actress Li Qinqin divorced her Japanese husband (known as 'Shan Gen' in Chinese) in 2008 partly because his work as a journalist meant that he was often away from home (Long Zhun 2008; Mu Xuan 2009). Actors Jiang Wen and Sandrine Chenivisse also divorced after long-term separation, because Jiang wanted them both to live in China while he pursued his career, but Chenivisse wanted to live and pursue her career in France ('Jiang Wen Faguo' 2006; 'He Faguo qizi' 2007; 'Quge yangniu' 2009).

Fourth, media reports suggest that extra-marital affairs, typically on the part of a foreign male partner, are the cause of some celebrity divorces. The case of Yang Erche Namu (hereafter Namu) is illustrative. Namu, from Yunnan Province in southwest China, is a writer and singer whose fame stems in part from her Mosuo ethnicity.[1] Namu left her native village while still a child to live in Yanyuan County in Sichuan Province. After arriving in Yanyuan, she joined a singing troupe, won a scholarship to study music in Shanghai at 13 years of age and later became a singer, writer and actress. She married an American photographer working for *National Geographic* magazine and moved to California with him in the early 1990s. They later divorced citing 'irreconcilable' cultural differences' ('Yang Erche Namu' 2004). In 1996, Namu met her second husband-to-be 'Shi Dantong', who was an official at the Norwegian Embassy in Beijing. However, after a relationship of seven years, which is described as a 'marriage' in many media articles, they 'divorced' because 'Shi Dantong' allegedly had slept with another woman in their bedroom ('Yang Er weishenme er' 2007;'Yuandu chongyang' 2009). Since her second 'divorce', Namu is reportedly focusing on career development, establishing a signature clothing and perfume brand, and assisting with the construction of a museum project in her native hometown of Lugu lake ('Yang Erche Namu' 2004).

Table tennis player and coach, Xiaoshan Zhili, similarly filed for divorce in 2000 because she suspected her husband Xiaoshan Yingzhi, a fellow table tennis champion and coach, of having an extra-marital affair with one of her colleagues in the Ikeda City, Osaka Bank Table Tennis Club ('Xiaoshan Zhili' 2007; 'Kuaguo hunyin' 2008; 'Zhongguo titan' 2008). As a result of these concerns, Xiaoshan Zhili failed to compete in the 1997 World Table Tennis Championship in

Manchester, UK, an event that she was expected to win as the world's number one table tennis player at the time. Xiaoshan Zhili filed for divorce, and was awarded millions of Japanese yen to compensate for lost earnings ('Kuaguo hunyin' 2008; 'Zhongguo titan' 2008).

Finally, some Chinese celebrities allegedly divorce their foreign spouses because of cruelty (*shou nue*) and sexual abuse (*xing nuedai*), although such reports are both limited and unconfirmed ('Chen Luyu zao' 2007; 'Kuaguo hunyin pinchuan' 2008; 'Zhongguo titan' 2008). The failure of Chinese news anchor, Chen Luyu's marriage offers one of the few examples of celebrity divorces that are attributed to sexual abuse by their foreign male partners. A 2007 online article reports that Chen Luyu went to the USA to 'revitalize' her career in 1995, where she met and married an American man that same year. However, they divorced in 1999 because of abuse ('Chen Luyu zao' 2007). Cruelty is also cited as a reason for Xiaoshan Zhili's divorce from her Japanese husband Xiaoshan Yingzhi, although the nature of that cruelty is not specified ('Zhongguo titan' 2008; 'Kuaguo hunyin pinchuan' 2008).

As with media accounts in the PRC of failed Chinese–foreign marriages in general, media reports of failed celebrity Chinese–foreign marriages typically place the blame for their failure on the (male) foreign marrying partners. An article in the *Chongqing Evening News* called 'Li Qinqin Recalls Her Two Intercultural Marriages, She Criticizes Her American Ex-Husband as Amoral' (*Li Qinqin huishou liangduan yiguo hunyin, pi Meiguo qianfu mei renxing*) is illustrative (Long Zhun 2008). It informs interested readers that actress Li Qinqin divorced her Japanese husband 'Shan Gen' and proceeded to marry an American whom she had met during the course of her first marriage. However, she eventually divorced him because of his alleged disloyalty and inability to establish a good relationship with her parents. The article refers to Li's second husband as the 'third-party' (*di sanzhe*) and attributes the failure of Li's first marriage to him (Long Zhun 2008). It then uses Li's description of her second husband as having 'no morals' (*mei renxing*) to imply that he was responsible for the failure of both of her marriages. The report never explicitly suggests that Li might have contributed to the failure of her first marriage by becoming involved in an extra-marital affair, but rather focuses readers' attention on the perceived misconduct of 'bad foreign husbands' (Long Zhun 2008). Other accounts of Li Qinqin's failed intercultural marriages place the blame for their failure on her new romantic interests described as an 'American man's intrusion' (*yige Meiguo ren de chuangru*) (Mu Xuan 2009; 'Mingxingmen' 2009). In doing so, such reports downplay any hint of misconduct on the part of Chinese celebrities, underscoring the perceived 'wrongdoings' of foreign spouses. This may indicate that due to limited time, space and resources, journalists have to rely on their available sources – the Chinese celebrities for quotes and comments. Given this scenario, the media serve as 'conduits for individuals eager to promote a certain perspective to a broader public audience' (Nelson *et al.* 1997: 568).

In summary, as with 'ordinary' Chinese–foreign marriages, celebrity intercultural marriages are framed as likely to end in divorce. However, unlike ordinary

Chinese–foreign divorces, celebrity divorces are associated with fewer problems. Moreover, these problems are briefly touched upon, and dealt with ambiguously, in media reports. In effect, such reports simply narrate the explanations provided by certain Chinese celebrities to journalists and hence the explanations are skewed towards presenting the Chinese celebrity in a positive light and the 'voices' of the foreign spouses in celebrity Chinese–foreign marriage are excluded. The singular perspective of such reports partly explains why Chinese celebrities are always in 'the right' and the attitudes and behaviour of foreign spouses are blamed for the perceived high incidence of celebrity Chinese–foreign divorce.

Also as with reports of 'ordinary' Chinese–foreign divorces, media accounts of Chinese–foreign celebrity divorce are gendered. Foreign males are usually although not exclusively 'blamed' for the failure of celebrity Chinese–foreign marriages, chiefly for engaging in extra-marital affairs and abusing their Chinese partners. Conversely, Chinese male celebrities are generally framed by default as not responsible for their divorces because such issues are simply not discussed in relation to the dissolution of their marriages. In the few cases where responsibility for the failure of a Chinese–foreign marriage is placed on a Chinese male celebrity, this responsibility is discussed in the context of rumour and speculation, as I now show.

Speculation and hearsay

Media coverage of celebrity divorce serves as a platform for public discussion and the enhancement of individual celebrity (Meyers 2009: 899). Such reportage is often speculative and based on hearsay, aiming not necessarily to impart information but rather to entertain and interest readers in the latest life-experiences of a celebrity (Guerin and Miyazaki 2006: 23). The recounting of hearsay allows readers to derive pleasure from speculating about the personality and actions of certain celebrities and the factors contributing to the failure of their marriages. Readers may also negotiate such reports in ways that are meaningful to them, either by rejecting or agreeing with them (Meyers: 894–904). Thus, as Graeme Turner (2004: 24) argues, celebrity gossip can be seen as 'an important social process through which relationships, identity and social and cultural norms are debated, evaluated, modified and shared'.

At the same time, reader interest in and speculation about a celebrity's private life serves to keep them in the public eye and augment their value as a branded celebrity-commodity, irrespective of whether that speculation is positive or negative. Some celebrities actively manipulate the reader-media relationship to enhance their fame and careers by selectively sharing stories about their 'intimate lives' with the public. Other celebrities whet public interest in their personal affairs by refusing to comment on rumours to the effect that their marriages are over, that they are divorcing, and/or that they have formed new romantic attachments. Celebrities who adopt the latter strategy get to 'stay in the news' whether they like it or not because media speculation is encouraged by the absence of conclusive information.

Speculation about celebrity divorce suspends temporarily the hierarchical boundary between the 'ordinary person' and the famous or 'extraordinary' person by suggesting that celebrity marriages are not 'sacred'. Celebrities are 'human' too and their divorces are often complicated just like those of 'ordinary' people. The notion of a 'real' celebrity who is just like the average person in unguarded moments and with whom a reader may or may not identify, is generated through the provision of perceived 'behind-the-scenes details' of the private life of the public figure (Holmes 2005: 24). This creates an illusion of intimacy between the reader and the celebrity in question (Meyers 2009: 892).

For example, recent media speculation about the marital problems of media magnate Rupert Murdoch and his wife Wendi Deng has extended from Australia to the PRC. Various Chinese media reports cite the Australian website *Crikey.com. au* to suggest that the couple now live apart, with some reports emphasizing the likelihood of divorce. For example, a 2009 online report carries the headline 'Analysing the Most Expensive Divorce Case – How Much Will It Cost Rupert Murdoch to Divorce Wendi Deng?'(*Pandian zuigui lihun an, Muo Duoke yu Deng Wendi lihun jiang sun duoshao*) ('Pandian zuigui' 2009). The headline aims to 'hook' readers with the implication that Murdoch and Deng are undergoing a costly divorce, although the text indicates that the Australian media only states that they are living apart. The report then suggests that divorce is not a good choice for a billionaire like Rupert Murdoch because of the cost involved, offering examples of costly divorces to underscore that conclusion, such as the £5.5 billion divorce of Chelsea football club owner Roman Abramovich from Irina Vyacheslavovna Malandina in 2007 and Murdoch's US$1.8 billion divorce from Anna Torv in 1999. The report's headline thus exploits the rumour of separation in order to speculate about the likelihood and cost of a divorce between Murdoch and Deng.

Conversely, other reports assert that rumours that Murdoch and Deng have separated are untrue, thereby repeating the same rumours while claiming to have a more credible source in the form of a celebrity 'friend'. For example, the *Guangzhou Daily* ran a 2009 story titled 'Wendi Deng Denies Rumours That She Has Separated From Rupert Murdoch Saying "We Are Still As Close As Before"' (*Yu 'Mo Duoke' hunyin wan'erwan? Deng Wendi piyao: women qinmi yijiu*) (Xiao Yu 2009). The report asserts that photographs uploaded on Deng's blog show the couple were together at recent events and therefore demonstrate they are not separated. The report also notes that a microblog written by Zhang Xin, a friend of Wendi Deng and co-founder of SoHo China, the largest real-estate developer in the PRC, further demonstrates that the couple are still happily married. In her microblog, Zhang indicated that she had asked Deng whether news of her separation from Murdoch was true and Deng had said no. In addition, Zhang had visited Deng and Murdoch recently at their home in New York, where she saw them living happily with their two daughters who spoke fluent Chinese (Xiao Yu 2009).[2]

Speculation about celebrity divorce also allows for additional media speculation about potential new celebrity romances. Actors Jiang Wen and Sandrine Chenivisse's relationship was the subject of three related rumours. The first rumour was that the couple had divorced in 2005 ('Jiang Wen Faguo' 2006; 'He Faguo qizi'

2007). The second rumour was that the divorce was the result of a romance between Jiang Wen and Chinese actress Zhou Yun ('Jiang Wen wei Zhou Yun' 2005). The third rumour was that Jiang Wen and Zhou Yun had married in secret ('Zhou Yun: suishu shi' 2007). None of these rumours has been confirmed by actor Jiang Wen to this day, although Jiang Wen and Zhou Yun are now living together and have a son.

A 2005 online article named 'Jiang Wen Divorces His Wife For Zhou Yun, Candid Photographs Show The Lover's Rendezvous' (*Jiang Wen wei Zhou Yun yu qi lihun, liangren qinmi youhui bei toupai*) provides images to suggest that Jiang must have divorced Chenivisse because available evidence indicated that he was involved in an intimate relationship with Zhou ('Jiang Wen wei Zhou Yun' 2005). The article explains that Zhou Yun had been to Jiang's office on two consecutive days and the two actors had been seen talking to each other with Jiang's arm around Zhou's waist. Two attached photographs of Jiang and Zhou together are included with the story to substantiate the reporter's claim to be exposing a secret relationship. The article concludes that both Jiang and Zhou deny rumours that they are involved in an intimate relationship, while also noting that rumours of their loving relationship have been circulating for months ('Jiang Wen wei Zhou Yun' 2005).

Speculation about Jiang's relationship with Zhou Yun in 2005 and hence the 'true' nature of Jiang Wen and Chenivisse's marital status, continued up to 2009. Journalists told readers that some people (*you de shuo*) claimed that the couple had never married in the first place, others claimed that they were married and had no plans to divorce, while others claimed that they had already divorced ('Jielu Jiang Wen' 2008). Journalists further informed readers that 'hearsay' (*you chuanwen cheng*) and 'rumoured news' (*chuanchu*) suggest that Jiang and Chenivisse must have divorced in 2005 because Chenivisse travelled to China from France with her daughter at that time, shortly after rumours surfaced to the effect that Jiang had married Zhou Yun ('Jiang Wen Faguo' 2006; 'He Faguo qizi' 2007; 'Mingxingmen' 2009).

Although Jiang Wen now lives with Zhou Yun and they have a son, he has never provided interviews about his marital status. It therefore remains unclear whether Jiang has divorced Chenivisse or not, when he started his relationship with Zhou Yun and whether he has married Zhou Yun or not. This suggests that some celebrities are reluctant to reveal details about their private lives publicly. In the case of Jiang Wen, this is perhaps because it would have attracted negative publicity on the grounds that divorce was the result of an extra-marital affair. However, in the absence of confirmation from authorized sources, readers are encouraged to speculate about the 'truth' of Jiang Wen's marital status and look for additional media coverage to confirm or alter their 'hunches'.

Similarly, publicized details of actress Ning Jing's long-term separation from American Paul Kersey while filming in different locations led to speculation that they had divorced and that Ning Jing was in a new relationship (Meng Qiaoli 2008). From the early 2000s up to 2008, China's media carried various stories speculating about whether Ning Jing and Paul Kersey had divorced or not. Some articles asserted that Ning Jing was living a stable life with her husband and son, concluding that reports of divorce were 'rumours' ('Ning Jing he Bao Luo' 2004; Wang Lu 2008). Other articles claimed that Ning Jing had divorced, and was in a new relationship ('Jiating guanxi' 2007; Zong He 2008).

For example, a 2008 report in the *Chongqing Shibao* (Chongqing Daily) uses the evocative headline, 'Ning Jing Seen on Date With Mystery Man, Speculation That She Has Already Met the In-Laws (*Ning Jing yu shenmi nan yuehui, bei yi jian weilai gongpo*) (Zong He 2008). The report argues that Ning Jing is divorced, and in a new relationship, even though her agent denies such rumours. It notes that Ning Jing was seen attending an Award Ceremony at the Fifteenth Beijing University Student Film Festival with a good looking, fair-skinned Chinese male around 40 years of age. Moreover, this man had stayed overnight at Ning Jing's residence and was seen with her the following day, having afternoon tea, later meeting an elderly couple who might be the mystery man's parents. The report concludes that 'the media suspect' (*bei meiti huaiyi*) and 'people guess' (*rang ren caice*) that the elderly couple are Ning Jing's future parents-in-law (Zong He 2008). The use here of opinion by 'the media' and 'the public', while referring to two broad and anonymous groups, gives the impression that the fact of Ning Jing's divorce and pending re-marriage is common knowledge. It thus has the effect of framing speculation as 'truth', while inciting further debate about the true nature of Ning Jing's marital affairs.

Other reports in 2008 suggested that Ning Jing's marriage was over even though she personally denied such 'rumours' (Qing Bao 2008). A report in the *Modern Life* titled 'Ning Jing Denies Rumour of Divorce, Although She Is Living Apart From Her Husband Paul Kersey' (*Ning Jing yu zhangfu 'Bao Luo' liangdi fenju, Ning Jing qifen fouren lihun chuanwen*) notes the ongoing speculation over Ning Jing's marital status. The journalist confirms for the readers that Ning Jing and Kersey are living apart – one in China and the other in the USA. However, when he asked Ning Jing to comment and confirm whether rumours that she had already divorced and planned to marry again were true, she reportedly replied in an angry fashion: 'What do you mean?' 'Who says I am divorced? Who says I will marry [again]?' (Qing Bao 2008).

In short, rumours of celebrity divorce and new post-marriage relationships are often presented in China's media as facts through the use of ambiguous reporting techniques and reliance on hearsay. Regardless of whether such stories appear on the Internet or in the print media, they use interviews with celebrities and 'friends' of celebrities combined with speculation and sensationalism to provide different 'true' stories about celebrity divorces and new relationships. Some reports simply mimic and/or copy other reports or cite them as authoritative sources, some rewrite the rumours reported in other media as new information, and yet others claim that stories of celebrity divorce as sensationalized by other media are false and purport to uncover the 'real truth' with their own coverage.

In doing so, China's media is able to profit from retelling the tantalizing rumours of extra-marital affairs and divorce in the commercially-driven new media market. The provision of rumours and speculation about celebrity divorces and relationships encourages interested readers to contemplate and further speculate about the nature of celebrity relationships, and hence to want to know more about them. At the same time, stories about celebrity divorce in China's media suggest that Chinese–foreign marriages are unstable, and consequently undesirable, as demonstrated by speculation over their failed marriages and extra-marital affairs.

Although celebrities such as actors Jiang Wen and Ning Jing proved reluctant to 'talk' to media reporters about their 'failed' intercultural marriages, other celebrities have given interviews to journalists or at least provided other forms of information designed to present their divorces in a positive light. The next section investigates how positive portrayals of celebrity Chinese–foreign divorce are manufactured through accounts that focus on the amicable severance of personal relationships and exemplary fatherhood based on alleged interviews and thus the personal testimony of certain celebrities.

Amicable divorces and exemplary fatherhood

Unlike media accounts of divorce involving 'ordinary' Chinese and intercultural marriages, which are typically portrayed as involving the severing of personal relations, failed celebrity Chinese–foreign marriages are sometimes portrayed positively as maintaining amicable relations after divorce. Scripts of post-marital relationships based on idealized conceptions of 'gratitude', 'family' and 'eternal friendship', suggest that despite the withdrawal of sexual love, the relationships between Chinese celebrities and their former foreign spouses remain not only amicable, but intimate on other levels. Couples retain friendship, gratitude, companionship and familial love beyond marriage.

The prevalence of such positive accounts owes much to the nature and essence of the 'fame game' especially in China, which calls for celebrities to remain in the public eye preferably as a positive role model rather than as a source of scandal. Celebrity divorcées often aim to 'stay in the news' and avoid negative speculation about their private lives by providing interviews or direct testimony about their idealized fairy-tale romances and equally idealized divorces. Certainly, media accounts often use quotations from celebrities as personal story tellers to reinforce suggestions that celebrity intercultural marriages are based on romantic love and in the event that such marriages fail, they are followed by peaceful divorces (*heping de*) and the maintenance of good personal relations (*youhao de*) (Wu Hai'ou 2005; 'Jiang Wen Faguo' 2006; 'Yang Erche Namu de' 2007; 'Li Donghua ren' 2008). Such accounts reinforce the dominant discourse of 'celebrity' as involving extraordinary characters, whose experiences of falling in and out of love are both spectacular and worthy of emulation, or, at the very least, everyday experiences with which their fans and followers can identify.

Media reports of amicable post-divorce relationships involve Chinese celebrities of both sexes. A 2007 online report called 'Yang Erche Namu's Romance and Love' (*Yangerche Namu de qingai siji*) describes how the ethnic minority singer and writer divorced amicably from her American husband, a photographer working for the *National Geographic* magazine ('Yang Erche Namu de' 2007). The report starts by posing the question on behalf of the readers: 'Do you hate [your former husband] Anchun Dan?' Namu replies: 'No. We are still good friends' (*buhui, women haishi hao pengyou*). To prove this point, Namu explains how her ex-husband and his new wife recently visited her hometown of Lugu Lake in Yunnan Province, where they not only stayed in her home but also met her mother and brothers ('Yang Erche Namu de' 2007).

A 2008 article somewhat differently describes Chinese film actress Chen Chong as experiencing feelings of profound gratitude (*chongman le ganji*) towards her ex-husband Jimmy Lau (Liu Qing), a Chinese–American actor ('Duoqi dianying ren' 2008). Chen was given the title of 'Movie Queen' in China at the age of 18 while studying at university, thanks to her exceptional performance in the film *Xiao Hua* (Little Flower) in 1979. After graduation, Chen left China to study filmmaking in the USA and worked part-time in Hollywood, where she met Lau who subsequently became her agent. Chen married Lau in 1986 and obtained American citizenship in 1989. She divorced Lau in 1990, with media reports in China citing Lau's jealousy and refusal to allow Chen to associate with other men as the reason for their separation ('Chen Chong' 2008; 'Duoqi dianying ren' 2008). While hinting that their divorce was not exactly amicable, media reports about their marriage and divorce in the 2000s conclude that Chen remains grateful to Lau for helping her to settle in the USA and star in such internationally acclaimed films such as *The Last Emperor* (dir. Bernardo Bertolucci 1987) ('Renwu jianjie' 2004; 'Duoqi dianying ren' 2008).

As with their female counterparts, many Chinese male celebrity divorcées apparently remain on good terms with their former foreign wives and feel grateful to them. A 2005 article in the *Heilongjiang Ribao* (Heilongjiang Daily) carries the headline, 'Zhang Tielin and His Wife Separate Peacefully: They Are Still a Family After Divorce' (*He qianqi heping fenshou, Zhang Tielin lihun hou haishi yi jiaren*) (Wu Hai'ou 2005). Actor Zhang Tielin, who is famous for his performance as an 'emperor' in the popular Chinese television series, *Huanzhu Gege* (Princess Pearl), reportedly separated from his UK-based Polish wife in the mid-1990s because they were pursuing different career paths in different countries. However, concluding with a quotation from Zhang, the report states: 'Who says divorce makes us enemies?' (*Shui shuo lihun shi yuanjia?*) 'We will always be a family because of our relationship with our daughter' (*Yinwei nü'er de guanxi, women yongyuan shi yijiaren*). A 2008 report in the *Dongfang Tiyu Ribao* (Oriental Sports Daily) similarly suggests that gymnast Li Donghua and his Swiss wife divorced on good terms in 2004. The report quotes Li as saying: 'I am grateful for her company during the 16-years [we were together] and we are still good friends …' (*wo feichang ganxie ta 16 nian de meihao peiban, xianzai women yiran shi hao pengyou*) ('Li Donghua ren' 2008).

Media reports sometimes use the alleged testimony of female foreign spouses to underscore the amicable nature of celebrity Chinese–foreign divorce. For example, the headline of a 2006 article in the *Huashang Chenbao* (China Business Morning Post) reads: 'Jiang Wen's French Ex-Wife Says First and Foremost, "We Still Love Each Other"' (*Jiang Wen Faguo qianqi shoudu kaikou: 'women yiran xiang'ai'*). This article states that Jiang and Chenivisse had divorced because of long-term separation, with Jiang living in China to work on a film and Chenivisse continuing to work in Paris. However, the report concludes by citing Chenivisse's emphasis on their continued love for each other. In Chenivisse's words, '[Jiang] is a great partner', 'He is the person I admire most, he is a genius, we still love each other' (*ta shi wo zui peifu de ren, shi ge tiancai, women yiran bici xiang'ai*) ('Jiang Wen Faguo' 2006).

The amicable severance discourse can be seen as an extended framing of idealized celebrity Chinese–foreign marriages. These narratives serve the interest of celebrities by highlighting their positive attitude, generosity and tolerance towards their partners and marriages and indicate that they exist within a broader concept of love rather than a narrow concept of heterosexual love between couples. They simultaneously mask the commonly perceived negativities of conflict, hostility and hatred between couples in the context of divorce. Hence such a construction effectively prohibits celebrity Chinese–foreign marriages from turning into a 'venue for moral evaluation' of celebrities themselves, who could have been assumed by the public as being 'morally deficient' (Adams and Coltrane 2006: 18). However, to examine this issue from a different perspective, the overall framing of 'good' celebrity Chinese–foreign divorces might have implicitly marginalized and stigmatized the 'ordinary' divorces in both Chinese–foreign and Chinese–Chinese families.

Some media reports underscore the notion that Chinese celebrities remain on good terms with and retain feelings of gratitude towards their former foreign spouses via portrayals of devoted fatherhood. A 2009 report in the *Wuhan Chenbao* (Wuhan Morning Post) titled 'Zhang Tielin: My Daughter Was My Lover in a Previous Life' (*Zhang Tielin: Nü'er shi qianshi qingren*) describes how actor Zhang Tielin was reconciled with his daughter Yueliang (Moon) after his divorce from her mother. Moon reportedly experienced depression following her parents' divorce, blaming her father Zhang for breaking up the family by choosing to divorce rather than to live in the UK with Moon and her mother (Bai Lu 2009). On one occasion when Zhang travelled from China to the UK to see Moon, he reportedly found her crying as she watched him acting in the role of a loving father in the television series Princess Pearl. Upon seeing this, Zhang held her close crying

> My baby girl, I am so sad … I had to separate from your mother, our marriage deteriorated because of long-term separation … but this doesn't affect our love for you … My silly girl … I have only one baby daughter in real life and that is you' (*Baobei, baba zhende feichang nanguo, wo he ni mama fenli de shijian taijiu, daozhi hunyin biande yuelai yue leng... dan zhe bingbu yingxiang women dui ni de ai … Sha haizi, baba zhe yisheng zhiyou ni yige baobei nüer*).

Upon hearing this, Moon's tears turned into smiles (Bai Lu 2009).

To offer another example, a 2009 article titled 'Celebrity Parents' Genes Revealed In Their Children' (*Jiyin yi zhuru, zaowan yao biaolu*) in the *Meiri Xinbao* (Daily News) discusses the relationship between actor Jiang Wen and his daughter from his marriage with Sandrine Chenivisse. Although Jiang is now known to be living with Chinese actress Zhou Yun and they have a son, the report states that Jiang Wen loves his daughter Jiang Yilang so much that he hangs her photographs everywhere in his office. It quotes Jiang claiming: 'My daughter is the most beautiful woman in the world' (*Wode nü'er shi shijie shang zui meili de nüren*). The report also describes Jiang Yilang as a quiet young woman who tends to keep things to herself rather than sharing her innermost feelings with Jiang Wen. However, as a father, Jiang respects her 'self-conscious awareness' (*ziwo yishi*) and is happy that she is 'herself' ('Jiyin yi zhuru' 2009).

In both examples, conceptions of responsible and loving fatherhood are used to promote positive images of Chinese men both in the context of celebrity Chinese–foreign divorces and masculinity in general. Fatherhood becomes in effect a 'vehicle for portraying masculine emotions, ethics and commitments and for re-directing masculine characterizations from spectacular achievements to domestic triumphs' (Jeffords 1993: 254). The focus on Jiang Wen and Zhang Tielin as responsible fathers, for example, suggests that parental love exists beyond the loss of sexual love between husband and wife and moves the narrative focus away from the friction of separation and divorce and towards notions of continued friendship and family relations between Chinese male celebrities and their former foreign wives. Such focus also discourages readers from assuming that children are victims of divorce and the associated parental responsibilities that celebrities should fulfil but perhaps might have failed to do so.

This focus on divorced mainland Chinese male celebrities as responsible fathers runs counter to popular constructions of male divorcées as irresponsible fathers in Chinese–Chinese marriages. In newspaper reports and legal cases, 'ordinary' Chinese men are often depicted as irresponsible fathers who refuse to share the responsibility for parenting with their ex-wives and even sever all ties with their ex-wives and children after they divorce (Wan 1998; 'Fuqin bujin' 2007; 'Nü'er yaoqiu' 2009). Hence, the construction of divorced Chinese male celebrities as responsible fathers also presents them as family role models.

Media accounts of failed celebrity Chinese–foreign marriages frequently present happy photographs of celebrities and their former spouses, which bear visual testimony to the amicable nature of their separation and continued friendship. For example, a 2009 online article named 'Bitterness after Sweetness: Many Celebrity Chinese–Foreign Marriages End in Divorce' (*Mingxingmen kuaguo hunlian nancheng zheng'guo, xiantianhouku lihun duo*) focuses on the perceived predictability of intercultural marriages failing, yet presents happy photographs of individual stars and their former spouses ('Mingxingmen' 2009). These include pre- and post-divorce images of couples at various locations hugging each other and smiling, holding hands, accompanying each other playing the piano and playing with their children ('Wei Wei zibao' 2005; 'He Faguo qizi' 2007; 'Zhongguo titan' 2008; 'Mingxingmen' 2009; 'Mingxing lihun' 2010).

Other media accounts provide happy photographs of divorced celebrity fathers with their children. They include photographs of actor Zhang Tielin hugging his daughter Moon, and smiling while sitting on the sofa at home ('Zhang Tielin hunxue' 2008; 'Zhang Tielin Bolan' 2009). They also include photographs of actor

Jiang Wen smiling happily at a film festival, carrying his daughter Jiang Yilang in one arm, who was around four years old at that time and with the other arm around his former wife Sandrine Chenivisse ('Jiang Wen hunxue' 2007; 'Jiyin yi zhuru' 2009).

The inclusion of happy domestic photographs emphasizes the positive aspects of celebrity Chinese–foreign marriage and divorce, shifting the audience focus away from the problems associated with divorce towards the positive aspects of the celebrity as a commercialized public persona and branded embodiment of an ideal life. Taken as a whole, narratives of 'peaceful' celebrity Chinese–foreign divorces are constructed through repeated scripts of 'profound gratitude', 'family', 'fatherhood' and 'eternal friendship'. These narratives are reinforced by visual images of happy ex-couples and their children. Such portrayals reframe love as the dominant motivation in celebrity Chinese–foreign marriage and suggest that particular bonds of love – such as friendship, family and parental love – continue to inform the relationship between celebrity intercultural couples even after divorce.

Reports adopting the amicable severance narrative in celebrity Chinese–foreign marriages can be placed within the particular social and political context of the mid- to late- 2000s, when the majority of these reports appeared in China's media. As discussed in previous chapters, this period was marked by emphatic portrayals in the media of renewed celebrity patriotism, a general reversal of migration patterns from the 'developed west' to China and the newfound cosmopolitanism of PRC citizens. The media stress on the harmonious nature of celebrity intercultural divorces perhaps also stems from the political policy goal of 'constructing a harmonious society' (*goujian hexie shehui*), which was raised by President Hu Jintao at the Fourth Plenum of the Sixteenth Central Committee of the Communist Party of China in 2004 and formally endorsed by the PRC Government in 2006 (Jiang Wandi 2005; 'CPC Seeks Advice' 2006). Harmonious society is the vision of Hu Jintao's administration for China's future socio-economic development. It advocates 'continued economic growth to provide prosperity, but it also sees the need for that prosperity to be broadly distributed and for economic growth to be balanced with social equality and environmental protection' (Jeffreys and Sigley 2009: 13). Developing a harmonious society is often equated with the maintenance of a stable domestic order and thus by extension with the maintenance of harmonious marital relationships (Chen Wei and Ran Qiyu 2009: 43; Zhang Xiamin 2010: 454; Xiao Huifaye 2011: 750).

However, these positive constructions of celebrity Chinese–foreign divorce also indicate that celebrities as spokespersons/objects exert some influence over how the media frame their personal, private choices vis-à-vis their family and professional lives. This appears to be especially the case in relation to China's female celebrities whose divorces are often framed in the media as an expression of female autonomy. The next section of this chapter consequently focuses on Chinese female celebrities to show how female autonomy is constructed in accounts of celebrity intercultural divorce.

Female autonomy and exemplary motherhood

Presenting divorce as a positive assertion of female autonomy helps to reinforce positive accounts of celebrity Chinese–foreign divorces. A 2011 report in the *China Daily*, 'Women Becoming Initiators of More Divorces', asserts that 'Chinese women are taking the lead in filing for divorce' (Cheng Yingqi and Cao Yin 2011). To demonstrate this point, the article cites statistics from the People's Court of Shunyi in northeast Beijing showing that 70 per cent of the 800 divorce cases handled by the local court in 2010 were initiated by women. It also cites a lawyer saying that female-initiated divorce has become a common phenomenon in China in recent years, with the Shunyi statistics mirroring a nationwide rise in the number of women initiating divorce chiefly because of domestic violence and their husbands' extra-marital affairs (Cheng Yingqi and Cao Yin 2011).

Although Chinese women in failed domestic marriages are initiating divorce proceedings, Chinese women in intercultural marriages are presented as unlikely to do so unless they happen to be either extraordinary and/or a celebrity. Women in Chinese–foreign marriages are typically portrayed as tolerating unhappy marriages and/or unable to escape domestic violence and abuse, especially when they live outside the PRC (Bauer *et al.* 2000: 38; Raj and Silverman 2002: 384; Liu Xiaoxiao 2005; 'Cong Xuenan'an kan' 2009). However, media reports frequently present Chinese female celebrities as the initiators of divorce proceedings in the context of failed intercultural marriages because their economic resources and social status reduce their dependence as women on men, giving them the capacity to become independent decision-makers.

The divorces of Chinese singers Wei Wei and Li Lingyu and actress Ning Jing, illustrate the media framing of female celebrities in the 2000s as career-oriented women who experience difficulties submitting to the role of a 'housewife' after marriage and who eventually chose to divorce of their own accord, in order to re-establish their careers. A 2004 online article entitled 'The Chinese-Style Divorces of Wei Wei and Li Lingyu' (*Wei Wei, Li Lingyu de Zhongguo shi lihun*) suggests that Wei Wei chose to divorce because she missed performing as a popular singer and could not endure a life of quiet domesticity ('Wei Wei, Li Lingyu' 2004; see also 'Gei lihun' 2007). In both that report, and a 2008 online report, singer Li Lingyu is similarly described as divorcing and returning to China after three years of residence and marriage to a Canadian, in part because she disliked abandoning her career for the role of a 'full-time housewife' wherein she cared for their child and two stepchildren from her husband's previous marriage ('Wei Wei, Li Lingyu' 2004; 'Tiange huanghou' 2008).

Another 2008 report in the *Wuhan Morning Post* titled 'Ning Jing: I Gave My Son to [His Father] My Former Husband' (*Ning Jing: Wo ba erzi tui gei le qianfu*) narrates the story of actress Ning Jing's career, marriage and divorce (Na Na 2008). Ning Jing married an American man, Paul Kersey in the USA in 1996 and after the birth of their son in 1998 reportedly took on the responsibility of child care and domestic duties with little help from Kersey. Ning Jing later returned to Beijing, re-established her career and initiated divorce proceedings. While domesticity is not cited as the sole reason for Ning Jing's alleged divorce from Kersey by 2008, the report implies that as a career woman Ning Jing found it difficult to endure a 'domestic or housewife lifestyle' (*jujia shenghuo*) (Na Na 2008).

Renowned Chinese news anchor, Chen Luyu is effectively framed as initiating divorce because she prioritizes her career over her marriage. Chen reportedly married an American citizen in 1995 while living in the USA and brought her husband to China when she started working at Phoenix Television in 1996. As host of the program *Fenghuang Zaoban Che* (Good Morning China), she had a long and complicated working routine, going to bed at around 7 p.m. each evening of the week so that she could start work at 4 a.m. each morning, with no breaks for holidays. Although this regime resulted in the deterioration of her marriage, Chen reportedly chose to prioritize her career and to end her marriage in 1999 when it became clear that, as a consequence, the relationship was failing ('Chen Luyu zao' 2007).

As can be seen, many female celebrities are portrayed as 'decision-makers' and the 'initiators' of celebrity Chinese–foreign divorce, with their career concerns either directly or indirectly contributing to the dissolution of their marriages. In other words, these women are constructed as modern, individualized career women to whom career is equal to or even more important than a successful marriage. They are neither constrained nor defined by marriage; instead, they are able to walk away from the traditional gender roles attached to women, make new choices and pursue their own individual interests. In this context, celebrity Chinese–foreign divorces are framed as a tool to liberate Chinese female celebrities from bad marriages rather than a bad consequence of their marriages.

Chinese female celebrities' reportedly positive attitude towards divorce further underscores their perceived autonomy in matters of modern-day marriage and divorce. Actor Li Qinqin has undergone two divorces, the first from a Japanese man and the second from an American, but maintains an allegedly optimistic and uncomplicated approach to what many people in China and elsewhere might view as her personal failures. In a 2004 article about her career and failed marriages, Li Qinqin rhetorically states that those people who think divorce is about failure or defeat are wrong (*shenme jiao shibai ya?*) ('Li Qinqin lijing' 2004). Instead, she says that divorce is simply a case of two people who can no longer continue living together and therefore must change their living arrangements ('Li Qinqin lijing' 2004; see also Long Zhun 2008). A 2008 report in the *Anqing Wanbao* (Anqing Evening News) further quotes Li as saying: 'Now [that I am divorced] I am acting in the films that I like and, apart from that, I cook. This [being single] is a perfect lifestyle for me' (*xianzai wo pai wo xihuan de xi, paixi zhiyu jingjingde zuo yixie jiachangcai, zhezhong zhuangtai jihao*) (Xiao Chen 2008).

Likewise, a 2004 report in the *Chongqing Shangbao* (Chongqing Commercial News), titled 'Wei Wei Announces that She Has Divorced Her Foreign Husband: Says It's Great To Be Single!' (*Wei Wei xuanbu he waiji zhangfu lihun, dushen ganjue taihaole*), quotes the famous Chinese singer as saying she felt 'free' following her divorce from the American composer, Michael Joseph Smith (Qu Yinghua 2004). In Wei Wei's words, 'It's great to be single. I can do whatever I feel like doing. I sing the songs I feel like singing, and can wear sexy clothes if I want to' (*wo juede dushen taihao le, wo xiang gan shenme jiu gan shenme, xiang chang shenme ge jiu chang shenme ge, xiang chuan shenme xing'gan de yifu dou suishi keyi chuan*). Along with reports stating that Wei Wei decided to free herself from a 'housewife lifestyle', divorce is presented here as giving Wei Wei the opportunity to rediscover herself. She allegedly lost these individual freedoms and claims to self-identity while acting in the role of a wife and mother rather than a performer prior to her divorce (Qu Yinghua 2004).

A 2005 report in the *Dongfang Zaobao* (Oriental Morning Post), 'Single Life Enables Wei Wei to Regain Confidence' (*Danshen shenghuo rang Wei Wei chongshi xinxin*), similarly quotes Wei Wei as saying that following her divorce she is once again devoted to her career; moreover, she is in 'good spirits' (*shencai yiyi*) having been relieved of a 'heavy load' (*rushi zhongfu*) (Li Yunling 2005). Adding to her happiness, Wei Wei informs the reader that her children are happy with their new life in China (Li Yunling 2005; see also Liu Zhonghua 2004). In this context, divorce is framed not only as an achievement of Wei Wei's individualized identity and motherhood, but also as a positive contribution to her revitalized stardom.

Director and actress Chen Chong is also framed in media reports as enjoying the single life of a divorcée. A 2007 report titled 'The Ups and Downs of Chen Chong's Two Intercultural Marriages' (*Liangci hunyin, liangdu chenfu*) in the *Chongqing Morning Post* paints a rose-coloured scene of her everyday life following her divorce from Jimmy Lau ('Liangci hunyin' 2007). Contrary to conventional depictions of the early post-divorce period as emotionally distressing, Chen describes herself as spending her days tidying up, buying roses, relaxing on the balcony and reading and writing while listening to music with a cup of tea. In her words, this is a period she is very proud of (*Wo ba wo de fangzi shoushi de zhengqi piaoliang, ziji gei ziji mai meigui, youkong zuozai yangtai shang, fang yipan datiqin qu, pao bei cha, xiexie dongxi Kankan shu,nashi yiduan zhide jiao'ao de rizi*) ('Liangci hunyin' 2007; see also 'Duoqi dianying' 2008).

By describing Chinese–foreign divorces as liberating for female celebrities, China's media redefine traditional conceptions of divorce. Divorce is constructed in an idealized fashion as a sign of female autonomy and empowerment, rather than as a source of emotional hardship and financial disadvantage (Whitehead 1997: 165). This stands in marked contrast to the routine depiction of 'ordinary' Chinese women in the context of failed intercultural marriages as victims of deception and abuse who are thus vulnerable and prone to emotional extremes (Liu Xiaoxiao 2005; Ni Yan 2005; Zhang Guannian 2007; Wang Jianwei 2008). Chinese female celebrities' reported acceptance and even embrace of divorce demonstrates that they are economically and psychologically self-sufficient. As celebrities are publicly recognized figures, their voices can exert a powerful influence on the public. The media thus rely on quotes from Chinese celebrities' to portray them within positive frames in the context of failed intercultural marriages. This effectively encourages 'ordinary' divorced women to be strong and embrace an independent future. However, such a construction simultaneously ignores the socio-economic complications of divorce.

While emphasizing the autonomy of Chinese female celebrities, media reports also stress that they are 'good and selfless mothers'. Pop singer Wei Wei is a case in point. Contrary to the allegedly amicable nature of other celebrity divorces, her divorce from Michael Joseph Smith was depicted as a 'battle' over child custody ('Wei Wei zibao' 2005; Yu Liangxin 2005; 'Mingxing lihun' 2010). In such reports, Smith is portrayed as a villain who not only threatened Wei Wei's life on many occasions, but also seized their three sons' passports and valued possessions when she initiated divorce proceedings. Conversely, Wei Wei is framed as a loving mother fighting hard for custody of her children because they are the most precious things in her life, even more important than her career ('Wei Wei zibao' 2005; Yu Liangxin 2005; 'Mingxing lihun' 2010). When she won custody of the children, Wei Wei reportedly cancelled concerts in order to spend more time with them, and introduce them to new activities such as sailing and skiing (Liu Zhonghua 2005). Singer Li Lingyu is similarly quoted in an online article, with the headline 'Insights Into Celebrity Chinese–Foreign Marriages' (*Quannei mingxing jia waiguoren neimu*), as saying that her son was the only thing she wanted to take away from her divorce from her Canadian husband in 2005 ('Quannei mingxing' 2010).

Actor Ning Jing is portrayed as loving and selfless mother who ceded custody of her son to his father because she had her child's best interests in mind. According to a 2008 article, Ning Jing took her son to China after quarrelling with her husband Paul Kersey in the USA in 2003 (Na Na 2008). While loving her son, as demonstrated by the claim that she was willing to give up a role in a film rather than not have her son by her side, Ning Jing eventually ceded custody of the child to Kersey in 2007. This reportedly agonizing decision was made after Ning Jing realized that her son preferred attending a kindergarten in the USA rather than one in China and that her ex-husband was a good father who would ensure that their son had the best education possible.

The 'loving and selfless mother' frames emphasize the motherly virtues displayed by Chinese female celebrities. However, this simultaneously overshadows the fatherly virtues of foreign men in celebrity Chinese–foreign marriages. Similar to exemplary fatherhood narratives, such frames may also reduce readers' assumptions of the (negative) effect of divorce on children in such marriages.

Individual photographs of celebrity Chinese women are published along with the stories of their divorce, which typically underscore the autonomy of the women in question by showing them happily working on their latest career project. For instance, a 2004 report on singer Wei Wei's divorce in the *Global Times* presents Wei Wei dressing in a dark costume and smiling as she plays her latest album for a journalist to hear (Liu Zhonghua 2004). A 2010 online article on the divorces of Chinese female entertainment stars presents photographs of singer Li Lingyu, singer Wei Wei and actress Ning Jing with smiling faces in front of a microphone while performing or addressing an audience on stage ('Gaodiao jia' 2010). Such photographs act as visual evidence of the celebrities' success as divorcées, mothers and independent career women, overturning gendered conceptions of women as the passive and disempowered objects of divorce.

To summarize the preceding remarks, China's media construct celebrity Chinese women in failed intercultural marriages as 'divorce initiators' and 'decision-makers'. Distinguished from 'ordinary' Chinese–foreign marriages, celebrity divorces are largely caused by Chinese female celebrities' career and ambitions and their rejection of traditional gender roles and the division of labour in the domestic sphere. By framing divorce as a form of liberation and empowerment to Chinese female celebrities in the context of failed intercultural marriages, the media champions an alternative conceptualization of divorce as a manifestation and celebration of Chinese female celebrities' achievement and development into modern individualized identities.

The inversion of traditional gender roles in media narratives of failed celebrity intercultural marriages adds to the perceived extraordinary nature of the celebrities in question. Celebrity Chinese women are portrayed as exercising power and authority in Chinese–foreign marriage, which disrupts the normative order of women being secondary to men in 'ordinary' patriarchal Chinese–foreign marital relationships. On the contrary, foreign husbands are sometimes overshadowed by their celebrity Chinese wives and sidelined for career ambitions, as in the case of Chen Luyu and Ning Jing. The positive spin on celebrity women divorcées as empowered modern individuals also overturns the stereotyped belief that divorced women in China are 'used items' who occupy an inferior social-economic position, as described by Cecilia Chan, Shirley Huang and Winnie Kung (2005: 148). However, traditional gender roles and the division of labour often do reassert themselves in reality after marriage and become a key factor leading to divorce as some celebrity wives are portrayed as being unhappy about being shouldered with the greater responsibility for domestic and childcare duties.

Conclusion

The chapter has examined different accounts of celebrity Chinese–foreign divorce in China's media. In negative constructions, as with accounts of 'ordinary' Chinese–foreign divorces, celebrity intercultural marriage is associated with a high incidence of divorce. In positive constructions and unlike ordinary intercultural divorces, celebrity Chinese–foreign divorce is associated with the amicable severance of marital relationships followed by either ongoing displays of friendship or exemplary parenthood. Celebrities themselves are not only able to gain from reports on their intercultural divorces as a means to enhance their public profiles, but in many cases present a counter-narrative of themselves in a positive light as the new generation of liberated divorcées – men becoming caring fathers and women as independent career-driven individuals.

At the same time, the popular discourse overturns traditional family values in China and facilitates the introduction of the modern notion of divorce – not as diametrically opposed couples but a well-negotiated result based on mutual interest; not as a source of detriment to women but a liberation and empowerment to them; not as an end of a good marriage but a good break from the previous one and perhaps a 'prerequisite to finding fulfilment in some later relationship' (Coltrane and Adams 2003: 371).

The negative and positive constructions of Chinese–foreign divorces appear contradictory to each other; however they embody the diverse ways in which celebrity Chinese–foreign marriage and divorce are framed in China's media. The dichotomous constructions have no clear-cut watershed either, as sometimes the negative can be read positively whereas the positive can be read negatively from another perspective. However, both negative and positive portrayals of celebrity Chinese–foreign divorce concentrate on individualized stories focused on sensationalizing news on a particular famous personality. In doing so, the PRC media somewhat disregards the complexity of the social issue of divorce as an outcome of political, economic and legislative changes.

Notes

1   The Mosuo ethnic group is known as 'the kingdom of women' (Nü'erguo). Mosuo culture is famous for its unique pattern of institutionalized sexual union practised by a majority of the Mosuo population, a system wherein 'husbands' and 'wives' do not live together as a couple as the heads of a single household and children are raised by the mother and her family. Both male and female members of the Mosuo continue to live with and work for their mother's household even after entering into a marital style relationship. 'Husbands' visit their 'wives' at their matrilineal home in the evening and they go back to their mother's household the next morning. It is a duolocal visiting sexual relationship based on agreement between the two partners rather than a legal form of marriage – the couple live in separate households and the sexual relationship is non-contractual, non-obligatory and non-exclusive ('Mosuo zouhun' 2004;'Walking Marriage' 2007; Shih 2010: 76).
2   Rupert Murdoch and Wendi Deng's divorce was later confirmed in June 2013 ('Murdoch Files for Divorce from Wife Wendi' 2013). Since then, disputes over their marriage dissolution have ceased. However, there have been new rumours centred on the reasons for their divorce and the ways in which property will be distributed.

7 Documenting Chinese–foreign marriage

The subject of intercultural marriage in the PRC has been a feature of Chinese television programmes since the early 2000s, in the form, for example, of news items, soap operas (*lianxuju*) and documentaries (*jilupian*). Television news items about intercultural marriage in the PRC are limited in number and short on content. They focus either on the romances, marriages and divorces of entertainment celebrities ('Wei Wei, Ning Jing de kuaguo hunyin' 2009; 'Deng Wendi cheng'gong jingying kuaguo hunyin' 2011), or else on the suffering experienced by 'ordinary' Chinese women because of the activities of illegal Chinese–foreign marriage introduction agencies ('Yang laogong miju' 2008; 'Kuaguo hunyin mengpo, zhongjie renqu loukong' 2009; 'Jizhe anfang, hunjie fuzeren luohuang'ertao' 2010).

At least three soap operas about intercultural marriage were produced and broadcast in the PRC during the early 2000s. For example, the Shanghai Film Studio (*Shanghai dianying zhipianchang*), in conjunction with Japan's Magnolia Film and Television Company (*Riben mulan yingshi gongsi*) produced 20 episodes of a series called *Yuanjia Riben* (hereafter Marrying Far Away in Japan) (dir. Zhang Jiabei and Tang Hong'gen 2001). The series aired in 2001 on Channel 8 of China Central Television Station (CCTV). CCTV-8 was launched in 1999 and is renowned for showing television dramas ('CCTV-8 dianshiju' 2011). *Marrying Far Away in Japan* narrates the stories of three women from Shanghai who married Japanese men and experienced hardship while living in Japan. CCTV produced 33 episodes of another programme called *Modeng Jiating* (hereafter Modern Family), with joint finance from Australian, Malaysian and South Korean media companies, which aired on CCTV-8 in 2002 (dir. Zeng Lizhen and Piao Lingzhu 2002). *Modern Family* tells the story of how two 'traditional' Chinese parents in Beijing handle the marriages of their three children to spouses from Australia, Italy and South Korea. In 2007, CCTV-8 broadcast 26 episodes of a programme called *Qingxi Xixili* (Love in Sicily), a co-production between Chinese and Italian media companies that narrates the life-stories of a Chinese–Italian family living in Hangzhou, the capital city of Zhejiang Province in eastern China and especially the daily 'conflict' between the Chinese mother and her Italian daughter-in-law (dir. Li Wei 2005). All of these soap operas focus on the nitty-gritty, albeit fictional, life-stories of 'ordinary' Chinese people in intercultural marriages in the PRC and overseas.

This chapter examines documentary-style television programmes about Chinese–foreign marriages in the PRC because they are more common and offer more detailed stories than other television programmes about intercultural marriage. The author collected a total of 57 documentaries produced in the PRC on the subject of intercultural marriage. Of these, 36 involved marriages between citizens of the PRC and Taiwan, the remainder involved marriages between citizens of the PRC and citizens of countries other than Taiwan (see Appendix 2). The author found no examples of documentary films that looked at marriages between citizens of mainland China and residents of Hong Kong and Macau, or marriages between citizens of mainland China and overseas Chinese.

The chapter first provides background information about the development of documentary film in the PRC and outlines the available sample of documentaries on Chinese–foreign marriage. These chiefly comprise documentaries of marriages between citizens of the PRC and citizens of Taiwan, which are commonly referred to as 'cross-Strait marriages' (*liang'an hunyin*) in modern Chinese and marriages between (rural) Chinese citizens and foreign nationals from countries other than Taiwan. By examining documentary films about these two different types of Chinese–foreign marriages, I show how their claims to represent the private life-stories of 'ordinary people' also operate as a platform for the distribution of political messages regarding the success of China's economic and social development.

New documentary and Chinese–foreign marriage

Although the term 'documentary' is conventionally understood as referring to a non-fictional film or video product that provides a historical record of 'real' people, things and events (Eitzen 1995: 81; Ren Yuan 1998: 33), it is widely acknowledged that documentary film, just like reality television, is not exactly an authentic representation or direct transmission of 'the real'. John Grierson (1898–1972), one of the founding fathers of British and Canadian documentary film, famously described the documentary form in the 1930s as 'the creative treatment of actuality' (Grierson and Hardy 1946: 11). Bill Nichols (1991), expands this definition of documentary film in a book called *Representing Reality* by describing documentary in effect as: 'the use of conventional means to refer to, represent, or make claims about historical reality' (Eitzen 1995: 84). In other words, the genre of documentary trades on the claim to represent reality in a truthful manner by using images and audiovisual materials that are directly obtained from real life. However, the 'truth' of that presented 'reality', is that it is constructed through the kinds of audiovisual techniques that are available through the artistic decisions and value judgments, made by the producers and editors of a documentary film, their sponsors and their imagined audiences.

The constructed nature of the genre of documentary is evident in the context of China where the genre has undergone a dramatic change in the reform period. Until recently, Chinese documentary functioned chiefly as a tool for the promotion of communist ideology and orthodoxy and focused on propagandizing the idealized life-stories of revolutionary heroes and model workers and cadres (Chu

Yingchi 2007: 29–30). The commercialization of China's film and television industries in the 1990s, along with access to western styles of documentary cinematic production, led to the increased production of entertainment-oriented documentaries, which catered for audience tastes and advertising markets, not strictly Party sensibilities (Chu Yingchi 2007: 30). A landmark event in this context was the PRC Government's decision to put the China Central Newsreel and Documentary Film Studio (*Zhongyang xinwen jilu dianying zhipianchang*) under the control of CCTV in 1993. This action made documentary film a part of television film production and programming ('Zhongyang xinwen' 2007; Chu Yingchi 2007: 28).

These changes have encouraged new styles of documentary films in China, which are collectively referred to as the 'new documentary movement' (*xin jilupian yundong*). Lü Xinyu, a Chinese media scholar, defines the new documentary movement as a genre of documentary film that emerged in the late 1980s and 1990s and in reaction to the focus during the late 1970s and early 1980s of government-sponsored documentaries on 'special topics' (*zhuanti pian*) – i.e., political education or propaganda-style documentaries with a historical focus and political themes (Chu Yingchi 2007: 29–30). Unlike 'old' documentaries, the new documentary movement examines Chinese society from a grassroots-up rather than top-down perspective. It features diverse subjects, narrative styles, modes of expression and production technologies and embraces new political themes by documenting the lives of social subjects who were marginalized by mainstream and official media, including the lives of ordinary people (Lü Xinyu 2003: 69; 'A Record of' 2004; Lin Xudong 2005; Chu Yingchi 2007: 28–33). New documentaries include independent and amateur work and film, television and online productions (Lü Xinyu 2003: 69; Wang Yiman 2005: 16; Chu Yingchi 2007: 33–4; Berry and Rofel 2010: 7).

Documentaries on Chinese–foreign marriage are produced and broadcast by various television stations in the PRC and appear to have emerged in the mid-2000s. A pertinent case in point is a documentary series broadcast on CCTV-4 called *Yuanfen* (dir. Guan Haiying and Yang Hua), which literally translates as 'Predestined Love' and is referred to hereafter as *Predestined Love*. The show aired every Sunday afternoon between 13.00 and 13.30 from 2006 to 2009. Roughly translated, the programme summary reads as follows:

> *Predestined Love*, produced by CCTV-4 in 2006, is an interview-based programme about human emotions and feelings which focuses on the lives of everyday people who are connected across the Taiwan Strait. The programme tells the touching stories and complex interactions between people across the Taiwan Strait as they go about their daily experiences of work, love and family life. It taps into the emotional connections between them, presents Chinese traditional virtues and displays the truth, goodness and beauty in life and human nature.
>
> ('Yuanfen lanmu' 2008)

Comprised of 150 episodes in total, *Predestined Love* devoted 44 episodes to the subject of intercultural marriage – 36 on marriages between people from the PRC and Taiwan, and, in apparent contradiction to its expressed mission, eight on marriages between citizens of the PRC and people from other parts of the world. Of the 36 marriages involving a citizen of the PRC and a Taiwanese citizen, 29 involved a marriage between a female citizen of the PRC and a male citizen of Taiwan and seven involved a marriage between a male citizen of the PRC and a female citizen of Taiwan. Of the eight episodes involving marriages between citizens of the PRC and citizens of countries other than Taiwan, six of these marriages involved female citizens of the PRC and two involved male citizens of the PRC. While there is no information about how the individuals featured in the documentaries were selected, the gendered composition of the marriages in question replicates the conventional understanding, as discussed in preceding chapters, that the majority of Chinese–foreign marriages are marriages between a female citizen of the PRC and a foreign man.

Predestined Love devoted 36 out of a total of 44 episodes on the subject of intercultural marriage to marriages between PRC citizens and people from Taiwan. This is because CCTV-4 is a Chinese-language TV channel targeting overseas Chinese and residents of Hong Kong, Macao and Taiwan. The channel is dominated by news reporting with a variety of cultural and entertainment shows and with a particular focus on coverage of news and entertainment related to Taiwan ('CCTV-4 guoji pindao' 2004).

The 36 episodes of *Predestined Love* about marriages between citizens of the PRC (29 women and seven men) and citizens of Taiwan (29 men and seven women) touch on different themes. While they usually narrate the stories of how couples met, fell in love and married and the challenges they face in their married lives, 15 of the 36 episodes focus on couples who have established joint businesses and live in the PRC. For example, 'Cross-Strait Couple Who Sell Fruit Vinegar' (*Mai guocu de liang'an fuqi*), which aired on 24 February 2008, narrates the story surrounding the marriage in 1997 of Jiang Zhenliang, a Taiwanese entrepreneur and Lin Xia, a Chinese woman from Fujian Province. The couple reportedly fell in love at first sight when Jiang met Lin while visiting a friend's company in Fujian Province. Jiang subsequently asked Lin to help him resolve some of the financial problems associated with a soft-drink company he had established in Hainan Province. Soon after, the couple married, and established a joint enterprise that sells fruit vinegar with over 40 sales representatives across the PRC. 'Marrying a Shandong Woman' (*Quge Shandong guniang dang laopo*), shown on 25 January 2009, similarly relates the story of the marriage between Guo Li, a 33-year old woman from Shandong Province and Wu Di, a 39-year old divorced entrepreneur from Taiwan with two children. The couple met in Shandong Province when they were both working in the tea industry and have opened more than 30 tea companies across 20 cities in the PRC since their marriage.

Of the 29 episodes of *Predestined Love* on marriages between PRC women and Taiwanese men, seven of these focus on the 'Taiwanese mother-in-law' and 'PRC daughter-in-law' relationship (*poxi guanxi*). An episode shown on 8 February 2009, entitled 'Wife and Mother-in-Law: Conflict in the Kitchen' (*Chufang li de poxi zhizheng*), narrates the story of the marriage between Fu Shuangye, a female lawyer from Wuhan and Shen Hengde, a male lawyer from Taiwan in 1995, with a particular focus on the mother-daughter-in-law relationship and its influence on the marital relationship. Likewise, an episode called 'A Close Cross-Strait Family: Mainland Chinese Wife and Taiwanese Mother-in-law' (*Liang'an poxi yijiaqin*), which was shown on 24 May 2009, focuses on the mother-daughter-in-law relationship following a marriage between Guo Zhenzhong, an entrepreneur from Taiwan who started a business in Changzhou City in Jiangsu Province, where he met and married Zhou Xia, a woman from Changzhou City who was working at another Taiwan-funded enterprise.

Although *Predestined Love* claims to focus on cross-Strait relationships, the programme devoted eight episodes to the subject of marriages between PRC citizens and citizens of overseas countries other than Taiwan; six of these eight episodes are concerned with marriages between Chinese women and foreign men. First, 'My Big Iranian Brother' (*Wo de Yilang pang gege*), shown on 22 March 2009, tells the story of the marriage between Hua Jiade, a 29-year-old Iranian man and Zhang Menghan, a 28-year-old woman from Henan Province. Zhang and Hua met while studying at the Beijing Language University. They married in Iran and now live in Beijing and Zhang has since become a Muslim. Second, 'Learning Chinese Kung Fu and Marrying a Chinese Woman Went Together' (*Quxifu xueyi liangbuwu*), shown on 29 March 2009, tells the story of Mike, a 28-year-old German man who married Li Qiaofang, the daughter of his Kung Fu master from Hubei Province, in 2007. The couple now lives in Wuhan City, Hubei Province. Third, 'Tianjin Girl Married a French Man' (*Tianjin guniang jiagei Faguo xiaohuo*), shown on 26 April 2009, narrates the marriage-story of a 35-year-old French man called 'Hang' to Chen Yin, a 31-year-old Chinese woman from Tianjin. The couple met and married in France in 2008 while Chen was studying for a master's degree and now live in France. Fourth, 'The Story of the Marriage Between My German Husband and I' (*Wo he Deguo zhangfu de hunyin gushi*), shown on 3 May 2009, relates the marriage-story of a German entrepreneur named John and a Chinese woman from Henan Province called Xiao Fan, who met in Shanghai and now live in Germany. Fifth, 'I Am Not a Wealthy Foreign Husband' (*Wo bushi youqian de yang zhangfu*), shown on 3 May 2009, tells the story of the marriage between a French man called Marc and a woman from Sichuan Province called Luo Yuehua. The couple met while working at the World Horticultural Exposition in Kunming in Yunnan Province in 1999. They are now married with five children and live in Wuhan City where Mark is employed, although they had previously lived in France.

Finally, a two-part episode called 'Falling in Love with Sichuan "Hot" Girls' (*Aishang Sichuan lameizi*), shown on 31 May 2009, tells the story of marriages between two Chinese women and a Canadian and American male respectively. The first part narrates the story of the marriage in 2003 between a Canadian man named Sam and a woman from Sichuan Province named Yang Li, who met while working for an unspecified foreign enterprise and who now live in Beijing with their daughter. The second part of the sixth episode relates the marriage-story of two divorcées with children from their first marriages – Tony, a 53-year old American man and Li Mei, a 38-year-old woman from Sichuan Province. The couple met in China in 2003. They now live in Lijiang in Yunnan Province where they promote local cultural activities, for example, by organizing a performance of the Lijiang Ethnic Song and Dance Troupe in the USA.

Two of eight episodes of *Predestined Love* on intercultural marriages between PRC citizens and people from overseas countries other than Taiwan involve marriages between Chinese men and foreign women. 'American Wife in Our Village' (*Cunli de Meiguo xifu*), which aired on 5 April 2009, tells the story of the marriage between Yang Jingying, a tertiary-educated Chinese man from a rural part of Shanxi Province and 'Yang Haili', an American woman 11 years younger than Yang, whom he met while studying at the University of Arkansas in the USA. The couple married in the USA but now live in Shanxi.

'South Korean Woman Searching for Love in China' (*Hanguo nühai Zhongguo xunyuan*), shown on 10 May 2009, tells the marriage-story of Jiang Xiaoyu, a Chinese television director from Fujian Province and Jin Jingxin, a 27-year-old female tour guide from South Korea. The couple met through an introduction from a friend and married in 2006. They now have a daughter and live in Beijing.

In addition to the documentary series called *Predestined Love*, the author collected 13 one-off documentaries on intercultural marriage produced for and broadcast by different television stations in the PRC. For example, Jiangxi Television (JXTV) aired a 27-minute documentary in 2007 entitled 'Foreign Son-in-law Comes to Our Village' (*Cunli laile ge yangnüxu*) as part of a series called *Chuanqi Gushi* (hereafter Legendary Stories), which started in January 2005 and is broadcast nightly between 10 p.m. and 10.30 p.m. ('Chuanqi gushi' 2011). According to the programme summary, *Legendary Stories*, like *Predestined Love*, tells 'social stories' that aim to reveal 'the true, the good and the beautiful' (*zhen-shan-mei*) and the ethical and rational nature (*de-yi-li*) of human life. 'Foreign Son-in-law Comes to Our Village' narrates the marriage-story of a male American university graduate and an unmarried mother from a rural part of Sichuan Province with a six-year-old son. The couple fell in love after they met in a street by chance; they are now married and live in rural Sichuan.

Shanghai Dragon Television (*Shanghai Dongfang weishi*) aired a 19-minute documentary in 2009 called 'Lijiang Love Story' (*Lijiang aiqing gushi*) as part of a series called *Zhenqing Shilu* (hereafter True Stories), which started in 2008 and is broadcast from Monday to Friday between 6 p.m. and 6.30 p.m. *True Stories* also analyses news items and social and topical issues from an emotional perspective, showing the concerns of 'ordinary people' and celebrating the 'beauty' of human nature ('Zhenqing shilu' 2008). 'Lijiang Love Story' tells the marriage-story of a man from Hubei Province and a South Korean woman who met in the tourist city of Dali in Yunnan Province. They married and now live in Lijiang in Yunnan Province, and have established a series of 'Cherry Blossom' bars across different cities in the PRC since their marriage.

Similarly, channel eight of Beijing Television aired a 26-minute documentary in 2009 named 'Intercultural Marriage in a Beijing Alley' (*Hutong li de kuaguo qingyuan*) as part of a series called *Beijing Yinxiang* (hereafter Beijing Impressions), which relates aspects of the lives of 'interesting' people in Beijing ('Beijing yinxiang' 2004). 'Intercultural Marriage in a Beijing Alley' tells the story of an established marriage between a Chinese man and a woman from Holland. The couple who met in Beijing during the 1960s have lived in Beijing for over 50 years.

Taken as a whole, documentaries about intercultural marriage in the PRC suggest that Chinese–foreign marriage is a subject that audiences will find interesting. They typically narrate in anecdotal fashion stories of intercultural love and marriage between ordinary couples in a Chinese–foreign marriage, providing interviews with the couples in question and concluding with a happy ending. Some documentaries provide detailed background information about the couples, including details about their age, educational level and occupation and the year of marriage, whereas other documentaries offer limited information. Yet other documentaries provide detailed background information about only one person in the marriage.

An analysis of the available sample of documentaries (see Appendix 2) indicates that intercultural marriage in the PRC has eight key features, reiterating the general characteristics of Chinese–foreign marriage identified in print media coverage. First, marriages between Chinese women and foreign men are more common than marriages between Chinese men and foreign women. Second, male spouses are generally older than their female partners; Taiwanese males, in particular, are usually much older than their Chinese wives, although in a few cases the women are older than the men. Third, the majority of individuals in Chinese–foreign marriages entered into such marriages in the 1990s and 2000s, although one documentary on *Beijing Impressions* features the pre-1978 marriage between a Chinese man and a Dutch woman. Fourth, the majority of marriages are between people who were single, and had no children from previous relationships, although some of the spouses were widowers or divorcées with children.

Fifth, Chinese citizens in intercultural marriages come from various cities and provinces across the PRC, including: the cities of Beijing, Shanghai, Dalian and Tianjin and the provinces of Shanxi in northern China; Hubei and Henan in Central China; Sichuan in western China; Shandong and Zhejiang in eastern China; and Hainan, Guangxi, Guangdong, Fujian and Jiangxi in southern China. Cross-Strait marriage, in particular, involves a number of people from eastern and southern China marrying Taiwanese citizens. Sixth, foreign spouses come from all corners of the globe, including: European countries such as France, Germany and the Netherlands; Asian countries such as Armenia; African countries such as Ethiopia; countries in the Asia–Pacific region such as Australia and South Korea; and other countries in the Americas such as the USA, Canada and Venezuela.

Seventh, people who enter into Chinese–foreign marriages according to documentary films produced in the PRC come from diverse occupational and educational backgrounds. Foreign men comprise company/factory managers, entrepreneurs, English-language teachers, university graduates, engineers and lawyers, and their Chinese wives are rural migrant workers, 'blue collar' workers, 'white collar' workers in foreign enterprises, professionals with a secondary school education and university students undertaking postgraduate courses overseas. Foreign women include entrepreneurs, English-language teachers and journalists. Their Chinese husbands can be rural migrant workers, or 'white collar' workers such as TV directors, doctors, company managers and people who have studied and worked overseas. However, in the case of cross-Strait marriages, the majority of the male marrying partners from Taiwan are entrepreneurs.

Finally, people who entered into intercultural marriages in the 2000s met their partners in different and diverse circumstances. Some couples met through an introduction from a friend, some met at work and some met by chance in the street and/or at public gatherings such as parties and at reunions organized by friends. Only one couple in the available sample of documentaries met through the Internet, although several couples used the Internet as a means to enhance their communication prior to marriage. Unsurprisingly, given that the documentaries were produced in the PRC, the majority of couples depicted in the documentaries had met each other in the PRC and live in the PRC post-marriage. The exceptions in this regard are a small number of Chinese people who met their partners while working abroad or undertaking a postgraduate university degree overseas.

As the documentary series *Predestined Love* chiefly focuses on PRC–Taiwan marriages, the next section provides some background information about the recent growth in the number of such marriages.

Cross-Strait marriage

The documentary series *Predestined Love* devoted 36 of 150 episodes to the subject of marriages between citizens of the PRC and citizens of Taiwan, which are described as 'cross-Strait marriages'. The term cross-Strait marriage (*liang'an hunyin*) follows from the politicized expression 'cross-Strait relations' (*haixia liang'an guanxi*). In 1949, with the Chinese Civil War turning decisively in the Communists' favour, the Chinese Communist Party established the People's Republic of China and Chiang Kai-shek, the leader of the rival Chinese Nationalist Party and the Republic of China (ROC), retreated with his government and military forces to Taiwan, an island off the southeast coast of mainland China and a territory of the ROC. From 1949 to 1979, the PRC and Taiwan maintained strained and confrontational relations, which restricted formal political and economic and informal private contacts across the Taiwan Strait. The PRC and ROC Governments claimed title as the legitimate ruler of 'China' understood as a single political entity that encompasses the mainland and the island of Taiwan. Both governments used the expression 'cross-Strait relations' rather than 'China–Taiwan' or 'PRC–ROC' to reinforce understandings that the mainland and Taiwan are not separate sovereignties and subsequently the term 'cross-Strait marriage' was used to refer to the unions between 'Chinese citizens' of a mutually contentious political status.

Political tensions between Taiwan and the PRC prevented the occurrence of cross-Strait marriages until the late 1980s. Taiwan was governed under Martial

Law until 1987, which placed a blanket ban on political, economic and private citizens' exchanges for any reason, including travel to the PRC for the purposes of family reunion, partly in order to avert attempts by the PRC to invade Taiwan (Liu Guofu 2005: 135). From 1949 to the early 1970s, the PRC underwent a programme of socialist development, which resulted in its economic and political isolation from the western world, whereas the ROC, aligned with the USA Government, adopted market-based economic policies, becoming known along with Hong Kong, South Korea and Singapore as one of Asia's Four Tigers for its export-driven economic success.

As part of wider foreign relations and economic reforms under Deng Xiaoping's leadership, the PRC formally shifted its confrontational stance to a policy of emphasizing peaceful reunification through dialogue with Taiwan in 1979 (Lampton 2001: 310). Between 1979 and 1987, the PRC initiated a series of political dialogues and policies seeking to normalize cross-Strait relations. In 1979 it proposed the 'Three Links' (*san tong*) of direct economic exchange in postal services, transportation and trade and the 'Four Exchanges' (*si liu*) for family, tourists, academics, cultural and sports groups between the Strait, which was rejected by the ROC Government (Lu 2008: 126). In 1983, Deng Xiaoping crystallized the concept of 'one country, two systems' to reunify China and Taiwan under one sovereign state (under the PRC), while allowing Taiwan continued political and economic autonomy as well as its own military force ('A policy of "One country, two systems" on Taiwan' 2000; Lu 2008: 126).

The ROC rejected the PRC's calls to normalize cross-Strait relations until the end of Martial Law in 1987. On 14 October 1987, the ROC lifted the blanket ban on private exchanges and allowed citizens to apply for travel permits to visit the mainland for the purpose of family reunification ('Cross-Strait Strains' 2004; Lu 2008: 127; Friedman 2010: 76). However, initial policies prohibited direct cross-Strait contact between businesses and travel agencies and travel permits limited the length and period of stay of Taiwan citizens on the mainland to one trip per year and three months per stay (Yu 1997: 23; Tu and Li Shaolin 1999: 511).

Hence, the first group of Taiwan nationals to enter the PRC was predominantly elderly veterans of the Nationalist Party who had retreated to Taiwan with the Nationalist army in 1949, and wished to visit their place of birth. These were also the first cohort to engage in cross-Strait marriage as they brought back younger spouses from their native homes back to Taiwan with them (Friedman 2010: 76; Tsai 2011: 244). This first cohort of 'mainland brides' was comprised largely of divorced and widowed women aged between 30 and 50 (Friedman 2010: 76).

The second wave of private cross-Strait interaction post-1987 stemmed from Taiwan's eventual recognition of, and desire to, benefit from the PRC's economic reforms and growth (Lu 2008: 126–7). In 1992, Taiwan officially legalized domestic businesses to invest in the PRC (before this, business interaction occurred predominantly through illegal networks). In January 2001, Taiwan formally allowed the 'three mini-links' of direct trade, travel and postal services; and permitted general direct cross-Strait trade in 2002. In June 2010, Taiwan signed a bilateral trade agreement (Economic Cooperation Framework Agreement) with the

PRC, evidence of the ROC's acknowledgement that stronger economic ties with the PRC are important for its own economic growth and expanding regional and international trade. These changes have increased the opportunities for cross-Strait marriages as the number of Taiwanese investors and entrepreneurs who work in the PRC is growing.

The most recent wave of private exchange between PRC and Taiwan flows from tourism, especially as cross-Strait charter flights have become available. Following the defeat of Taiwan's eight-year-ruling Democratic Progressive Party in 2008, the PRC lifted official restrictions on tourists travelling from the PRC to Taiwan because the island adopted a more China-friendly administration ('Chinese mainland tourists' 2009; Fan 2010: 268). The PRC now actively promotes travel to Taiwan through various policies and incentives, such as direct flights, reduced tourism costs and document approval times and tourism promotion campaigns (Fan 2010: 270). An estimated 1.66 million people from the PRC visited Taiwan as tourists in 2010, an increase of 68.6 per cent from 2009 (China National Tourism Administration 2011). This number looks set to increase as a new policy introduced in Taiwan in July 2011 allows individual travellers from the PRC, whereas only tour groups were permitted previously. Conversely, 3.66 million people travelled from Taiwan to the PRC in 2002. That figure rose to 4.48 million people in 2009 and 5.14 million in 2010 (China National Tourism Administration 2002, 2010, 2011).

At the same time, as discussed in Chapter 1, the PRC has instituted a series of legal and administrative reforms to formally recognize, manage and simplify the registration of Chinese–foreign marriages, including marriages between mainland citizens and citizens from Taiwan (see *Guanyu Taiwan tongbao yu Dalu gongmin zhijian banli jiehun dengji youguan wenti de tongzhi* 1988 and *Dalu jumin yu Taiwan jumin hunyin dengji guanli zanxing banfa* 1998). The PRC has also standardized the exit and entry requirements for foreigners and Chinese citizens, which has encouraged foreign nationals to visit and live in the PRC, paving the way for an increasing number of intercultural marriages. These laws and administrative regulations include the 1986 Law of the PRC on the Control of the Entry and Exit of Aliens, the 1986 Law of the PRC on the Control of the Exit and Entry of Citizens, the 1992 Measures for the Control of Chinese Citizens Travelling To and From the Region of Taiwan, the 2004 Measures for the Administration of Examination and Approval of Foreigners' Permanent Residence in China and the 2010 regulations on Residence Permits for Foreigners, which supplement the exit and entry regulations for foreigners in the PRC (*Zhonghua Renmin Gongheguo waiguoren rujing chujing guanli fa* 1986; *Zhonghua Renmin Gongheguo gongmin chujing rujing guanli fa* 1986; *Zhongguo gongmin wanglai Taiwan diqu guanli banfa* 1992; *Waiguoren zai Zhongguo yongjiu juliu shenpi guanli banfa* 2004; *Waiguoren juliu xuke* 2010).

Figure 7.1 below illustrates the number of cross-Strait marriages that were registered in the PRC between 1990 and 2011. It shows that approximately 500 people from Taiwan registered a marriage with citizens of mainland China in the PRC in 1990. That figure more than doubled the following year, and the number of cross-Strait marriages registered in the PRC continued to rise rapidly until 2003. More than 10,000 people from Taiwan registered a marriage with citizens of mainland China in the PRC in 1997, that figure reached a peak of over 37,000 persons in 2003, before decreasing to around 11,000 persons in 2011.

The growth in the number of cross-Strait marriages reflects these three waves of cross-Strait interaction, although the ROC Government has been reluctant to allow citizens of the PRC to reside in Taiwan. The ROC first allowed spouses from the PRC to enter Taiwan through a tightly controlled immigration process in 1992. Taiwan's Civil Code establishes the procedures for entry and exit and residence in cases of marriages between Taiwanese citizens and foreigners and for recognizing the educational qualifications of the foreign spouse. However, spouses from the PRC are placed under the '1992 Statute Governing Relations Between People of the Taiwan Area and Mainland Area', which is overseen by the Ministry of Interior and the Mainland Affairs Council and places restrictions on migration through a cross-Strait marriage. Chinese spouses are not allowed to work in Taiwan without legal residency status. They are only eligible to apply for temporary residency (*juliu*) after two years of marriage, or the birth of a child and the permission of residency is subject to an annual quota allowance (King 2011: 181). Only after two years of temporary residency, with restrictions of two visitor visas of 90 days' duration per year, can Chinese spouses apply for permanent residency (*dingju*) and then Taiwanese citizenship (King 2011: 181). While amendments to the 1992 Statute in 1999 allowed for the more lenient handling of cases involving children, elderly family and ailing or incapacitated spouses, Taiwan's annual quota for immigrants in cross-Strait marriages falls well below the growing number of applications. In 1992 there were 954 applications, which was four times the quota of 240, in 1997 there were 5,821 applications, which was five times greater than the

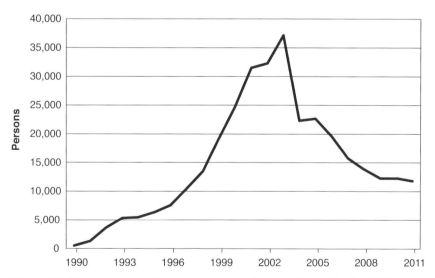

Figure 7.1 Taiwan spouses in cross-strait marriages registered in the PRC (1990–2011)

Source: *Zhongguo Minzheng Tongji Nianjian* (China Civil Affairs Statistical Yearbook, 1991–2012).

142 *Documenting Chinese–foreign marriage*

quota of 1,080 for that year (King 2011: 183). Until the late 1990s and early 2000s, spouses from the PRC also received limited access to health and welfare services in Taiwan and were granted restricted work permits. Not until August 2009, were spouses from mainland China granted equalized status to other foreign marital immigrants in terms of residency and work rights upon their first arrival in Taiwan (Friedman 2013: 157).

Despite these restrictions, the number of women migrating from the PRC to Taiwan through marriage has increased because of increased business connections, tourism, the Internet and introductions from friends and marriage introduction agencies (Friedman 2010: 76–7). Melody Lu (2008: 192) categorizes these marriage introduction agencies into three main types: 1) institutionalized brokering companies and agencies; 2) individual entrepreneurs and matchmakers and 3) the more informal practices of women from the PRC who are married to men from Taiwan acting as matchmakers in both the sending and receiving communities. Such introductions commonly involve Taiwanese men providing money in order to marry a woman from the PRC. Hence, cross-Strait marriages are sometimes viewed as a more commodified and 'inferior' type of marriage when compared to PRC–PRC and Taiwan–Taiwan marriages (Hsieh Ching-yu and Wang 2008: 102).

Table 7.1 below suggests that the majority of intercultural marriages that are registered in Taiwan occur between a Taiwanese male and a female citizen of the

Table 7.1 Number of marriages registered in Taiwan (1998–2011)*

Year	Total number of registered marriages (couples)	Foreign spouses** (persons)	PRC spouses Total (persons)	Male Number	(%)	Female Number	(%)
1998	145,976	10,454 (7.2%)	12,167 (8.3%)	382	3.1	11,785	96.9
1999	173,209	14,674 (8.5%)	17,288 (10.0%)	697	4	16,591	96
2000	181,642	21,338 (11.8%)	23,297 (12.8%)	686	3	22,611	97
2001	170,515	19,405 (11.4%)	26,516 (15.6%)	834	3.1	25,682	96.9
2002	172,655	20,107 (11.7%)	28,603 (16.6%)	1,436	5	27,167	95
2003	171,483	19,643 (11.5%)	34,685 (20.2%)	3,060	9	31,625	91
2004	131,483	20,338 (15.5%)	10,642 (8.1%)	256	2.4	10,386	97.6
2005	141,140	13,808 (9.8%)	14,258 (10.1%)	282	2	13,976	98
2006	142,669	9,524 (6.7%)	13,964 (9.8%)	323	2.3	13,641	97.7
2007	135,041	9,554 (7.1%)	14,721 (10.9%)	371	2.6	14,350	97.4
2008	154,866	8,957 (5.8%)	12,274 (7.9%)	371	3	11,903	97
2009	117,099	8,620 (7.4%)	12,796 (10.9%)	452	3.5	12,344	96.5
2010	138,819	8,169 (5.9%)	12,807 (7.9%)	562	4.4	12,245	95.6
2011	165,327	8,053 (4.9%)	12,800 (7.7%)	686	5.4	12,114	94.6

* Table adapted from Neizhenbu, Huzhengsi (Department of Household Registration, Ministry of the Interior). Online. Available at www.ris.gov.tw/version96/population_01_C_05.html (accessed 24 October 2012).
** Foreign Nationals exclude citizens from mainland China, Hong Kong and Macau; percentage of total registered marriages in brackets.

PRC. The number of women from the PRC who registered a marriage with a Taiwanese male in Taiwan increased from nearly 12,000 in 1998 to reach a peak of over 31,000 women in 2003, before declining to around 10,000 women in 2004. This sudden decline was partly attributed to the strict border screening scheme implemented by the Taiwan immigration agency, which requested that couples be interviewed with regard to issuing a residential visa to mainland spouses (Yeh 2010: 202). This figure maintained a level of around 12,000 to 14,000 women per year between 2005 and 2011.

The growth in numbers of Taiwan–PRC marriages throughout the 1990s and early 2000s attracted differing media scrutiny in both areas. In Taiwan, the gendered nature of such marriages first attracted attention as a sign of the PRC's economic and social inferiority. Conversely, recent newspaper reports and television programmes in the PRC stress the openness of China with regard to Taiwan–PRC marriages, interpreting the growing number of couples in such marriages who now live in the PRC as a sign of China's economic growth and attractiveness to the outside world.

Cross-Strait marriage in the media

Following the establishment of the ROC Government in Taiwan after 1949, Taiwan looked to the United States as a model for rapid industrialization and associated modernization. Between the early 1960s and 1990s, Taiwan became a regional economic powerhouse based on the exports of manufacturing goods to developed countries. The economically developed nature of Taiwanese society in the early 1990s compared positively to the situation in the PRC, which only adopted a programme of market-based economic reforms in December 1978 and retained a relatively rigid social system throughout the 1990s (Chia *et al.* 1997: 138–9).

The disadvantaged position of the PRC compared to Taiwan at that time is reflected in Taiwanese newspaper coverage of cross-Strait marriages between the 1990s and the 2000s, which provide negative depictions of 'mainland brides' as hypergamous 'gold diggers' and 'prostitutes' (Shih 1998: 295–303; Hsia 2007: 55–62; Lu 2008: 168–9; Tsai 2011: 245). In such reports, women from the PRC who migrated to Taiwan through marriage and especially those who migrated via the medium of marriage brokers, were called 'mainland sisters' (*dalumei*). Although the term implies a horizontal form of cultural and linguistic connection, it has derisive connotations in practice. 'Mainland sisters' were stereotyped in newspaper discussions as 'gold diggers' who married Taiwanese men for economic gain (Hsia 2007: 61). They were also associated with bogus marriage for migration and stigmatized as providers of commercial sexual services in Taiwanese entertainment venues (Shih 1998: 297). In short, women from the PRC who migrated through marriage to Taiwan were stigmatized in Taiwanese newspapers as an inferior species of 'Chinese women' who were contaminating the purer moral framework of Taiwanese society (Hsia 2007: 55; Tsai 2011: 246).

In a similarly negative tone, Taiwanese men who married women from the PRC often were portrayed as undesirable from the perspective of Taiwanese women

(Hsia 2007: 63–4; Kuo 2010: 86). Such men were portrayed as disadvantaged in domestic marriage markets because their financial circumstances were limited vis-à-vis other Taiwanese men. Moreover, they often had lower than average levels of education and were deemed to be physically and psychologically challenged and unattractive.

Newspapers in the PRC began covering in a limited fashion the growing phenomenon of cross-Strait marriage in the 1990s and up until the early 2000s the majority of these reports also focused on the negative aspects of such marriages. Journalists expressed concerns about female citizens of the PRC who experienced economic hardship and social stigmatization in Taiwan after migrating via real or 'bogus' marriages (Min Jun 1993; Zhao Baosheng 2000a; Dai Honghong and Liu Laihong 2004). They also expressed concerns about the emerging practice of Taiwanese entrepreneurs keeping female citizens of the PRC as mistresses or 'second wives' (*bao er'nai*) in the PRC ('Liang'an hunyin mianmian guan' 1992; Min Jun 1993; Zhao Baosheng 2000a; 'Dalu peiou' 2004).

From the mid- to late 2000s, while newspapers in the PRC still focused on the hardships experienced by female citizens of the PRC who had married Taiwanese men and migrated to live in Taiwan, they began to focus on an additional set of both negative and positive issues. These issues included further tales of hardship stemming from the rising incidence of cross-Strait divorce, which was viewed as an inevitable consequence of women from the PRC entering into 'flash or blitz' marriages (*shanhun*) with Taiwanese men (Sun Ziming 2006; Xu Qiaona 2008a; Mo Xueqing 2009). At the same time, journalists started to attribute the growing incidence of cross-Strait marriage to increased economic and cultural interaction across the Taiwan Strait. This resulted in a new focus on the positive experiences of mainland Chinese women who married Taiwanese men and migrated to live in Taiwan and, conversely, on the positive experiences of Taiwanese women who married male citizens of the PRC and migrated to live in the PRC (Xu Qiaona 2008b; Xiao Shiyan and Shi Wei 2009; Xu Chen and Zhao Huanhuan 2009; Zhou Jianchang 2009).

Starting in the late 2000s, newspaper reports about the phenomenon of cross-Strait marriages in the PRC became both more commonplace and positive in tone. Journalists began to focus on the new trend of women from Taiwan marrying men from the PRC and migrating from Taiwan to live in the PRC (Yuan Zhonghai and Sun Xianglan 2007; 'Taiwan lang Xiamen quqin' 2009; 'Taiwan nü jia Dalu nan' 2010; Ren Bo 2011). For example, a 2007 report in the *Global Times*, entitled 'Taiwanese Women Who Are Brides On the Mainland' (*Jiadao Dalu de Taiwan xin'niang*), states that female Taiwanese citizens marry men from the PRC both for love and because life in the PRC offers them good work and living conditions (Yuan Zhonghai and Sun Xianglan 2007). Similarly, a number of reports note that men from Taiwan are marrying women from the PRC and living in the PRC for reasons of love and career development ('Liang'an hunyin xin xianxiang' 2011; Ren Bo 2011).

In newspaper reports in the PRC since the late 2000s, the perceived reverse direction of migration from Taiwan to the PRC via cross-Strait marriage is framed as reflecting the continued rapid growth of the PRC's economy, enhanced cross-Strait interactions and the declining economic and political position of Taiwan in the region vis-à-vis the PRC. Media accounts of the perceived reverse direction of migration from Taiwan to the PRC via cross-Strait marriage suggest a repositioning of the PRC as the superior rather than inferior partner in cross-Strait relations. This understanding is reinforced by media coverage of marriages between Taiwanese female celebrities and male entrepreneurs from the PRC. Such marriages include the marriage between Taiwanese actress and model Meng Guangmei and Beijing entrepreneur Ji Zenghe in 2010, Taiwanese actress Xu Xiyuan and Beijing entrepreneur Wang Xiaofei in 2010 and Taiwanese actress Liu Ruoying and an entrepreneur from Zhejiang Province called Zhong Shi in 2011 (Taiwan nü jia Dalu nan' 2010; 'Liang'an hunyin xin xianxiang' 2011). The new incidence of such marriages points to the heightened economic and cultural prowess of the PRC in the region.

In the documentary series called *Predestined Love*, positive audience understandings of improved cross-Strait relations are encouraged via a focus on the personal relationships between women from the PRC and their Taiwanese mothers-in-law (*poxi guanxi*). For example, an episode called 'Wife and Mother-in-Law: Conflict in the Kitchen', narrates the story of the struggle for acceptance from her Taiwanese mother-in-law of Fu Shuangye, a lawyer and career-oriented woman from Wuhan City ('Chufang li de poxi zhizheng' 2009). The initial relationship between the two women is described as a 'silent war' (*wusheng de zhanchang*), because the mother-in-law was prejudiced by negative stereotypes of 'mainland brides', and Fu failed to meet her expectations of a good Chinese woman as a 'housewife', or as someone whose life is organized around the private life of the home and not the public domain of paid employment.

Fu tells the reporter from *Predestined Love* that the mass media in Taiwan have played a major role in encouraging Taiwanese people to hold negative views of the PRC and its citizens as inferior, in part through the use of labels such as 'mainland sister'. As Fu explains, '[television hosts in Taiwan] perhaps do not think that such labels discriminate against us [mainland women living as brides in Taiwan], but we find it is a very insulting mode of address' (*Tamen keneng bu renwei zhezhong chengwei shi dai yizhong qishixing de, dui women laijiang shi yige hen quruxing de chenghu*). Fu concludes that her mother-in-law was predisposed to view her negatively, despite her high educational level and good professional reputation, because of the Taiwanese media portrayal of women from the PRC who marry men from Taiwan as 'gold diggers' and 'prostitutes'. Fu claims to have spent considerable time and effort trying to please her mother-in-law by spending time talking and shopping with her and learning songs in local dialect from her, so as to erase what Fu describes as her 'mainland hue' (*Dalu laide biaozhi/secai*).

Another episode of *Predestined Love* called 'A Close Cross-Strait Family: Mainland Chinese Wife and Taiwanese Mother-in-law' similarly narrates the story of the struggle for acceptance from her Taiwanese mother-in-law of Zhou Xia, a 'white collar' worker from Jiangsu Province ('Liang'an poxi yijiaqin' 2009). Zhou met her husband, Guo Zhenzhong, a Taiwanese entrepreneur, in 1998 while he was working in Jiangsu Province and they married despite substantial opposition from his parents, in particular. A series of anecdotal stories recounts how Zhou did her best to please her mother-in-law after moving to Taiwan with her husband, dutifully cooking and cleaning to prove that she is a worthy daughter-in-law despite never having performed such domestic chores prior to her marriage.

The episode concludes that Zhou and Guo have since achieved family harmony in their ten-year-long cross-Strait marriage. Guo's parents now love his 'mainland bride' (*Dalu xifu*) and are glad that he has such a dutiful and capable wife (*xianhui neng'gan de qizi*). As Zhou tells the reporter, she knows that her Taiwanese mother-in-law loves her because of her actions: she remembers Zhou's birthday and buys her gifts. In Zhou's words: 'she buys me shoes, clothes and purses … Her love for me is demonstrated by her actions. I can feel it. I think [Guo's] mother is a great mother!' (*Ta hui bang wo mai xiezi, mai yifu, mai baobao… ta zhege ai shi yong xingdong biaoda chulai de, wo neng ganshou dao. Wo yizhi juede ta mama shi yige henbang de mama*). At the same time, interviews with Zhou's parents are presented to show that they like their Taiwanese son-in-law (*Taiwan nüxu*), Zhou's mother praises Guo for caring about her husband and herself. In her words, 'he arranges travel for us every year and it's been quite a few years now. I am very satisfied with my son-in-law' (*Ta meinian dou anpai women liang'ge laode chuqu lüyou yici, yijing lianxu hao jinian le. Suoyi, wo dui zhege nüxu shi bijiao manyi de*). Zhou's father adds that Guo is a good and kind son to them.

> 'Whenever we eat together, he serves us first. He remembers both of our birthdays and buys us birthday cake every year … Filial piety, I strongly feel this from him' (*Women zai yiqi chifan, ta doushi diyige – tang, fan, xiangei women chi. Shengri dou jide, women shengri, gei women shengri mai dangao, meinian doushi zheyang … xiaoxin, xiaoxin zhe yidian wo shi feichang ganjue dao de*).

By framing all of the relationships involved in this particular marriage as loving, the episode suggests that the initial opposition of both sets of parents to the marriage of Zhou and Guo was a misplaced product of the historical conflict between Taiwan and the PRC. Prejudice and opposition to cross-Strait marriages in the 1990s is now replaced by love and understanding in the 2000s, mirroring the gradual improvement of wider cross-Strait relations during this decade.

The mother and daughter in-law narratives in *Predestined Love* thus serve as a metaphor for the wider and changing political relationship between the PRC and Taiwan in the contemporary period. The efforts of women from the PRC vis-à-vis their Taiwanese mothers-in-law reflects for PRC audiences the PRC Government's ongoing efforts to unite the PRC and Taiwan via the concept of 'peaceful development' (*heping fazhan*). This concept was articulated by President Hu Jintao of the PRC at the Seventeenth National Congress of the Chinese Communist Party in October 2007 and at celebrations held for the ninetieth anniversary of the founding of the Chinese Communist Party at the People's Great Hall in July 2011 ('Hu Jintao's report' 2007; Xin Qiang 2009: 59; 'Promote Peaceful Development' 2011).

Such constructions also symbolically convey to Taiwan and PRC audiences that the cross-Strait policy of the PRC Government and the ROC Government are converging. President Hu Jintao of the PRC proposed a 16-character guideline for cross-Strait relations in April 2008 which advocates promoting 'peaceful development' and 'creating a win-win situation (*gongchuang shuangying*)', by 'building mutual trust' (*jianli huxin*) while 'laying aside differences' (*gezhi zhengyi*) and 'seeking consensus while shelving differences' (*qiutong cunyi*). President Ma Ying-jeou of Taiwan also proposed a 16-character guideline for cross-Strait relations in July 2009, which advocates creating a mutually beneficial relationship (*gongchuang shuangying*), by 'facing realities' (*zhengshi xianshi*), 'building mutual trust' (*jianli huxin*)' and 'laying aside differences' (*gezhi zhengyi*) (Zhang Yong 2008; 'Song Qiang: Hu zongshuji' 2009). The fact that women and men from the PRC and Taiwan have married and overcome the initial opposition of their families to such marriages suggests that the PRC and Taiwan can work together to build a happy and perhaps unified relationship, by overcoming the cultural barriers created by a history of political conflict.

Predestined Love's documentary portrayals of cross-Strait marriages seeks to further break down the cultural wall of distrust between PRC and Taiwanese citizens by presenting positive constructions of PRC women who marry Taiwanese men. In this documentary series, female citizens of the PRC who marry Taiwanese men are not 'gold diggers' or 'seductresses', but rather women who have good educational levels, good family backgrounds and high social status. For example, they are university graduates, lecturers, lawyers, actors, models and managers of businesses ('Yibosanzhe de liang'an hunyin' 2008; 'Chufang li de poxi zhizheng' 2009; 'Hunqian hunhou buyiyang' 2009). They also migrate to Taiwan after marrying men of recognizable quality, such as rich entrepreneurs, rather than marrying a man who has limited currency in the local Taiwanese marriage market. However, these women, like the men they marry, do so primarily for reasons of love not strictly socio-economic advancement, as illustrated by the fact they go to Taiwan for different reasons. After registering a marriage in the PRC, many such women travel to Taiwan to visit their parents-in-law and/or to give birth, eventually returning to live and work in the PRC ('Mai guocu de liang'an fuqi' 2008; 'Taiwan Fujiazi aishang Hainan guniang' 2008; 'Tianjin guniang Taiwan lang' 2008).

In fact, numerous episodes of *Predestined Love* frame the 'mainland bride' as a capable career woman who is an equal partner with her Taiwanese husband both in marriage and in business. For example, an episode entitled 'My Wife Helped Me Become a Billionaire' (*Qizi bangwo chuangzao shangyi caichan*), which aired on 2 March 2008, tells the story of a hardworking woman from the northern Chinese city of Dalian who has worked in partnership with her Taiwanese husband to start up and manage a successful joint business endeavour, after battling a series of financial set-backs. Likewise, an episode called 'Zipper Business Helps Zhejiang Woman and Taiwan Man Tie the Knot' (*Zhejiang xifu Taiwan lang yu lalian jieyuan*), which aired on 11 February 2007, tells the story of a woman from Zhejiang Province who met and married a Taiwanese entrepreneur who is renowned in China as the 'Zipper King' (*lalian dawang*). They now run zipper and café businesses in the PRC.

In an episode of *Predestined Love* called 'Wife and Colleague' (*bange xifu bange tongshi*), which aired on 2 November 2008, the female citizen of the PRC who marries a man from Taiwan is portrayed as an even more capable entrepreneur than her husband. The woman named Hong Yi originally worked as an employee and subordinate of the man she married, a man named Chen. However, she went on to establish her own successful company, and appointed her husband as the company manager, under her leadership as the director of the company. At the end of the episode, Chen comments that:

> This is the tenth year of our marriage … I love her more and more … she has never stopped improving herself... She takes good care of me, and she even 'stole' my job. She is in charge of all the work by herself now, both inside and outside the family … Imagine if I lost her … What would I do? I cannot imagine. It would be horrible!' (*jin'nian shi jiehun yihou de di 10 nian … wo yuelaiyue ai ta … ta buduan ba ziji gaode yuelaiyue youxiu … ranhou zai shenghuo shang zhaogu dao wo yijing buzhidao gai zenmeban, gongzuo bei ta qiang'guang le, xianzai gongzuo doushi ta zaizuo, jia limian shiqing yeshi ta zaizuo… wo ruguo you yitian shiqu ta le … wo hui zenmeban? Canburendu bugan xiangxiang*).

This construction of the PRC bride as a competent 'business partner' demonstrates the perceived capacity of women from mainland China in both the public and marital domain. They are portrayed as performing a significant role in helping their Taiwanese husbands to settle down and work in the PRC, gain access to local resources and build up the social networks that form the foundations of their subsequent business successes on the mainland. PRC brides thus become economic actors and drivers who contribute to the development of both local industry and bilateral social-economic engagement and interdependence. These women are domestically capable and financially independent, signifying the new-found positional superiority of the PRC vis-à-vis Taiwan in Asia.

To summarize the preceding remarks, the *Predestined Love* documentaries produced in the PRC on cross-Strait marriages claim to look at society from the viewpoint of the lives of 'ordinary people'. In turn, this focus provides a platform for the delivery of seemingly non-politicized political messages regarding the improved nature of cross-Strait relations and the strategic significance of 'peaceful development' in maintaining cross-Strait relations. Simultaneously, the documentaries rectify the negative image of 'mainland brides' as stereotyped in the Taiwanese media so as to reveal the changing landscape of cross-Strait marriages in contemporary China led by the PRC's strengthening economic power. In doing so, the documentaries suggest that tensions between families and individuals across the Taiwan Strait are simply misunderstandings stemming from a recent history of political division.

Rural Chinese and foreign nationals

Apart from the 36 documentaries on cross-Strait marriages produced by *Predestined Love*, the author collected another 21 documentaries on marriages between citizens of the PRC and people from other parts of the world. Nine of these 21 documentaries – one episode of *Predestined Love* and eight of the 13 one-off documentaries on intercultural marriage – focus on a specific type of Chinese–foreign marriage; namely, marriages between foreign nationals and people from rural parts of China. Five of these nine documentaries look at marriages between men from the PRC and foreign women and four look at marriages between women from the PRC and foreign men. While it is not possible to generalize from such a small sample, this focus suggests that intercultural marriages between foreign nationals and rural Chinese and especially between foreign women and rural Chinese men, are viewed as unusual and hence of particular interest to potential audiences.

The roughly equal number of documentaries concerned with the intercultural marriages of rural Chinese citizens reflects the growing presence of rural people in cultural representations of a future urban China. Despite rapid urbanization, China is an agricultural country, and the rural population still accounts for approximately 50 per cent of the total population of the PRC (National Bureau of Statistics of China 2011a). Yet, by the end of 2010, an estimated 242 million people have migrated from rural parts of China to towns and cities to look for work (National Bureau of Statistics 2011b). Rural migrant workers initially were stereotyped in media accounts of them as poor, uncouth outsiders in the city and even as thieves and criminals. Such representations stand in marked contrast to the depiction of rural people in Maoist-era China as pure of heart and the emphasis on 'going down to the countryside' to learn from the peasants (Kipnis 1997: 168). Concomitantly, the nature of life in contemporary rural China did not attract substantial media coverage until recently, other than in the form of 'anti-corruption' narratives – i.e., stories about corrupt rural officials victimizing local peoples in violation of state policies (Li Fengjie 2005; Sun Wanning 2008: 36–7). Representations of corruption in the countryside and of rural migrant workers in the cities as lower quality citizens both drew on and reinforced a rural-urban hierarchy that privileges the urban as modern and the rural as backward.

In recent years, media accounts of rural migrant workers and rural life have become more positive in tone, both in response to changing government agendas and as rural migrants have become a familiar and established component of everyday life in China's cities. Media accounts of rural migrants working in Chinese cities started to become more sympathetic in tone from the late 1990s and especially in the early 2000s (Dong Xiaoyu and Hu Yang 2010), as the rural migrant workforce increased to around 40 per cent of the urban labour force in 2004 (Wang Dewen 2008) and a new generation of the children of migrant workers grew up, and were educated in the cities where their parents were working. This particular generation reportedly not only want better jobs and better opportunities, but also view the city that they live in as 'home' and intend to stay there permanently. In the mid-2000s, China's media also began to increase positive reporting of rural migrant workers and life in rural China to promote the PRC Governments' political agenda as articulated in the Eleventh Five-Year Plan for National Economic and Social Development from 2006 to 2010. The Eleventh Five-Year Plan encouraged various provincial governments to redefine rural migrant workers in cities as 'new urban citizens' (*xin shimin*) with accompanying rights to welfare and services (Shi Zhiyong and Liang Juan 2006; 'Duihua "xin shimin"' 2008). It also promoted the modernization of rural China under the rubric of creating a 'new socialist Chinese countryside' (*shehui zhuyi xin nongcun*) (Zhonggong zhongyang guanyu zhiding guomin jingji he shehui fazhan di 11 ge 5 nian guihua de jianyi 2005; see also Sun Wanning 2008: 39; Gao Haijian 2008: 114–15; Dong Xiaoyu and Hu Yang 2010).

Documentaries about marriages between rural Chinese and foreign nationals are both a part of the new documentary movement's emphasis on giving voice to marginalized members of society and part of a broader rethinking of the place of rural China in a future China. As discussed previously, newspaper reports about intercultural marriage in the PRC emphasize the increasing popularity of intercultural marriages among urban Chinese and highlight a reversed migration trend wherein foreigners from wealthy industrial countries migrate to live with their Chinese spouses in the developing new 'global cities' of Shanghai, Shenzhen and Beijing (Du Zhanfan 2001; Zhao Junhui 2007; Wu Xuemei and He Xin 2007a). In contrast, documentaries on intercultural marriage produced in the PRC focus on a perceived more recent trend wherein foreign nationals marry rural Chinese citizens and migrate to live with them in the remote rural countryside or in small towns in underdeveloped regions, such as China's northern Shanxi Province, eastern Shandong Province, Henan Province in Central China and southwest Sichuan Province ('Cunli laile ge yangnüxu' 2007; 'Mima qingshu' 2008; 'Yangxifu de chengshi meng' 2008; 'Cunli de Meiguo xifu' 2009).

In such documentaries, people from rural communities, unlike their urban counterparts, are framed as being unused to dealing with foreigners, and therefore as excited by having a foreign person in their physical proximity ('Cunli laile ge yangnüxu' 2007; 'Mima qingshu' 2008; 'Cunli de Meiguo xifu' 2009; 'Yangnüxu qiuhun ji' 2010). For example, a 20-minute documentary called 'A Foreign Bride Comes to Our Village' (*Cunli laile yangxifu*)' relates the story of the marriage between Cai Xiaohau from Runan County in Henan Province and an American woman referred to as 'Di Fan'ni' ('Cunli laile yangxifu' 2008). The couple met when Cai was working as a security guard in Guangdong Province. They married in Cai's native village in 2008 and now live and work in a city in Henan Province. The documentary portrays the couple's wedding ceremony which was held in Cai's native home and witnessed by a large number of villagers. It was shown as part of a series called *Jiangshu* (hereafter Stories) on CCTV-10 in 2008, which first aired in July 2001 and is broadcast daily from 9 p.m. to 9.23 p.m. and claims to 'present the extraordinary stories of ordinary people to inspire viewers' ('Jiangshu' 2011). In the documentary, an elderly villager is asked by a reporter if she has ever seen a foreign bride before. She smiles shyly and replies 'no'. This is the first time she has ever seen a foreign woman in the flesh.

A 26-minute documentary named 'American Wife in Our Village' (*Cunli de Meiguo xifu*), produced by *Predestined Love* and shown on CCTV-4 in 2009,

Documenting Chinese–foreign marriage 151

relates a similar tale ('Cunli de Meiguo xifu' 2009). The documentary tells the story of the marriage between a Chinese man named Yang Jingying from rural Shanxi Province and an American woman and violin teacher called 'Yang Haili (hereafter Haili). Yang met Haili while he was studying for a doctorate in biology at the University of Arkansas. After their marriage in the USA, they returned to the PRC to live in Yang's home town in rural Shanxi Province. As Yang explains to the interviewing journalist, when Haili first came to the village, everybody came to visit him in order to see her. One elderly man, in particular, could not stop staring at her and was fascinated by her blonde hair.

This curiosity is made more explicit in a five-minute news documentary called 'A Rural Woman From Xintai City Marries a "Foreign-son-in-law"' (*Xintai nongjianü qule 'yang nüxu'*). Shown in 2009 on Xintai Television Station, which is based in Shandong Province, the documentary covers the story of the marriage between Yin Li and a Russian man named 'Jili'er Chenguang' (hereafter Chenguang). In an interview, a villager states in front of the camera: 'I have never heard of anyone [in our village] marrying a "foreign son-in-law". That is why we have all come here to watch [Chenguang]. He is handsome, so cute and looks fabulous. It's great!' (*Qule ge yang nüxu, an hai conglai mei tingshuo guo, zhebu dajiahuo doulai kankan, zhang de hen shuaiqi, tai piaoliang le, hen jingshen, tai bangle!*)

Conversely, the documentaries present such 'exotic' foreign spouses as coming from privileged backgrounds, and hence as initially being unused to the physical hardships, and lack of modern conveniences associated with life in rural China. Among the sample group of nine couples involved in a rural Chinese–foreign marriage, the foreign spouses are portrayed as coming from affluent families, and having good occupations, and a high social status in their own countries of origin. The four foreign men comprise a lawyer, an engineer, an English-language teacher, and a university graduate, whereas their Chinese wives may be a teacher, a bus ticket seller, a grocery store assistant or an agricultural worker. The five foreign women comprise a 'white-collar' worker, a journalist, a nurse, a music teacher and an English-language teacher, whereas their Chinese spouses are a company manager, a researcher, a freelance worker, a security guard and an agricultural worker. In short, the foreign marrying partners, especially men, are presented as being socially and economically superior to their rural Chinese spouses ('Mima qingshu' 2008; 'Yangxifu de Chengshimeng' 2008; 'Cunli de Meiguo xifu' 2009).

In the CCTV documentary 'American Wife in Our Village', Yang Jingying and his American wife Haili arrive in Yang's native village in Shanxi Province exhausted after the 36-hour journey from the USA. Haili reportedly threw herself onto a bed, thinking it would be soft and comfortable. However, she experienced a rude shock as the bed was a wooden board without a mattress (*muban chuang*), which meant that she was unable to feel comfortable, and fall asleep, despite her exhaustion.

Likewise, an 18-minute documentary called 'A Foreign Wife's Urban Dream' (*Yang xifu de chengshimeng*), as part of the series *True Stories* on Shanghai Dragon TV in 2008, tells of the hardships experienced by Nu Nei, a woman from an affluent family in urban Armenia, when she arrives at the rural hometown of her Chinese husband, Deng Zhonggang ('Yang xifu de chengshi meng' 2008). As she tells the interviewing reporter: 'I felt extremely uncomfortable when I first arrived [at Deng's home]. It was dark, filthy and dirty and they were burning grass' (*jinjia yihou, heihei de, nongcun bu ganjing, shaocao, zangzang de, wo kan le yihou xinli feichang bushufu, feichang bushufu*). 'You have no idea how I felt then. I [looked and thought] this family has nothing, it's dreadful' (*renhe ren dou buzhidao wo nage shihou shi shenme ganshou, zhege jia shenme dou meiyou, name buhao*).

In a somewhat different vein, a 19-minute documentary called 'Coded Love Letter (*Mima qingshu*), also as part of the series *True Stories* on Shanghai Dragon TV in 2008, focuses on the difficulties associated with such marriages because of the use of different languages ('Mima qingshu' 2008). The documentary tells the story of the marriage between Fang Qin, a rural migrant woman and a British engineer named John. The couple met in a grocery store in Wukang, a small town in Zhejiang Province, where John was working on a company project. Fang worked in the grocery store and often helped John, who could not speak Chinese with his purchases. The couple married in 2008 and they now live in Wukang.

John reportedly wrote a letter to Fang Qin to express his interest in starting a relationship with her by using Google translation software. However, his letter shocked Fang as the translation was incorrect and confusing. In the letter, he wrote: 'Hi, my name is John', which the translation software translated into Chinese as 'Hi, I am a prostitute client (*piaoke*), using the term 'john' as a synonym for prostitute client rather than as a proper name. The documentary used this letter both as a humorous starting point for the documentary and as its title.

While the emphasis of such documentaries on the exotic nature of foreign spouses and the difficulties they face in living and communicating with their Chinese spouses is clearly intended to entertain watching audiences, it also reverses the conventional positioning of Chinese–foreign and rural–urban hierarchies. On the one hand, such frames reveal an unequally distributed power relation between rural Chinese–foreign couples. Rural Chinese partners apparently possess the dominant resources in their home territory whereas their foreign partners as 'strangers' are marginalized and are associated with cultural inconveniences, anxieties and insecurities. On the other hand, by showing that the foreign spouses come from more privileged backgrounds than their rural Chinese partners, the documentaries imply by default that the rural Chinese spouses of foreign nationals must have high forms of human and social capital because otherwise foreign nationals would not fall in love with them and be willing to 'marry down'. The documentaries imply that rural Chinese citizens who marry foreigners have professional intelligence in communicating with the 'external world' – they are attractive, capable and 'open' intellectually and sexually as demonstrated by the nature of their relationships. Hence they are representatives of a newly emerging modern (rural) Chinese masculinity and femininity.

The attractiveness of the rural Chinese spouses in question is underscored in the documentaries by the fact that their foreign spouses are willing to stay with them and work together to overcome hardship. In 'A Foreign Wife's Urban Dream',

Nu Nei works hard with her husband to overcome his family's poverty and the couple eventually prosper after opening a small battery farm for chickens. From that time on, Nu Nei says she began to enjoy living in China. The documentary then shows scenes of Nu Nei declaring her happiness at her thirty-fifth birthday celebration surrounded by well-wishers. After narrating the story of how the couple subsequently moved from the countryside with their two daughters to a small town to run a café business, the episode ends with Nu Nei saying: 'I am a truly lucky woman. I have a good husband and two good children. This is a gift to me from God' (*Wo zhenshi yige feichang xingfu de nüren, wo you yige hao laogong, you liang'ge feichanghao de haizi, wo zhidao zhe keneng jiushi Laotian gei wo de*).

A 30-minute documentary called 'Foreign Son-in-law Comes to Our Village' (*Cunli laile ge Yangnüxu*), which aired as part of *Legendary Stories* on Jiangxi TV in 2007, similarly tells the story of how an American man Alan is willing to overcome multiple complications to marry a rural Chinese woman called Chen Yan ('Cunli laile ge yangnüxu' 2007). The couple fell in love and married in 2003 after they met in the street by chance in 2001. When they met, Chen, a former agricultural worker who had migrated for work to Chengdu City, had only a middle-school education, and was an unmarried mother with a four-year-old son, whereas Alan was studying Chinese at Sichuan University. They now live in Chen Yan's hometown, Zhenwu village in Sichuan Province, along with Chen's son and the parents of her son's father. Speaking to the interviewing reporter in Chinese, Alan says he was not afraid of moving to a small Chinese village and taking on the responsibility of looking after a child, and the child's extended family. In his words: 'I am not scared of being poor and having no money, that's the way it is. It isn't a big problem because our situation will improve' (*Wo bupa ku rizi, wo bupa meiyou qian de shihou... yijing na yangzi le... yueguo yuehao, meiyou shenme da wenti*). The documentary suggests that Alan's willingness to overcome hardship to secure his marriage is demonstrated by the fact that the child now loves him, and calls him 'Dad'.

Another documentary entitled 'Story of a Foreign-Son-in-Law's Marriage Proposal' (*Yangnüxu qiuhunji*), which aired as a part of *Stories* on CCTV-10 in 2010, tells the story of how an Australian lawyer named 'Rui En' married Tian Weili, a female rural migrant worker in Zhuhai, after overcoming the suspicions of her family (Yangnüxu qiuhunji 2010). Tian met her Australian husband, who did not speak Chinese at the time, when he was travelling as a tourist in China, and she was working as a bus ticket seller in Zhuhai. The couple communicated through the Internet after Rui En returned to Australia, and eventually married after he made three trips to China to see her. Tian apparently refused his first marriage proposal because her parents doubted his marital motivations, and his claim to be a lawyer. Rui En subsequently paid 170,000 yuan (US$21,250) for private investigators to examine his background and prove to Tian's parents that he was an unmarried lawyer with genuine feelings for their daughter. Tian's mother is shown saying to the interviewing reporter that his actions won their trust. In her words: '[Rui En] has a great personality and a good heart, he is a good person!' (*wo kan zhege ren xing'ge tebie hao, xin ye tebie hao, ta shige haoxin ren*).

154 *Documenting Chinese–foreign marriage*

These narratives of the foreign spouse who is willing to overcome difficulties to be with the rural Chinese person they love, even though they have in effect 'married down', stands in marked contrast to print media constructions of hypergamous Chinese female citizens who marry a foreigner and move overseas. Chinese women who marry foreign nationals and live in rural areas overseas typically are presented as experiencing isolation, hardship and tragedy, as the dreams associated with their goal of 'marrying up' are always dashed (Liu Xiaoxiao 2005; Ni Yan and Xu Xiuyou 2006; Zhang Guannian 2007; 'Jiadao Riben' 2007). In contrast, 'marrying up' is presented as a consequence rather than the motivation of rural Chinese citizens in Chinese–foreign marriage in the sample group of documentaries, with 'love' rather than hypergamy being presented as the motivating factor for such marriages.

The source of love in such marriages is presented as being tied up with the Chinese virtues of self-sacrifice, honesty and filial piety, which are viewed as being undermined by rapid urbanization. In the documentaries discussed above, rural Chinese people who marry foreign nationals are presented as being 'modern' yet embodying those traditional values. Nu Nei falls in love with Deng Zhonggang because he displays concern for her, and is willing to endure hardship for her. When they first began to see each other, Deng waited in freezing weather for her to arrive for a friend's party on a long overdue bus rather than assuming that she was not coming and/or leaving her to find her own way to the gathering. Chen Yan wins Alan's love because she is honest with him about her background and circumstances, and she is a good mother and displays filial piety to her son's extended family. The Australian lawyer Rui En falls in love with Tian Weili because she helps him when she first meets him as a tourist in China. Shortly after their first meeting, she gave him money out of her own limited wages to buy an expensive train ticket when he was unable to access cash.

These narratives, by highlighting the purity of love and the positively endorsed virtues of human nature, act as exemplars to encourage society to embrace the narratives' proclaimed moral principles and social practices. Simultaneously, such narratives are constructed partly in response to the 'false, bad and evil' phenomenon, or the previously discussed emerging social problems that perhaps are associated with 'China's rapid social changes and mores', such as hypergamy, deception, domestic violence and extramarital affairs (Guo Yingjie 2010: 65).

In summary, documentaries about rural Chinese–foreign marriages produced in the PRC present a new pattern of social mobility wherein an increasing number of foreign nationals are marrying rural Chinese citizens and living in villages, small towns and less developed cities in the PRC, as opposed to the cosmopolitan cities of Beijing, Shanghai and Shenzhen. In doing so, the documentaries suggest that Chinese–foreign marriage is no longer a practice associated solely with urbanites and celebrities or privileged sectors of Chinese society. Instead, members of the large underclass of rural Chinese citizens are now entering into Chinese–foreign marriages. This implies that rather than being bounded by the once common feudal practice of arranged marriages or mercenary marriages of the past, contemporary rural Chinese citizens are enjoying liberated marriages that are based on free spousal choice, individualism and romance. This also shows that rural Chinese citizens are increasingly embracing cosmopolitanism and rural China is gradually becoming more 'urban' and modern in the process of constructing the 'the new socialist countryside' in the reform-era.

Conclusion

Documentaries about Chinese–foreign marriage in the PRC have emerged as part of the new documentary movement. Such documentaries claim to focus on the lives of ordinary people in extraordinary situations, and thus to provide insights into both the proclaimed beauty of human nature and the political, economic and social transformations that are taking place in contemporary China. On the one hand, they give a voice to people in Chinese–foreign marriages by creating opportunities for them to comment on, and share information about their personal lives with television audiences. On the other hand, many such documentaries are not as removed from broader political agendas as their focus on the lives of 'ordinary' individuals might suggest. The documentaries' presentation of the changing dynamics of Chinese–foreign marriages, especially the increased incidence of cross-Strait marriages and rural Chinese–foreign marriages, highlight the relationship between new types of marriages and China's economic and social transformations and changing political policies.

8 Television talk shows and Chinese–foreign marriage

This chapter examines television talk shows produced in the PRC, involving both 'ordinary' and celebrity Chinese–foreign marriages. It explores in four stages the ways in which personal stories and intimate information about Chinese–foreign marriages are narrated and transformed into public entertainment. The first section introduces the development of the genre of television talk shows in the PRC and provides an outline of the sample talk shows used in the study. The second section examines the content of television talk shows that involve couples in a Chinese–foreign marriage as guests, showing how some foreign spouses are Sinicized as 'Chinese'. Conversely, the third section shows how foreign spouses are also often portrayed as 'foreign-country bumpkins' and objects of humour. The fourth section examines how marital conflicts in intercultural marriages are dramatized and made 'fun' of in television talk shows. I conclude that these televisual framings of foreign spouses, which involve discussions of their marital/family relations and perceived degree of familiarity with aspects of Chinese culture, serve three purposes. They provide a framework for audiences to affirm the assumed superiority of Chinese culture, they affirm common-sensical understandings of the nature of intimate relationships, and they highlight the increasingly more open attitude of many Chinese people towards the public discussion of love, marriage and sex.

Television talk shows in the PRC

Television talk shows are a popular, often criticized, hybrid, an adaptable media format. The origins of the television talk show are usually attributed to the development of interactive radio in the United States in the 1930s (Priest 1995: 11; Ilie 2006: 489). Although critics maintain that television talk shows have replaced 'objective journalism' with a form of journalism 'that is based on subjective points of view combined with entertainment' (Penz 1996: 1–2), the genre is popular with many audiences partly because it combines entertainment with 'expert' and 'lay' commentary on matters ranging from 'the sensational and bizarre to the conventional and advisory to politics and world affairs' (Munson 1993: 3). A typical talk show is organized around a host, who encourages diverse people to debate, narrate, confess and supply testimony, on particular subjects (Ilie 2006: 489–94).

The 'western' television talk show format was adopted in China and adapted into a localized form during the early 1990s (Guo Minxiu and Peng Hongping 2008: 86). In January 1993, the *Shanghai Dongfang Dianshitai* (Shanghai Oriental Television) broadcast the first such talk show in the PRC called *Dongfang Zhiboshi*[1] (hereafter Oriental Live Studio) (Lu Xin 2009: 64; Zuo Hanying 2009). *Oriental Live Studio* is broadcast on prime-time television every evening from 7 p.m. to 7.30 p.m., competing with *Xinwen Lianbo* (China Central News Daily) on CCTV-1. It is a live TV programme that invites audiences to the studio to discuss with the host and guest speakers the 'hot' social topics in the news (Yi Wen 2004: 39). The initial popularity of *Oriental Live Studio* with television audiences meant that the show format was soon copied by other provincial and municipal television broadcasting stations, for example, stations in Heilongjiang, Guangdong and Shandong (Yi Wen 2004: 39). However, as all of these local television stations did not have satellite broadcasts in 1993, the initial audiences for talk shows were limited (Yi Wen 2004: 39; Lu Xin 2009: 64).

Talk show programmes started to gain popularity in the PRC following the broadcast of a programme called *Shihua Shishuo* (hereafter *Tell It Like It Is*) in March 1996 on CCTV-1, China's major state-owned national television channel. The programme was apparently inspired by *The Oprah Winfrey Show* in the USA (Luo Yunjuan 2009: 294; 'Zhongguo Tuokou xiu' 2003; Zhang Kexuan 2004). According to the programme summary, *Tell It Like It Is* turns on group conversation, creating a light atmosphere for the host, the guest speakers, and the studio audiences, to discuss topical social issues and individual life-experiences, thereby encouraging the expression of different opinions and increasing communication and understanding among the participants ('Shihua shishuo' 2011). The programme was broadcast every Sunday night on CCTV-1 from 1996 to 2009 between 9.15 p.m. and 10.00 p.m. It was cancelled after running for over 13 years in September 2009, with the show's declining ratings being blamed on the departure of its original male host, Cui Yongyuan in 2002 (Martinsen 2009; 'Shoushilü' 2009). However, for many years, *Tell It Like It Is* was ranked one of the most popular programmes on Chinese television because of its fresh format, involving a humorous hosting style, and proclaimed focus on 'real people, authentic lives, and truthful revelations' and thus the lives of 'ordinary, grassroots people' as opposed to those of 'elites' (Zhang Yingjin 2010: 121; Yi Wen 2004: 40).

The evident popularity of *Tell It Like It Is* encouraged the proliferation of talk show programmes across the PRC, with both central and local television stations in different cities and provinces producing their own shows ('Zhongguo Tuokouxiu' 2003; Zhang Kexuan 2004; Yi Wen 2004: 40). These copied and modified versions of *Tell It Like It Is* similarly focused on the discussion of social issues. Some notable examples of other popular talk shows in the PRC are: *Wenhua Shidian* (Cultural View), which aired on CCTV-3 in 1996 and was broadcast every Wednesday; *Youhua Dajiashuo* (Let Us Talk), which aired on Shanghai TV in 1998, and was broadcast every Sunday; and the Saturday programme of *Yingshi Tongqisheng* (Movie Express), which aired on CCTV-8 in 1999 (Yi Wen 2004: 40).

The flourishing market for talk shows in the PRC subsequently led to an increased production of talk shows which centred on celebrity and entertainment and these shows gradually came to occupy a dominant position among other types of shows on numerous television channels (Yi Yuhan 2009: 31). Fierce competition for audiences and advertising revenue encouraged China's television stations to shift from a previous focus on education and the propagandization of state policies and ideologies towards entertainment and celebrity formats, ultimately blurring the boundaries between entertainment and non-entertainment programmes. Celebrity-style entertainment programmes, including a wide range of talk shows, have since become a common feature of television programming in the PRC, fuelled in part by the popularity of Taiwanese entertainment and talk shows among China's youth (Bai Ruoyun 2005: 8; Chen Lei 2011: 164; Yi Yuhan 2009: 31).

In the late 1990s and early 2000s, a number of television talk shows about love and marriage were broadcast in the PRC, the majority of these shows were entertaining in nature. In July 1998, Hunan TV produced *Meigui Zhi Yue* (hereafter Red Rose Date), a talk show programme modelled on the Taiwanese talk show *Feichang Nan'nü* (Extraordinary Men and Women). *Red Rose Date* invited 'ordinary' men and women to come into the television studio and air their opinions about love, marriage and family. *Red Rose Date* is the earliest example of a talk show on love and marriage on PRC television. The popularity of the show with television audiences generated a 'cloning effect' whereby approximately 20 similar talk shows on love and marriage were produced by different local television stations. These shows included *Yuanfen Tiankong* (A Match Made in Heaven) on Chongqing TV, *Haonan Haonü* (Good Men, Good Women) on Shaanxi TV and *Shui Rang Ni Xindong* (Who Moves Your Heart) on Henan TV (Yi Wen 2004: 40). As these talk shows remain situated in the indigenous Chinese context and their guest speakers, audiences and other participants were predominantly Chinese nationals, they focused on love and marriage among Chinese couples rather than touching on the subject of intercultural love and marriage.

In December 1999, Channel One of Beijing television station produced an international talk show programme called *Guoji Shuangxingxian* (hereafter Common Ground), one of the earliest talk shows on television in the PRC to invite foreign nationals to join in a televised public discussion with Chinese people (Yi Wen 2004: 40). *Common Ground* invites both Chinese and foreign guest speakers and audiences to the studio and all participants are provided with simultaneous interpretation equipment (Chinese–English, English–Chinese) throughout the show. According to the programme introduction, *Common Ground* acts as a cultural link between China and the world, 'the programme focuses on the common topics that interest people all around the world and devotes itself to discussing the cultural differences between the East and the West' ('Common Ground' 2011).

However, *Common Ground* did not address the topic of Chinese–foreign marriage until the 2000s, a period when fierce competition among television stations had encouraged more diverse content in talk shows. In 2000, there were more than 80 talk shows in the PRC. That number rose to 179 talk shows in 2001 and there are currently more than 200 television talk shows on air in the PRC (Lu

Xin 2009: 64; Yi Wen 2004: 40). According to a report by CSM Media Research, an organization that specializes in TV and radio audience research ('About CSM' 2011), within only the 100 days from 1 January to 10 April in 2009, 190 talk shows had broadcast over 5,400 hours from 6 p.m. to 12 a.m. across 153 cities in China. These figures highlight the popularity of talk show formats and suggest strong competition among producers of the genre (Zuo Hanying 2009). This competition has encouraged different content and ways of interacting with audiences, for example, including 'real life exposés' by 'real people', adding competitions, quizzes, games and performance aspects to the shows and the use of telephone and Internet hotlines to facilitate audience interaction (Li Bing 2002: 72; Yi Wen 2004: 40). It has also led to criticisms of the genre for being sensationalist, repetitive and catering to low-brow tastes, for example, by focusing on extramarital affairs and incest (Chen Lei 2011: 164; Su Hong 2011: 80; Sun Yuhao 2011: 97; Zeng Wanyu 2011: 27).

The subject of Chinese–foreign marriage began to feature as a component of talk shows in the PRC in the late 2000s. Although there are no television talk shows in the PRC that are solely about intercultural marriage, a number of talk shows devote episodes or segments of the show to discussions of Chinese–foreign marriage. In such programmes, the talk show host(s) usually invite celebrities and 'ordinary' people who are involved in a Chinese–foreign marriage, to talk about their experience of love and marriage with the studio audience.

The author collected 20 episodes of television talk shows produced in the PRC that deal with the subject of Chinese–foreign marriage. Of these, 10 episodes focus on 'ordinary' Chinese–foreign marriages, the other ten episodes focus on celebrity Chinese–foreign marriages (see Appendix 3). Each of the selected episodes feature the marriage of a different Chinese–foreign couple, although sometimes the same couples, especially when the couple are celebrities, are invited to speak on different talk show programmes. All of these samples focus on marriages between citizens of the PRC and foreign nationals. The author was unable to find any examples of talk shows centred on marriages between mainland Chinese citizens with citizens from Hong Kong, Macau, Taiwan or overseas Chinese. This is presumably because Chinese–foreign marriages that involve a foreign rather than the Chinese partner generate more topics for discussing and 'showing' the nature of love and marriage, because of differences in nationalities, ethnicities, cultures and languages.

The ten episodes of television talk shows produced in the PRC that focus on 'ordinary' Chinese–foreign marriages were shown on the following programmes and channels. *Common Ground* on Beijing TV-1 devoted three episodes to the subject of non-celebrity Chinese–foreign marriage. *Common Ground* is an international talk show that started in 1999. It is broadcast between 1.05 p.m. and 1.55 p.m. every Sunday; its target audiences are people with good educational background and with average or higher levels of income. Two episodes of a talk show series called *Lu Yu You Yue* (A Date with [host] Lu Yu) were devoted to the subject of non-celebrity Chinese–foreign marriages. The programme started on the Hong Kong-based Phoenix TV in 1998 and transferred to Hunan TV in 2008 and then to Anhui TV in 2010. *A Date with Lu Yu* is broadcast between 10.05 a.m. and

10.55 a.m. from Monday to Friday and features people with unique experiences and stories.

Jiating Yanboshi (hereafter Family Television Studio) on the Shanghai Oriental TV Entertainment Channel devoted two episodes to the subject of non-celebrity Chinese–foreign marriage. Starting in 2002, *Family Television Studio* is a celebrity talk show that invites celebrities and their family members, and sometimes 'ordinary' guest speakers, on to the show to share their personal stories with audiences. It is broadcast between 7.20 p.m. and 8.20 p.m. every Friday night with the operating slogan of: 'revealing true feelings from daily life, celebrities are ordinary people too' (*Pingfan zhizhong jian zhenqing, mingxing ye shi lao baixing*).

Yue Ce Yue Kaixin (hereafter More Talk Makes for Happiness) on Hunan TV devoted one episode to the subject of non-celebrity Chinese–foreign marriage. *More Talk Makes for Happiness* is an entertainment talk show that started in 2002 and was repackaged in 2006. It is broadcast between 8.50 p.m. and 10 p.m. every Saturday evening. *Xiang Yue* (hereafter A Date with the Countryside) on CCTV-7 devoted one episode to the subject of non-celebrity Chinese–foreign marriage. *A Date with the Countryside* started in 2003 and is broadcast every Saturday evening between 9.17 p.m. and 10.07 p.m. It is filmed outdoors and features stories from the Chinese countryside. *Xingfu Wandianming* (hereafter Happy Evening Roll Call) on Jiangsu TV also devoted one episode to the subject of non-celebrity Chinese–foreign marriage. *Happy Evening Roll Call* is a talk show focused on fashion and targeting youth audiences that started in 2010. It is broadcast between 10.50 p.m. and 12 a.m. from Monday to Thursday and between 11.05 p.m. and 12.15 a.m. on Friday evening.

The ten episodes of television talk shows produced in the PRC that focus on non-celebrity Chinese–foreign marriages involved 17 Chinese–foreign couples, the majority of whom had married in the 2000s. Nine of those marriages were between foreign men and Chinese women and eight of those marriages were between foreign women and Chinese men. The foreign spouses in Chinese–foreign marriages came from various countries, including Argentina, Armenia, France, Germany, Russia, South Korea, Switzerland, the UK and Ukraine. The Chinese spouses in Chinese–foreign marriages came from various cities and provinces across the PRC, including the cities of Beijing and Shanghai and the provinces of Henan, Hunan, Shaanxi and Zhejiang. The occupational backgrounds of male foreign spouses included entrepreneurs, language teachers, an engineer and a self-employed person and their Chinese wives were overseas students, an actor, a university teacher, a manager assistant, a self-employed person and a rural migrant worker. The occupational backgrounds of the female foreign spouses included overseas students, a model, a designer and a nurse and their Chinese husbands were entrepreneurs, a politician, a TV director, a radio host and a farmer. The majority of these married couples live in the PRC, as would be expected given that they feature on television talk shows produced in the PRC.

The ten episodes of television talk shows produced in the PRC that focus on celebrity Chinese–foreign marriages were shown on the following programmes and channels. *Feichang Fuqi* (hereafter Extraordinary Husband and Wife) on Beijing

TV-3 devoted six episodes to the subject of celebrity Chinese–foreign marriage. Renamed in 2009, *Extraordinary Husband and Wife* was first broadcast in 2002 under the title of *Fuqi Juchang* (Husband and Wife Theatre). It is a talk show that features conversation between the host and celebrity couples on the topics of love, marriage and family and is broadcast between 8 p.m. and 8.45 p.m. on Thursday evenings. *A Date with Lu Yu* and *Feichang Jing Juli* (hereafter Talking With Li Jing) devoted two episodes respectively to the subject of celebrity Chinese–foreign marriage. Starting on Anhui TV in 2009, *Talking With Li Jing* is a celebrity entertainment talk show which is broadcast from 11 p.m. to 11.40 p.m. every evening.

These ten episodes involved ten couples, the majority of whom married in the 2000s and live in the PRC. One marriage was between a foreign woman and a Chinese man – a female celebrity from Germany and a Beijing taxi driver. The remaining nine marriages were between foreign men and Chinese women. Of these nine marriages, one was a marriage between a foreign male celebrity and a Chinese female celebrity – both are world champion chess players. Two were marriages between foreign male celebrities and ordinary Chinese women (an actor and a blue-collar worker). The remaining six marriages were between foreign men without celebrity status (two entrepreneurs, an editor, a musician, a referee and an athlete) and six Chinese female celebrities (four entertainment celebrities and two sports celebrities). The countries of origin of the foreign spouses include: Australia, Germany, Russia, Switzerland, Ukraine, the USA and Qatar. The places of origin of Chinese spouses include the cities of Beijing and Nanjing and the provinces of Guizhou, Hebei, Hubei, Jilin, Sichuan, Yunnan and Zhejiang.

Taken as a whole, the majority of television talk shows in the PRC on the subject of Chinese–foreign marriage are produced by provincial or municipal television stations. Many of the shows are shown in the evening, and are approximately 40 minutes in length. Some shows invite individual couples whereas other shows have several Chinese–foreign couples as guests in an individual episode. All of the 20 television talk shows under discussion are based on the provision of entertainment, and are characterized by their use of celebrity or previously unknown hosts who are either known or have become known for their unique style of television hosting. All of the 20 television talk shows present intercultural marriage in a positive light, typically by narrating anecdotal stories and personal experiences that generate discussions of different cultures in Chinese–foreign marriages.

Regardless of the specific topics that are discussed, the majority of these shows focus on the foreign rather than the Chinese spouse. Hence the next section takes a closer look at how foreign partners in Chinese–foreign marriages are presented in television talk shows produced in the PRC, with a focus on how foreign partners are portrayed as becoming or 'almost Chinese'.

Foreign Chinese

Television talk shows about Chinese–foreign marriage that are produced in the PRC often Sinicize the foreign spouses by presenting them as 'almost Chinese' or 'foreign Chinese'. Foreign spouses on such shows are called by Chinese names

162   Television talk shows

and distinguished by their capacity to demonstrate their 'Chinese-ness' by showing near-native or native linguistic competence in *Putonghua*, i.e., Mandarin, the official standard language of the PRC. Some foreign spouses further display their mastery of Chinese language and culture by speaking in classical Chinese and in local dialects.

An episode of *Extraordinary Husband and Wife* that aired on Beijing TV-3 in February 2010 illustrates how foreign spouses are Sinicized in television talk shows by (self-)presenting their 'Chinese' talents. The episode entitled 'Foreign Bride and Local Groom' is about a German woman, Esther Haubensack (Hao Lianlu) and her Chinese husband, Wang Hongye. Wang, a Beijing taxi driver, met Haubensack when she was studying Chinese language at Beijing University. The couple who married in 1995, have a son and live in Beijing ('Wailai de xifu, bendi de lang: Hao Lianlu, Wang Hongye' 2010).

The host of *Extraordinary Husband and Wife* presents Haubensack as an extraordinary 'foreign Chinese', rather than an ordinary foreign resident in China, with reference to 'Hao Lianlu's' growing celebrity as a foreign cross-talk[2] performer and sitcom actor in the PRC. After answering some basic questions about her background, Haubensack tells the host and audience about how she met Wang and how he became her second, informal, Chinese teacher. She further explains how she learnt Chinese [and performance] from Ding Guangquan, a renowned, professional cross-talk artist. The programme then shows a comedy sketch called *Yangqiang Yangdiao* (Speaking Chinese with Foreign Accents), performed by Haubensack and Ding for the prestigious Chinese New Year Spring Festival Gala on Beijing TV in 1997, which is accompanied by audience applause. The sketch demonstrates Haubensack's comic talents and fluency in Mandarin. The programme later shows a segment from the television drama series *Wailai Xifu Bendilang* (Local men and Foreign Brides), which aired on Guangdong TV (dir. Lu Xiaoguang, Wang Gang, Liu Weiping and Yang Jianian 2000). In that segment, Haubensack acts as the American wife of a Guangzhou man and speaks standard Cantonese. The show thus highlights Haubensack's skills in mastering the two main Chinese languages and her proficiency in interpreting Chinese art and culture.

Another episode of *Extraordinary Husband and Wife* that aired on Beijing TV-3 in October 2010 similarly illustrates how foreign spouses are Sinicized in television talk shows by (self-)presenting their 'Chinese' talents. The guests of an episode entitled 'Ukrainian Man and His Chinese Love' are a Ukrainian actor called Braby Kon (known as Zhao Bo in Chinese) and his wife, Zhang Wenting, a Chinese actress ('Wukelan xiaohuo de Zhongguo qingyuan: Zhang Wenting he Bo Biken' 2010). Kon is the only foreign apprentice of Zhao Benshan, a famous comedy and sitcom actor in the PRC. The couple met each other when they were making a film in Hong Kong in 1998. They married in 2009, and live in Beijing.

After stating that their initial performances as a husband and wife duo met with audience derision, Kon explains that they have worked hard to please Chinese audiences by conveying cultural competence. Most notably, Kon has learnt to perform acts that are popular with Chinese audiences, but that are not often performed by contemporary entertainers, whether Chinese or 'foreign'. As Kon tells the host of the talk show, he can sing revolutionary songs from Shandong Province such as *Balujun La Dashuan* (The Eighth Route Army Pulls the [Rifle] Bolt), a claim that generates immediate applause from the live studio audience. Kon then proceeds to sing the song along with the talk show host and the applauding audience. Kon also performs, to the obvious delight of the live audience, comedy sketches based on characters from a classic Chinese novel, the *Water Margin*, a 'dwarf walk' (*zou aizi*), which is a skill required for Beijing Opera performance. He further performs a 'Song-and Dance Duet' (*Er'ren zhuan*), a popular folk art in northeast China, with his wife and plays an ethnic flute-like instrument (a *hulusi*) from Yunnan Province.

Although the preceding examples deal with foreign spouses who have become minor celebrities in the PRC, non-celebrity foreign spouses also perform their 'Chinese-ness' in television talk shows by talking about their love of things 'Chinese'. A case in point is an episode of *Family Television Studio* that aired on Shanghai Oriental TV in November 2009 entitled 'The Life of a German Bride in China' ('Deguo yangxifu de Zhongguo shenghuo' 2009). The German woman known as 'Sa Tangya' in Chinese (hereafter Tangya) is a model who met a Chinese actor called Sa Gangyun by chance in a beauty salon in Shanghai. The couple married in 2008, and live in Shanghai with their twin children, a boy and a girl.

As Tangya tells the talk show host and viewers, she has lived in China for more than 12 years, and had dreamt of coming to China ever since she was a child in Germany. That dream was enhanced by her admiration of the Chinese film *Red Sorghum* (dir. Zhang Yimou 1987), the music of Deng Lijun (1953–1995), a Taiwanese Mando-pop singer and the kung-fu comedy films of Jacky Chan. She learnt the lyrics of Deng Lijun's songs and looked for the meaning of the words in a Chinese dictionary, thereby learning Chinese by studying song lyrics. Tangya further explains to the audience how her mother thought she was suffering psychological problems and took her to see a counsellor because as a 14-year-old she used chopsticks, not knives and forks and collected Chinese porcelain and curios.

Upon hearing this, the talk show host says to Tangya: 'You look like a foreigner, but you have a Chinese heart' (*ren suiran zhangde shi waiguoren, danshi xin que shi yike Zhongguoren de xin*). Tangya affirms this statement by saying yes in Chinese and vigorously nodding her head, adding that she has lots of Chinese friends in Germany. The talk show host replies to this with audience applause that Tangya is a *cao jidan*, the egg of a free-range chicken on the Chinese grasslands – white on the outside but very yellow in the middle, meaning that Tangya has white skin but she thinks and feels like a Chinese person inside.

Tangya's claim to have been 'Chinese' since her childhood is enhanced by her professed claim to have always wanted to meet and marry a Chinese man. Asked by the programme's host whether she had ever thought of marrying a Chinese man, Tangya laughingly replies to audience applause: 'Absolutely, I've wanted to find a Chinese husband [since I was 14-years-old] (*dangran xiang, wo jiushi yao zhao yige Zhongguo laogong*). Tangya explains that she was attracted to Chinese men because her idol at the age of 14 was Guo Fucheng, a Hong Kong singer, dancer and actor. She found him more attractive than German men and therefore decided to come to China to find a man just like him.

An episode of *More Talk Makes for Happiness* called 'Intercultural Marriage' (*kuaguo hunyin*), which aired on Hunan TV in January 2011, offers an example of non-celebrity foreign spouses performing their love of China in television talk shows about Chinese–foreign marriage. In this episode, the British husband of a woman from Shaanxi Province is held up as a 'foreign Lei Feng'. Lei Feng (1940–1962), a soldier of the People's Liberation Army is a national role model, renowned for his selflessness, modesty and love of the Chinese Communist Party and the Chinese people (see Edwards 2010: 26–30). When the host of the talk show asks the British man called 'Da Ming' why he is wearing a Lei Feng T-shirt, Da Ming strikes a resolute pose associated with the image of Lei Feng, and says that he likes Lei Feng because Lei Feng is a good Chinese person (*hao Zhongguoren*). The host then tells the audience that Da Ming was awarded a prize by the Xinjiang Government for his contributions to the social and economic development of the province, thereby implying that he is a foreigner who has adopted and promotes the 'Lei Feng spirit (*Lei Feng jingshen*) by helping the Chinese people and supporting social development in China.

A different example of non-celebrity foreign spouses showing their love of China is provided in an episode of *Common Ground* entitled 'Three Generations of Intercultural Love in One Family' ('Yijia sandai kuaguo qing' 2010). The episode, which aired on Beijing TV-1 on 17 January 2010, invited a Ukrainian woman called 'Lian Na' and her Chinese husband, a TV director called Liu Xuan, to talk about their marriage. Liu met 'Lian Na' when he was working on a television series with her in Ukraine. They married in the early 2000s and now live with their son in Beijing. Their family is presented as unusual because Liu is the grandchild of Li Lisan, a communist leader during the Maoist period, who married a Russian woman known in Chinese as Li Sha, while he was studying Leninism in the former Soviet Union during the 1930s. Li Lisan and Li Sha had a daughter called Li Yingnan who is Liu's mother. Li Sha went to live in China with her husband in 1946 and renounced her Russian citizenship and became a citizen of the PRC following the collapse of Sino-Soviet relations in the 1960s. Li Yingnan, a university professor, remarried at some stage to a Russian professor for reasons that are unspecified and hence Liu Xuan's family is considered unusual because it involves a history of three generations of Chinese–foreign marriage.

A short video about the family history of intercultural marriage shows Li Sha, a 95-year-old woman, telling the interviewing reporter in Chinese and with clear excitement in her voice: 'I have been living in China for 60 years. I love China!' (*Wo lai Zhongguo yijing 60 nian le, Zhongguo, wo yijing aishang le Zhongguo!*). While clearly designed to protect herself and her family from political repercussions with potentially life-threatening consequences, the footage suggests that Li Sha's decision to stay in China and become 'Chinese' was the 'right' decision because she has grown to love China. Moreover, her family is living a good life in China.

Some talk shows also underscore the 'Chinese-ness' of the children of couples in an intercultural marriage with reference to their fluency in Mandarin and local Chinese dialects. For example, in an episode of *Extraordinary Husband and Wife* in April 2009, the eldest son of Shi Ke, a famous Chinese actress from Hubei Province and her German husband Christian Könitzer, demonstrates his ability to speak in a Hubei dialect ('Shi Ke, Ke Lize' 2009). In an episode of *A Date With the Countryside* in October 2009, the twin daughters of Deng Zhonggang, a man from Shandong Province, and his Armenian wife, Nu Nei, speak a dialect from the northeast of Shandong Province known as Wei Hai ('An cun de Yangxifu' 2009). In an episode of *More Talk Makes for Happiness*, the son of Liu Jia from Hunan Province, and her British husband speaks in a dialect associated with Changsha, the capital city of Hunan Province ('Kuaguo hunyin' 2011). Likewise, in an episode of *Extraordinary Husband and Wife*, the son of Beijing taxi driver, Wang Hongye, and German comedian, Esther Haubensack, shows that he is able to speak Cantonese, just like his mother ('Wailai de xifu, bendi de lang: Hao Lianlu, Wang Hongye' 2010). In short, the Chinese-speaking children of Chinese–foreign marriages are presented as symbols of a successful process of Sinification. Regardless of how many languages these children speak, their fluency in Mandarin and local Chinese dialects suggest that they are more 'Chinese' than they are 'foreign', a product of both their Chinese parent and the Chinese-ness of their non-Chinese parent.

In summary, the Chinese-ness of the foreign spouses in Chinese–foreign marriage talk shows is constructed through demonstrations of their Chinese linguistic competence, cultural skills and love of China and through the performances of their children. Many of these selected 'foreign Chinese' have not only migrated to China to live with their spouses and to raise a family in China, but also enjoy some professional success as actors, entertainers, models and academics. In turn, the portrayal of these foreign spouses as 'almost Chinese' suggests that China has the power to 'absorb' and/or 'transform' foreigners and that Sinicization enables foreign spouses to create new lives and careers for themselves and their children.

However, not all foreign spouses are presented as 'virtually Chinese' in television talk shows about Chinese–foreign marriage that are produced in the PRC. Some foreign spouses are presented as 'foreign-country bumpkins'. The foreign-country bumpkin trope provides a different way of entertaining interested audiences.

Foreign spouses as country bumpkins

Television talk shows about Chinese–foreign marriage that are produced in the PRC sometimes frame foreign spouses as 'uncultured' being unfamiliar with Chinese language and customs and thus 'foreign-country bumpkins'. The *Longman Dictionary of Contemporary English* (2003: 358) defines a 'country bumpkin' as 'someone who is considered to be stupid because they are from an area outside towns and cities'. In the context of Chinese–foreign marriage talk shows, foreign spouses are sometimes framed as 'country bumpkins' in the sense that they are portrayed as educated, well-meaning people, who appear 'stupid', and hence

166 *Television talk shows*

comical, because they have limited understanding of the Chinese language and Chinese customs.

Foreign husbands who have difficulties in communicating in the Chinese language are a particular focus of this kind of framing and humour. For example, an episode of *Extraordinary Husband and Wife* that aired in September 2011, entitled 'The Love of Skeet Shooting Zhang Shan and Zhang Desheng (Dexter Barnes)' refers to the marriage between Zhang Shan, a Chinese Olympic champion and Dexter Barnes, an Australian skeet shooting champion ('Ai de feidie: Zhang Shan, Zhang Desheng' 2011). Zhang Shan tells the host and studio audience that Barnes has lived in China for seven years but speaks little Chinese. Moreover, since Zhang is often travelling, her relatives and friends have to help take care of Barnes whose lack of linguistic competence prevents him from doing basic domestic tasks.

To the entertainment of listening audiences, Zhang Shan explains that Barnes sometimes calls her for help on the telephone when she is travelling because he does not know how to turn on the air-conditioner in their home, which was made in China, even though she has explained how the machine functions several times. When the host asks whether this means that Barnes is hot when he wants to be cold and vice versa, Zhang replies that Barnes rings her for instructions and then she calls her Aunt who goes to the house to resolve the problem. To audience laughter and applause, the host responds: 'Oh my, such a waste [of time and energy] to keep a foreigner at home – you need an Auntie as well!' (*Aiya, na jiali mian yang yige laowai ke gou fei de zhege, haide yubei yi er'sao, ni kan*).

Zhang Shan goes on to explain that Barnes' inability to speak Chinese has enhanced her relationships with family and friends. According to Zhang, she is often in touch with relatives and friends when she travels, as they always ask about whether Barnes will eat with them, and what he would like to eat, and when. In response, the host exclaims, again to audience laughter and applause: 'It seems that there is not a foreigner at home, but a deaf and dumb friend who needs special care!' (*zhe ganjue shang bushi jiali you ge waiguoren, shi you ge longya pengyou – haide you ren zhuanmen zhaogu!*) Zhang Shan laughingly replies: 'I think that my friends and I are getting closer because we have this person who doesn't speak Chinese' (*suoyi yinwei you zheme yige butong yuyan de zheme yige ren, keneng rang wo he wo shenbian de henduo pengyou de guanxi haoxiang hai gengjin le*).

An episode of *A Date with Lu Yu*, entitled 'Chinese–British Marriage', which aired on Anhui TV in January 2011 similarly frames 'John' a British engineer and husband of a rural migrant women called Fang Qin, as an object of humour because of his limited knowledge of the Chinese language ('Zhong Ying kuaguo hunyin' 2011). The couple met in a grocery store where Fang Qin worked in Zhejiang Province. They married in 2008, have a son and now live in Zhejiang Province. The host of the talk show, Lu Yu, invites John to tell the audience the number of Chinese words he has learnt and is able to use. John replies to audience laughter that he has learnt around 20 words and can put them in short sentences, such as 'I don't understand' (*tingbudong*). After John pronounces various other words in Chinese with a strong foreign accent, Lu Yu asks John to say his wife's name, which he does correctly but with a predictably thick accent. Lu Yu then asks him to say her name, noting that it is more difficult to pronounce than 'Fang Qin' and that non-native speakers usually pronounce it incorrectly as 'Luyou'. To audience laughter and applause, John proceeds to pronounce Lu Yu's name in exactly the incorrect manner predicted.

Likewise, an episode of *More Talk Makes for Happiness* that aired on Hunan TV in January 2011, entitled 'Intercultural Marriage', interviews two Chinese–British couples, which include a Chinese woman named Liu Jia and her husband 'Simon' ('Kuaguo hunyin' 2010). The couple met and married in the UK where Liu obtained a master's degree. They now live in Hunan Province with their son and a daughter. One of the talk show's hosts tells the audience that Simon had practised how to ask Liu's mother for her consent to the marriage. He had learnt to say in Mandarin: *'Wo keyi he nin nü'er jiehun ma?'* (Would you grant me permission to marry your daughter?). To the evident delight of the audience, Liu Jia proceeds to explain that Simon's request, although clearly articulated, did not achieve its desired effect because her mother speaks a dialect from Hunan Province and has a limited understanding of Mandarin, let alone Mandarin spoken with a foreign accent. As a result, Liu's mother had listened to Simon and then turned to Liu, asking: 'Does he want a cola?' (*ta shi yao kele ba?*). Simon is thus portrayed as an object of humour for 'bungling' his attempt to ask his girlfriend's mother for formal permission to marry her daughter and failing to recognize the linguistic complexity of their family life.

Understandably, these foreign males who do not speak Chinese lack the power base for daily communication when living in their Chinese partners' home territory. However, instead of framing the foreign partners as 'powerless', the media focus on certain (positive) power dynamics between couples in these kinds of marriages. In doing so, the media translate the culturally marginalized circumstances of 'foreign bumpkins' to those of circumstance-changers. That is, rather than presenting foreign males as being dominated by their Chinese partners, their lack of language skills are constructed as an 'insulation from power' (Rosenblatt 2009: 14). Similarly, rather than framing foreign spouses as being isolated from the mainstream culture, they are presented as attention-makers who have the power to enrich the 'flavour' of life thanks to their cultural uniqueness. They are also highlighted as individuals who can alter the potential power relations between their partners, and their partners' friends and social networks.

The second type of 'country bumpkin' in television talk shows about Chinese–foreign marriage are foreign spouses who speak good Chinese, but who are unfamiliar with complicated phrases, idioms and metaphors, that are a part of everyday Chinese culture nonetheless. Talk show hosts typically make comments about a particular marriage and then ask the foreign spouse as an invited guest on the show to demonstrate their understanding of the host's comments by explaining the nature of those comments to the audience, or else by demonstrating their familiarity with the local dialects spoken by their Chinese partners and their partners' families. In turn, audiences are enjoined to laugh at the predictable failure of foreign spouses of both sexes to comprehend the literal meanings of certain turns of speech.

This point can be illustrated with reference to an episode of *Happy Evening Roll Call* on Jiangsu TV that aired in June 2010 entitled 'Can Intercultural Love Bring True Happiness?' ('Yiguolian zhende hui xingfu ma?' 2010). The two hosts of the programme talk to a Chinese woman named Zhang Wenjie from Beijing and her Argentinean husband 'Gao Wei', a couple who married despite experiencing long-distance separation, financial difficulties and parental interference. Describing their love story as astonishing, the male host says to the audience: 'Their love story "draws tears" (*cuiren leixia*) and it "shakes the universe and moves the gods"' (*Jing tiandi, Qi guishen*). The female host asks Gao Wei if he understands what the Chinese references mean, and when he replies in the affirmative, she asks him to explain what they mean in his own words. To the delight of the audience, Gao Wei responds that the reference means that China and Argentina are on opposite sides of the globe, a conclusion which he has derived from watching the female host point to the ceiling when referring to the heavens and pointing to the ground when referring to the underworld. The two hosts proceed to evoke further laughter from the audience by asking what is the relationship between heaven, the gods and the geographical location of China and Argentina, which leaves Gao Wei looking bemused.

In a similar vein, an episode of *Family Television Studio* entitled 'Intercultural Marriage' that aired on Shanghai Oriental TV in April 2010 questions three foreign spouses about their understanding of local Shanghainese idioms ('Kuaguo hunyin' 2010). The three couples invited onto the show are: a Shanghai entrepreneur named Xu Liang, and his Russian wife 'You Liya'; a Chinese white-collar worker named Chen Jieqi, and her German husband 'Wu Keduo'; and a Chinese actor named Sa Gangyun and his German wife 'Tangya'. Holding up a piece of paper with Shanghainese idioms written on it, the host asks if any of the foreign spouses invited onto the show know the meaning of the expression '*Daiyan luojing*', which means 'to attract attention'. To the amusement of viewers, the foreign spouses respond with incorrect answers. For example, Wu Keduo replies mistakenly that '*Daiyan luojing*' means 'fake eyes' (*jia yanjing*) and Tangya responds that it means 'shining eyes' (*yanjing henguang*). The host then asks the foreign spouses if they know the meaning of the Shanghainese idiom '*goupi daozao*', which means 'stingy' and 'calculating', or else refers to a person of low moral character or quality and hence someone who cannot be trusted to deal with matters in a proper or reliable manner. Again to audience laughter and applause, Wu Keduo replies incorrectly that the expression means 'copy-cat' or 'persistent follower' (*genpichong*) and Tangya says it means 'sassy' or 'thick-skinned' (*hou lianpi*).

The third type of 'country bumpkin' in television talk shows about Chinese–foreign marriages are those spouses who display unfamiliarity with aspects of everyday life in China. An episode of *A Date with the Countryside* on CCTV-7 entitled 'A Foreign Bride in Our Village', which aired in October 2009, is about a rural Chinese man called Deng Zhonggang, and his Armenian wife 'Nu Nei' ('An cun de Yangxifu' 2009). Following some preliminary conversation, the host of the show asks Nu Nei whether she used a washing machine to wash laundry when she first came to China. Nu Nei replies that she wanted to do some washing on her second day in China, and looked for a washing machine in the home of her parents-in-law. Eventually she saw a large black pot in the kitchen with a fire underneath, and assumed it must be a cauldron for boiling clothes. She proceeded to wash the clothes in this fashion despite concerned gesturing and talking on the part of her mother-in-law whose local dialect Nu Nei did not understand. The audience burst into laughter when Nu Nei shows how her mother-in-law was yelling to Deng Zhonggang: 'Zhonggang, come and see what your wife is doing! Washing clothes in the cooking pot!' (*Zhonggang qu Kankan ni laopo gande shenme! Zai guoli mian xi yifu! Maya!*).

Other foreign spouses are made figures of fun for their ignorance of basic aspects of everyday life in China, such as food. An episode of *Extraordinary Husband and Wife*, which aired on BTV-3 in February 2009, invited Chinese actress Shen Danping, her German husband 'Wu Wei' (Uwe Kraeuter) and their two daughters on to the show. The host asks the family to answer a question: 'Who is the least clever person in the family?' (*jiali shui zui bu congming?*), with Shen Danping getting the highest vote. Shen responds by saying that even a silly person like herself is cleverer than her non-Chinese literate husband, who compliments people on their cooking skills when they give him a bowl of instant noodles, and does not know how to cook basic and 'fast' Chinese food such as frozen dumplings.

In short, television talk shows about Chinese–foreign marriage that are produced in the PRC at times frame foreign spouses as 'foreign-country bumpkins' who are unfamiliar with basic aspects of everyday life in China, especially those aspects of everyday life that relate to the use of local languages and customs. Talk show hosts typically entertain their audiences by highlighting the 'naïvety' or 'clumsiness' of the foreign spouses in question. The 'country bumpkin' nature of the foreign spouses in Chinese–foreign marriages is framed in a manner that is intended to be amusing rather than offensive – the entertainment-oriented nature of such programmes ensures that their 'ignorance' is portrayed as 'funny', 'cute' and 'endearing', rather than as a source of genuine marital problems. The humour associated with the depiction of foreign spouses as 'country bumpkins' clearly also functions to affirm a sense of cultural superiority for watching Chinese audiences.

Making marital conflict 'fun'

Discussing the nature and resolution of conflict in an intercultural marriage is an important component of television talk shows about Chinese–foreign marriages that are produced in the PRC. Marital conflicts are often dramatized, and made an object of humour to entertain the studio and anticipated television audiences. Such conflicts are discussed in a conversational, or testimonial and confessional manner and typically include disagreements over parenting stemming from cultural differences, quarrels about lifestyle choices and low-level physical altercations.

Conversations about marital conflicts on talk shows about Chinese–foreign marriage serve, perhaps counter-intuitively, to underscore the perceived romantic and intimate nature of such marriages. The intimate nature of intercultural marriage is highlighted with reference to certain 'truisms' about relationships, such as the importance of expressing love on a daily basis, the notion that absence makes the heart grow fonder, and the understanding that harsh words and deeds are often a sign of affection. These tropes are a particular feature of talk shows with celebrity guests. Celebrities are professional performers who are good at disclosing the 'right' private conflict at the 'right' time in the 'right' place. By exposing their marital conflicts and 'washing their dirty linen' in public, they strategically 'advertise' the ultimately loving nature of their foreign spouses and their intercultural marriages to watching audiences.

The importance of saying 'I love you' as an antidote to the banality of daily marital bickering is the focus of an episode of *Talking With Li Jing* entitled 'Shout about Your Love', which aired on Anhui TV in November 2010 ('You ai dasheng shuo' 2010). Ma Yashu, a renowned Chinese actress and her American husband James Hayes, are guests on the show. The host asks the couple if they say 'honeyed words' (*tianyan miyu*) to each other on a regular basis. To the amusement of the audience, Ma Yashu laughingly replies that Hayes says 'I love you' to her every day. Moreover, if they quarrel, and she sulks, and refuses to talk to him, Hayes will not stop saying 'I love you' to her, until she reluctantly starts to talk to him, and eventually says that she loves him too. Ma Yashu's entertaining description of their quarrel and the laughter it produces on the part of the studio audience, suggests that bickering and female sulking are viewed as common facets of married life that are easily resolved by verbal expressions of love, which, in turn, reaffirm the bonds of marital love.

The notion that temporary separation may create problems between a couple yet ultimately also revives the bonds of marital love is highlighted in an episode of *Extraordinary Husband and Wife*, broadcast by Beijing TV-3 in May 2010, entitled 'Cao Cao and Li Zhiyin: We Won't Break Up' ('Cao Cao, Li Zhiyin: Women buneng san' 2010). American actor Jonathan Kos-Read, a well-known actor in China known as Cao Cao and his Chinese wife Li Zhiyin, are guests on the show. Kos-Read tells the host and audience they often quarrel when he is away filming, with Li suspecting him of infidelity and fearing that he no longer loves her. To underscore the unnecessary nature of her fears, Kos-Read explains that he once brought Li and his daughter to live in a rented house in Shanghai while he was filming there, although he was obliged to stay in a hotel with the rest of film production crew. When Li confesses that she still suspected her husband of infidelity, and thought he no longer loved her, the host exclaims: 'What! How could you doubt his love when he took you [and your daughter] to Shanghai [to be near him]?' (*dou jie dao Shanghai le zenme hai bu ai ni le?*). To laughter and applause from the audience as the 'victim' of a jealous wife, Kos-Read leans forward and says in a loud voice: 'See how I am treated! It's so unfair' (*Shibushi! Wo yuan a*!) ('Cao Cao, Li Zhiyin' 2010).

Having revealed her jealous insecurities, Li Zhiyin proceeds to further entertain the studio audience by stating that in reality she often quarrels with Kos-Read when he is at home for extended periods and wishes he was working away. Laughing along with the audience at the seeming contrariness of his wife, Kos-Read asserts that short business trips are a positive thing. Couples who experience short-term separation miss each other, and are reminded of what they like about each other, whereas couples who are together constantly think about each other's negative aspects, just like an 'aged husband and wife' (*laofu laoqi*). Kos-Read then hugs and kisses Li Zhiyin, saying 'our love is completely restored as a result [of occasional separation]' (*nage ganqing dou buman le*) ('Cao Cao, Li Zhiyin' 2010). The fact that this action attracts spontaneous applause from the studio audience suggests that it affirms popular understandings of the nature of intimate relationships such as 'familiarity breeds contempt', and 'absence makes the heart grow fonder'.

Disagreements over different approaches to parenting are the focus of an episode of *Common Ground* entitled 'Travelling With Our Baby', which aired on Beijing TV-1 in July 2010, and features a Chinese woman called Yu Ziru and her Swiss husband 'Fei Bin', who both enjoy travelling ('Daizhe baobao qu lüxing' 2010). The couple talk about their perceived unique way of child-rearing, which involves broadening their young daughter's horizon through travel. The couple took their daughter with them to watch the Beijing Olympic Games when she was only four months old. She went with them to her father's hometown in Switzerland when she was only nine months old. The couple also took their one-year-old daughter with them to see the Meri Snow Mountain in Yunnan Province, the scenic sites of Guilin in the Guangxi Zhuang Autonomous Region, the Great Wall outside Beijing, the Shanghai World Expo and various international sports competitions.

After discussing their experiences of travelling with their daughter, the host asks Yu Ziru and Fei Bin if they ever have had any conflicts over child-rearing, to which the couple reply that they have. They disagree over what to do when their daughter has a fever, Yu Ziru always wants to take her immediately to hospital, whereas Fei Bin believes that too much medicine, and doctors are a bad thing. Fei Bin allows their daughter to play wherever she wants, and to touch whatever she wants, whereas Yu discourages her daughter from touching objects and places that she thinks are unclean. The couple note that they also cannot agree over which language their daughter should learn as her main language, because Yu Ziru's mother tongue is Chinese, Fei Bin's mother tongue is German, and Yu and Fei communicate with each other in English. Another guest on the show, an expert in early child development, tells the audience that children under three years of age should not be taught multiple languages unless they have a special linguistic capacity. To the apparent delight of the audience, the host replies that 'Yu Ziru and Fei Bin will quarrel once again when they hear what you have to say!' (*ni shuo zhege tamenliang you dei chaojia*). The delighted reaction of Yu Ziru and Fei Bin to the host's interjection reflects the understanding that minor disagreements originating from cultural differences are seen as a normal and often (retrospectively) amusing part of married life, the ongoing nature of which can serve to affirm or strengthen bonds of intimacy.

Disagreements over parenting stemming from cultural differences may also strengthen family ties, according to an episode of *Family Television Studio* entitled 'Intercultural Marriage' (*Kuaguo hunyin*), which aired on Shanghai Oriental TV in April 2010. The guests on this episode are a Shanghai-based entrepreneur called

172 *Television talk shows*

Xu Liang and his Russian wife 'You Liya' and the couple's two daughters and Xu Liang's mother. The host of the talk show asks Xu Liang's mother if she has ever had any conflict with You Liya. The mother proceeds to explain to the delight of the studio audience that she has disagreed with her daughter-in-law on numerous occasions. As a Chinese mother and grandmother, she wanted to pick up her grandchildren when they were toddlers if they fell over while learning to walk, but her daughter-in-law wanted the children to learn how to get back on their feet by themselves. She wanted to help her grandchildren to eat by putting the spoon to their mouths for them, but her daughter-in-law wanted the children to feed themselves. She wanted to accompany the grandchildren to school, but her daughter-in-law wanted them to walk to school by themselves. She wanted to help the children tidy up, but her daughter-in-law wanted the children to clean up by themselves ('Kuaguo hunyin' 2010).

The mother-in-law's account of different styles of parenting entertains the studio audience by juxtaposing a 'good Chinese grandmother' and a 'good foreign mother'. The former is stereotyped as someone who wants to 'spoil' her grandchildren by demonstrating love and care and the latter is stereotyped as someone who wants her children to learn to do things for themselves, even if that means unsettling the children. However, the tensions between the Chinese mother and the foreign daughter-in-law are resolved and hence the Chinese ideal of family harmony is restored, when the mother concludes that these conflicts are a thing of the past because the children have grown up and seem more independent and capable than their peers. In the mother's words: 'I have to thank my son for finding me such a great daughter-in-law!' (*Wo shuo wo yao xiexie erzi, zhaodao zheme haode xifu*) ('Kuaguo hunyin' 2010).

Low-level physical altercations between couples in intercultural marriages are also presented as 'fun' in some talk shows about celebrity Chinese–foreign marriages. For example, the famous Chinese actress Shen Danping and her German husband Uwe Kraeuter and their two daughters, Dan Dan and Shan Shan, are guests on an episode of *Extraordinary Husband and Wife* entitled 'Shen Danping and Wu Wei', which aired on Beijing TV-3 in February 2009 ('Shen Danping, Wu Wei' 2009). Shortly after the start of the show, the host asks the family: 'Who is the fiercest person in the family? (*jiali shui zui lihai*), to which they all reply that Shen Danping is.

When asked to explain how fierce Shen Danping is and whether that means she dares to beat her husband, Dan Dan replies that Shen once kicked Kraeuter out of the marital bed. Kraeuter explains to the host and audience that Shen Danping is the person who starts most of the arguments between them and those quarrels usually end with him refusing to talk to her. Shen adds that the time she kicked Kraeuter was because she wanted him to stop being silent, with Kraeuter standing up to show the now laughing audience exactly how the kick was done.

The host then quotes a famous Chinese saying: 'Beating is (a sign of) affection, (and) scolding is (a sign of) love' (*da shi qin, ma shi ai*), which means that harsh words or deeds may express love, and extends the quote by adding that 'kicking when angry may also resolve problems' (*jile yong jiao chuai*). Upon hearing this,

Kraueter smiles and says, to audience laughter and applause, that he agrees with that saying, and therefore loves Shen Danping. The host then proceeds to make Shen laugh by saying it is a pity she did not join the Chinese women's soccer team, because she is such a good kicker. When Shen apologizes for making a fool and public spectacle of herself, the host replies that there is no need for her to be embarrassed because many men of his age (men in their late forties) would be more than happy to be kicked by her.

This shows that low-level physical conflict among married couples, at least when initiated by women, is seen retrospectively as 'cute' and endearing. The narrative of Shen Danping 'kicking' her foreign husband presents a highly gendered conception of 'fierce' Chinese women, while ultimately exposing the fallacy of the stereotype via reference to Shen's physical beauty, and lack of genuine physical strength. In doing so, the narrative effectively projects an idealized view of Chinese–foreign marriage as being characterized by equality (of both nation and gender). While it trivializes genuine domestic violence, it reinforces a popular Chinese conception of minor or 'fake' physical altercations initiated by women as a funny, and a permitted form of interaction between husband and wife, which by virtue of its prohibition outside a romantic context must strengthen the bonds of marital intimacy. The fact that this perceived 'truism' may also be applied to intercultural marriage also allows Chinese–foreign marriages to be placed under the umbrella of 'normal' marital relations.

The stereotype of the 'fierce' Chinese woman demonstrating her love through low-level physical altercations is reiterated in another celebrity episode of *Extraordinary Husband and Wife* called 'Ukrainian Man and His Chinese Love: Zhang Wenting and Bobi Ken (Braby Kon)', which aired on Beijing TV-3 in October 2010 ('Wukelan xiaohuo de Zhongguo qingyuan: Zhang Wenting he Bobi Ken' 2010). The invited guests on the show are actress Zhang Wenting and her Ukrainian husband Braby Kon, who is a comic actor and minor celebrity in China. After introducing how they met and fell in love, the couple's conversation with the talk show host turns in part on the reasons behind their temporary separation and reconciliation prior to their marriage registration.

When asked about the reasons for their temporary separation, Kon keeps the host in suspense by saying that he is often bullied by Zhang Wenting. In response, Zhang says, to audience laughter and applause, that although it is usually men who beat women, she once hit Kon when he was drunk. When the host asks whether it was a serious fight, Zhang replies that she ripped his collar when she grabbed him because he refused to go home. Kon responds that he was drunk because he was drinking with a group of Chinese men who were drinking heavily. The host then teases Zhang and underscores the unusual nature of her behaviour by adding that the girlfriends of other men presumably did not tear their respective boyfriend's clothes.

Following this story, Kon explains that the real reason he had separated from Zhang Wenting for a long period of time was because she 'nagged' him to stop smoking cigarettes, and take care of his health, but he did not want to quit. As a result, Kon had left home and lived for a year with his teacher (Zhao Benshan, a famous Chinese skit and sitcom actor). However, Zhang had continued to help Kon during their separation by providing his details to people wanting to hire comic performers. The couple eventually resumed their relationship after they met at a dinner arranged by their friends.

The audience laughs when Kon says that Zhang Wenting asked him to come back to her first and Zhang replies that her husband is lying as usual because Kon had in fact asked her to come back to him first. The host comments on the altercation:

> If he said it [first], then he should have said 'if I come back, will you still beat me?'. If you said it [first], you should have said 'If you come back, then I won't beat you anymore' (*ta ruguo shuo de hua, ta hui zheme shuo 'wo huilai ni hai da wo me?' Ni yao xian shuo, ni de zheme shuo, 'ni huilai ba, ni huilai wo jiu zai ye bu da ni le!'*).
>
> ('Wukelan xiaohuo de Zhongguo qingyuan: Zhang Wenting he Bobi Ken' 2010)

Zhang replies, with more laughter from the audience, that it would not be possible for her to keep that promise, for example, she will inevitably continue to initiate low-level physical fights.

As the cheerful response of the audience suggests, the televisual strategy of making the 'good Chinese wife' the seeming perpetrator of low-level domestic violence and portraying the foreign spouse as the 'henpecked' husband, is clearly attractive to many viewers. It reinforces the understanding that minor physical altercations initiated by women are a permitted form of interaction between husband and wife, which are amusing in retrospect, and thus strengthen the bonds of marital intimacy. By playing on the adage that 'beating is affection, scolding is love', talk shows about Chinese–foreign marriage reaffirm 'commonsensical' understandings of married life as characterized by the interplay between bickering and intimacy. In instances where celebrities are involved, the exploitation of certain 'truisms' about intimate relationships enables audiences to identify with celebrities and their daily lives via the suggestion that extraordinary people are ordinary people too.

Conclusion

Television talk shows in the PRC are localized versions of a western television format that provide a forum for the public discussion of Chinese–foreign marriage. The diverse ways in which an intercultural marriage may complicate or even challenge cultural norms and day-to-day habits offers relatable, entertaining and reasonably relevant material for dialogue. Stories of foreign spouses internalizing and mastering traditional Chinese art forms, and local languages, or else being unable to master the proper 'Chinese way of doing things', serve to affirm the superiority of Chinese culture. At the same time, entertaining stories about the conflicts between foreign spouses and their Chinese counterparts highlight both the perceived universal aspects of intimate relationships, such as the importance of expressing love on a daily basis, the notion that absence makes the heart grow fonder, and the understanding that harsh words and deeds are often a sign of affection. In doing so, they also highlight the progressively more open attitude of many Chinese people towards the public discussion of love, marriage and sex.

Notes

1   This programme shares the same name but is different from the programme *Oriental Live Studio*, which started in March 2010 on Shanghai Dragon television (Shanghai Dongfang weishi).
2   The Chinese performance of cross-talk, or '*Xiangsheng*' in Chinese, is a type of folk vocal art originally from North China. Cross-talk can be divided into three types in terms of the number of performers, this includes two-person comic cross-talk (*duikou xiangsheng*), monologue comic-talk (*dankou xiangsheng*) and more-than-two-persons comic cross-talk (*duokou xiangsheng*). Cross-talk performance aims to entertain the audience through the telling of jokes and involves comic ways of speaking and singing, as well as asking and answering questions. Cross-talk is commonly used to satirize the subjects in question. However, it has also been used in recent years to compliment and endorse new people and new things ('Xiangsheng' 2012).

9 Concluding comments

The growth of Chinese–foreign marriage as a distinguishing feature of love and marriage in globalising China is a recent and largely unexplored phenomenon. This book has examined the prior obstacles, the evolution of legal frameworks, official statistics and the media presentations of Chinese–foreign marriage in the PRC between 1979 and 2011. I conclude the study by summarizing the main insights of the preceding chapters, and outline some potential avenues for further research on the subject of Chinese–foreign marriage.

Defining and counting Chinese–foreign marriages

Chinese legal regulations divide Chinese–foreign marriages into three categories. These are marriages between citizens of mainland China and people categorized as foreign nationals (including Chinese with foreign nationalities), citizens of Hong Kong, Macau and Taiwan and overseas Chinese. Statistical data shows that the number of Chinese–foreign marriages registered in the PRC increased significantly throughout the 1980s and 1990s, and reached a peak in 2001 before starting a decreasing trend between 2002 and 2011. Approximately 8,460 couples registered a Chinese–foreign marriage in the PRC in 1979. That figure climbed to a peak of nearly 79,000 couples in 2001 and decreased to around 48,000 couples in 2011 (Zhonghua renmin gongheguo minzhengbu 1979, 2002, 2012, see Appendix 1).

The most common form of Chinese–foreign marriage registered in the PRC until the late 2000s was between citizens of mainland China and citizens of Hong Kong, Macau and Taiwan. Nearly 8,000 people from Hong Kong, Macau and Taiwan married citizens of mainland China in 1979 (Zhonghua renmin gongheguo minzhengbu 1979, see Appendix 1). That figure peaked at slightly more than 48,000 people in 2003 (Zhonghua renmin gongheguo minzhengbu 2004, see Appendix 1). However, the number of such marriages has been declining on average since 2003, with less than 18,000 people from Hong Kong, Macau and Taiwan marrying mainland Chinese citizens in 2011 (Zhonghua renmin gongheguo minzhengbu 2012, see Appendix 1). In other words, the type of marriage that accounts for the largest number of Chinese–foreign marriages registered in the PRC since 1979 has become less popular.

At the same time, data from Taiwan illustrates that between 1998 and 2011, over 246,000 marriages registered in Taiwan involved a mainland spouse. This number grew rapidly from around 12,000 in 1998 to more than 34,000 in 2003. It declined sharply to the lowest level of 10,600 in 2004, before stabilizing at around 12,000 after 2008 (Neizhengbu Huzhengsi 2011). Data from Hong Kong indicates that from 1986 to 2011, approximately 197,000 marriages that were registered in Hong Kong involved a spouse from mainland China. This number skyrocketed from around 780 in 1986 to a peak of 21,600 in 2006. It then declined before reaching over 20,400 in 2011 (Xianggang tebie xingzhengqu 2011).

Marriages between citizens of mainland China and foreign nationals started to become the most common form of Chinese–foreign marriage registered in the PRC in 2008. Around 300 foreign nationals entered into this type of Chinese–foreign marriage in 1979 (Zhonghua renmin gongheguo minzhengbu 1979, see Appendix 1). That figure climaxed at over 26,000 people in 2001 and declined to a figure of around 25,000 people in 2011 (Zhonghua renmin gongheguo minzhengbu 2002, 2012, see Appendix 1). The number of registered marriages in the PRC that involve citizens of mainland China and foreign nationals has therefore increased significantly since 1979 and remained relatively stable since the early 2000s.

Marriages between citizens of mainland China and overseas Chinese comprise the least popular category of Chinese–foreign marriage registered in the PRC. In 1979, less than 200 overseas Chinese married citizens of mainland China (Zhonghua renmin gongheguo minzhengbu 1979, see Appendix 1). That figure increased steadily on an annual basis and reached a high of more than 7,500 people in 2005 and declined to a figure of just over 7,100 people in 2011 (Zhonghua renmin gongheguo minzhengbu 2006, 2012, see Appendix 1). The number of such marriages has remained fairly constant since the late 1990s.

The majority of mainland Chinese citizens registered as entering into Chinese–foreign marriages in the PRC are women, both historically and in the present day. In 1979, around 8,100 Chinese female citizens registered a marriage with a foreign spouse in the PRC. That figure rose steadily throughout the 1980s and early 1990s to reach a peak of over 67,800 women in 2001. Since then, the number of female citizens of the PRC registering a marriage with a foreign spouse in the PRC has declined steadily to reach a low of 35,400 women in 2011, which is less than the figures from the mid-1990s to 2000s.

The number of male citizens of the PRC registering a marriage with a foreign spouse in the PRC has remained consistently low when compared to the number of Chinese women, although those figures increased in the 2000s. In 1979, only about 250 male citizens of the PRC registered a marriage with a foreign spouse in the PRC. That figure rose in a variable fashion throughout the 1980s and 1990s to reach a figure of around 5,800 men in 1999. It then rose steadily to reach a peak of 20,000 men in 2005. Since then, the proportion of male citizens of the PRC registering a marriage with a foreign partner in the PRC has remained at a relatively consistent albeit low level, with about 11,900 men registering such marriages in 2011.

Most of these marriages were registered in China's economically advanced cities and provinces on the eastern seaboard. The large numbers of Chinese–foreign marriages registered in mainland China include the provinces of Guangdong, Fujian, Zhejiang and Shanghai city. (Zhonghua renmin gongheguo minzhengbu 1979 to 2012). In addition, Chinese–foreign marriages were also popular in China's northern provinces of Heilongjiang and Jilin and the capital city of Beijing (Zhonghua renmin gongheguo minzhengbu 1979 to 2012).

In comparison, the economically undeveloped areas of western China recorded limited numbers of registered Chinese–foreign marriages during the same period. These places include Gansu, Ningxia, Qinghai and Tibet Autonomous Region (Zhonghua renmin gongheguo minzhengbu 1979 to 2012).

Data compiled by the PRC Ministry of Civil Affairs reveals that from 1987 to 1998, the percentage of second, and subsequent Chinese–foreign marriages increased whereas that of the first-time marriages declined. In 1987, slightly more than 2,600 persons with previous marital experience registered a Chinese–foreign marriage, which comprised only 6.7 per cent of the total for that year. This figure grew rapidly and exceeded 27,300 persons in 1998, which accounted for 27.2 per cent of the total (Zhonghua renmin gongheguo minzhengbu 1987, 1999). Conversely, in 1987, nearly 37,500 persons registered a Chinese–foreign marriage for the first time, which constituted 93.3 per cent of the total number of persons who registered a Chinese–foreign marriage in that year. In 1998, this figure reached 73,300 persons; however its percentage declined to 72.8 per cent (Zhonghua renmin gongheguo minzhengbu 1987, 1999). This indicates that Chinese–foreign marriages have become a popular alternative for divorcées seeking new marriages.

There is no sufficient data available for a comprehensive evaluation of the sociodemographic characters of Chinese–foreign marriages registered in the PRC. However, scholarly literature suggests that there are several common features of Chinese–foreign marriage registered in particular cities/regions in and outside the PRC. First, Chinese–foreign marriages commonly occur between younger Chinese women and older foreign males and the average age of couples entering into a Chinese–foreign marriage is generally older than couples in Chinese–Chinese marriages (e.g., Zhang Guoxiong 1997: 37; Ding Jinhong *et al.* 2004: 69; Gao Ying *et al.* 2013: 33). Second, the average educational level of Chinese–foreign couples is higher than couples in domestic marriages. In particular, a large percentage of foreign males have acquired graduate diplomas and bachelor's degrees (Ding Jinhong *et al.* 2004: 69; Gao Ying *et al.* 2013: 32). Third, until recently, the number of marriages between Chinese citizens and foreign nationals has been growing rapidly and appeared to become more popular than marriages that involved a spouse from Hong Kong, Macau, Taiwan and overseas Chinese (Ye Wenzhen and Lin Qingguo 1996: 22; Ding Jinhong *et al.* 2004: 68).

Data compiled by foreign countries such as Japan, Korea and Australia shows that marriages registered in these countries that involved a Chinese spouse have increased rapidly since the 1990s and these kinds of marriages were also predominantly between Chinese women and foreign males. For instance, prior to the 1980s, there were less than 1,000 Chinese who registered a marriage to Japanese in Japan. However, the number rose from around 1,100 in 1980 to almost 6,000 in 1995, before reaching its peak of nearly 15,000 persons in 2001 (Ministry of

Health, Labour and Welfare, Japan). Doo-Sub Kim's study of cross-border marriage in Korea suggests that China had become the main providing country for intercultural marriages registered in Korea by mid-1990s. The number of Chinese brides was under 2,500 persons a year prior to the early 1990s. However it grew rapidly and exceeded 20,600 in 2005 (Kim 2010: 136). Similarly, the number of Chinese males remained at the lower level of under 500 persons per year from the 1990s to the early 2000s. This figure grew rapidly and became the largest group of foreign husbands by 2004 (Kim 2010: 136–7). In Australia, the total number of registered marriages involving a Chinese spouse was under 2,000 each year from 1994 to 2002. The figure jumped to over 2,200 in 2003, before increasing to more than 6,300 persons in 2011 (Australian Bureau of Statistics 1994 to 2011).

More recently, the number of Chinese–foreign divorces registered in the PRC has increased. The data demonstrates that, with fluctuations, divorces between mainland Chinese citizens and citizens of other countries/regions maintained a steady growth from around 80 couples in 1979 to around 1,100 couples in 2000 (Zhonghua renmin gongheguo minzhengbu 1979, 2001, see Appendix 1). That figure jumped to over 2,800 couples in 2001 and skyrocketed to nearly 9,500 couples in 2008 (Zhonghua renmin gongheguo minzhengbu 2002, 2009, see Appendix 1). The number of such divorces then decreased to around 5,700 couples in 2011 (Zhonghua renmin gongheguo minzhengbu 2012, see Appendix 1). Unsurprisingly, the divorce rate was recorded as proportionately higher in the provinces of Guangdong, Fujian, Zhejiang and Shanghai city where most Chinese–foreign marriages were registered.

Media discussions of Chinese–foreign marriage

A small number of newspaper and magazine reports started to discuss the growing phenomenon of Chinese–foreign marriage in the PRC in the 1980s and 1990s, initially focusing on the growing incidence of intercultural marriage in major cities on China's developing eastern seaboard ('Shanghai shewai hunyin jianwen' 1988; Ling Zaiming 1992; 'Hainan shewai hunyin' 1993). These reports noted that Chinese–foreign marriages mainly comprised marriages between young women from mainland China and older foreign men, especially men from Hong Kong, Macau and Taiwan, although some marriages involved men from European countries, Japan and the USA. Many such women reportedly entered into a Chinese–foreign marriage to ensure upward socio-economic mobility, but often with tragic consequences.

Early print media reports similarly characterized some celebrity Chinese–foreign marriages as motivated by hypergamy. They condemned the Chinese celebrities in question for naïvely believing that their careers and lives would be improved overseas and for their alleged lack of patriotism as demonstrated by their decision to leave China – their country of origin, and the place where their appreciative fans had made them famous (Feng Xinzi 1994: 34; Shi Qing 1997: 18–19; Wang Dazhao 1998). However, other media reports described celebrity Chinese–foreign marriages as romantic fairy-tales, and constructed Chinese celebrities as role models who entered into intercultural marriages for reasons of 'love' rather than socio-economic advancement (Xu Baokang 1993; Li Jun 1994a; Du Pin 1995; Juan Zi 1996).

Intercultural marriage became a more common feature of media reporting in the 2000s, just when the number of Chinese–foreign marriages registered in the PRC began to decrease in China's eastern coastal cities. Journalists interpreted this trend as a sign of China's urban development, arguing that improved living standards, more opportunities to interact with the outside world and new social values of 'rational' decision-making towards spousal selection, had decreased the number of Chinese–foreign marriages motivated by socio-economic considerations. They asserted that love had replaced hypergamy as the dominant motivation for intercultural marriage, as evidenced by the narrowing gaps in age, educational level and financial status between mainland Chinese citizens and their foreign spouses (Jiang Zhongyi 2007; 'Shewai hunyin dengji' 2007; Tan Lujie 2009). Celebrity Chinese–foreign marriages were also commonly characterized as motivated by love, with celebrities being held up as exemplary people with fairy-tale romances (Hao Xiaohui 2004: 20; Xu Xuelian 2005; 'Zhu Chen: weinai' 2008; 'Mingxing Shi Ke' 2009). At the same time, media reports in the 2000s highlighted a new pattern of marriage-related mobility, noting that increasing numbers of divorced, middle-aged Chinese women were seeking foreign husbands for multiple purposes, with many hoping to realize a 'fresh start' in life, albeit sometimes in the name of 'love' and 'romance' (Pang Fan and Wen Huangwei 2005; Hu Yongmou 2007; 'Bei youhuo' 2008; 'Nüzi wanglian' 2008).

Journalists further underscored the proclaimed shift to Chinese–foreign marriage based on romantic love in the 2000s by noting that foreign spouses come from an increasingly diverse range of countries and not predominantly from Hong Kong, Macau and Taiwan. The countries of origin of the foreign partners in Chinese–foreign marriages registered in the PRC now include Australia, Japan, Malaysia, New Zealand, South Korea, Vietnam, the USA and some African countries, although the majority come from the developed nations of Australia, Canada, Japan and the USA (Meng Xiaoyun 2001; Chen Liyu 2003; Yuan Lanhua and Du Zhanfan 2005; Pan Meihong 2006). An increasing number of couples in celebrity and 'ordinary' Chinese–foreign marriages are now also choosing to live in mainland China, or are (re)migrating from overseas countries, such as Hong Kong, Macau and Taiwan, to live in mainland China, rather than marrying and settling abroad (Du Zhanfan 2001; 'Siqin Gaowa: Ruishi' 2006; Zhao Junhui 2007; 'Mingxing Shi Ke' 2009; 'Chen Lu, Den Nisi' 2009).

Print media reports about intercultural marriage in the 2000s began to focus on the new topic of failed marriages or Chinese–foreign divorce, a phenomenon highlighted in statistical data released by the PRC's Ministry of Civil Affairs. Journalists attributed the growing number of Chinese–foreign divorces registered in the PRC mainly to domestic violence, extramarital affairs and bigamy, as well as the activities of illegal Chinese–foreign marriage introduction agencies (Liu Xiaoxiao 2005; Ye Xiaonan 2006; Zhang Guannian 2007; Wang Jianwei 2008). The behaviours of male foreign spouses, especially men from places other than

Hong Kong, Macau and Taiwan, were blamed for the failure of such marriages, creating a dichotomous and gendered image of foreign male aggressors and Chinese female victims. While noting increased incidences of celebrity Chinese–foreign divorce, journalists typically portrayed such divorces as being characterized by amicable severance, continued friendship and exemplary parenting (Wu Hai'ou 2005; 'Jiang Wen Faguo' 2006; 'Yang Erche Namu de' 2007; 'Li Donghua ren' 2008; Na Na 2008). They suggested in effect that female celebrities in failed intercultural marriages were empowered by their divorces and did not experience the emotional and financial hardships associated with the divorces of 'ordinary' Chinese women.

Chinese–foreign marriage became a feature of television programmes broadcast in the PRC in the mid- to late 2000s. News stories, soap operas, talk shows, game shows, and especially documentaries, capitalized on the range of interested audiences associated with print media and online reports of intercultural marriage in the PRC by incorporating more anecdotal stories about people in intercultural marriages. Television documentaries about Chinese–foreign marriage focus on cross-Strait marriages, and marriages between foreign nationals and people from rural China, in particular (see Appendix 2). Marriages between mainland Chinese citizens and citizens of Taiwan are presented as examples of successful love and business partnerships, which also show how mainland Chinese women have worked to establish harmonious relationships with their extended Taiwanese families, especially their mothers-in-law ('Qizi bangwo chuangzao shangyi caichan' 2008; 'Mai guocu de liang'an fuqi' 2008; 'Liang'an poxi yijiaqin' 2009; 'Chufang li de poxi zhizheng' 2009). In the process, documentaries about cross-Strait marriages reinforce for PRC audiences the PRC Government's proclaimed efforts to improve political and cultural relations with Taiwan and provide a positive counter image to the negative images of 'mainland brides' that circulate in Taiwan.

Television documentaries on Chinese–foreign marriages that involve rural Chinese citizens emphasize an unconventional pattern of social mobility in which foreign nationals marry rural Chinese nationals, and choose to live with them in poor and undeveloped parts of China ('Cunli laile ge yang nüxu' 2007; 'Mima qingshu' 2008; ('Yang xifu de chengshi meng' 2008; 'Cunli de Meiguo xifu' 2009). Foreign spouses in these circumstances are constructed as exotic 'others' who are prepared to overcome cultural differences and experience lower standards of living in order to be with their 'loved' Chinese partners. While highlighting the difficulties of everyday life in many parts of rural China, this focus presents a romantic view of intercultural marriage and rural China as 'authentic' and offering unadulterated as in non-hypergamous examples of 'modern-day love' between 'remarkable yet ordinary' representatives of the 'East and the West' in the twenty-first century.

The growing popularity of talk shows in the PRC has resulted in an increasing number of programmes featuring diverse 'personal discussions' of love and marriage, including Chinese–foreign marriage. Talk shows typically present the foreign spouses in Chinese–foreign marriages in one of two ways. The first is as a Sinophile or 'foreign Chinese' who entertains audiences by demonstrating a strong and even expert interest in aspects of China's languages, cultures and people. The second is as a 'foreign ignoramus' who entertains audiences by revealing their limited understanding of China's languages, cultures and people, despite their marriage to a PRC citizen. Marital conflicts are another staple feature of talk shows about Chinese–foreign marriage in the PRC. Conflict in the context of intercultural marriages is typically portrayed in terms of ultimately humorous disagreements and even low-level physical altercations stemming from cultural differences, which serve to consolidate the seemingly unique yet universal bonds of marital intimacy.

While designed to entertain, documentaries and talk shows on Chinese–foreign marriage serve other functions. They provide a platform in China's increasingly commercialized media for Chinese–foreign couples to share their personal stories and opinions on intercultural marriages with broader audiences. At the same time, they reiterate political messages regarding China's enhanced position on the world stage. Documentaries and talk shows about Chinese–foreign marriage therefore reflect the expansion of commercial culture and the existence of more open attitudes towards discussions of love, marriage and sex in the public sphere in the PRC today. They also illustrate how stories about 'intimate relations' may be used to convey political messages regarding the 'modern' nature of twenty-first-century China.

In analysing media coverage of Chinese–foreign marriage in the PRC, this book highlights three issues that reflect both processes of social change in reform-era China and China's enhanced status in the world. First, it reveals altered patterns of marriage-related mobility in the Chinese context. While a significant number of Chinese women who marry foreign nationals continue to do so as a means to achieve socio-economic advancement, statistical data and media reports indicate that intercultural marriages in contemporary China are neither a 'women only' nor unidirectional (East goes West) phenomenon. Some intercultural marriages now reportedly end in divorce because they are bogus in the first place, i.e., they are based on the personal and financial exploitation of vulnerable Chinese women by foreign men (Ni Yan 2005; 'Nüzi wanglian' 2008; 'Weizhuang haiwai' 2009). Contrary to conventional depictions of Chinese women in intercultural marriages as ruthless passport hunters, recent media reports suggest that foreign men also use deceptive promises of marriage to inveigle financial support from Chinese women (Hu Yongmou 2007; Wang Si 2008; 'Cong Xuenaiyin'an kan' 2009).

The analysis of media coverage of Chinese–foreign marriage in the PRC in this book also suggests that an increasing number of foreign spouses in Chinese–foreign marriages are developing businesses and careers in the PRC, thereby reconfiguring conventional constructions of intercultural marriage as enabling a generic group of mainland Chinese women to marry and live abroad. James Farrer (2008a: 10–11) describes how men from the developed 'West' work and subsequently marry in Shanghai, using the social, economic and cultural resources made available by their Chinese spouses to enhance their local business-making capacity. Media reports about Chinese–foreign marriage in the PRC similarly show that some marriages between both male and female citizens of mainland China and citizens of Hong Kong and Taiwan are related to the development of careers and businesses in the PRC (Yuan Zhonghai and Sun Xianglan 2007; 'Gangnü qinglai Dalunan' 2007; Liang'an hunyin xin xianxiang' 2011; Ren Bo 2011). In addition, foreign nationals from either the developed West or developing countries are now marrying people from 'backward' rural parts of China, and many of them are choosing to live and work in underdeveloped regions of the PRC. Such marriages are presented in recent media reports as highlighting an altered pattern of marriage-related mobility. Instead of marriages based on business and career development, some foreign nationals are portrayed as willing to 'marry down' for love to 'authentic' rural Chinese who embody traditional Chinese virtues of 'self-sacrifice', 'honesty' and 'filial piety', values that have allegedly been abandoned by the more 'westernized' urban citizens of China.

Second, analysis of media coverage of Chinese–foreign marriage in the PRC in this book suggests that China's enhanced socio-economic status is reflected in media coverage of altered mate selection preferences in the context of intercultural marriages. Recent media reports suggest that some foreign women now view Chinese men as attractive marriage partners because they are 'diligent', 'reliable' and 'good husband material', whereas foreign women previously viewed them as 'unattractive partners' both physically and economically. Concomitantly, recent media reports suggest that some Chinese men now view foreign women as attractive marriage partners with 'traditional' feminine Chinese characters whereas Chinese men previously were repelled by the perceived 'assertive and aggressive' character of foreign women. These altered conceptions of 'cultural attractiveness' are reinforced by media reports that play on the 'Sinicized' nature of foreign spouses in intercultural marriages and the internationalized and cosmopolitan identity of 'modern Chinese'. Such reports suggest a greater accommodation by Chinese of 'foreignness' and of 'Chineseness' by foreigners. In doing so, media presentations of this kind perhaps also reflect a revived sense of Chinese cultural superiority.

Finally, the analysis of media coverage of Chinese–foreign marriage in the PRC suggests that an (economically) stronger China is presented as not only affording Chinese women an improved status as being equal to Chinese men, but also as inverting the conventional gender power relationships between men and women in intercultural marriages. This strategy is particularly evident in media portrayals of failed intercultural marriages involving celebrities. In contrast to media accounts of 'ordinary women' as 'dependent wives' and 'victims' of foreign men, Chinese female celebrities are masculinized as 'breadwinners', 'career women' and 'initiators of divorce'. At the same time, the foreign husbands of celebrity Chinese women are feminized as 'househusbands' and 'good caretakers', rather than as (patriarchal) 'swindlers' and 'abusers'. Such inversion is further enhanced by talk shows on celebrity Chinese–foreign marriages, with some PRC female celebrities being presented as dominant and physically aggressive figures, whereas their foreign spouses are presented as 'henpecked' husbands.

Nevertheless, the embedded meaning of mediated images of intercultural marriages is far beyond the intimate level between couples. Instead, the topic of intercultural marriage is incorporated by the PRC media, which cooperates in partnership with the PRC Government, as part of its nation-bonding and rejuvenating effort to demonstrate China's socio-economic progress, national achievement and increasing multiculturalism. It is used to encourage public pronouncements of Chinese patriotism, and promote exemplary citizenship, domestic harmony and bilateral relations. It is used to provide moral education to the mass audience in line with traditional Chinese virtues and government policies. It is also used as a means to prompt public participation in discussing, debating and negotiating issues of modernism, globalisation, gender inequality, as well as ethnic and cultural diversity in contemporary China.

Potential avenues for further research

Media presentations of Chinese–foreign marriage in the PRC, while sometimes reinforcing negative stereotypes, mainly seek to convey positive understandings of Chinese–foreign interactions in the personal domain, and highlight the 'cosmopolitan' nature of modern China. This rendition of China's cosmopolitanism – a nation that is at home in the wider world and comfortable with different cultures – is achieved in the context of intercultural marriage by either downplaying or eliding the 'voices' of the foreign spouses in Chinese–foreign marriages, including overseas Chinese and citizens of Hong Kong, Macau and Taiwan. This is especially the case in discussion of Chinese–foreign divorces, as (male) foreign nationals are often blamed for the problems associated with intercultural marriages, such as deception, domestic violence, bigamy and extramarital affairs.

While this downplaying of the 'voices' of the foreign spouses in Chinese–foreign marriages stems from practical considerations, it suggests additional areas for research. Media reports about intercultural marriage in the PRC are produced by journalists in mainland China for mainland Chinese audiences, and are disseminated via China's media. From a practical perspective, it is cheaper and more efficient to interview mainland citizens and couples residing on the mainland. However, further research could be based on interviews with the foreign partners in Chinese–foreign marriages, and especially in instances where the couples reside in the PRC, in order to provide a more nuanced and comparative perspective. Further research could also examine how Chinese–foreign marriage has been presented in the media of other countries both historically and in the present day.

The new social dynamics of commercially facilitated Chinese–foreign marriage matchmaking provide other potential research directions. Chinese–foreign marriage matchmaking services are prohibited in the PRC because the PRC Government views such services as a source of harm to Chinese women and damaging to China's national reputation (Guowuyuan bangongting guanyu jiaqiang shewai hunyin jieshao guanli de tongzhi 1994). Media reports consequently focus on the problematic nature of such businesses, for example, their capacity to extort money from clients (usually women) based on false promises. However, there is clearly a demand for such services. This demand is demonstrated by the continued existence of illegal Chinese–foreign matchmaking services and the recent proliferation of 'matchmaking channels' on Internet forums, online dating websites, television matchmaking/dating shows and new social media. While many of these forums target women and men seeking domestic partners, they also target women and men seeking foreign partners and intercultural relationships.

Last, but not least, mainland China's recent shift to being a 'receiving' rather than a 'sending' country for 'foreign brides' provides another potential avenue for research. Recent media interviews with Chen Shiqu, Director of the Anti-human Trafficking Office under the PRC's Ministry of Public Security indicate that an increasing number of young women from Southeast Asia, mostly from rural areas of Vietnam, Burma and Laos, are entering the PRC illegally, aided by human trafficking organizations (Cui Xiaolin and Wen Shan 2010: 8–9; Zhang Yan 2011; Yu Zeyuan 2011). On the one hand, trafficking organizations capitalize on the desires of some of these women to improve their socio-economic circumstances by smuggling them into China in exchange for money. Some of these women may enter into such transactions based on deceptive promises of well-paid work in China's big cities and the opportunity to meet 'wealthy' Chinese men as potential marriage partners. On the other hand, trafficking organizations capitalize on the growing market for 'foreign brides' in the PRC fuelled by socio-economic imbalances in China's marriage market. Middle-aged rural Chinese men in the less developed regions of Sichuan, Fujian and Henan provinces who cannot afford to marry a local woman are reportedly eager to pay traffickers a negotiated price for a 'foreign Southeast Asian bride'. This particular nexus of supply and demand has led to a growing number of young women from rural areas of Vietnam, Burma and Laos entering China to work illegally, entering the sex industry via deceptive recruiting methods and marrying older Chinese men residing in poor and remote rural areas of China (Cui Xiaolin and Wen Shan 2010: 8; Ji Beibei 2010). Further study on Chinese–foreign marriage in the PRC could therefore examine new patterns of marriage-related mobility 'into' rather than 'out of' the PRC.

As the preceding examples show, an examination of Chinese–foreign marriages sheds light on multiple dynamics of social change in both China and other regions of the world. Numerous avenues exist for further research.

Appendix 1
Sources of statistical information on marriages and divorces registered in the PRC

Zhonghua renmin gongheguo minzhengbu [PRC: Ministry of Civil Affairs] (1979) 'Shewai hunyin dengji qingkuang' [Chinese–Foreign Marriage Registration], *Quanguo minzheng tongji ziliao* [China Civil Affairs Statistical Data], Beijing: Zhongguo tongji chubanshe, pp. 135–6.

Zhonghua renmin gongheguo minzhengbu [PRC: Ministry of Civil Affairs] (1980) 'Shewai hunyin dengji qingkuang' [Chinese–Foreign Marriage Registration], *Quanguo minzheng tongji ziliao* [China Civil Affairs Statistical Data], Beijing: Zhongguo tongji chubanshe, p. 72.

Zhonghua renmin gongheguo minzhengbu [PRC: Ministry of Civil Affairs] (1981) 'Shewai hunyin dengji qingkuang' [Chinese–Foreign Marriage Registration], *Quanguo minzheng tongji ziliao* [China Civil Affairs Statistical Data], Beijing: Zhongguo tongji chubanshe, pp. 71–2.

Zhonghua renmin gongheguo minzhengbu [PRC: Ministry of Civil Affairs] (1982) 'Shejihuaqiao, Gang Ao Tai tongbao, waijihuaren, waiguoren de hunyin' [Marriage Registrations Involving [Citizens of the PRC and] Overseas Chinese, Compatriots from Hong Kong, Macau and Taiwan, Chinese with Foreign Nationalities and Foreign Nationals], *Quanguo minzheng tongji nianbao* [China Civil Affairs Statistical Yearbook], Beijing: Zhongguo tongji chubanshe, pp. 88–9.

Zhonghua renmin gongheguo minzhengbu [PRC: Ministry of Civil Affairs] (1983) 'Zai hunyin dengji zhong: Shewai ji huaqiao, Gang Ao Tai tongbao hunyin qingkuang' [Marriage Registrations Involving Foreign Nationals, Overseas Chinese and Compatriots from Hong Kong, Macau and Taiwan], *Quanguo minzheng tongji nianbao* [China Civil Affairs Statistical Yearbook], Beijing: Zhongguo tongji chubanshe, pp. 22–3.

Zhonghua renmin gongheguo minzhengbu [PRC: Ministry of Civil Affairs] (1984) 'Zai hunyin dengji zhong: Sheji waiguoren, huaqiao, Gang Ao Tai tongbao hunyin de qingkuang' [Marriage Registrations Involving Foreign Nationals, Overseas Chinese and Compatriots from Hong Kong, Macau and Taiwan], *Quanguo minzheng tongji nianbao* [China Civil Affairs Statistical Yearbook], Beijing: Zhongguo tongji chubanshe, pp. 31–2.

Zhonghua renmin gongheguo minzhengbu [PRC: Ministry of Civil Affairs] (1987) 'Shewai ji huaqiao, Gang Ao Tai tongbao hunyin' [Marriages Involving [Citizens of the PRC and] Foreign nationals, Overseas Chinese and Compatriots from Hong Kong, Macau and Taiwan], *Quanguo minzheng shiye tongji ziliao* [China Civil Affairs Statistical Data], Beijing: Zhongguo tongji chubanshe, pp. 156–7.

Zhonghua renmin gongheguo minzhengbu [PRC: Ministry of Civil Affairs] (1988) 'Shewai ji huaqiao, Gang Ao Tai tongbao hunyin' [Marriages Involving [Citizens of the PRC and] Foreign nationals, Overseas Chinese and Compatriots from Hong Kong, Macau and Taiwan], *Quanguo minzheng shiye tongji ziliao* [China Civil Affairs Statistical Data], Beijing: Zhongguo tongji chubanshe, pp. 166–7.

Zhonghua renmin gongheguo minzhengbu [PRC: Ministry of Civil Affairs] (1990) 'Shewai ji huaqiao, Gang Ao Tai tongbao hunyin dengji qingkuang' [Marriage Registrations Involving [Citizens of the PRC and] Foreign Nationals, Overseas Chinese and Compatriots from Hong Kong, Macau and Taiwan], *Zhongguo minzheng tongji nianjian* [China Civil Affairs Statistical Yearbook], Beijing: Zhongguo tongji chubanshe, pp. 252–3.

Zhonghua renmin gongheguo minzhengbu [PRC: Ministry of Civil Affairs] (1991) 'Shewai ji huaqiao, Gang Ao Tai tongbao hunyin' [Marriages Involving Foreign Nationals, Overseas Chinese and Compatriots from Hong Kong, Macau and Taiwan], *Zhongguo minzheng tongji nianjian* [China Civil Affairs Statistical Yearbook], Beijing: Zhongguo tongji chubanshe, pp. 172–3.

Zhonghua renmin gongheguo minzhengbu [PRC: Ministry of Civil Affairs] (1992) 'Shewai ji huaqiao, Gang Ao Tai tongbao hunyin' [Marriages Involving Foreign Nationals, Overseas Chinese and Compatriots from Hong Kong, Macau and Taiwan], *Zhongguo minzheng tongji nianjian* [China Civil Affairs Statistical Yearbook], Beijing: Zhongguo tongji chubanshe, pp. 176–7.

Zhonghua renmin gongheguo minzhengbu [PRC: Ministry of Civil Affairs] (1993) 'Shewai ji huaqiao, Gang Ao Tai tongbao hunyin' [Marriages Involving Foreign Nationals, Overseas Chinese and Compatriots from Hong Kong, Macau and Taiwan], *Zhongguo minzheng tongji nianjian* [China Civil Affairs Statistical Yearbook], Beijing: Zhongguo tongji chubanshe, pp. 172–3.

Zhonghua renmin gongheguo minzhengbu [PRC: Ministry of Civil Affairs] (1994) 'Shewai ji huaqiao, Gang Ao Tai tongbao hunyin' [Marriages Involving Foreign Nationals, Overseas Chinese and Compatriots from Hong Kong, Macau and Taiwan], *Zhongguo minzheng tongji nianjian* [China Civil Affairs Statistical Yearbook], Beijing: Zhongguo tongji chubanshe, pp. 178–9.

Zhonghua renmin gongheguo minzhengbu [PRC: Ministry of Civil Affairs] (1995) 'Shewai ji huaqiao, Gang Ao Tai tongbao hunyin' [Marriages Involving Foreign Nationals, Overseas Chinese and Compatriots from Hong Kong, Macau and Taiwan], *Zhongguo minzheng tongji nianjian* [China Civil Affairs Statistical Yearbook], Beijing: Zhongguo tongji chubanshe, pp. 148–9.

Zhonghua renmin gongheguo minzhengbu [PRC: Ministry of Civil Affairs] (1996) 'Shewai ji huaqiao, Gang Ao Tai tongbao hunyin' [Marriages Involving Foreign Nationals, Overseas Chinese and Compatriots from Hong Kong, Macau and Taiwan], *Zhongguo minzheng tongji nianjian* [China Civil Affairs Statistical Yearbook], Beijing: Zhongguo tongji chubanshe, pp. 298–9.

Zhonghua renmin gongheguo minzhengbu [PRC: Ministry of Civil Affairs] (1997) 'Shewai ji huaqiao, Gang Ao Tai tongbao hunyin' [Marriages Involving Foreign Nationals, Overseas Chinese and Compatriots from Hong Kong, Macau and Taiwan], *Zhongguo minzheng tongji nianjian* [China Civil Affairs Statistical Yearbook], Beijing: Zhongguo tongji chubanshe, pp. 258–9.

Zhonghua renmin gongheguo minzhengbu [PRC: Ministry of Civil Affairs] (1998) 'Shewai ji huaqiao, Gang Ao Tai tongbao hunyin dengji qingkuang' [Marriage Registrations Involving [Citizens of the PRC and] Foreign Nationals, Overseas Chinese and Compatriots from Hong Kong, Macau and Taiwan], *Zhongguo minzheng tongji nianjian* [China Civil Affairs Statistical Yearbook], Beijing: Zhongguo tongji chubanshe, pp. 280–1.

Zhonghua renmin gongheguo minzhengbu [PRC: Ministry of Civil Affairs] (1999) 'Shewai ji huaqiao, Gang Ao Tai tongbao hunyin dengji qingkuang' [Marriage Registrations Involving [Citizens of the PRC and] Foreign Nationals, Overseas Chinese and Compatriots from Hong Kong, Macau and Taiwan], *Zhongguo minzheng tongji nianjian* [China Civil Affairs Statistical Yearbook], Beijing: Zhongguo tongji chubanshe, pp. 200–1.

Zhonghua renmin gongheguo minzhengbu [PRC: Ministry of Civil Affairs] (2000) 'Jiehun dengji qingkuang' [Marriage Registration], *Zhongguo minzheng tongji nianjian* [China Civil Affairs Statistical Yearbook], Beijing: Zhongguo tongji chubanshe, pp. 254–5.

Zhonghua renmin gongheguo minzhengbu [PRC: Ministry of Civil Affairs] (2000) 'Lihun dengji qingkuang' [Divorce Registration], *Zhongguo minzheng tongji nianjian* [China Civil Affairs Statistical Yearbook], Beijing: Zhongguo tongji chubanshe, p. 256.

Zhonghua renmin gongheguo minzhengbu [PRC: Ministry of Civil Affairs] (2001) 'Jiehun dengji qingkuang' [Marriage Registration], *Zhongguo minzheng tongji nianjian* [China Civil Affairs Statistical Yearbook], Beijing: Zhongguo tongji chubanshe, pp. 238–9.

Zhonghua renmin gongheguo minzhengbu [PRC: Ministry of Civil Affairs] (2001) 'Lihun dengji qingkuang' [Divorce Registration], *Zhongguo minzheng tongji nianjian* [China Civil Affairs Statistical Yearbook], Beijing: Zhongguo tongji chubanshe, pp. 240–1.

Zhonghua renmin gongheguo minzhengbu [PRC: Ministry of Civil Affairs] (2002) 'Jiehun dengji qingkuang' [Marriage Registration], *Zhongguo minzheng tongji nianjian* [China Civil Affairs Statistical Yearbook], Beijing: Zhongguo tongji chubanshe, pp. 226–7.

Zhonghua renmin gongheguo minzhengbu [PRC: Ministry of Civil Affairs] (2002) 'Lihun dengji qingkuang' [Divorce Registration], *Zhongguo minzheng tongji nianjian* [China Civil Affairs Statistical Yearbook], Beijing: Zhongguo tongji chubanshe, pp. 228–9.

Zhonghua renmin gongheguo minzhengbu [PRC: Ministry of Civil Affairs] (2003) 'Jiehun dengji qingkuang' [Marriage Registration], *Zhongguo minzheng tongji nianjian* [China Civil Affairs Statistical Yearbook], Beijing: Zhongguo tongji chubanshe, pp. 282–3.

Zhonghua renmin gongheguo minzhengbu [PRC: Ministry of Civil Affairs] (2003) 'Lihun dengji qingkuang' [Divorce Registration], *Zhongguo minzheng tongji nianjian* [China Civil Affairs Statistical Yearbook], Beijing: Zhongguo tongji chubanshe, pp. 284–5.

Zhonghua renmin gongheguo minzhengbu [PRC: Ministry of Civil Affairs] (2004) 'Jiehun dengji qingkuang' [Marriage Registration], *Zhongguo minzheng tongji nianjian* [China Civil Affairs Statistical Yearbook], Beijing: Zhongguo tongji chubanshe, pp. 100–1.

Zhonghua renmin gongheguo minzhengbu [PRC: Ministry of Civil Affairs] (2004) 'Lihun dengji qingkuang' [Divorce Registration], *Zhongguo minzheng tongji nianjian* [China Civil Affairs Statistical Yearbook], Beijing: Zhongguo tongji chubanshe, pp. 102–3.

Zhonghua renmin gongheguo minzhengbu [PRC: Ministry of Civil Affairs] (2005) 'Jiehun dengji' [Marriage Registration], *Zhongguo minzheng tongji nianjian* [China Civil Affairs Statistical Yearbook], Beijing: Zhongguo tongji chubanshe, pp. 118–19.

Zhonghua renmin gongheguo minzhengbu [PRC: Ministry of Civil Affairs] (2005) 'Lihun banli' [Divorce Registration], *Zhongguo minzheng tongji nianjian* [China Civil Affairs Statistical Yearbook], Beijing: Zhongguo tongji chubanshe, pp. 120–1.

Zhonghua renmin gongheguo minzhengbu [PRC: Ministry of Civil Affairs] (2006) 'Jiehun dengji' [Marriage Registration], *Zhongguo minzheng tongji nianjian* [China Civil Affairs Statistical Yearbook], Beijing: Zhongguo tongji chubanshe, pp. 120–1.

Zhonghua renmin gongheguo minzhengbu [PRC: Ministry of Civil Affairs] (2006) 'Lihun banli' [Divorce Registration], *Zhongguo minzheng tongji nianjian* [China Civil Affairs Statistical Yearbook], Beijing: Zhongguo tongji chubanshe, pp. 124–5.

Zhonghua renmin gongheguo minzhengbu [PRC: Ministry of Civil Affairs] (2007) 'Jiehun dengji' [Marriage Registration], *Zhongguo minzheng tongji nianjian* [China Civil Affairs Statistical Yearbook], Beijing: Zhongguo tongji chubanshe, pp. 148–9.

Zhonghua renmin gongheguo minzhengbu [PRC: Ministry of Civil Affairs] (2007) 'Lihun banli' [Divorce Registration], *Zhongguo minzheng tongji nianjian* [China Civil Affairs Statistical Yearbook], Beijing: Zhongguo tongji chubanshe, pp. 152–3.

Zhonghua renmin gongheguo minzhengbu [PRC: Ministry of Civil Affairs] (2008) 'Jiehun dengji' [Marriage Registration], *Zhongguo minzheng tongji nianjian* [China Civil Affairs Statistical Yearbook], Beijing: Zhongguo tongji chubanshe, pp. 144–5.

Zhonghua renmin gongheguo minzhengbu [PRC: Ministry of Civil Affairs] (2008) 'Lihun banli' [Divorce Registration], *Zhongguo minzheng tongji nianjian* [China Civil Affairs Statistical Yearbook], Beijing: Zhongguo tongji chubanshe, pp. 148–9.

Zhonghua renmin gongheguo minzhengbu [PRC: Ministry of Civil Affairs] (2009) 'Jiehun dengji' [Marriage Registration], *Zhongguo minzheng tongji nianjian*

[China Civil Affairs Statistical Yearbook], Beijing: Zhongguo tongji chubanshe, pp. 144–5.

Zhonghua renmin gongheguo minzhengbu [PRC: Ministry of Civil Affairs] (2009) 'Lihun banli' [Divorce Registration], *Zhongguo minzheng tongji nianjian* [China Civil Affairs Statistical Yearbook], Beijing: Zhongguo tongji chubanshe, pp. 148–9.

Zhonghua renmin gongheguo minzhengbu [PRC: Ministry of Civil Affairs] (2010) 'Jiehun dengji fuwu' [Marriage Registration Service], *Zhongguo minzheng tongji nianjian* [China Civil Affairs Statistical Yearbook], Beijing: Zhongguo tongji chubanshe, pp. 482–3.

Zhonghua renmin gongheguo minzhengbu [PRC: Ministry of Civil Affairs] (2010) 'Lihun banli fuwu' [Divorce Registration Service], *Zhongguo minzheng tongji nianjian* [China Civil Affairs Statistical Yearbook], Beijing: Zhongguo tongji chubanshe, pp. 486–7.

Zhonghua renmin gongheguo minzhengbu [PRC: Ministry of Civil Affairs] (2011) 'Jiehun dengji fuwu' [Marriage Registration Service], *Zhongguo minzheng tongji nianjian* [China Civil Affairs Statistical Yearbook], Beijing: Zhongguo tongji chubanshe, pp. 510–11.

Zhonghua renmin gongheguo minzhengbu [PRC: Ministry of Civil Affairs] (2011) 'Lihun banli fuwu' [Divorce Registration Service], *Zhongguo minzheng tongji nianjian* [China Civil Affairs Statistical Yearbook], Beijing: Zhongguo tongji chubanshe, pp. 514–15.

Zhonghua renmin gongheguo minzhengbu [PRC: Ministry of Civil Affairs] (2012) 'Jiehun dengji fuwu' [Marriage Registration Service], *Zhongguo minzheng tongji nianjian* [China Civil Affairs Statistical Yearbook], Beijing: Zhongguo tongji chubanshe, pp. 670–1.

Zhonghua renmin gongheguo minzhengbu [PRC: Ministry of Civil Affairs] (2012) 'Lihun banli fuwu' [Divorce Registration Service], *Zhongguo minzheng tongji nianjian* [China Civil Affairs Statistical Yearbook], Beijing: Zhongguo tongji chubanshe, pp. 674–5.

Appendix 2
Documentary films on Chinese–foreign marriage (57 episodes)

Aishang Sichuan lameizi [Falling in Love with Sichuan 'Hot' Girls] 2009, Yuanfen, CCTV-4, Beijing, 31 May.

Bange xifu bange tongshi [Wife and Colleague] 2008, Yuanfen, CCTV-4, Beijing, 2 November.

Banlu fuqi de suantian kula [The Joys and Sorrows of a Couple Who Have Had Previous Marriages] 2008, Yuanfen, CCTV-4, Beijing, 15 June.

Bu fushu de Liang'an hunyin [The Cross-Strait Couple Who Refuse to Concede Defeat] 2007, Yuanfen, CCTV-4, Beijing, 28 October.

Chufang li de poxi zhizheng [Wife and Mother-in-Law: Conflict in the Kitchen] 2009, Yuanfen, CCTV-4, Beijing, 8 February.

Cunli de Meiguo xifu [American Wife in Our Village] 2009, Yuanfen, CCTV-4, Beijing, 5 April.

Cunli laile ge yangnüxu [Foreign Son-in-Law Comes to Our Village] 2007, Chuanqi gushi, Jiangxi TV, Jiangxi, 28 March.

Cunli laile yangxifu [A Foreign Bride Comes to Our Village] 2008, Jiangshu, CCTV-10, Beijing, 3 December.

Dalu xin'niang weihe liulei? [Why Was the Mainland Bride Crying?] 2007, Yuanfen, CCTV-4, Beijing, 2 December.

Haixiao yusheng: Li Qinghui yu Liu Wei [Surviving the Tsunami: Li Qinghui and Liu Wei] 2008, Yuanfen, CCTV-4, Beijing, 26 May.

Hanguo nühai Zhongguo xunyuan [South Korean Woman Searching for Love in China] 2009, Yuanfen, CCTV-4, Beijing, 10 May.

Henan xiaohuo qima yong batai dajiao yingqu Meilianshe nü jizhe [Henan Man Uses Eight-Bearer Sedan to Marry Associate Press Reporter] 2011, Digital Video, *Youku* website, 23 February.

Huan'nan fuqi jian zhenqing [True Love Conquers Difficulties in Marriage] 2007, Yuanfen, CCTV-4, Beijing, 6 May.

Hunqian hunhou bu yiyang [Life is Different Before and After Marriage] 2009, Yuanfen, CCTV-4, Beijing, 19 April.

Hutong li de kuaguo qingyuan [Intercultural Marriage in a Beijing Alley] 2009, Beijing TV-8, Beijing, 20 January.

Jiagei ta wo bu houhui [I Do Not Regret Marrying Him] 2007, Yuanfen, CCTV-4, Beijing, 8 July.

Jimao suanpi wu xiaoshi [Trivial Matters] 2008, Yuanfen, CCTV-4, Beijing, 28 December.

Kafei shu xia de aiqing [Love Under the Coffee Tree] 2007, Yuanfen, CCTV-4, Beijing, 17 August.

Kuaguo hunyin beihou de suantian kula [The Sweetness and Bitterness of Intercultural Marriage] 2009, Rang'ai zhu wojia, Guangxi TV, Guangxi, 8 May.

Liang'an fuqi gongdu qing'gan nanguan [Cross-Strait Couple Work Hard to Overcome Emotional Difficulties] 2008, Yuanfen, CCTV-4, Beijing, 16 March.

Liang'an hunyin yichang dubo [Cross-Strait Marriage Is a Gamble] 2008, Yuanfen, CCTV-4, Beijing, 6 July.

Liang'an hunyin yixian qian [Tying the Cross-Strait Knot] 2007, Yuanfen, CCTV-4, Beijing, 7 September.

Liang'an hunyin: Wang Qiuli he Zhu Zhongjia [Cross-Strait Marriage: Wang Qiuli and Zhu Zhongjia] 2007, Yuanfen, CCTV-4, Beijing, 17 December.

Liang'an poxi yijiaqin [A Close Cross-Strait Family: Mainland Chinese Wife and Taiwanese Mother-in-Law] 2009, Yuanfen, CCTV-4, Beijing, 24 May.

Liang'an yinyuan gushiduo [Stories about Love and Cross-Strait Marriages] 2009, Yuanfen, CCTV-4, Beijing, 17 May.

Lijiang aiqing gushi [Lijiang Love Story] 2009, Zhenqing shilu, Shanghai Dragon TV, Shanghai, 24 April.

Liuxun laoren kuaguo lian [The Intercultural Love of a Couple in Their 60s] 2007, Jilu Zhongguo, FSTV, Guangdong, 8 April. No information available about date of broadcast.

Mai guocu de liang'an fuqi [Cross-strait Couple Who Sell Fruit Vinegar] 2008, Yuanfen, CCTV-4, Beijing, 24 February.

Mima qingshu [Coded Love Letter] 2008, Zhenqing shilu, Shanghai Dragon TV, Shanghai, 7 October.

Mugua yuan li de aiqing [Love in the Papaya Garden] 2008, Yuanfen, CCTV-4, Beijing, 27 April.

Nan'ren beihou de nüren men [The Women behind the Men] 2008, Yuanfen, CCTV-4, Beijing, 28 January.

Neimenggu liulanghan yu ta de Taiwan xin'niang [Inner Mongolian Tramp and His Taiwanese Bride] 2006, Yuanfen, CCTV-4, Beijing, 9 July.

Nü daxuesheng jiagei Taiwan chanong [Female University Student Marries a Taiwanese Tea Merchant] 2008, Yuanfen, CCTV-4, Beijing, 26 October.

Qizi bangwo chuangzao shangyi caichan [My Wife Helped me Become a Billionaire] 2008, Yuanfen, CCTV-4, Beijing, 2 March.

Quge Shandong guniang dang laopo [Marrying a Shandong Woman] 2009, Yuanfen, CCTV-4, Beijing, 25 January.

Quxifu xueyi liangbuwu [Learning Chinese Kung Fu and Marrying a Chinese Woman Went Together] 2009, Yuanfen, CCTV-4, Beijing, 29 March.

Shandian jiehun zhihou de kunao [The Worries That Follow a Speedy Marriage] 2007, Yuanfen, CCTV-4, Beijing, 27 May.

Taibei guniang yu Naxi xiaohuo de qingyuan [The Love Story of a Taibei Woman and a Naxi Man] 2006, 19 February.

Taiwan fujianü aishang bing gege: Lai Minying yu Ma Lin [Wealthy Taiwanese Woman Falls in Love with a Mainland Soldier: Lai Minying and Ma Lin] 2007, Yuanfen, CCTV-4, Beijing, 4 February.

Taiwan Fujiazi aishang Hainan guniang [Wealthy Taiwanese Man Falls in Love With a Woman From Hainan] 2008, Yuanfen, CCTV-4, Beijing, 27 April.

Taiwanren de xiangcun aiqing [A Taiwanese Man Finds Love in the Countryside] 2008, Yuanfen, CCTV-4, Beijing, 21 September.

Tianjin guniang jiagei Faguo xiaohuo [Tianjin Girl Married a French Man] 2009, Yuanfen, CCTV-4, Beijing, 26 April.

Tianjin guniang Taiwan lang [Tianjin Woman and Her Taiwanese Man] 2008, Yuanfen, CCTV-4, Beijing, 20 July.

Wo bushi youqian de yang zhangfu [I Am Not a Wealthy Foreign Husband] 2009, Yuanfen, CCTV-4, Beijing, 3 May.

Wo de Yilang pang gege [My Big Iranian Brother] 2009, Yuanfen, CCTV-4, Beijing, 22 March.

Wo jia de Feizhou xifu [My African Wife] 2010, Baqu gushi, BTV-8, Beijing, 29 October.

Wo shi zhangfu de xian neizhu [I'm an Understanding and Helpful Wife] 2008, Yuanfen, CCTV-4, Beijing, 17 August.

Wo zai Taiwan dang xifu de rizi [When I was a Bride in Taiwan] 2007, Yuanfen, CCTV-4, Beijing, 22 July.

Yang Xifu hui pojia [Foreign Bride Visits Her Husband's Family] 2006, Xiangyue siji, Yuzhou TV, Henan, 12 September.

Yangnüxu qiuhunji [Story of a Foreign Son-in-Law's Marriage Proposal] 2010, Jiangshu, CCTV-10, Beijing, 1 September.

Yangxifu de chengshimeng [A Foreign Wife's Urban Dream] 2008, Zhenqing shilu, Shanghai Dragon TV, Shanghai, 21 November.

Yibosanzhe de liang'an hunyin [Ups and Downs of a Cross-Strait Marriage] 2008, Yuanfen, CCTV-4, Beijing, 6 April.

Yige Taiwan nüren de xinqing gushi [The Inner Story of a Taiwanese Woman] 2006, Yuanfen, CCTV-4, Beijing, 2 July.

Yuanjia Deguo [Marrying Far Away in Germany] 2006, Dongfang quan jilu, Shanghai Dragon TV, Shanghai, 28 August.

Yuanjia yiguo de Zhongguo guniang [Chinese Women Who Married Abroad] 2009, Yuanfen, CCTV-4, Beijing, 3 May.

Zhejiang xifu Taiwan lang yu lalian jieyuan [Zipper Business Helps Zhejiang Woman and Taiwan Man Tie the Knot] 2007, Yuanfen, CCTV-4, Beijing, 11 February.

Zhenjian dui maiming de Liang'an hunyin: Liu Jie and Wang Xun [The Cross-Strait Marriage of Liu Jie and Wang Xun: Tit for Tat] 2008, Yuanfen, CCTV-4, Beijing, 4 January.

Appendix 3
Television talk shows on Chinese–foreign marriage (20 episodes)

Ai de feidie: Zhang Shan, Zhang Desheng [The Love of Skeet Shooting: Zhang Shan and Zhang Desheng (Dexter Barnes)] 2011, Feichang fuqi, BTV-3, Beijing, 8 September.

An cun de Yangxifu [A Foreign Bride in Our Village] 2009, Xiangyue, CCTV-7, Beijing, 10 October.

Bing shang ailü: Chenlu, Dan Nisi [Loving Couple On the Ice: Chen Lu and Dan Nisi (Denis Alekseyevich Petrov)] 2008, Luyu youyue, Anhui TV, Anhui, 14 February.

Cao Cao, Li Zhiyin: Women buneng san [Cao Cao (Jonathan Kos-Read) and Li Zhiyin: We Won't Break Up] 2010, Feichang fuqi, BTV-3, Beijing, 6 May.

Daizhe baobao qu lüxing [Travelling With Our Baby] 2010, Guoji shuangxingxian, BTV-1, Beijing, 18 July.

Deguo yangxifu de Zhongguo shenghuo [The Life of a German Bride in China] 2009, Jiating yanboshi, Shanghai Oriental TV, Shanghai, 13 November.

Ganyi jiazu de kuaguo qingyuan [The Intercultural Love of the Cognac Family] 2010, Guoji shangxingxian, BTV-1, Beijing, 5 September.

Hanguo xifu Zhongguo lang de aiqing gushi [Love Story of a South Korean Bride and a Chinese Groom] 2007, Luyu youyue, Anhui TV, Anhui, 23 August.

Kuaguo hunyin [Intercultural Marriage] 2010, Jiating yanboshi, Shanghai Oriental TV, Shanghai, 16 April.

Kuaguo hunyin [Intercultural Marriage] 2011, Yue ce yue kaixin, Hunan TV, Hunan, 25 January.

Shen Danping, Wu Wei [Shan Danping and Wu Wei (Uwe Kraeuter)] 2009, Feichang fuqi, BTV-3, Beijing, 12 February.

Shi Ke, Ke Lize [Shi Ke and Ke Lize (Christian Könitzer)] 2009, Feichang fuqi, BTV-3, Beijing, 17 April.

Tan Te zhige: Gong Lin'na [The Song Tan Te: Gong Linna] 2011, Feichang Jing juli, Anhui TV, Anhui, 14 January.

Wailai de xifu, bendi de lang: Hao Lianlu, Wang Hongye [Foreign Bride and Local Groom: Hao Lianlu (Esther Haubensack) and Wang Hongye] 2010, Feichang fuqi, BTV-3, Beijing, 11 February.

Wukelan xiaohuo de Zhongguo qingyuan: Zhang Wenting he Bobi Ken [Ukrainian Man and His Chinese Love: Zhang Wenting and Bobi Ken (Brabykon)] 2010, Feichang fuqi, BTV-3, Beijing, 15 October.

Yijia sandai kuaguo qing [Three Generations of Intercultural Love in One Family] 2010, Guoji shuangxingxian, BTV-1, Beijing, 17 January.

Yiguolian zhende hui xingfu ma? [Can Intercultural Love Bring True Happiness?] 2010, Xingfu wandianming, Jiangsu TV, Jiangsu, 24 June.

You ai dasheng shuo [Shout about Your Love] 2010, Feichang Jing juli, Anhui TV, Anhui, 9 November.

Zhong Ying kuaguo hunyin [Chinese–British Marriage] 2011, Luyu youyue, Anhui TV, Anhui, 28 January.

Zhu Chen: Wo de meili qiyuan [Zhu Chen: My Beautiful Encounter with Chess] 2006, Luyu youyue, Anhui TV, Anhui, 14 January.

Appendix 4
Children in celebrity Chinese–foreign marriages (examples)

Couples (nationalities)	Number of children
Haubensack Esther (German)/Wang Hongye (Chinese)	1 son
Jiao Zhimin (Chinese–South Korean)/Ahn Jae-hyun (South Korean)	1 son
Kos-Read Jonathan (American)/Li Zhiyin (Chinese)	1 daughter
Li Donghua (Chinese–Swiss)/Friedli Esperanza (Swiss)	1 daughter
Li Lingyu (Chinese)/'Jerry' (Canadian)	1 son
Li Qinqin (Chinese)/'Shan Gen' (Japanese)	1 son
Ning Jing (Chinese)/Kersey Paul (American)	1 son
Wu Qihua (Chinese–Hong Kong)/Shi Yangzi (Chinese)	1 daughter
Zhang Tielin (Chinese–British)/'Marissa' (Polish)	1 daughter
Chen Chong (Chinese–American)/Xu Yimin (Chinese–American)	2 daughters
Chen Lu (Chinese)/Alekseyevich Petrov Denis (Russian)	1 son and 1 daughter
Deng Wendi (Chinese–American)/Murdoch Rupert (Australian–American)	2 daughters
Fu Mingxia (Chinese)/Liang Jingsong (Chinese–Hong Kong)	1 daughter and 2 sons
Jiang Wen (Chinese)/Chenivisse Sandrine (French)	1 daughter (from previous marriage) and 2 sons
Liu Ye (Chinese)/Martane Anais (French)	1 son and 1 daughter
Ma Jingtao (Chinese–Taiwan)/Wu Jiani (Chinese)	1 daughter (from previous marriage) and 2 sons
Roswell Mark (Canadian)/Gan Lin (Chinese)	1 son and 1 daughter
Shen Danping (Chinese)/Kraeuter Uwe (German)	2 daughters
Shi Ke (Chinese)/Könitzer Christian (Swiss)	2 sons
Siqin Gaowa (Chinese–Swiss)/Chen Liangsheng (Chinese–Swiss)	1 son and 1 daughter (both from previous marriage)
Wei Wei (Chinese)/Smith Joseph Michael (American)	3 sons
Zhu Chen (Chinese–Qatarian)/Al-Modiahki Ahmed Mohammed (Qatarian)	2 daughters

References

A Hen (1996) 'Siqin Gaowa: Zhongguo dianying wo de gen' [Siqin Gaowa: My Roots Are in Chinese Film], *Lüyou*, 9: 38–9.
'A Policy of "One Country, Two Systems" on Taiwan' (2000) *Zhonghua renmin gongheguo waijiaobu*, 17 November. Online. Available at www.fmprc.gov.cn/eng/ziliao/3602/3604/t18027.htm (accessed 10 September 2011).
'A Record of the New Documentary Movement in China' (2004) *Zhongguo wang*, 23 August. Online. Available at www.china.org.cn/english/culture/104848.htm (accessed 21 June 2011).
'About CSM' (2011) *CSM Media Research*. Online. Available at www.csm.com.cn/en/about.php?action=About (accessed 5 October 2011).
Adams, M. and Coltrane, S. (2006) 'Framing Divorce Reform: Media, Morality and the Politics of Family', *Family Process*, 46(1): 17–34.
Akhavan-Majid, R. (2004) 'Mass Media Reform in China', *Gazette: The International Journal for Communication Studies*, 66(6): 553–65.
Akhavan-Majid, R. and Ramaprasad, J. (1998) 'Framing and Ideology: A Comparative Analysis of US and Chinese Newspaper Coverage of the Fourth United Nations Conference on Women and the NGO Forum', *Mass Communication and Society*, 1(3/4): 131–52.
'Asian Men Seek Poor Brides' (2010) *Agence France Press*, 6 July. Online. Available at www.hurriyetdailynews.com/n.php?n=asian-men-seeks-poor-brides-2010-07-06 (accessed 3 October 2010).
Ata, A.W. (2005) *Mixed Marriage: Catholic/Non–Catholic Marriages in Australia*, Ringwood: David Lovell Publishers.
Bai Lu (2009) 'Zhang Tielin: Nü'er shi qianshi qingren' [Zhang Tielin: My Daughter Was My Lover in a Previous Life], *Wuhan chenbao*, 20 February.
Bai Ruoyun (2005) 'Media Commercialization, Entertainment and the Party–State: The Political Economy of Contemporary Chinese Television Entertainment Culture', *Global Media Journal*, 4(6): 1–21.
Bauer, H. M., Rodriguez, M. A., Quiroga, S. S. and Flores-Ortiz, Y. G. (2000) 'Barriers to Health Care For Abused Latina and Asian Immigrant Women', *Journal of Health Care For the Poor and Underserved*, 11(1): 33–44.
'Bei youhuo de nüren – Zhongguo nüren de shewai hunlian suipian yu Guangzhou shewai hunjie miju' [Tempted Women –The Mysterious Guangzhou Chinese–Foreign Marriage Agency and the Destruction of Chinese Women's Hopes for Intercultural Love and Marriage] (2008) *Nanfang ribao*, 20 February.
'Beijing yinxiang' [Beijing Impressions] (2004) *360buy.com*. Online. Available at http://mvd.360buy.com/20011584.html (accessed 17 August).

198 References

Berry, C. and Rofel, L. (2010) 'Introduction', in Berry, C., Lü Xinyu and Rofel, L. (eds) *New Chinese Documentary Film Movement: For the Public Record*, Hong Kong: Hong Kong University Press, pp. 3–14.

Bi Ran (2008) 'Jiehun 3 nian, jiu dale 3 chang lihun guansi – jian'nan xiudiao yangqi, xiaohuo yisheng tanxi' [Chinese Man Sighs over Filing for Third Divorce after Three Years of Marriage], *Wujin ribao*, 2 May.

Brady, A-M. (2003) *Making the Foreign Serve China: Managing Foreigners in the People's Republic*, Lanham, MD: Rowman and Littlefield.

Brady, A-M. (2007) *Marketing Dictatorship: Propaganda and Thought Work in Contemporary China*, Lanham, MD: Rowman and Littlefield.

Brand, R., Markey, C., Mills, A. and Hodges, S. (2007) 'Sex Differences in Self-Reported Infidelity and Its Correlates', *Sex Roles*, 57(1): 101–9.

Bray, D. (2005) *Social Space and Governance in Urban China: The Danwei System From Origins to Reform*, Stanford, CA: Stanford University Press.

Breger, A. R. and Hill, R. (1998) 'Introducing Mixed Marriages' in Breger, A. R. and Hill, R. (eds) *Cross-Cultural Marriage: Identity and Choice*, Oxford: Berg Publishers, pp. 1–32.

Brown, M. (2004) *Is Taiwan Chinese? The Impact of Culture, Power and Migration on Changing Identities*, Berkeley, Los Angeles and London: University of California Press.

Brugger, B. (1980) *China Since the 'Gang of Four'*, London: Croom Helm.

Bui, H. N. and Morash, M. (1999) 'Domestic Violence in the Vietnamese Immigrant Community: An Exploratory Study', *Violence Against Women*, 5: 769–95.

Bureau of Reeducation-through-Labor Administration (1979) 'Guowuyuan guanyu laodong jiaoyang de buchong guiding' [Supplementary Decision of the State Council On Reeducation through Labor], *Sifabu laodong jiaoyang guanliju*, 29 November. Online. Available at www.legalinfo.gov.cn/moj/ldjyglj/content/2007-05/16/content_19616.htm?node=258 (accessed 16 July 2010).

Cang Lide and Mu Ya (1993) 'Xiaohua duchuang Haolaiwu, suantiankula shuiren zhi' [*Little Flower* Singlehandedly Takes on Hollywood, No One Knows Her Joys or Sorrows], *Huanqiu shibao*, 11 April.

Cao Guangyu (2008) 'Hunjie jingli jie shewai hanjie heimu' [Marriage Broker Reveals Insights Into Chinese–Foreign Marriage Service], *Dongya jingmao xinwen*, 5 March.

Cao Wei (2000) 'Wei Wei yinwei you ai, yinwei you jiating' [Wei Wei: Because I Have Love and a Family], *Zhongguo minzu bolan*, 3: 25–46.

'CCTV-4 guoji pindao' [CCTV-4 International Channel] (2004) *Zhongyang dianshitai*. Online. Available at www.cctv.com/homepage/profile/04/index.shtml (accessed 6 October 2011).

'CCTV-8 dianshiju pindao jieshao' [Introduction to TV Drama Channel: CCTV-8] (2011) *Baidu wenku*, 18 January. Online. Available at http://wenku.baidu.com/view/1a3f73f79e 31433239689355.html (accessed 10 August).

Chan, K. W. (1992) 'Economic Growth Strategy and Urbanizaton Policies in China, 1949–1982', *International Journal of Urban and Regional Research*, 16(2): 275–305.

Chan, L. W. C., Huang, S. L. S. and Kung, W. W. (2005) 'Rediscovery of the "Self": Culturally Sensitive Intervention for Chinese Divorced Women', in Young, K. and Fok, A. (eds) *Marriage, Divorce and Remarriage: Professional Practice in the Hong Kong Cultural Context*, Hong Kong: Hong Kong University Press, pp. 143–68.

Chang Jian (2008) 'Chang Jian: Zhongguo duiwai kaifang de lishi jincheng' [Chang Jian: Historical Process of China's Opening-up]. *Guojia fagai wei hongguan yuan tiguan suo*, 28 September. Online. Available at www.cas.cn/zt/jzt/ltzt/dlqzgxdhyjltwx/dhbg/200809/t20080928_2671087.shtml (accessed 16 March 2010).

Chang Jui-shan (1999) 'Scripting Extramarital Affairs: Marital Mores, Gender Politics and Infidelity in Taiwan', *Modern China*, 25(1): 69–99.

Chao, E. (2005) 'Cautionary Tales: Marriage Strategies, State Discourse and Women's Agency in a Naxi Village of Southwestern China', in Constable, N. (ed.) *Cross-Border Marriages: Gender and Mobility in Transnational Asia*, Philadelphia: University of Pennsylvania Press, pp. 34–52.

Chen Bao (2003) 'Shanghai pandian 20 nian shewai hunyin' [Two Decades of Chinese–Foreign Marriage in Shanghai], *Renmin ribao*, 4 June.

'Chen Chong: Rang ao'yun jixu' [Chen Chong: Let the Olympic Games Go On] (2008) *Ai sixiang wang*, 10 April. Online. Available at www.aisixiang.com/data/detail.php?id=18329 (accessed 26 March 2011).

Chen Daoqiang (2008) 'Yi aide mingyi zhujiu xingfu yiguo qingyuan' [Building up Happiness in the Name of Love in Intercultural Marriage], *Yibin wanbao*, 11 May.

Chen Lei (2011) 'Qianxi guonei yule tanhua jiemu de fazhan' [A Brief Analysis of the Development of Entertainment Television Talk Shows in China], *Xinwen chuanbo*, 4: 164.

Chen Liyu (2003) 'Hu shewai hunyin jiankang fazhan wanli yinyuan qianshou ge dazhou' [Shanghai–Foreign Marriage Maintains Healthy Growth, Love Links All Continents], *Renmin ribao*, 11 June.

'Chen Lu, Den Nisi: yueguo Zhong E aihe, women yiqi feixiang' [Chen Lu and Denis Petrov: Fly across China–Russia Border] (2009) *Zhonghua mingren*, no date. Online. Available at www.zhmrmqmp.com/wenzhang/90/mrgs2.htm (accessed 26 August 2010).

'Chen Luyu zao Meiguo zhangfu xing nuedai' [Chen Luyu Suffers Sexual Abuse from Her American Husband] (2007) *Zhong'an zaixian*, 17 July. Online. Available at http://entertainment.anhuinews.com/system/2007/07/17/001796429.shtml (accessed 23 January 2011).

Chen Wei and Ran Qiyu (2009) 'Goujian hexie de hunyin jiating guanxi' [The Construction of Harmonious Marriage and Family Relationship], *Hebei Law Science*, 27(8): 43–9.

Chen Zhonghe (2007) 'Yang Xiaoxing de Zhongguo hunyin' [Foreign Comedian's Chinese Marriage], *Jiating shenghuo daobao*, 16 December.

Chen Zikun (1993) 'Shen Danping dongren de kuaguo hunyin' [Shen Danping's Emotionally Moving Intercultural Marriage], *Zhongguo jiankang yuekan*, 12: 38–9.

Cheng Yingqi and Cao Yin (2011) 'Women Becoming Initiators of More Divorces', *China Daily*, 4 March.

Chew, M. (2009) 'Research on Chinese Nightlife Cultures and Night-Time Economies', *Chinese Sociology and Anthropology*, 42(2): 3–21.

Chia, R. C., Allred, L. J. and Jerzak, P. A. (1997) 'Attitudes toward Women in Taiwan and China: Current Status, Problems and Suggestions for Future Research', *Psychology of Women Quarterly*, 21: 137–50.

Childs, C. E. (2005) *Navigating Interracial Borders: Black–White Couples and Their Social Worlds*, New Brunswick, NJ: Rutgers University Press.

'China Domestic Violence Complaints Soar 70 pct' (2007) *Reuters*, 25 November. Online. Available at www.reuters.com/article/idUSPEK264585 (accessed 20 October 2010).

'China Income Distribution' (2009) *China Hong Kong Travel Guide*. Online. Available at www.china-hongkong-travelguide.com/china-income.html (accessed 20 July 2010).

China Internet Network Information Center (CNNIC) (1997) 'Statistical Report of the Development of Chinese Internet', *CNNIC*, October 13. Available at www.cnnic.net.cn/download/manual/en-reports/1.pdf (accessed 3 July 2011).

China Internet Network Information Center (CNNIC) (2002) '10th Statistical Survey on the Development of Internet in China', *CNNIC*, July 15. Available at www.cnnic.net.cn/download/manual/en-reports/10.pdf (accessed 3 July 2011).

China Internet Network Information Center (CNNIC) (2008) 'CNNIC fabu "di 22 ci Zhongguo hulian wangluo fazhan zhuangkuang tongji baogao"' [CNNIC Releases 'The 22nd Statistical Report on the Internet Development in China'], July 24. Available at www.cnnic.net.cn/html/Dir/2008/07/23/5233.htm (accessed 17 September 2010).

China Internet Network Information Center (CNNIC) (2009) 'The 23rd Statistical Survey Report on the Internet Development in China', *CNNIC*, 13 January. Available at www.cnnic.net.cn/uploadfiles/pdf/2009/3/23/153540.pdf (accessed 4 June 2011).

China Internet Network Information Center (CNNIC) (2012) 'The 29th Statistical Report on the Internet Development in China', *CNNIC*, January. Online. Available at www1.cnnic.cn/IDR/ReportDownloads/201209/P020120904421720687608.pdf (accessed 24 March 2013).

China Labour Bulletin (2004) 'Working Women in China – Second Class Workers'. Online. Available at www.china-labour.org.hk/en/node/3442 (accessed 22 May 2010).

China National Tourism Administration (2002) '2002 nian Zhongguo lüyouye tongji gongbao' [China Tourism Statistics Report 2002]. Online. Available at www.chinadmd.com/search.do?nkey=2002%E5%B9%B4%E4%B8%AD%E5%9B%BD%E6%97%85%E6%B8%B8%E4%B8%9A%E7%BB%9F%E8%AE%A1%E5%85%AC%E6%8A%A5 (accessed 9 July 2014).

China National Tourism Administration (2010) '2009 nian Zhongguo lüyouye tongji gongbao' [China Tourism Statistics Report 2009]. Online. Available at www.cnta.gov.cn/html/2010-10/2010-10-20-10-43-69972.html (accessed 9 July 2014).

China National Tourism Administration (2011) '2010 nian Zhongguo lüyouye tongji gongbao' [China Tourism Statistics Report 2010]. Online. Available at www.cnta.gov.cn/html/2011-11/2011-11-1-9-50-68041.html (accessed 9 July 2014).

'China's TV Industry: An Overview' (2006) *China Radio International*, 26 October. Online. Available at www.china.org.cn/english/entertainment/186489.htm (accessed 24 December 2010).

'Chinese Mainland Issues New Policies to Ease Cross-Strait Travel' (2008) *Xinhuawang*. Online. Available at www.chinadaily.com.cn/china/2008-09/07/content_7005998.htm (accessed 5 March 2013).

'Chinese Mainland Tourists Make 350,000 Trips to Taiwan after Travel Ban Lifted' (2009) *Renmin Wang*, 28 June. Online. Available at http://english.peopledaily.com.cn/90001/90782/92900/6687896.html (accessed 25 September).

Chu Yingchi (2007) *Chinese Documentaries: From Dogma to Polyphony*, London and New York: Routledge.

Chuanqi gushi' [Legendary Stories] (2011) *Baidu*. Online. Available at http://baike.baidu.com/view/420771.htm (accessed 9 July 2011).

Chuanqi nüren Deng Wendi de hunyin shenghuo' [The Married Life of Legendary Woman, Wendi Deng] (2008) *Taisha wang*, 9 September. Online. Available at www.taisha.org/abroad/sh/gs/200809/20080909113708.html (accessed 27 August 2010).

Clark, C. D. (2001) 'Foreign Marriage, "Tradition" and the Politics of Border Crossings', in Chen, N., Clark, C. D., Gottschang, Z. S. and Jeffery, L. (eds) *China Urban: Ethnographies of Contemporary Culture*, Durham, NC and London: Duke University Press, pp. 104–22.

Coltrane, S. and Adams, M. (2003) 'The Social Construction of the Divorce "Problem": Morality, Child Victims and the Politics of Gender', *Family Relations*, 52(4): 363–72.

'Common Ground' (2011) *BTV.com.cn*. Online. Available at www.btv.org/btvweb/btvwzlm/2007-05/16/content_179353.htm (accessed 9 October).

'Cong Xuenaiyin'an kan Zhong Ao kuaguo hunyin: Zhongguo xin'niang de beiju' [Observing Chinese–Australian Marriage from the Perspective of the Xuenaiyin Case – Chinese Bride's Tragedy] (2009) *Beifang xinbao*, 23 June.

Constable, N. (2003) *Romance on a Global Stage: Pen Pals, Virtual Ethnography* and *'Mail-Order' Marriages*, Berkeley: University of California Press.

Constable, N. (2005a) 'A Tale of Two Marriages: International Matchmaking and Gendered Mobility' in Constable, N. (ed.) *Cross-Border Marriages: Gender and Mobility in Transnational Asia*, Philadelphia: University of Pennsylvania Press, pp. 166–86.

Constable, N. (2005b) 'Introduction: Cross-Border Marriages, Gendered Mobility and Global Hypergamy', in Constable, N. (ed.) *Cross-Border Marriages: Gender and Mobility in Transnational Asia*, Philadelphia: University of Pennsylvania Press, pp. 1–16.

'CPC Seeks Advice on Building Harmonious Society' (2006) *Xinhua News Agency*, 13 October. Online. Available at www.china.org.cn/english/government/183853.htm (accessed 28 April 2011).

'Cross-Strait Strains' (2004) *Time Magazine World*, 8 March. Online. Available at www.time.com/time/magazine/article/0,9171,501040315-598583,00.html (accessed 10 September 2011).

Cui Xiaolin and Wen Shan (2010) 'Jiejiu Mian nü' [Rescuing Burmese Women], *Zhongguo jingji zhoukan*, 5: 7–12.

Dai Honghong and Liu Laihong (2004) 'Ningbo cheng jia she Tai hunyin gao shuchu di' [High Incidence of Bogus Cross-Strait Marriages in Ningbo], *Dongfang zaobao*, 9 April.

Dalu jumin yu Taiwan jumin hunyin dengji guanli zanxing banfa [Administration of The Registration of Marriages between Mainland Residents and Taiwan Residents Tentative Procedures] (1998) *Ministry of Civil Affairs*, 10 December. Online. Available at http://news.xinhua net.com/tai_gang_ao/2006-04/06/content_4391758.htm (accessed 7 August 2008).

'Dalu peiou zai Tai qiuzhi nan' [Mainland Spouses Experience Difficulties Finding Jobs in Taiwan] (2004) *Dongfang zaobao*, 5 October.

Dashan wangzhai (2010) 'Who is Dashan?', *Dashan wangzhai*. Online. Available at www.dashan.com/en/index.htm (accessed 3 December 2010).

Davidson, J. R. (1991) 'Black–White Interracial Marriage: A Critical Look at Theories About Motivations of the Partners', *Journal of Intergroup Relations*, XVIII(4): 14–19.

Davin, D. (2005) 'Marriage Migration in China: The Enlargement of Marriage Markets in the Era of Market Reforms', *Indian Journal of Gender Studies*, 12(2/3): 173–88.

Davin, D. (2007) 'Marriage Migration in China and East Asia', *Journal of Contemporary China*, 16(50): 83–95.

De Vreese, C. H. (2005) 'News Framing: Theory and Typology', *Information Design Journal and Documentary Design*, 13(1): 51–62.

Del Rosario, V. O. (1994) 'Lifting the Smoke Screen: Dynamics of Mail-Order Bride Migration from the Philippines', PhD thesis, The Hague: Institute of Social Studies.

Deng Hong (2005) 'Titan kuaguo hunyin zhi nashi huakai, 4 duan yinyuan chuanwei meitan' [Four Chinese–Foreign Marriages in the Chinese Sports Industry] (2005) *Beijing yule xinbao*, 19 April.

Deng Huajuan (1993) 'Jingti shewai hunyin zhong buzhengchang xianxiang' [Be on Guard Against an Unusual Phenomenon in Intercultural Marriage], *Renmin ribao*, (article provided by *Shanghai jiefang ribao*), 3 April.

Deng Kaisong (1999) *Aomen lishi 1840–1949* [History of Macau 1840–1949], Zhuhai: Zhuhai chubanshe.

Deng Wendi chenggong jingying kuaguo hunyin [Wendi Deng's Successful Intercultural Marriage] 2011, television news programme, Zhengwu 30 fen, Shenzhen TV, Shenzhen, 21 July.

'Deng Wendi: Moduoke yu wo yijian zhongqing' [Wendy Deng: Murdoch and I Fell in Love at First Sight] (2009) *Zhongxin wang*, 7 December. Online. Available at http://news.cnwest.com/content/2009-12/07/content_2628381.htm (accessed 17 December 2010).

Di san qi Zhongguo funü shehui diwei diaocha zhuyao shuju baogao [Report on Major Results of the Third Wave Survey on the Social Status of Women in China] (2011) *All-China's Women's Federation and National Bureau of Statistics*, 21 October. Online. Available at www.wsic.ac.cn/academicnews/78621.htm (accessed 23 January 2013).

'Difang "guoji hongniang"' [Be Wary of 'International Matchmakers'] (1992) *Hangzhou ribao*, 30 April.

Ding Jinhong, Yang Hongyan, Zhou Shaoyun, Zhou Jixiang, Lin Kewu and Zhang Yuzhi (2004) 'Lun xinshiqi Zhongguo shewai hunyin de tezheng yu zouxiang' [Characteristics and Trends of Cross-Nation Marriage in Modern Shanghai (sic)], *Chinese Journal of Population Science*, 3: 66–80.

'Domestic Violence Increases in China' (2009) *Xinhua News Agency*, 7 March. Online. Available at www.chinadaily.com.cn/china/2009-03/07/content_7551147.htm (accessed 20 October 2010).

Donald, S., Keane, M. and Yin Hong (2002) *Media in China: Consumption, Content and Crisis*, London: RoutledgeCurzon.

Dong Xiaoyu and Hu Yang (2010) 'Dushi lei meiti zhong nongmin gong xingxiang liubian yanjiu' [The Changing Images of Rural Migrant Workers in the Mainstream Media], *Renmin wang*, 8 November. Online. Available at http://media.people.com.cn/GB/22114/206896/206904/13157563.html (accessed 1 October 2011).

Du Pin (1995) 'Shen Danping: mai huochai de xiao nühai' [Shen Danping: The Little Match-Girl], *Zhongguo fushi bao*, 24 November.

Du Zhanfan (2001) 'Tuijin shewai hunyin fuwu zhiduhua guifanhua jianshe' [Standardizing and Institutionalizing Chinese–Foreign Marriage Services], *Zhongguo shehuibao*, 27 September.

Duihua "Xin shimin"' [Dialogue: 'New Urban Citizens'] (2008) *Juzhou wang*, 27 October. Online. Available at www.jzw.gov.cn/fcontent.php?id=13 (accessed 3 October 2011).

'Duoqi dianying ren Chen Chong de liangduan hunyin' [Multi-Film Actor Chen Chong's Two Marriages] (2008) *Jiaren*, 3 December. Online. Available at http://lady.163.com/08/1203/11/4S82EK7P00262AEH.html (accessed 15 January 2011).

Earnshaw, G. (1981) 'Fiancee of Diplomat "Hooligan"', *Danwei: Chinese Media, Advertising and Urban Life*, 16 April. Online. Available at www.danwei.org/the_earnshaw_vault/hooligan_crime.php (accessed 8 January 2010).

Edmonds, R. (1992) 'The Changing Geograpy of Taiwan, Hong Kong and Macau', in Chapman, G. and Baker, K. (eds) *The Changing Geography of Asia*, London: Routledge, pp. 160–94.

Edwards, L. (2010) 'Military Celebrity in China: The Evolution of "Heroic" and "Model" Servicemen', in L. Edwards and E. Jeffreys (eds) *Celebrity in China*, Hong Kong: Hong Kong University Press, pp. 21–44.

Edwards, L. and Jeffreys, E. (eds) (2010) *Celebrity in China*, Hong Kong: Hong Kong University Press.

'Eguo kongjie wanli chizhui Zhongguo xiaohuo' [Russian Airhostess Chases after Chinese Man for Thousands of Miles] (2008) *Wujin ribao*, 16 January.

Eitzen, D. (1995) 'When is a Documentary? Documentary as a Mode of Reception', *Cinema Journal*, 35(1): 81–102.

Emerton, R., Laidler, K. and Petersen, C. (2007) 'Trafficking of Mainland Chinese Women Into Hong Kong's Sex Industry: Problems of Identification and Response', *Asia–Pacific Journal on Human Rights and the Law 2*, pp. 35–84.

Entman, R. B. (1993) 'Framing: Toward Clarification of a Fractured Paradigm', *Journal of Communication*, 43: 51–8.

Erwin, K. (1999) 'White Women, Male Desires: A Televisual Fantasy of the Transnational Chinese Family' in Yang Mei-Hui M. (ed.) *Spaces of Their Own: Women's Public Sphere in Transnational China*, Minneapolis and London: University of Minnesota Press, 4: 232–57.

Evans, H. (1997) *Women and Sexuality in China, Dominant Discourses of Female Sexuality and Gender Since 1949*, Cambridge: Polity Press.

Ewing, K. (2010) 'Foreign Workers (and Wives) Pour Into China', *Asia Times*, 30 April. Online. Available at www.atimes.com/atimes/China/LD30Ad01.html (accessed 1 October 2010).

Fallows, D. (2007) 'China's Online Population Explosion', *PewResearchCenter Publications*, 12 July, Online. Available at http://pewresearch.org/pubs/537/china-online (accessed 4 July 2011).

'Family Violence Becomes Public Evil in China' (2003) *Xinhua News Agency*, 7 March. Online. Available at www.china.org.cn/english/China/57629.htm (accessed 20 October 2010).

Fan, C. (2008) 'Migration, Hukou and the City' in Yusuf, S. and Saich, T. (eds) *China Urbanizes: Consequences, Strategies and Policies*, Washington, D.C.: World Bank Publications, pp. 65–89.

Fan, C. C. and Huang, Y. (1998) 'Waves of Rural Brides: Female Marriage Migration in China', *Annals of the Association of American Geographers*, 88(2): 227–51.

Fan, C. C. and Li, L. (2002) 'Marriage and Migration in Transitional China: A Field Study of Gaozhou, Western Guangdong', *Environment and Planning A*, 34(4): 619–38.

Fan, C.S. and Lui, H.-K. (2004) 'Extramartial Affairs, Marital Satisfaction and Divorce: Evidence from Hong Kong', *Contemporary Economic Policy*, 22(4): 442–52.

Fan, S.-P. (2010) 'The Effects of China's Tourism Diplomacy and a "United Front"', *China: An International Journal*, 8(2): 247–81.

Fang, H. (2008) 'Shen Daning huiyi dangnian kuaguo hunyin, danian chuer bei hongchu jiamen' [Shen Danping Recalls Her Intercultural Marriage, She Was Kicked Out of the Family House at New Year], *Bandao chenbao*, 6 July.

Fang, N. Wang Bingquan and Ma Lijun (2002) *Chengzhang de Zhongguo* [Growing China], Beijing: Renmin chubanshe.

'Fanyi gongsi weigui gao shewai hunjie: yi nü hua bawan jiage 74 sui yang laogong' [Translation Company Provides Illegal Chinese–Foreign Matchmaking Serivce, Woman Spent 80,000 Yuan to Marry a 74-year-old Foreigner] (2009) *Shengxin daokan*, 16 February.

Farrer, J. (2008a) 'From "Passports" to "Joint Ventures": Intermarriage between Chinese Nationals and Western Expatriates Residing in Shanghai', *Asian Studies Review*, 32(1): 7–29.

Farrer, J. (2008b) 'Play and Power in Chinese Nightlife Spaces', *China: An International Journal*, 6(1): 1–17.

Farrer, J. (2010) 'A Foreign Adventurer's Paradise? Interracial Sexuality and Alien Sexual Capital in Reform Era Shanghai', *Sexualities*, 13(1): 69–95.

'Fensui sirenbang' [Smashing the 'Gang of Four'] (2009) *Xinhua News Agency*, 23 September. Online. Available at http://hxd.wenming.cn/gq60n/2009-09/23/content_48342.htm (accessed 24 December 2010).

Feng Junyu and Su Xiaohuan (2001) *Zhongguo jingtou 2001* [China Lens 2001], Beijing: Wuzhou chuanbo chubanshe.

Feng Manlou (2008) 'Shewai hunyin jiufen 8 cheng yuanyu jiating baoli' [Eighty Per Cent Chinese–Foreign Marriage Conflict Caused by Domestic Violence], *Qingdao caijing ribao*, 29 October.

Feng Xinzi (1994) 'Nümingxing, yangren men hui chong ni ma?' [Female Stars: Can Foreigners Love You?], *Chuangye zhe*, 10: 34.

Feng Xu (2009) 'Governing China's Peasant Migrants: Building Xiaokang Socialism and Harmonious Society', in Jeffreys, E. (ed.) *China's Governmentalities: Governing Change, Changing Government*, New York: Routledge, pp. 38–62.

'Foreigners Enjoy Living, Travelling in China' (2004) *Xinhua News Agency*, 4 October. Online. Available at www.chinadaily.com.cn/english/doc/2004-10/04/content_379676.htm (accessed 16 July 2010).

'Fourth World Conference on Women' (1995) *UN.org*, 4 September. Online. Available at www.un.org/womenwatch/daw/beijing/dpibrochure.html (accessed 19 October 2010).

Freeman, C. (2005) 'Marrying Up and Marrying Down: The Paradoxes of Marital Mobility for Chosonjok Brides in South Korea', in Constable, N. (ed.) *Cross-Border Marriages: Gender and Mobility in Transnational Asia*, Pennsylvania: University of Pennsylvania Press, pp. 80–100.

Friedman, S. L. (2010) 'Marital Immigration and Graduated Citizenship: Post-Naturalization Restrictions on Mainland Chinese Spouses in Taiwan', *Pacific Affairs*, 83(1): 73–93.

Friedman, S. L. (2013) 'Mobilizing Gender in Cross-Strait Marriages: Patrilineal Tensions, Care Work Expectations and a Dependency Model of Marital Immigration,' in Wen-hsin Yeh (ed.) *Mobile Horizons: Dynamics across the Taiwan Strait*, Institute of East Asian Studies Publications Series, Berkeley: University of California.

Fu Guiming (2007) 'Gongli qudong, nan jie liangyuan, kuaguo hunyin liyi pansheng' [Marriage Driven By Hypergamy Is Unlikely to Succeed, Divorce Rate Hikes in Intercultural Marriages], *Shenyang ribao*, 16 October.

Fu Hualing (2005) 'Re-education Through Labor in Historical Perspective', *The China Quarterly*, 184: 811–30.

'Fuqin bujin jiating yiwu, fayuan panjue fuyang' [Law Court Requires Man to Comply with His Obligation for Parenting] (2007) *Zhelin lüshi wang*, 29 August. Online. Available at www.zjzllawyer.com/news_view.asp?newsid=124 (accessed 16 May 2011).

Gamson, W. A. and Modigliani, A. (1989) 'Media Discourse and Public Opinion on Unclear Power: A Constructionist Approach', *American Journal of Sociology*, 95(1): 1–37.

'Gang Tai zai neidi jiujing you duoshao ernai?' [How Many 'Second Wives' of Hong Kong and Taiwan Men Are from Mainland China?] (2003) *Sohu wang*. Online. Available at http://women.sohu.com/6/0204/41/blank219134150.shtml (accessed 13 October 2010).

'Gangnü qinglai Dalunan, Beijia geli rizeng, 20 nian fanle 9 bei'[Hong Kong Women Favour Mainland Men, Such Marriages Are Increasing in Northern China on a Daily Basis and Have Increased Ninefold over the Last Two Decades] Xingdao huanqiu wang, 21 November. Online. Available at www.stnn.cc/hongkong/200711/t20071121_673588.html (accessed 5 October 2011).

Gao Baoliang (2009) 'Chuguo wugong chengjiu yiduan meili kuaguo yinyuan, Jiangdu pinhan mugong qulai piaoliang Yuenan xin'niang' [Poor Worker from Jiangdu Obtained Pretty Vietnamese Wife When Working Abroad], *Yangzhou shibao*, 5 August.

Gao Haijian (2008) 'Meiti dui xin nongcun jianshe baodao de yicheng jiangou' [On the Agenda of Media's Report on the New Rural Construction (sic)], *Journal of Neijiang Normal University*, 23(3): 114–16.

Gao Jian Sheng (1995) *Zhongguo 21shiji de hunyin jiating* [Family and marriage in the twenty-first-century China], Shanxi: Shanxi renmin chubanshe.

Gao Li (2009) 'Liyi daoxiang zai shewai hunyin lingyu zhubu ruohua' [Profit-oriented Motivation Weakens in Intercultural Marriage], *Zhongguo funü bao*, 10 November.

Gao Ying (2005) 'Henan meizi jiagei Bolan zhunzongtong yidinghui daizhe zhangfu hui niangjia' [Henan Girl Marries Polish Presidential Candidate, She Will Bring Him to Her Native Home], *Dahe bao*, 10 July.

Gao Ying, Zhang Xiulan and Zhu Weilong (2003) 'Beijing jinnian shewai hunyin zhuangkuang yanjiu' [A Study on Cross-Nation Marriage of Beijing in Recent Years (sic)], *Population and Economics*, 1(196): 27–36.

'Gaodiao jia laowai que yi lihun shouchang de nüxing' [Female Stars' High Profile Marriages with Foreigners End in Divorce] (2010) *Hualong wang*, 1 November. Online. Available at http://news.0898.net/2010/11/01/598793.html (accessed 31 January 2011).

'Gei hunyin lai ci Zhongwai hezi' [Make Marriage a 'Chinese–Foreign Joint Venture'] (2008) *Dangdai shenghuobao*, 15 August.

'Gei lihun zhaoge liyou' [The Reasons for Divorce] (2007) *Jinri wanbao*, 15 December.

'Geren yewu' [Personal Business] (2005) *Zhonghua renmin gongheguo gong'anbu*, Online. Available at www.mps.gov.cn/n16/n1555903/n1555963/n1556023/n1556143/n1640809/1712259.html (accessed 5 March 2013).

'German Jumps Cultural Wall' (2004) *China Daily*, 14 April. Online. Available at www.chinadaily.com.cn/english/doc/2004-04/14/content_323159.htm (accessed 19 August 2010).

Glodava, M. and Onizuka, R. (1994) *Mail Order Brides: Women for Sale*, Colorado: Alakan.

Glosser, S. L. (2003) *Chinese Visions of Family and State, 1915–1953*, Berkeley, Los Angeles and London: University of California Press.

'Gonganbu: Jiezhi 2011 niandi, 4,752 ren chiyou waiguoren yongjiu juliuzheng' [Ministry of Public Security: 4,752 Foreigners Obtained a Permanent Residence Permit by End of 2011] (2012) *Xinhua wang*. Online. Available at http://news.xinhuanet.com/politics/2012-04/25/c_111838822.htm (accessed 24 March 2013).

Grierson, J. and Hardy, F. (1946) *Grierson on Documentary*, London: Collins.

Gu Hui (2007) 'Kuaguo hunyin jinqu nei anxiang caozui' [International Marriage Introduction Agencies Operate in a Black-Box Environment], *Zhongguo jingyingbao*, 10 September, C08 edn.

'Guanyu aizibing yu maiyin renyuan de diaocha baogao' [Investigative Report On Sex Sellers and HIV/AIDS] (2002) *Zhongguo aizibing jiance wang*. Online. Available at www.aids120.com/00/0xingxue/lunli/20040115162407.htm (accessed 13 October 2010).

'Guanyu dui nongcun maimai hunyin xianzhuan de sikao' [An Analysis of Mercenary Marriages in Rural Areas] (2010) *Neimenggu xinwen wang*, 5 March. Online. Available at http://news.nmgnews.com.cn/xam/article/20100305/231161_1.html (accessed 27 October 2010).

Guanyu neidi jumin she Gang shengyu wenti de guiding [Regulations of Birth Control of Chinese Mainland Citizens in Chinese–foreign Marriages Involving Citizens from Hong Kong] (1998) *National Population and Family Planning Commission*, 11 December. Online. Available at www.gsjsw.gov.cn/html/gjrkfg/11_30_39_487.html (accessed 30 October 2012).

Guanyu jieding huaqiao waiji huaren guiqiao qiaojuan shenfen de guiding [Regulations on Defining Overseas Chinese, Chinese with Foreign Nationalities, Returned Overseas Chinese and Family Members of Overseas Chinese] (2009) *Overseas Chinese Affairs of the State Council*, 24 April. Online. Available at www.qhwq.gov.cn/html/4331/143675.html (accessed 30 October 2012).

Guanyu sheqiao jihua shengyu zhengce de ruogan yijian [Suggestions on the Birth Control Regulations of Chinese Mainland Citizens in Chinese–Foreign Marriages Involving Overseas Chinese] (2009) *NPFPC, the Ministry of Public Security and the Overseas Chinese Affairs Office of the State Council*, 30 December. Online. Available at www.gqb.gov.cn/news/2010/0224/18685.shtml (accessed 30 October 2012).

Guanyu Taiwan tongbao yu Dalu gongmin zhijian banli jiehun dengji youguan wenti de tongzhi [Notice on Issues Relating to Marriage Registration between Taiwan Compatriots and Mainland Citizens] (1988) *Ministry of Civil Affairs, Central Taiwan Affairs Leading Group Office, Ministry of Foreign Affairs, Ministry of Public Security and Ministry of Justice*, 31 March. Online. Available at www.lawtime.cn/info/hunyin/hunyinfagui/2007070520266.html (accessed 18 March 2012).

Guanyu Zhongguo neidi jumin shewai shengyu wenti de guiding [Regulations of Birth Control of Chinese Mainland Citizens in Chinese–Foreign Marriages Involving Foreign Nationals] (1998) *National Population and Family Planning Commission*, 11 December. Online. Available at www.gsjsw.gov.cn/html/gjrkfg/11_30_39_487.html (accessed 30 October 2012).

Guerin, B. and Miyazak, Y. (2006) 'Analyzing Rumors, Gossip and Urban Legends Through Their Conversational Properties', *The Psychological Record*, pp. 23–34.

Guo Minxiu and Peng Hongping (2008) 'Zhongguo dianshi tanhua jiemu de bentu wenhua tese' [On the Local Cultural Characteristics of Chinese Television Talk Show (sic)], *Jiangxi lantian xueyuan yuebao*, 3(2): 86–9.

Guo Yingjie (2010) 'China's Celebrity Mothers: Female Virtues, Patriotism and Social Harmony', in Edwards, L. and Jeffreys, E. (eds) *Celebrity in China*, Hong Kong: Hong Kong University Press, pp. 45–66.

Guo Yuandan (2007) 'Jizhe jiu shewai hunyin xiang'guan wenti caifang Yang xiaolin lüshi' [Chinese–Foreign Marriage: Interview with Lawyer Yang Xiaolin], *Fazhi wanbao*, 28 February.

'Guowuyuan bangongting guanyu jiaqiang shewai hunyin jieshao guanli de tongzhi' [Notice on 'Strengthening the Management of International Marriage Introduction Agencies] (1994) *General Office of the State Council*, 6 December. Online. Available at www.zge.gov.cn/bmfw/content/2008-02/18/content_75067.htm (accessed 4 November 2010).

Gustafsson, B. and Li Shi (2000) 'Economic Transformation and the Gender Earnings Gap in Urban China', *Journal of Population Economics*, 13(2): 305–29.

'Hainan shewai hunyin renshu zengduo' [Hainan Sees More Intercultural Marriages] (1993) *Hangzhou ribao*, 20 January.

Hao Xiaohui (2004) 'Wu Wei: wo jia gei le Shen Danping' [Wu Wei: I Married Shen Danping], *Beijing jishi*, 7: 18–21.

Harding, H. (1993) 'The Concept of Greater China: Themes, Variations and Reservations', *The China Quarterly*, 136: 660–86.

'He Faguo qizi yiguo fenju, Jiang Wen shouci hunyin lihun shouchang' [Jiang Wen Separates from French Wife, His First Marriage Ends in Divorce] (2007) *Xinlang yule*, 19 October. Online. Available at www.huanqiu.com/www/191/2007-10/14107.html (accessed 10 October 2010).

He Jingru (2006) 'Xianggang, Aomen tebie xingzhengqu' [Special Administrative Regions: Hong Kong and Macau], *Xinhua News Agency*, 24 February. Online. Available at http://politics.people.com.cn/GB/8198/58703/58709/4138413.html (accessed 18 March 2010).

He Ying (1999) 'Dashan: xingfu de Zhongguo nüxu' [Dashan: Happy Chinese Son-in-Law], *Hainan ribao*, 5 May.

'Heping, Youyi, Xingfu' [Peace, Friendship and Happiness] (1989) *Hangzhou ribao*, 20 February.

Hershatter, G. (2011) *The Gender of Memory: Rural Women and China's Collective Past*, Berkeley, Los Angeles and London: University of California Press.

Hiseh Ching-yu and Wang Ching-yi (2008) 'Immigrant Wives and Their Cultural Influence in Taiwan', *Shida xuebao*, 53(2): 101–18.

Holmes, S. (2005) 'Off-guard, Unkempt, Unready?' Deconstructing Contemporary Celebrity in Heat Magazine', *Journal of Media and Cultural Studies*, 19(1): 21–38.

Hong Junhao (2002) 'The role of media in China's democratisation', *WACC*. Online. Available at www.waccglobal.org/en/20021-mass-media-and-the-democratisation-of-eastern-europe/702-The-role-of-media-in-Chinas-democratisation-.html (accessed 28 April 2012).

'Hong Kong Man Too Tied up to Visit China Mistress' (2006) *Bangkok Post*, 7 November. Online. Available at http://chinaview.wordpress.com/2006/11/08/hong-kong-man-too-tied-up-to-visit-china-mistress/ (accessed 4 October 2010).

Hooks, B. (1995) *Killing Rage: Ending Racism*. New York: Henry Holt.

Hsia, Hsiao-Chuan (2007) 'Imaged and Imagined Threat to the Nation: The Media Construction of the 'Foreign Brides Phenomenon' as Social Problems in Taiwan', *Inter-Asia Cultural Studies*, 8(1): 55–85.

'Hu Jintao's Report at 17th Party Congress' (2007) *Zhongguo wang*, 15 October. Online. Available at www.china.org.cn/english/congress/229611.htm#10 (accessed 24 September 2011).

Hu Shufeng and Xiong Yunbin (2007) 'Jiehui da queqiao, yinzhen chuan hongxian – Nanyang 'Li shi zhenjiu' chuanren xiqu Riben xin'niang' [(Pharmaceutical) Festival: Li, the Son of the Well-known Family of Acupuncturists Marries His Japanese Bride at Nanyang City (Henan Province)], *Nanyang ribao*, 10 September.

Hu Yongmou (2007) 'Jieshao shewai hunyin, weifa!' [International Marriage Introduction Agencies: They Are Illegal!] *Chutian dushibao*, 15 September.

Huang Mei-Ying (2003a) 'Improving Human Rights in China: Should Re-education Through Labor Be Abolished?', *Columbia Journal of Transnational Law*, 41(303): 303–26.

Huang Mei-Ying (2003b) 'Reassessing Reeducation Through Labor', *China Rights Forum*, 2: 35–41.

Huang Qizao (1994) 'Huang Qizao: zai quanguo fulian 7 jie 2 ci zhiweihui shangde gongzuo baogao' [Work Report by Huang Qizao at the Second Executive Committee of the 7th National Women's Conference]. *Zhongguo funü yanjiu wang*, 18 November. Online. Available at www.wsic.ac.cn/internalwomenmovementliterature/13326.htm (accessed 4 November 2010).

Huang Youqin (2001) 'Gender, *Hukou* and the Occupational Attainment of Female Migrants in China (1985–1990)', *Environment and Planning*, 33: 257–79.

'Huangruo geshi de mingxing gushi' [Remembering Celebrities' Stories of Yesteryear] (2008) *Suqian wanbao*, 29 November.

Huaqiao tong guonei gongmin, Gang Ao tongbo tong neidi gongmin zhijian banli jiehun dengji de jixiang guiding [Rules On Marriage Registration between Chinese Citizens and Overseas Chinese and Hong Kong and Macau Compatriots] (1983) *Ministry of Civil Affairs*, 10 March. Online. Available at www.xuanhan.gov.cn/Html/shiminpindao/shiminbanshi/hunyin/shewaihunyin/29587110.html (accessed 12 August 2009).

'Hunyin dengji banfa' [Marriage Registration Procedures] (1955) *Ministry of Internal Affairs*, 1 June. Online. Available at www.docin.com/p-258741725.html (accessed 5 March 2012).

'Hunyin dengji banfa' [Marriage Registration Procedures] (1980) *Ministry of Civil Affairs*, 11 November. Online. Available at www.mhhsx.com/ShopData/ShopData.aspx?Nid=SP2011062823540001 (accessed 5 March 2012).

'Hunyin dengji banfa' [Marriage Registration Procedures] (1986) *Ministry of Civil Affairs*, 15 March. Online. Available at www.people.com.cn/item/flfgk/gwy/msfg/860315.html (accessed 5 March 2012).

'Hunyin dengji guanli tiaoli' [The Regulations on Marriage Registration] (1994) *Ministry of Civil Affairs*, 1 February. Online. Available at www.people.com.cn/GB/shehui/212/3576/3577/3593/20020318/689673.htm (accessed 7 August 2008).

'Hunyin dengji tiaoli' [The Regulation on Administration of Marriage Registration] (2003) *General Office of the State Council*, 1 October. Online. Available at www.people.com.cn/GB/shizheng/1026/2023057.html (accessed 7 August 2008).

'Hunyin jieshao fuwu jigou guanli qingkuang jianjie' [Introduction to the Circumstances Surrounding the Management of Marriage Introduction Agencies] (2008) *Zhun ge'er zhichuang*, 18 February. Online. Available at www.zge.gov.cn/bmfw/content/2008-02/18/content_75067.htm (accessed 20 October 2010).

'Hunyin: tongxiang ziyou de bainian zhilu' [The Journey to Marriage Freedom over the Last Hundred Years] (2010) *Zhongguo funü bao*, 2 March. Online. Available at www.chinawoman.com/rp/main?fid=open&fun=show_news&from=view&nid=55160 (accessed 27 October 2010).

Hvistendahl, M. (2005) 'China's Pulse Races', *Los Angeles Times*, 24 July.

Ichikawa, T. (2006) 'Chinese in Papua New Guinea: Strategic Practices in Sojourning', *Journal of Chinese Overseas*, 2(1): 111–32.

Ilie, C. (2006) 'Talk Shows' in Brown, K. (ed.) *Encyclopedia of Language and Linguistics*, 2nd edn., Oxford: Elsevier, pp. 489–94.

'International Marriage Broker Sent to Prison' (2008) *Danwei: Chinese Media, Advertising and Urban Life*, 20 November. Online. Available at www.danwei.org/front_page_of_the_day/international_match_maker.php (accessed 20 October 2010).

Jeffords, S. (1993) 'Can Masculinity be Terminated?' in Cohan, S. and Rae, H. (eds) *Screening the Male: Exploring Masculinities in Hollywood Cinema*, London and New York: Routledge, pp. 245–262.

Jeffreys, E. (2006) 'Debating the Legal Regulation of Sex-related Bribery and Corruption in the People's Republic of China', in Jeffreys, E. (ed.) *Sex and Sexuality in China*, London and New York: Routledge, pp. 159–178.

Jeffreys, E. and Edwards, L. (2010) 'Celebrity/China', in Edwards, L. and Jeffreys, E. (eds) *Celebrity in China*, Hong Kong: Hong Kong University Press, pp. 1–20.

Jeffreys, E. and Sigley, G. (2009) 'Governmentality, Governance and China', in Jeffreys, E. (ed.) *China's Governmentalities: Governing Change, Changing Government*, New York: Routledge, pp. 1–23.

Ji Beibei (2010) 'Vietnamese Authorities Tackle Human Trafficking Into China', *Global Times*, 24 February. Online. Available at www.globaltimes.cn/china/society/2010-02/507487.html (accessed 5 December 2011).

Ji Zhe (1996) 'Mengduan Bageda' [Dream Ends in Baghdad], *Zhejiang ribao*, 22 June.

'Jiadao Riben fangzhi "jinguixu" shi "qiongguangdan"' [After Marrying and Moving to Japan She Discovered Her Rich Husband Was a Pauper] (2007) *Changjiang ribao*, 16 November.

'Jianadaren Dashan: shi waiguoren que bushi wairen' [Canadian Da Shan – A Foreign National But Not an Outsider] (2008) *Wenhui bao*, 10 July.

Jiang Wandi (2005) 'Scholar Explores Harmonious Society Concept', *Zhongguo wang*, 4 March. Online. Available at www.china.org.cn/english/2005/Mar/121746.htm (accessed 28 April 2011).

'Jiang Wen Faguo qianqi shoudu kaikou: "Women yiran xiang'ai"' [Jiang Wen's French Ex-Wife Says First and Foremost, 'We Still Love Each Other'] (2006) *Huashang chenbao*, 1 November.

'Jiang Wen hunxue nü'er baoguang, liang ren "qizi" jie cheng xian neizhu' [Jiang Wen's Mixed-Race Daughter Exposed, His 'Two Wives' Are Both Helpful] (2007) *Sohu wang*, 7 August. Online. Available at http://yule.sohu.com/20070807/n251449910.shtml (accessed 2 May 2011).

'Jiang Wen wei Zhou Yun yu qi lihun, liangren qinmi youhui bei toupai' [Jiang Wen Divorces His Wife For Zhou Yun, Candid Photographs Show the Lover's Rendezvous] (2005) *Qianlong wang*, 8 July. Online. Available at www.hsw.cn/fun/2005-07/08/content_2031920.htm (accessed 17 May 2011).

Jiang Haishun (1999) 'Dui Zhong Han shewai hunyin ruogan wenti de tantao' [Discussing Issues about Chinese–Korean Marriages], *Journal of Yanbian University*, 32(3): 128–31.

Jiang Zhongyi (2007) 'Woshi shewai hunyin shuliang yousuo xiajiang' [Intercultural Marriage Decreases in Our City], *Jinhua ribao*, 26 September.

'Jiangshu' [Stories] (2011) *Baidu*. Online. Available at http://baike.baidu.com/view/99076.htm (accessed 9 July 2011).

'Jiating guanxi jinzhang, yu jingji ren lian'ai, Ning Jing tanyan lihun' [Ning Jing Confesses to Divorce after Family Tensions and Starts New Relationship with Her Agent] (2007) *Xingchen yule*, 29 April. Online. Available at http://ent.changsha.cn/yltt/200606/t20060615_486131.htm (accessed 17 May 2011).

'Jielu Jiang Wen yu qianqi lihun neimu' [Divorce between Jiang Wen and His Ex-French Wife Revealed] (2008) *Shenzhen xinwan wang*, 22 November. Online. Available at www.sznews.com/home/content/2008-11/22/content_3410333.htm (accessed 17 April 2011).

Jin Mei (2009) 'Zhongguo fan jiating baoli fa pingshu' [Analysis of China's Law Against Domestic Violence], *Journal of Jiangsu Police Officer College*, 24(1): 53–60.

Jing Lin (2003) 'Chinese Women Under the Economic Reform: Gains and Losses', *Harvard Asia Pacific Review*, 7(1): 88–90.

'Jingji tequ' [Special Economic Zones] (2002) *Zhongguo wang*, 22 September. Online. Available at http://lianghui.china.com.cn/chinese/zhuanti/208123.htm (accessed 15 March 2010).

'Jiyin yi zhuru, zaowan yao biaolu' [Celebrity Parents' Genes Revealed in Their Children] (2009) *Meiri xinbao*, 28 November.

Jizhe anfang, hunjie fuzeren luohangertao [Marriage Introduction Agency Operator Flees from an Unexpected Visit by Journalist] 2010, television news programme, Gongtongguanzhu, CCTV-13, Beijing, 16 December.

Jones, G. and Shen Hsiu-hua (2008) 'International Marriage in East and Southeast Asia: Trends and Research', 12(1): 9–25.

Juan Zi (1996) 'Chen Chong: weixi hunyin de mijue shi zhongcheng' [Chen Chong: Loyality is the Key to A Successful Marriage], *Dangdai dianshi*, 5: 5.

Keane, M., Fung, A. and Moran, A. (2007) *New Television, Globalization and the East Asian Cultural Imagination*, Hong Kong: Hong Kong University Press.

Khulpateea.V. L. (2007) 'State of the Union: Cross Cultural Marriages in Nineteenth-Century Literature and Society', PhD Thesis, Binghamton: State University of New York.

Kim, Doo-Sub (2010) 'The Rise of Cross-border Marriage and Divorce in Contemporary Korea', in Yang, Wen-Shan and Lu, Melody Chia-Wen (eds) *Asian Cross-border Marriage Migration: Demographic Patterns and Social Issues*, Amsterdam: Amsterdam University Press, pp. 127–53.

King, W. (2011) 'Taiwanese Nationalism and Cross-Strait Marriage: Governing and Incorporating Mainland Spouses' in Schubert, G. and Damm, J. (eds) *Taiwanese Identity in the 21st Century: Domestic, Regional and Global Perspectives*, London and New York: Routledge, 176–96.

Kipnis, A. (1997) *Producing Guangxi: Sentiment, Self and Subculture in a North China Village*, Durham, NC: Duke University Press.

Kong Qingjing (2004) 'Cross-Taiwan Strait Relations: What Are the Legitimate Expectations from the WTO', *Minnesota Journal of Global Trade*, 14(1): 91–110.

Kuaguo hunyin mengpo zhongjie renqu loukong [Dream of Intercultural Marriage Destroyed, Marriage Introduction Agency Disappears] 2009, television news programme, Diyi shijian, CCTV-2, Beijing, 14 September.

'Kuaguo hunyin pinchuan lihun, He Zhili yuanjia Riben shoudao nuedai' [Intercultural Marriages Keep Ending in Divorce, He Zhili Abused after Marrying a Japanese] (2008) *Guangzhou ribao*, 19 January.

Kuo, Yi-Hsuan (2010) 'Subversions of the Social Hierarchy: Social Closure as Adaptation Strategy by the Female Marriage Migrants of Taiwan', *Journal of Comparative Research in Anthropology and Sociology*, 2(1): 85–101.

Lampton, M. D. (2001) *The Making of Chinese Foreign and Security Policy in the Era of Reform, 1978–2000*, Stanford, CA: Stanford University Press.

Lang, G. and Smart, J. (2002) 'Migration and the Second Wife in south China: Toward Cross-Border Polygyny', *International Migration Review*, 36(2): 546–69.

Lauser, A. (2006) 'Philippine Women on the Move: A Transnational Perspective on Marriage Migration', *International Asian Forum, International Quarterly for Asian Studies*, 37(3/4): 321–37.

Lee, F. (2004) 'Constructing Perfect Women: the Portrayal of Female Officials in Hong Kong Newspapers', *Media Culture and Society*, 26(2): 207–25.

Lee Hye-Kyung (2008) 'International Marriage and the State in South Korea', *Pai Chai University*. Online. Available at www.cct.go.kr/data/acf2006/multi/multi_0303_Hye%20Kyung%20Lee.pdf (accessed 18 August 2009).

Lee, T. V. (1997) *Foreigners in Chinese Law*, New York and London: Garland Publishing.

Lewise, R., Yancey, G. and Bletzer, S. (1997) 'Racial and Nonracial Factors That Influence Spouse Choice in Black/White Marriages', *Journal of Black Studies*, 28(1): 60–78.

Li Bing (2002) 'Dianshi tanhua jiemu qianxi' [A Brief Analysis of Television Talk Shows], *Dangdai dianshi*, 4: 72–3.

Li Demin (2004) 'Shewai hunyin zai bianhua' [Chinese–Foreign Marriage is Changing], *Renmin ribao*, 3 November.

'Li Donghua ren Ruishi daibiao tuan tebie dashi, nüyou shi huayi guzheng shou' [Li

Donghua Assigned as Special Ambassador to Swiss Delegation, His Chinese Girlfriend Plays the Zither (Guzheng)] (2008) *Dongfang tiyu ribao*, 3 August.

Li Erwei (1994) 'Siqin Gaowa yinxiang – zuoren congyi dou zhencheng' [Siqin Gaowa: Sincere On and Off Stage], *Xiandan funü*, 2: 32–3.

Li Fengjie (2006) 'Meiti "Chengshi hua" yu nongcun xinxi "huangmo hua"' [The 'Urbanization' of the Media and the 'Desertification' of Rural News], *Qingnian jizhe*, 10: 42.

Li Hongguang (2006) 'Queqiao buzai – kuaguo lihun shenli nan' [Love Broken: The Difficult Trials of Intercultural Divorce Cases], *Zhongguo funü bao*, 10 October.

Li Hui (2007) 'Yiwei Meiguo xiaohui zai Anqing de aiqing' [An American Guy Finds Love in Anqing City], *Anqing Wanbao*, 24 October.

Li Jing (2010) 'Xiagang nügong ruhe yingdui jiuye nan wenti' [How Do Laid-off Female Workers Cope with the Difficult Employment Situation], No. 2, General No. 74, Fushun: Bianjiang jingji yu wenhua, pp. 55–6.

Li Juan and Long Yao (2008) 'Zhong Yue bianjing kuaguo hunyin wenti yanjiu – yi Guangxi Daxin xian Aijiang cun weili' [A Study of Cross Border Marriage in the Sino-Vietnamese Border Regions: A Case of Aijing Village, Daxin County, Guangxi Province (sic.)], *South China Population*, 23(89): 34–41.

Li Jun (1994a) 'Wei Wei: Xingfu yougui' [Wei Wei:Journey to Love and Happiness], *Yinyue tiandi*, Vol. 9.

Li Jun (1994b) 'Wei Wei: shenghuo zhong xuyao langman' [Wei Wei: Life Needs Romance], *Shidai chao*, 5: 73–4.

Li Ping (2008) 'Dashan: woshi Chongqing nüxu, Guo Donglin laizai chunwan buzou' [Dashan: I am a Chongqing Son-in-law; Actor Guo Donglin Refuses to Leave the New Year's Party], *Chongqing chenbao*, 18 April.

'Li Qinqin lijing liangci shewai hunyin, re'ai shenghuo xiangshou shenghuo' [Li Qinqin: Loving Life after Two Intercultural Marriages] (2004) *Xinlang yule*, 1 September. Online. Available at http://ent.sina.com.cn/s/m/2004-09-01/1756491161.html (accessed 2 May 2011).

Li Ranran (1999) 'Dianping Siqin Gaowa' [Comments on Siqin Gaowa], *Dazhong dianying*, 11: 62.

Li Sha (2009a) 'Kuaguo hunyin jin 30 nian zengzhang 5 bei' [Chinese–Foreign Marriage Increases Five Fold over the Last Three Decades], *Fazhi wanbao*, 18 October, 22nd edn.

Li Sha (2009b) 'Lianyin qingjia xianjin yi fugai quan shijie' [Chinese–Foreign Marriage Is Global], *Fazhi wanbao*, 19 October, 23rd edn.

Li Yan (2005) 'Shi Ke de langman zhi lü' [Shi Ke's Romantic Trip], *Wenzhai bao*, 10 February.

Li Yan (2008) 'Dashan: wo shi Chongqing nüxu' [Dashan: I am a Chongqing Son-in-Law], *Chongqing wanbao*, 18 April.

'Li Yang lihun'an kaiting, fayuan tiaojie weiguo' [Li Yang Divorce Case Opens in Court, Mediation was Unsuccessful] (2011) *Xinhuawang*. Online. Available at http://news.xinhuanet.com/local/2011-12/15/c_111247787.htm (accessed 9 January 2012).

Li Yunling (2005) 'Danshen shenghuo rang Wei Wei chongshi xinxin' [Single Life Enables Wei Wei to Regain Confidence], *Dongfang zaobao*, 28 September.

Li Zijun (2005) 'Zai guowai deng guang'gao zhao laogong? Shewai hunyin "hei zhongjie" xianshen Nanjing' [Advertising for a Husband Overseas? Chinese–Foreign Marriage "Go-betweens" Appear in Nanjing City], *Nanjing ribao*, 28 April.

Liang Hongying (2002) 'Shewai hunyin laofushaoqi xianxiang jianshao' ['Old Husband–Young Wife' Phenomenon Decreases in Chinese–Foreign Marriages], *Wenhuibao*, 1 July, 8th edn.

Liang Ying and Peng Xuemei (2008) 'Shewai hunyin, cong gongli dao rang ai zuozhu' [Chinese–Foreign Marriage: From Hypergamy to Love], *Xijiang dushibao*, 27 November.

'Liang'an hunyin mianmianguan' [The Characteristics of Cross-Strait Marriages] (1992) *Hangzhou ribao*, 17 December.

'Liang'an hunyin xin xianxiang: Taiwan nü jia Dalu nan' [New Phenomenon of Cross-Strait Marriage: Taiwan Women Marry Mainland Men] (2011) *Xiamen shangbao*, 11 April.

'Liangci hunyin, liangdu chenfu' [The Ups and Downs of Chen Chong's Two Intercultural Marriages] (2007) *Chongqing chenbao*, 16 December.

'Lianyungang kaiban shewai hunyin jieshaosuo' [Chinese–Foreign Marriage Introduction Agency to be Established in Lianyungang] (1992) *Xinxi ribao*, 26 September.

Liao, C. and Heaton, T. (1992) 'Divorce Trends and Differentials in China', *Journal of Comparative Family studies*, 23(3): 413–29.

Liaw Kao-Lee, Ochiai, E. and Ishikawa, Y. (2010) 'Feminization of Immigration to Japan: Marital and Job Opportunities', in Yang, Wen-Shan and Lu, Melody (eds) *Asian Cross-border Marriage Migration: Demographic Patterns and Social Issues*, Amsterdam: Amsterdam University Press: 49–86.

'Lihun'an jin sicheng you jiating baoli suozhi' [40 Per Cent Divorce Cases Stem from Domestic Violence] (2010) *Renmin wang*. Online. Available at http://tv.people.com.cn/GB/14644/135863/13382849.html (accessed 23 January 2013).

'Lihunlü gao! Zhongguo nümingxing yuanhe dou leyi jiagei waiguo ren?' [High Divorce Rate! Why do Chinese Female Celebrities Prefer to Marry Foreigners?] (2007) *Zhongguo wang*, 14 September. Online. Available at www.china.com.cn/info/txt/2007-09/14/content_8877700.htm (accessed 15 January 2011).

Lin Guifen (2008) 'Shewai hunyin: cong 3 dui dao 30 duo dui' [Chinese–Foreign Marriage: From Three to over Thirty Couples], *Xiamen shangbao*, 9 October.

Lin Xudong (2005) 'Documentary in Mainland China', trans. by Cindy Carter, *International Documentary Film Festival*, August. Online. Available at www.yidff.jp/docbox/26/box26-3-e.html (accessed 22 June 2011).

Ling Zaiming (1992) 'Yang guniang luohu "tiantang"' [Foreign Women Settle Down in 'Heaven'], *Zhejiang ribao*, 15 October.

Liu Gong and Wang Tingfeng (1999) 'Haikou shewai hunyin rizeng' [Chinese–Foreign Marriages Increase in Haikou], *Hainan ribao*, 8 June.

Liu Guofu (2005) 'The Right to Leave and Return and Chinese Migration Law', PhD thesis, Sydney: University of Technology, Sydney.

Liu Guofu (2009) 'Changing Chinese Migration Law: From Restriction to Relaxation', *Journal of International Migration and Integration*, 10(3): 311–33.

Liu Josie (2007) 'Suggestion on Abolishing Illegal Cohabitation Triggered Debate', *Josieliu.blogspot.com*, 11 March. Online. Available at http://josieliu.blogspot.com/2007/03/2007-npc-cppcc-journal-day-7.html (accessed 17 July 2010).

Liu Jun (1994) 'Aichao zhong de Shen Danping' [Shen Danping: In the Nest of Love], *Dangdai dianshi*, 8: 27–9.

Liu Lihui and Liu Hong (2008) 'Boundary-Crossing Trough Cyberspace' in Kuah-Pearce, K. E. (ed.) *Chinese Women and the Cyberspace*, Amsterdam: Amsterdam University Press, pp. 249–70.

Liu Meng and Chan Cecilia (1999) 'Enduring Violence and Staying in Marriage: Stories of Battered Women in Rural China', *Violence Against Women*, 5: 1469–92.

Liu Meng and Chan Cecilia (2000) 'Family Violence in China: Past and Present', *Journal of Comparative Social Welfare*, 16(1): 74–87.

Liu Shuyong (1996) *Xiang'gang de lishi* [The History of Hong Kong], 1st edn, Beijing: Xinhua chubanshe.
Liu Xiaoxiao (2005) 'Zhiji Zhongguo kuaguo hunyin mingmen' [Striking at the Heart of Chinese–Foreign Marriages] (2005) *Fazhi zaobao*, 11 December.
'Liu Ye Yinglai langman kuaguo lianqing, Faji meinü you wangfu yun' [Liu Ye Welcomes Intercultural Love, French Beauty Brings Him Luck] (2007) *Nanjing chenbao*, 24 January.
Liu Zhonghua (2004) 'Wei Wei shuo ziyou de ganjue zhenhao' [Wei Wei Says It's Great to be Single], *Huanqiu shibao*, 31 May.
Liu Zhonghua (2005) 'Wei Haizi buxi shang fating, mang yanchu liangguo laihui pao' [(Wei Wei) Goes to Court for Her Children, Busy Performing Across Two Countries], *Huanqiu shibao*, 11 April.
Liu Zhonghua and Zhang Xuejun (2004) 'Wei Wei, kuaguo hunyin zoudao jintou' [Wei Wei's Intercultural Marriage Comes to an End], *Huanqiu shibao*, 26 April.
Long Zhun (2008) 'Li Qinqin huishou liangduan yiguo hunyin, pi Meiguo qianfu mei renxing' [Li Qinqin Recalls Her Two Intercultural Marriages, She Criticizes Her American Ex-Husband as Amoral], *Chongqing wanbao*, 27 January.
Longman Dictionary of Contemporary English (2005) Harlow, UK: Pearson Education.
Lu Aiguo (2002) 'Economic Reforms and Welfare Changes in China' in Lu Aiguo and Montes, M. F. (eds) *Poverty, Income Distribution and Well-Being in Asia During the Transition*, Basingstoke: Palgrave Macmillan, pp. 83–103.
Lü Guojiang (2002) 'Qianxi xin hunyinfa guanyu chonghun de guiding' [Analysis of the Regulations on Bigamy in the New Marriage Law] (2001), *Journal of Social Science of Jiamusi University*, 4(20): 21–2.
Lu Man (2011) 'Li Yang chengren jiabao, xiang qizi daoqian' [Li Yang Admits Domestic Violence, Apologizes to His Wife], *Xin jingbao*, 11 September.
Lü Suozhi (2005) 'Xingfu nüren Shen Danping zhuanfang: rang Deji nüer liuxue Zhongguo' [Interview With Happy Woman, Shen Danping: She Lets Her German Daughter Study in China], *Wuhan wanbao*, 19 April.
Lu Xin (2009) 'Zhongguo dianshi "tuokouxiu" jiemu de xianzhuang yu fazhan' [The Development of Chinese Television Talk Show], *Xinwen chuanbo*, 6: 64–5.
Lü Xinyu (2003) 'Jilupian de lishi yu lishi de jilu' [The History of Documentary and Documenting History], *Xinwen daxue*, 1: 69–73.
Lu Yilong (2002) '1949 nian hou de Zhongguo huji zhidu: jiegou yu bianqian' [The Structure of and Changes to China's Household Registration System after 1949], *Journal of Peking University (Humanities and Social Sciences)*, 39(2): 123–30.
Lu, M. (2007) 'Transnational Marriage in Asia', Leiden: International Institute for Asian Studies. Online. Available at https://openaccess.leidenuniv.nl/handle/1887/12805 (accessed 18 September 2008).
Lu, M. (2008) 'Gender, Marriage and Migration: Contemporary Marriages between Mainland China and Taiwan', PhD thesis, Leiden: Leiden University.
Luo Bin (2008) 'Chuguo biaoyan aishang Riben nanzi, jiehun buman yizhou laoyan fenfei, kuaguo yinyuan jiehun rongyi lihun nan' [Marriage is Easy, Divorce is Hard: (Chongqing Woman) Falls in Love With and Marries a Japanese Man While On a Business Tour – They Separate after One Week of Marriage], *Chongqing wanbao*, 7 January.
Luo Bin (2009) 'Baogao jingcha: wode Meiji zhangfu chonghun shengzi' [Report to the Police: My American–Chinese Husband is a Bigamist with Two Families and Children] (2009) *Chongqing wanbao*, 10 June.
Luo Ronghua (2009) 'Wei jia yanglaogong bushao nüzi zhong heizhao – yenei renshi baoguang shewai hunjie qian guize' [Many Women Seeking Foreign Husbands Fall into

a Trap – Insiders Reveal the 'Rules' of Chinese–Foreign Marriage Matchmaking Services], *Nanguo jinbao*, 11 October.

Luo Wenqing (2006) 'Heping yu jiaowang: Guangxi bianjing diqu kuaguo hunyin wenti chutan' [Peace and Communication: Exploration of Transnational Marriage in the Frontiers of Guangxi Province (sic.)], *Journal of Guangxi Normal University: Philosophy and Social Sciences*, 42(1): 52–6.

Luo Yunjuan (2009) 'Chinese Television' in Sterling, C. (ed.) *Encyclopedia of Journalism*, Thousand Oaks, CA: Sage Publications, pp. 292–4.

Ma Xin (2009) 'Shewai hunyin yushijujin bianhua duo, nianling chaju xiao suzhi zai tigao' [Chinese–Foreign Marriages Undergo Significant Changes: Age Gap Decreases and Education Level Increases], *Jin wanbao*, 17 September.

Ma Zhongdong, Lin Ge and Zhang, Frank (2010) 'Cross-border Marriage in Hong Kong: 1998–2005', in Yang, Wen-Shan and Lu, Melody (eds) *Asian Cross-border Marriage Migration: Demographic Patterns and Social Issues*, Amsterdam: Amsterdam University Press, pp. 87–101.

'Mainland Entry Permits More Accessible to Taiwanese' (2013) *Xinhuawang*. Online. Available at http://news.xinhuanet.com/english/china/2013-01/30/c_132139097.htm (accessed 5 March 2013).

'Map of Nanjing City' (2010) *Chinatouristmaps.com*. Online. Available at www.chinatouristmaps.com/city/nanjing.html (accessed 18 March 2010).

Martinsen, J. (2009) 'CCTV Cancels a Talk Show and Shifts Its Focus toward Entertainment', *Danwei.org*, 25 September. Online. Available at www.danwei.org/tv/shihua_shishuo_gets_cancelled.php (accessed 30 September).

Marxists Internet Archive (2009) 'Resolution on CPC History (1949–81)' *Foreign Languages Press*. Online. Available at www.marxists.org/subject/china/documents/cpc/history/index.htm (accessed 1 December 2010).

McCombs, M., Shaw, D. and Weaver, D. (1997) *Communication and Democracy: Exploring the Intellectual Frontiers in Agenda-Setting Theory*, Hillsdale, NJ: Erlbaum.

Measures for the Administration of Examination and Approval of Aliens' Permanent Residence in China (*Waiguoren zai Zhongguo yongjiu juliu shenpin guanli banfa*) (2004) Approved by the State Council on 13 December 2003 and promulgated by the Ministry of Public Security and the Ministry of Foreign Affairs on 15 August 2004, Decree No. 74. Online. Available at http://news.sina.com.cn/c/2004-08-20/10304086859.shtml and www.enghunan.gov.cn/Tourism/ThingsToKnow/Practical_Information/LawsPolicies/201104/t20110419_336121.htm (accessed 28 March 2012).

'Meiman de kauguo hunyin – Zhu Chen yu ta laogong de aiqing gushi' [Happy Intercultural Marriage – The Love Story of Zhu Chen and Her Husband] (2003) *Chongqing wanbao*, 2 December.

Meng Qiaoli (2008) 'Ning Jing lai Fei jiangshu yiguo hunyin' [Ning Jing Visits Hefei (Capital City of Anhui Province) and Talks about Her Intercultural Marriage], *Anhui shichang bao*, 24 June.

Meng Xiaoyun (2001) 'Yang xifu, yang nüxu: Zhongguo ren kuaguo hunyin yipie' [Foreign Sons and Daughters-in-Law: A Glimpse of Chinese–Foreign Marriages], *Renmin ribao*, 6 February.

Meyers, E. (2009) 'Can You Handle My Truth?": Authenticity and the Celebrity Star Image', *The Journal of Popular Culture*, 42(5): 890–907.

'Miandui jiabao, zenyang shuo "bu"' [How To Say "No" to Domestic Violence] (2011) *Xinhuawang*, 13 October. Online. Available at http://news.xinhuanet.com/society/2011-10/13/c_122152006_4.htm (accessed 9 January 2012).

Miao Hui (2006) 'Shewai hunyin "sanbuqu" bubu you mangdian' [The 'Blind Spots' of Chinese–Foreign Marriage], *Jiating zhoumobao*, 8 June.

Min Jun (1993) 'Haixia liang'an tonghun youxilu' [The Joys and Woes of Cross-Strait Marriages], *Hangzhou ribao*, 24 June.

Min Zheng (1994) 'Yihun nü pian zhengming zaijia yangren jiu chacuo yan faji chonghun you zui' [Married Woman Falsifies Marriage Registration Papers to Marry a Foreigner in a Bigamous and Illegal Fashion], *Hangzhou ribao*, 1 June.

Ming, K. (2005) 'Cross-border Traffic: Stories of Dangerous Victims, Pure Whores and HIV/AIDS in the Experiences of Mainland Female Sex Workers in Hong Kong', *Asia Pacific Viewpoint*, 46(1): 35–48.

'Mingren mingxing shewai hunlian, beixi guan shuiqing' [Celebrity Chinese–Foreign Marriage – Who Cares?] (2007) *Nanguo dushibao*, 6 July.

'Mingxing lihun zheng caichan sipo lian, Wei Wei zao qianfu an'suan xian sangming' [Celebrity Divorce Ends in Property Dispute, Wei Wei Almost Murdered By Ex-Husband] (2010) *Beiqing wang*, 16 November. Online. Available at http://ent.ynet.com/view3.jsp?oid=73597309 (accessed 5 March 2011).

'Mingxingmen kuaguo hunlian nancheng zhengguo, xiantianhouku lihun duo' [Bitterness after Sweetness: Many Celebrity Chinese–Foreign Marriages End in Divorce] (2009) *Zhongxin wang*, 8 August. Online. Available at http://news.enorth.com.cn/system/2009/08/08/004154354.shtml (accessed 18 January 2011).

'Mingxing Shi Ke yu laowai zhangfu de kuaguo hunyin' [Intercultural Marriage of Celebrity Shi Ke and Her Foreign Husband] (2009) *Wenhua jiaoliu*. Online. Available at www.iouclub.com/newsdetail-392.html (accessed 25 August 2010).

'Minzhengbu guanyu banli hunyin dengji zhong jige shewai wenti chuli yijian de pifu' [Reply from the Ministry of Civil Affairs to [the Shanghai Civil Affairs Bureau] on Issues Related to Foreign Applicants for Marriage Registration] (1983) Ministry of Civil Affairs, 9 December. Online. Available at http://acwf.people.com.cn/GB/99042/100629/6180066.html (accessed 21 March 2012).

Mo Xueqing (2009) 'Taiwan "fu laogong" yuanshi qiong'guangdan' [Rich Taiwanese Husband Is A Poor Catch (i.e. Is Poor)], *Chongqing wanbao*, 26 March.

Modeng jiating [Modern Family] 2002, television series, CCTV-8, Beijing, 24 January.

'Mosuo zouhun' [Walking Marriage of Mosuo Ethnicity] (2004) *Yunnan sheng renmin zhengfu menhu wangzhan*, 13 December. Online. Available at www.yn.gov.cn/yunnan,china/74595266874834944/20041213/3563.html (accessed 8 February 2011).

Mu Xuan (2009) 'Mingxing kauguolian weisha lihun duo' [Why Do the Intercultural Marriages of Most Stars End in Divorce?], *Daqing ribao*, 21 August.

Mu Zi (1999) 'Wei Wei he ta de erzi' [Wei Wei and Her Sons], *Hunyin yu jiankang*, 4: 44.

Munson, W. (1993) *All Talk: The Talkshow in Media Culture*, Philadelphia: Temple University Press.

'Murdoch Files for Divorce from Wife Wendi' (2013) *Chinadaily. com.cn*. Online. Available at www.chinadaily.com.cn/world/2013-06/14/content_16618513.htm (accessed 14 June 2013).

Na Na (2008) 'Ning Jing: Wo bai erzi tui gei le qianfu' [Ning Jing: I Gave My Son to (His Father) My Former Husband], *Wuhan chenbao*, 30 September.

Nakamatsu, T. (2003) 'International Marriage through Introduction Agencies: Social and Legal Realities of "Asian" Wives of Japanese Men', in Piper, N. and Roces, M. (eds) *Wife or Worker? Asian Women and Migration*, Lanham, MD: Rowman and Littlefield Publishers, pp. 181–201.

Nan Chen (2007) 'Zhang Tielin: Danxin ta buhui jiang Zhong'guohua' [Zhang Tielin: Worries His Daughter Cannot Speak Chinese], *Dushi chenkan*, 31 May.

Narayan, U. (1995) '"Male-Order" Brides: Immigrant Women, Domestic Violence and Immigration Law', *Hypatia*, 10(1): 104–19.

National Bureau of Statistics of China (2011a) '2010 nian di 6 ci quanguo renkou pucha zhuyao shuju gongbao [Di 1 hao]' [Communiqué of the National Bureau of Statistics of People's Republic of China on Major Figures of the 2010 Population Census [1] (No 1)]. Online. Available at www.stats.gov.cn/tjgb/rkpcgb/qgrkpcgb/t20110428_402722232.ht (accessed 30 September 2011).

National Bureau of Statistics of China (2011b) '2010 nian nongmingong jiance baogao' [2010 Report on Rural Migrant Workers], *Zhongguo fazhan baogao* [China Development Report], Beijing: Zhongguo tongji chubanshe, pp. 99–105.

Neizhengbu Huzhengsi [Department of Household Registration, Ministry of the Interior of Taiwan] (2011) Online. Available at www.ris.gov.tw/zh_TW/web/guest;jsessionid=3 BB7F66227EE55A3142BDCA3405C6D66 (accessed 9 September 2011).

Nelson, E. T., Clawson, A. R. and Oxley, M. Z. (1997) 'Media Framing of a Civil Liberties Conflict and Its Effect on Tolerance', *The American Political Science Review*, 91(3): 567–83.

Ni Yan (2005) 'Shewai hunyin lihun renshu nianzeng 57%' [Chinese–Foreign Divorces Increase 57 Per cent Yearly], *Nanjing ribao*, 28 April.

Ni Yan and Xu Xiuyou (2006) 'Qunian Jiangsu baiyudui shewai hunyin polie' [Hundreds of Chinese–Foreign Marriages Ended in Divorce Last Year in Jiangsu Province], *Nanjing ribao*, 13 February.

Nichols, B. (1991) *Representing Reality: Issues and Concepts in Documentary*, Bloomington and Indianapolis: Indiana University Press.

'Ning Jing he Bao Luo, reqing yu lengjing zhijian' [Ning Jing and Paul (Kersey): between Passion and Calmness] (2004) *Qingnian shibao*, 26 November.

'Nü'er yaoqiu fuqin fu fuyang fei an' [Law Case: Daughter Wants Child Support from Father] (2009) *Zhonggu falü wang*, 6 May. Online. Available at http://news.9ask.cn/hyjt/znfy/201105/1175161.shtml (accessed 16 May 2011).

'Nüzi wanglian qingxin waiguo "fushang", shenmi xiangzi pianzou jukuan 23 wan' [Chinese Woman Dates Online, Tricked by 'Mr. Rich's' 'Overseas Baggage' [and the Opportunity To Go Overseas] She Loses 230,000 Yuan] (2008) *Shenyang ribao*, 17 April.

'One in Five Marriages End in Divorce in China' (2010) *Thaindian News*, 12 June. Online. Available at www.thaindian.com/newsportal/health/one-in-five-marriages-end-in-divorce-in-china_100379046.html (accessed 5 October 2010).

Ong, R. (2007) *China's Security Interests in the 21st Century*, Abingdon: Routledge.

Oxfeld, E. (2005) 'Cross-Border Hypergamy? Marriage Exchanges in a Transnational Hakka Community', in Constable, N. (ed.) *Cross-Border Marriages: Gender and Mobility in Transnational Asia*, Philadelphia: University of Pennsylvania Press, pp. 17–33.

Pan Meihong (2006) 'Shewai hunyin Binhai shengwen' [Chinese–Foreign Marriage Booms in Binhai], *Beifang jingji shibao*, 19 May A01 edn.

Pan Suiming (2006) 'Transformations in the Primary Life Cycle: The Origins and Nature of China's Sexual Revolution', in Jeffreys, E. (ed.) *Sex and Sexuality in China*, London and New York: Routledge, pp. 21–42.

Pandian mingxing beican kuaguo lian' [Celebrities' Tragic Intercultural Love Stories] (2009) *Zhongguo xinwen wang*, 19 October. Online. Available at http://fashion.people.com.cn/GB/10212458.html (accessed 26 March 2011).

Pandian zuigui lihun an, "Muo Duoke yu Deng Wendi lihun jiang sun duoshao' [Analysing the Most Expensive Divorce Case – How Much Will It Cost Rupert Murdoch to Divorce Wendi Deng?] (2009) *Zhongguo jingji wang*, 8 December. Online. Available at http://news.cnwest.com/content/2009-12/08/content_2630482.htm (accessed 17 May 2011).

Pang Fan and Wen Huangwei (2005) 'Zhongnian funü kaishi zhuiqiu shewai hunyin wei bo huanyan kuxue yingyu' [Middle-aged Women in Pursuit of Intercultural Marriage Study Hard at English to Please Foreigners], *Shidai Xinbao*, 28 September.

Parsons, P. and Xu Xiaoge (2001) 'News Framing of the Chinese Embassy Bombing by the People's Daily and the New York Times', *Asian Journal of Communication*, 11(1): 51–67.

Penny, J. and Khoo, S-E. (1996) *Intermarriage: A Study of Migration and Integration*, Canberra: Australian Government Publishing Service.

Penz, H. (1996) *Language and Control in American TV Talk Shows: An Analysis of Linguistic Strategies*, Tübingen: Gunter Narr Verlag.

Perilla, J. L. (1999) 'Domestic Violence as a Human Rights Issue: The Case of Immigrant Latinos', *Hispanic Journal of Behavioral Sciences*, 21: 107–33.

Perry, B. and Sutton, M. (2006) 'Seeing Red over Black and White: Popular and Media Representations of Inter-racial Relationships as Precursors to Racial Violence', *Canadian Journal of Criminology and Criminal Justice*, 48(6): 887–904.

Perry, C. M., Shams, M. and Deleon, C. C. (1998) 'Voices from an Afghan Community', *Journal of Cultural Diversity*, 5: 127–31.

'Pilu: shezu yiguolian de Zhong'guo nüxing' [Chinese Female Stars in Intercultural Marriage] (2008) *Tengxun nüxing pindao*, 12 June. Online. Available at www.803.cn/lady/HTML/lady_33280.html (accessed 27 August 2010).

Piper, N. (2003) 'Wife or Worker? Worker or Wife? Marriage and Cross-Border Migration in Contemporary Japan', *International Journal of Population Geography*, 9: 457–69.

Poston, D. and Glover, K. (2005) 'Too Many Males: Marriage Market Implications of Gender Imbalances in China', paper presented at XXV International Population Conference, Tours, France, 18–23 July, pp. 1–26.

Prasso, S. (2005) *The Asian Mystique: Dragon Ladies, Geisha Girls and Our Fantasies of the Exotic Orient*, 1st edn, New York: Publish Affairs.

Priest, P. J. (1995) *Public Intimacies: Talk Show Participants and Tell All TV*, Cresskill, NJ: Hampton Press.

'Promote Peaceful Development of Relations Across Taiwan Straits: Hu Jintao' (2011) *Xinhuawang*, 1 July. Online. Available at http://news.xinhuanet.com/english2010/china/2011-07/01/c_13960438.htm (accessed 24 September 2011).

Pu Liu (2002) 'Ning Jing yu Baoluo de yiguo qingyuan: cong xizhong qinglü dao zhixin airen' [Ning Jing and Paul (Kersey's) Intercultural Love: From On Screen Couples to Real Life Lovers] *Beijing qingnian bao*, 21 June.

Qi Xinxin (2008) 'Guangzhou Yiguanglian feifa congshi shewai hunyin bei chafeng' [Illegal Marriage Agency in Yiguanglian, Guangzhou, Is Closed Down], *Nanfang ribao*, 15 March.

Qian Zhenchao and Lichter, D. T. (2007) 'Social Boundaries and Marital Assimilation: Interpreting Trends in Racial and Ethnic Intermarriage', *Amercian Sociological Review*, 72: 68–94.

Qing Bao (2008) 'Yu zhangfu Baoluo liangdi fenju, Ning Jing qifen fouren lihun chuanwen' [Ning Jing Lives Apart from Her Husband Paul, Angrily Denies Divorce Rumour], *Dangdai shenghuo bao*, 21 November.

Qingxi Xixili [Love in Sicily] 2007, television series, CCTV-8, Beijing, 2 January.
Qiu Ying (2007) 'Jia: Zhongguo yiban, Jianada yiban' [Home is Both in China and in Canada], *Shangqiu baoye wang*, 1 October. Online. Available at www.sqrb.com.cn/gb/misc/2007-10/01/content_848677.htm (accessed 22 December 2010).
'Qizi changqi jiating baoli, zhangfu xinji lihun huozhun' [Wife Abuses Husband Long-term: Frightened Husband Files for Divorce] (2010) *Nanfang ribao*, 12 October. Online. Available at http://msn.china.ynet.com/view.jsp?oid=69751532 (accessed 15 October 2010).
Qu Hailin and Lam, S. (1997) 'A Travel Demand Model for Mainland Chinese Tourists to Hong Kong', *Tourism Management*, 18(8): 593–97.
'Qu waiguo nüren de Zhongguo nanren' [Chinese Men Who Have Married Foreign Women] (2005), *Xinhua wang*, 29 December. Online. Available at www.ah.xinhuanet.com/news2005/2005-12/29/content_5928554.htm (accessed 5 October 2011).
Qu Yinghua (2004) 'Wei Wei xuanbu he waiji zhangfu lihun: dushen ganjue tai hao le' [Wei Wei Announces that She Has Divorced Her Foreign Husband: Says It's Great to Be Single], *Chongqing shangbao*, 20 April.
'Quannei mingxing jia waiguoren neimu' [Insights into Celebrity Chinese–Foreign Marriages] (2010) *Shenzhen xinwen wang*, 2 July. Online. Available at www.sznews.com/photo/content/2010-07/02/content_4715760_27.htm (accessed 9 March 2010).
Quan Xiaoshu (2005) 'Cong jinxingpai dao lüka: waiguoren zai zhongguo yuelai yue ziyou' [From 'No go' to Green Card: Foreigners Enjoy More Freedom in China]. Online. Available at http://news.jxgdw.com/gnxw/539503.html (accessed 4 June 2009).
'Quge yangniu zuo laopo' [Get a Foreigner for a Wife] (2009) *Luoyang wanbao*, 11 July.
Raj, A. and Silverman, J. (2002) 'Violence Against Immigrant Women: The Roles of Culture, Context and Legal Immigrant Status on Intimate Partner Violence', *Violence Against Women*, 8: 367–98.
Rallu, L. J. (2002) 'International Migration in South-East Asia: The Role of China', paper presented at the IUSSP Conference on Southeast Asia's Population in a Changing Asian Context, Chulalongkorn University, Bangkok, pp. 1–20.
Ren Bo (2011) 'Haixia bian yinhe, jiaoliu da queqiao' [The [Taiwan] Strait Became the Milky Way; Communication Has Built the Bridge of Magpies], *Meiri xinbao*, 5 August.
Ren Yuan (1998) 'Dongxi fang dianshi jilupian duibi yanjiu' [A comparative analysis of eastern and western television documentaries], *Shijie dianying*, 5: 32–4.
Renwu jianjie: Chen Chong' [Chen Chong's Biography] (2004) *Zhongguo yingshi ziliao guan*. Online. Available at www.cnmdb.com/bio/343 (accessed 26 March 2011).
Roberts, I. D. (2010) 'China's Internet Celebrity: Furong Jiejie' in Edwards, L. and Jeffreys, E. (eds) *Celebrity in China*, Hong Kong: Hong Kong University Press, pp. 217–36.
Robinson, K. (1996) 'Of Mail-Order Bride and "Boys" Own" Tales: Representations of Asian-Australian Marriages', *Feminist Review*, 52: 53–68.
Romano, D. (1988) *Intercultural Marriage: Promises and Pitfalls*, Yarmouth, ME: Intercultural Press.
Romano, D. (1997) *Intercultural Marriage: Promises and Pitfalls*, 2nd edn, Yarmouth, ME: Intercultural Press.
Romano, R. (2003) *Race Mixing: Black–White Marriage in Postwar America*, Cambridge, MA: Harvard University Press.
Rong Weiyi (2004) 'Jiating baoli jiexi' [Analysing Domestic Violence], *Xin anquan*. Online. Available at www.people.com.cn/GB/paper2515/11573/1043275.html (accessed 25 October 2010).

Rosenblatt, P. C. (2009) 'A System Theory Analysis of Intercultural Couple Relationships', in Karis, T. A. and Killian, K. D. (eds) *Intercultural Couples: Exploring Diversity in Intimate Relationships*, New York and London: Routledge, pp. 3–20.

Rosenthal, E. (1998) 'In China, 35 + and Female = Unemployment', *The New York Times*, 13 October.

'Ruci hunlian zhe jie' [Such (hypergamy-led) Marriage Shall Stop] (1990) *Hangzhou ribao*, 14 July.

Schein, L. (2005) 'Marrying Out of Place: Hmong/Miao Women Across and Beyond China', in Constable, N. (ed.) *Cross-Border Marriages: Gender and Mobility in Transnational Asia*, Pennsylvania: University of Pennsylvania Press, pp. 53–79.

Scheufele, D. A. (1999) 'Framing as a Theory of Media Effects', *Journal of Communication*, 49(1): 103–22.

Shan Danping (1995) *Yangguangxia de Piaobo: Wo de Yishu yu Hunlian* [Life in the Sun: My Art, Love and Marriage], Beijing: Zhongguo huabao chubanshe.

Shang Bin (2008) 'Mengxiang kuaguo hunyin: 80 duo ming nüzi bei pianqianpianse' [Dreaming of Intercultural Marriage: Over 80 Women Cheated], *Huanqiu shibao*, 31 December.

Shanghai Municipal Statistics Bureau (2007) 'Shanghai tongji nianjian' [The Shanghai Statistical Yearbook]. Online. Available at www.statssh.gov.cn/2003shtj/tjnj/nje07.htm?d1=2007tjnje/e0312.htm (accessed 7 August 2008).

'Shanghai shewai hunyin danhua gongli secai' [Utilitarianism Fades in Intercultural Marriage in Shanghai] (2002) *Liaoning ribao*, 29 November.

'Shanghai shewai hunyin jianwen' [Chinese–Foreign Marriage in Shanghai] (1988) *Renmin ribao*, (article provided by *Shanghai fazhibao*), 11 January.

Shanghai shi shewai hunyin guanli zanxing banfa [Interim Procedures of Shanghai Municipality on the Administration of Foreign-related Marriage] (2000) *Shanghai Municipality*, 1 January. Online. Available at www.hjxh.cn/news/news_show.asp?news_id=266 (accessed 8 November 2010).

Shao Zhen and Liang Hongying (2004) 'Shewai hunyin zaoyu 7 nian zhiyang' [Chinese–Foreign Marriage Encounters "Seven-Year-Itch"], *Wenhui bao*, 7 September.

'Shehui zhuyi hexin jiazhi tixi' [Socialist Core Value System] (2006) *Xinhua wang*. Online. Available at http://news.xinhuanet.com/ziliao/2009-04/08/content_11150446.htm (accessed 28 November 2012).

'Shehui zhuyi jingshen wenming jieshe de tichu yu fazhan' [Development of the Concept of Construction of Socialist Spiritual Civilization] (2003) *Xinhua wang*. Online. Available at http://news.xinhuanet.com/ziliao/2003-01/20/content_697927.htm (accessed 21 Febraury 2013).

Shen Hsiu-Hua (2005) 'The First Taiwanese Wives and the Chinese Mistresses: the International Division of Labour in Familial and Intimate Relations across the Taiwan Strait', *Global Networks*, 5(4): 419–37.

Shen Hsiu-Hua (2008) 'The Purchase of Transnational Intimacy: Women's Bodies, Transnational Masculine Privileges in Chinese Economic Zones', *Asian Studies Review*, 32: 57–75.

Shen Jianfa (2003) 'Cross-Border Connection between Hong Kong and Mainland China Under "Two Systems" Before and Beyond 1997', *Geogr. Ann.*, 85B(1): 1–17.

Sheu, Yea-huey (2007) Full Responsibility with Partial Citizenship: Immigration Wives in Japan, *Social Policy and Administration*, 41(2): 179–96.

'Shewai hunjie shu feifa' [International Marriage Introduction Agencies Are Illegal] (2008) *Nanfang ribao*, 20 February.

'Shewai hunyin dengji shuliang wei jin 4 nian zuidi, kuaguo yinyuan buzai shou wenzhouren qinglai' [Records of Chinese–Foreign Marriage Lowest in Four Years: Cross-Cultural Love Is No Longer Favoured by Wenzhounese] (2007) *Taizhou wanbao*, 17 September.

Shi Ping (1999) 'Mingxing "jiating xinwen" heqiduo' [Lots of Celebrity 'Family News'], *Hainan ribao*, 8 June.

Shi Qing (1997) 'Cong Ning Jing waijia shuoqi' [About Ning Jing's Intercultural Marriage], *Dianying pingjie*, 5: 18–19.

Shi Yanrong (2009) 'Zhong Ri kuaguo hunyin wenti fenxi' [Analysis of China–Japan Marriages], *Lilun yu xiandaihua*, 4: 88–92.

Shi Zhiyong and Liang Juan (2006) 'Nongmingong bian shen "xin shimin": mingcheng gaibian de zhenglun' [Rural Migrant Workers Are Now 'New Urban Citizens': the Controversy Behind the Name Change], *Xinhua wang*, 12 December. Available at http://news.xinhuanet.com/focus/2006-12/12/content_5449637.htm (accessed 30 May 2011).

Shih Chuan-kang (2010) *Quest for Harmony: The Moso Traditions of Sexual Union and Family Life*, Stanford, CA: Stanford University Press.

Shih Shu-mei (1998) 'Gender and New Geopolitics of Desire: The Seduction of Mainland Women in Taiwan and Hong Kong Media', *Signs*, 23(2): 287–319.

'Shihua shishuo' [Tell It Like It Is] (2011) *CCTV.com*. Online. Available at www.cctv.com/program/talkshow/index.shtml (accessed 5 October 2011).

'Shiwei jiagei waiguo mingren de Zhongguo nüxing' [Ten Chinese Women Who Married Foreign Celebrities] (2008) *Zhiyin*, 31 March. Online. Available at http://lady.163.com/08/0331/09/48BR5GS900262AEH.html (accessed 26 August 2010).

'Shiyi jie sanzhong quanhui kaipi shehui zhuyi shiye fazhan xin shiqi' [Third Plenum of the Eleventh National Party Congress Central Committee Paves Way For New Era of Development of Socialism] (2008) *Zhongguo gongchandang xinwan wang*, 16 September. Online. Available at www.jrsx.com.cn/ponews.asp?id=9304&owen1=%B5%B3%CA%B7%B3%A4%C0%C8 (accessed 5 December 2010).

'Shoushilü lian'nian xiajiang, *Shihua shishuo* bei Zhongyang dianshitai quxiao' [China Central TV Station Cancels *Shihua shishuo* [CCTV Cancels Talk Show *Tell It Like It Is* Because of Falling Ratings] (2009) *Zhongguo xinwen wang*, 27 September. Online. Available at http://news.21315.com/xinwendongtai/shxw/2009-09-27/37071.html (accessed 30 September 2011).

Shu Enyu (1996) '"Kuaguo zhuihun zhe" shen' [Pursuers of Transnational Marriage – Be Cautious], *Hangzhou ribao*, 10 October.

Shuai Yong and Jiang Yu (2007) 'Nanjing meinian qianyu ren jiaqu laowai' [Over One Thousand People Enter Into an Intercultural Marriage in Nanjing City Each Year], *Nanjing ribao*, 9 September, A06 edn.

'Siqin Gaowa: Ruishi bushi wo de jia' [Siqin Gaowa: Switzerland is Not My Home] (2006) *Beijing qingnianbao*, 22 February.

'Sirenbang fandang shijian de tongzhi' [Notification on the Anti-communist Behaviour of the 'Gang of Four'] (1992) *Zhonghua renmin gongheguo chunqiu shilu*, January. Online. Available at http://old.hybsl.cn/lz-d-01.htm (accessed 2 December 2010).

So, A. (2003) 'Cross-border Families in Hong Kong: The Role of Social Class and Politics', *Critical Asian Studies*, 35(4): 515–34.

'Song Qiang: Hu zongshuji yu Ma Yingjiu "16 zi fangzhen"de yitong' [Song Qiang: The Similarities and Differences between the '16-Character Guidelines' of CCP General Secretary Hu Jintao and Ma Yingjiu] (2009) *Fenghuang wang*, 28 July. Online. Available at http://opinion.nfdaily.cn/content/2009-07/28/content_5433536.htm (accessed 24 September 2011).

Stroud, M. (1986) 'The Love Match That Rocked China – French Diplomat, Chinese Artist Find Respite at Stanford', *Los Angeles Times*, 24 August. Online. Available at http://articles.latimes.com/1986-08-24/news/vw-17507_1?pg=3 (accessed 5 November 2009).

Su Hong (2011) 'Tanxi qing'ganlei dianshi tanhua jiemu de fazhan ji qushi' [Exploring the Development Trends of Emotive TV Talk Shows], *Jin chuanmei*, 3: 79–81.

Su Hongjun (2005) 'Reinserting Woman Into Contemporary Chinese National Identity: A Comparative Reading of Three New Immigrant Plays from 1990s Shanghai', *Theatre Journal*, 57(2): 229–46.

Sun Wanning (2008) 'The Curse of the Everyday: Politics of Representation and New Social Semiotics in Post-socialist China', in Sen, K. and Lee, T. (eds) *Political Regimes and the Media in Asia*, Abingdon and New York: Routledge, pp. 31–48.

Sun Yuan'er (2003) 'Shewai hunyin, Zhongnan wainü bili shenggao' [Intercultural Marriage: More Chinese Men Are Marrying Foreign Women], *Huanqiu shibao*, 26 September.

Sun Yuhao (2011) 'Qianxi Zhongguo diansh tanhua jiemu' [A Brief Analysis of Chinese Television Talk Shows], *Dongfang qiye wenhua*, 4: 97.

Sun Ziming (2006) 'Jianmian dangtian jiu jiele hun, xianzai yao lihun que lian duifang zhu na dou buzhidao' [Married after First Meeting, Now She Wants a Divorce But Has No Idea Where He Is], *Dushi kuabao*, 1 November.

'Taiduo gongli mengbi shuangyan' [Hypergamy Prevents Clear Sight] (2008) *Yangcheng wanbao*, 22 October.

Taiwan Fujiazi aishang Hainan guniang [Wealthy Taiwanese Man Falls in Love With a Woman from Hainan] 2008, Yuanfen, CCTV-4, Beijing, 27 April.

'Taiwan lang Xiamen ququin tianmi jiu "gouben"' [Taiwan Men Marry Xiamen Women for Love] (2009) *Xiamen shangbao*, 23 November.

'Taiwan nü jia Dalu nan: dangbuzhu de chaoliu' [Taiwan Women Marry Mainland Men: An Inevitable Trend] (2010) *Luoyang wanbao*, 25 November.

Tan Lujie (2009) '22 ge yang meimei qunian jiadao Chongqing – zuiduo de shi Yuenan guniang, qici fenbie wei Hanguoren, Ribenren he Xinjiapo ren' [22 Foreign Women Married in Chongqing Last Year – Most Were Vietnamese, Followed By South Korean, Japanese and Singaporean Women], *Chongqing wanbao*, 10 April.

Tang Ying (1995) *Meiguo laide qizi* [Wife from America], Shanghai: Shanghai yuandong chubanshe.

Tewksbury, D. and Scheufele, D. A. (2009) 'News Framing Theory and Research', in Bryant, J. and Oliver, M. B. (eds), *Media Effects: Advances in Theory and Research*, 3rd edn, London and New York: Routledge, pp. 17–33.

Thai, Hung Cam. (2005) 'Clashing Dreams in the Vietnamese Diaspora: Highly Educated Overease Brides and Low-Wage U.S. Husbands', in Constable, N. (ed.) *Cross-Border Marriages: Gender and Mobility in Transnational Asia*, Philadelphia: University of Pennsylvania Press, pp. 145–65.

The Basic Law of the Hong Kong Special Administrative Region of the People's Republic of China (1997) Adopted on 4 April 1990 by the Seventh National People's Congress of the People's Republic of China at its Third Session, Effective on 1 July 1997. Online. Available at www.basiclaw.gov.hk/en/basiclawtext/index.html (accessed 22 December 2011).

The Basic Law of the Macau Special Administrative Region of the People's Republic of China (1999) Adopted on 31 March 1993 by the Eight National People's Congress of the People's Republic of China at its First Session, Effective on 20 December 1999. Online. Available: http://web.parliament.go.th/parcy/sapa_db/cons_doc/constitutions/data/Macao/Basic%20Law%20of%20the%20Macao%20Special%20Administrative%20

Region%20of%20the%20People'%20s%20Republic%20of%20China.htm (accessed 4 March 2012).
Thiagarajan, M. (2007) 'A Qualitative Exploration of First-generation Asian Indian Immigrant Women in Cross-Cultural Marriages', PhD thesis, Michigan: Western Michigan University.
'Tiange huanghou Li Lingyu liangci shibai de hunyin' [Sweet Song Queen Li Lingyu's Two Failed Marriages] (2008) *A'boluo xinwan wang*, 6 March. Online. Available at www.aboluowang.com/ent/data/2008/0306/article_11749.html (accessed 15 January 2011).
'Tianjinshi shewai hunyin zhunian zengduo' [Chinese–Foreign Marriage Increases Every Year in Tianjin] (2006) *Dazhong kejibao*, 12 September.
Tsai, Ming-Chang (2011) '"Foreign Brides" Meet Ethnic Politics in Taiwan', *International Migration Review*, 45(2): 243–68.
Tu, E. (2007) 'Cross-Border Marriage in Hong Kong and Taiwan', *Population and Society*, 3(2): 29–43.
Tu, E. and Li Shaomin (1999) 'Inter-regime Marriage and Mobility: The Case of Mainland China and Taiwan', *Journal of Contemporary China*, 8(22): 499–516.
Tuchman, G. (1978) *Making News: A Study in the Construction of Reality*, New York: Free Press.
Turner, G. (2004) *Understanding Celebrity*, London: Sage Publications.
'Understanding the Attraction to Foreign Men' (2007) *Middlekingdomlife.com*. Online. Available at http://middlekingdomlife.com/guide/understanding-attraction-foreign-men-china.htm (accessed 4 October 2010).
UNICEF (2000) 'Domestic Violence Against Women and Girls'. Online. Available at www.unicef-irc.org/publications/pdf/digest6e.pdf (accessed 28 October 2010).
'Waiguoren juliu xuke' [Long-term Residence Permit for Foreigners] (2010) *Ministry of Public Security*, 1 June. Online. Available at www.bjgaj.gov.cn/web/detail_getZwgkInfo_44643.html (accessed 1 May 2012).
Wailai xifu bendi lang [Local Men and Foreign Brides] 2000, television series, Guangdong TV, Guangdong, 4 November.
'Walking Marriage of Mosuo People' (2007) *Cultural-china.com*. Online. Available at www.cultural-china.com/chinaWH/html/en/14Traditions342.html (accessed 8 February 2011).
Wan, Y. E. (1998) 'China's Divorce Problem', *The Tech*, 10 November. Online. Available at http://tech.mit.edu/V118/N57/wan.57c.html (accessed 16 May 2011).
Wang Dazhao (1998) 'Tiyu de guojie' [National Boundary in the Sports Circle], *Huanqiu shibao*, 15 February.
Wang Dewen (2008) 'Rural–Urban Migration and Policy Responses in China: Challenges and Options', *ILO Asian Regional Programme on Governance of Labour Migration Working Paper No. 15*. Online. Available at http://pstalker.com/ilo/resources/WP15%20-%20Internal%20Migration%20China.pdf (accessed 3 October 2011).
Wang Fang (2006) 'Dengji jiehun dan wei gongtong shenghuo shewai hunyin caichan ruhe fange' [Distributing Property is Difficult in Cases of Intercultural Marriage Where Couples Register For Marriage But Do Not Live Together], *Fazhi ribao*, 27 September.
Wang Jianwei (2008) 'Shanhun jitian hou yangxinniang "taopao"' [Foreign Bride Runs Away after Flash Marriage], *Nanguo jinbao*, 16 August.
Wang Lin (2010) 'Laodong zhidu de feizhi yuekuai yuehao' [Abolishing Reeduction Through Labor: the Faster, the Better], *Xin jingbao*, 24 June. Online. Available at www.news365.com.cn/xwzx/gd/201006/t20100624_2747598.htm (accessed 22 July 2010).

Wang Linchang (1999) 'Jiao Zhimin: Hanguo xifu Zhongguo piqi' [Jiao Zhimin: A South Korea Daughter-in-Law with a Chinese Temperament], *Huanqiu shibao*, 26 February.

Wang Lu (2008) 'Ning Jing lumian cheng huiyin zhengchang' [Ning Jing Says Her Marriage is Normal], *Shandong shangbao*, 6 March.

Wang Na (2009) '"Guoji hongniang" beikong liancai baiwan' ['International Matchmaker' Company Accused of Seizing Millions of Dollars] *Guangzhou ribao*, 4 November.

Wang Shengtian and Bao Wenfeng (2008) 'Yang nüxu yang xifu de lingyiban' [Foreign Sons-in-Law and Daughters-in-Law (In Dalian)], *Renmin ribao*, 26 January, 7th edn.

Wang Si (2008) 'Zhongduo beipian nüshi jiangshu ziji de shangxin wangshi, "yang laogong" wan shizong "shanhun" hou lihun nan' [Numerous Women Tell Their Sad Stories: Foreign Husbands Play the Disappearing Game, Flash Marriages Are Easy to Enter Into and Hard to Get Out Of], *Dangdai shenghuo bao*, 26 November.

Wang Tao (1987) *Zhongguo chengyu dacidian* [Dictionary of Chinese Idioms and Phrases], Shanghai: Shanghai cishu chubanshe.

Wang Tianfu, Wang Yuebin and Xiao Bo (2009) 'Qianli yinyuan yixianqian, Yuenan nü fanyi jiadao Tianmuhu' [Vietnamese Translator Marries at Tianmu Lake: Knot of True Love Tied across Thousands of Miles], *Changzhou ribao*, 5 March.

Wang Yiman (2005) 'The Amateur's Lightning Rod: DV Documentary in Post Socialist China', *Film Quarterly*, 58(4): 16–26.

Wang Yingxia (2009) 'Huang Fenglan: Taiguo wangzu de Zhongguo xifu' [Huang Fenglan: Chinese Daughter-in-Law of a Wealthy Thailand Family], *Changshu ribao*, 19 May.

Wang Zhaihua (2001) 'Lun woguo laodong jiaoyang zhidu de xianzhuang ji fazhan' [Analysis of the Current State of China's Labor Reeducation System and Future Development], *Dangdai faxue*, 1: 58–60.

Wei Jiang (1997) 'Zou chu *Honghegu* de Ning Jing' [Ning Jing's Life after the *Red River Valley*], *Zhongguo jiaotong bao*, 29 June.

Wei Minghui (2009) 'Zhe 32 ge nüde bei huyou canle' [These 32 Women Were Truly Cheated], *Fushan wanbao*, 8 June.

'Wei Wei, Li Lingyu de Zhongguo shi lihun' [The Chinese-style Divorces of Wei Wei and Li Lingyu] (2004) *Fazhi wanbao*, 22 September. Online. Available at www.people.com.cn/GB/yule/1082/2800722.html (accessed 31 January 2011).

Wei Wei, Ning Jing de kuaguo hunyin [Wei Wei and Ning Jing's Intercultural Marriages] 2009, television news programme, Yingshi fengyunbang, CETV, Beijing, March.

Wei Wei zibao lihun neimu: qianfu qiche zuoshoujiao hai qiming' [Wei Wei Reveals Details about Her Divorce: Ex-Husband Tries to Murder Her by Tampering With Her Car] (2005) *Jinyang wang*, 29 August. Online. Available at http://news.xinhuanet.com/ent/2005-08/29/content_3416897.htm (accessed 10 March 2010).

'Weihai gaikuang' [Weihai Overview] (2004) *Weihai.gov.cn*. Online. Available at www.weihai.gov.cn/gk/index.asp (accessed 18 March 2010).

'Weihun tongju weifa ma?' [Is Non-Marital Cohabitation Illegal?] (2009) *Quanmin jiankang wang*, 7 May. Online. Available at www.hrb.fx120.net/eden/qgtd/nnqg/200905/52300.htm (accessed 17 July 2010).

'Weizhuang haiwai chenggong renshi yinman hunyin zhuangkuang' [Tricking Women into Marriage by Pretending to Be Successful Overseas Men] (2009) *Xinxi ribao*, 18 September.

Wen, J.J. and Tisdell, C.A. (2001) *Tourism and China's Development: Policies, Regional Economic Growth and Ecotourism*, Singapore: World Scientific Publishing.

'Wenzhou gailan' [Wenzhou Overview] (2010) *Wenzhou gailan*. Online. Available at www.wenzhou.gov.cn/col/col4276/index.html (accessed 18 March 2010).
'Western Wives, Chinese Husbands' (2010) *Middlekingdomlife.com*. Online. Available at http://middlekingdomlife.com/blog/newest-articles/western-wives-chinese-husbands/ (accessed 3 October 2010).
Whitehead, D. B. (1997) *The Divorce Culture: How Divorce Became a Psychological Entitlement and How it is Blighting the Lives of Our Children*, New York: Alfred A. Knopf.
Whyte, M. K. and Parish, W. L. (1984) *Urban Life in Contemporary China*, Chicago: University of Chicago Press.
Williams, L. and Yu Mei-Kuei (2006) 'Domestic Violence in Cross-Border Marriage – A Case Study from Taiwan', *International Journal of Migration, Health and Social Care*, 2(3/4): 58–69.
Wing Lam and Zenobia Lai (2005) 'Reform of the Reeducation Through Labor System', *China Rights Forum*, 2: 31–3.
'Wo qu yangniu zuo laopo' [I Married a Foreign Woman] (2009) *Zhonggong wang*, 10 December. Online. Available at http://character.workercn.cn/c/2009/12/10/141349180 863781.html (accessed 5 October 2011).
'Wo weishenme yao chengwei Meiguoren?' [Why Do I Want to Become American?] (2008) *Wuhan wangbao*, 21 November.
Wu Changhua (2008) 'Mengduan kuaguo hunlian nüshi shicai 17 wan' [Woman Lost 170,000 Yuan in Pursuit of Intercultural Marriage], *Chutian dushibao*, 17 October.
Wu Fulong and Webber, K. (2004) 'The Rise of "Foreign Gated Communities" in Beijing: between Economic Globalization and Local Institutions', *Cities*, 2(3): 203–13.
Wu Hai'ou (2005) 'He qianqi heping fenshou, Zhang Tielin lihun hou haishi yi jiaren' [Zhang Tielin and His Wife Separate Peacefully: They Are Still a Family after Divorce], *Heilongjiang ribao*, 2 July.
Wu Hui (2008a) 'Baoshou jiating baoli shanghai, waiguo qizi zoujin fating' [Foreign Wife Goes to Court Because of Domestic Violence], *Qidu wankan*, 31 January.
Wu Hui (2008b) 'Yi xingqi kuaguo hunyin lishi liangnian de jietui' [Entering Into An Intercultural Marriage Marriage Takes One Week, Divorce Takes Two Years], *Qidu wankan*, 26 January.
Wu Wei (1994) 'Shen Danping yu zhangfu Wu Wei gongchang yitai xi yige shaonü he liang'ge nanhai paijun' [Shen Danping and Her husband Wu Wei Collaborate on a Film *One Girl and Two Boys*], 15 July.
Wu Xiaoyan (2008) 'Shewai hunyin xingfu yu tiaozhan tongxing' [Intercultural Marriage: Happiness Goes Along with Challenges], *Zhongguo gaigebao*, 26 December.
Wu Xiuyun (2008) 'Weifa shewai hunjie shou fuwufei 1511 wan (yuan) – "Yiguanglian" fuzeren huoxing 10 nian, bing chu fajin 200 wan yuan' [The Illegal Chinese–Foreign Marriage Agency, Yiguanglian', Made 15,110,000 Yuan – Owner Is Sentenced to 10 Years (in Prison) and a Two Million Yuan Fine], *Nanfang dushibao*, 20 November.
Wu Xuemei and He Xin (2007a) 'Shewai hunyin mianmianguan' [Intercultural Marriages], *Renmin ribao*, 13 June, 4th edn.
Wu Xuemei and He Xin (2007b) 'Shewai hunyin huigui yu ai' [Love Matters in Chinese–Foreign Marriage], *Jingli ribao*, 16 June, 5th edn.
'Wuhan xiaohuo Feizhou zuo zhiyuanzhe yisheng, qu heiren nühai weiqi' [Volunteer Doctor in Africa from Wuhan City Marries a Black Woman] (2009) *Wuhan wanbao*, 15 January.
Xiang'gang tebie xingzhengqu, Zhengfu tongjichu, renkou tongji zu [Demographic Statistics Section, Census and Statistics Department, The Government of the Hong Kong Special

Administrative Region] (2011) 'Marriages and Divorces', *Demographic Trends in Hong Kong: 1981–2011*, p. 88.

'Xiangsheng' [Cross Talk] (2012) *Baidu baike*. Online. Available at http://baike.baidu.com/view/6749.htm (accessed 24 January 2012).

Xiao Chen (2008) 'Huishou liangduan yiguo hunyin, Li Qinqin houhui jia laowai' [Li Qinqin Recalls Her Marriages, She Regrets Marrying Foreigners], *Anqing wanbao*, 28 January.

Xiao Huifaye (2011) 'Love is a Capacity: The Narrative of Gendered Self-development in Chinese-Style Divorce', *Journal of Contemporary China*, 19(66): 735–53.

'Xiao shancun li de yang guye' [Small Village Foreign Son-in-Law] (2007) *Qibin wanbao*, 18 September.

Xiao Shiyan and Shi Wei (2009) 'Taibei you ge "Dalu xinniang" zhijia' [Mainland Brides Form a Family (an Organized Group) in Taibei], *Huanqiu shibao*, 13 March.

Xiao Yu (2009) 'Yu "Mo Duoke" hunyin wanwan? Deng Wendi piyao: Women qinmi yijiu' [Wendi Deng Denies Rumours That She Has Separated from Rupert Murdoch Saying 'We Are Still as Close as Before'], *Guangzhou ribao*, 11 December 2009.

'Xiaoshan Zhili lihun hou juexin zai bujia Ribenren, kewang chongzu jiating' [Divorcee Xiaoshan Zhili Is Determined Not to Marry Another Japanese, But Hopes to Have a Family Once Again] (2007) *Chengdu shangbao*, 1 March.

Xie Rong and Ding Li (2000) 'Ning Jing yu Bao Luo de yinse gushi' [Ning Jing and Paul (Kersey's) Silver Stories], *Jiankang tiandi*, 128: 66–8.

Xie Xiao and Shen Yangwen (2001) 'Shen Danping zhizuo de jilupian zai De shou huanying' [Shen Danping's Documentary is Popular in Germany]. *Nanfang dushi bao*, 7 August. Online. Available at www.people.com.cn/GB/wenyu/64/129/20010807/529824.html (accessed 6 December 2010).

'Ximei: Zhongguo nanren dao Dongnanya "mai laopo"' [Spanish Media: Chinese Men "Buying" Wives from Southeast Asia], *Xinhua wang*, 15 September. Online. Available at http://china.huanqiu.com/eyes_on_china/economy/2011-09/2007439.html (accessed 5 October 2011).

Xin Kai and Ye Xiaochuan (2008) 'Meishan xin'niang Meiguolang shangyan "Zhong" guoshi jiehun' [Meishan Woman and American Man Stage Chinese–style Wedding], *Sichuan meishan ribao*, 10 January.

Xin Li (2005) 'Siqin Gaowa: "quanli nüren" de mianchang rouqing' [Siqin Gaowa: Ongoing Affection for a 'Powerful Woman'] (2005) *Xiandai funü*, 2: 11–13.

Xin Qiang (2009) 'Mainland China's Taiwan Policy Adjustments', *China Security*, 5(1): 53–64.

Xintai nongjianü qule 'yangnüxu' [A Rural Woman from Xintai City Marries a 'Foreign Son-in-Law'], 2009, television news program, Xintai TV, Shandong, 9 May.

Xu Baokang (1993) 'Jiao Zhimin qingxi niangjia' [Jiao Zhimin's Love Ties to Her Family], *Huanqiu shibao*, 14 November.

Xu Chen and Zhao Huanhuan (2009) 'Qieshi baohu "Dalu xin'niang" zai Tai quanyi' [Protecting the Interests of the "Mainland Brides" in Taiwan], *Yangcheng wanbao*, 26 April.

Xu Qiaona (2008a) 'Rending youyi, liang'an "shanhun" yi shenxing' [Be Cautious of "Flash Marriage" as Marriage Registration Varies across the Straits], *Xiamen shangbao*, 14 April.

Xu Qiaona (2008b) 'Kuahai xiangqin, Taibao buke xinji' [Taiwan Compatriots: Don't Rush into a Cross-Strait Marriage by Using a Matchmaker], *Xiamen shangbao*, 7 April.

Xu Shiwen, Wu Shuliang and Wang Minlin (2010) 'Xin kuaguo hunyin, duojin nan dao Yuenan zhao laopo' [New Transnational Marriage: Rich Men Seek Wives in Vietnam],

Sohu wang, 6 April. Online. Available at http://women.sohu.com/20100406/n271338684.shtml (accessed 5 October 2011).

Xu Xianzhong (2007) 'Xiao shangpincheng zhong de yang hunyin' [Chinese–Foreign Marriage in Small Businesses], *Zhejiang ribao*, 4 January.

Xu Xiao, Zhu Fengchuan, Campo, P., Koenig, M. A., Mock, V. and Campbell, J. (2005) 'Prevalence of and Risk Factors For Intimate Partner Violence in China', *American Journal of Public Health*, 95(1): 78–85.

Xu Xuelian (2005) 'Zhang Shan vs. Barnes: Shenqiang jizhong caipan wenrou, guanjun feiyue aiqing haiyang' [Zhang Shan vs. Barnes: Bulls-eye Straight Into the Referee's Heart, Skeet Shooting Champion is Propelled over the Sea of Love], *Fazhi wanbao*, 15 February.

Xu Zhensheng (2002) *Xinhua chengyu cidian* [Xinhua Idioms and Phrases Dictionary], Beijing: shangwu yinchuguan.

'Xun'ai 10 nian, ta zhongyu zhaodaole Deguo ai'ren' [Hunting for Love for Ten Years, She Finally Found Her German Partner] (2009) *Wuhan wanbao*, 6 January.

Yan Jin (2009) 'Bei aiqing yiwang de jiaoluo' [A Love-Forsaken Corner], *Renmin wang*, 27 August. Online. Available at http://ent.people.com.cn/GB/115513/167215/9942309.html (accessed 7 December 2010).

'Yang Cao Cao he tade Zhongguo xifu' [Foreign Man Cao Cao and His Chinese Wife] (2010) *Tianshi wang*, 9 June. Online. Available at http://tjtv.enorth.com.cn/system/2010/06/09/004756814.shtml (accessed 12 December 2010).

'Yang Er weishenme er' [Why Does Yang Er Appears Silly?] (2007) *Qingdao zaobao*, 3 June.

'Yang Erche Namu de qingai siji' [Yang Erche Namu's Romance and Love] (2007) *Ruili nüxing wang*, 15 October. Online. Available at www.rayli.com.cn/0013/2007-10-15/L0013005_264652.html (accessed 10 April 2011).

'Yang Erche Namu: mei taoguo 7 nian zhiyang' [Yang Erche Namu Has Not Escaped the Seven-Year-Itch] (2004) *Shenzhen shangbao*, 15 June. Online. Available at http://eladies.sina.com.cn/2004-06-15/97424.html (accessed 23 November 2010).

Yang Jie (2010) 'Qiong Tai lianyin: nianzeng 500 dui' [Hainan–Taiwan Marriage Increases by 500 Couples Per Year], *Haikou wanbao*, 24 May.

Yang laogong miju [Foreign Husband 'Trap'] 2008, television news programme, Shehui zongheng, Guangdong TV, Guangdong, 19 March.

Yang Lijun and Lim (2010) 'Three Waves of Nationalism in Contemporary China: Sources, Themes, Presentations and Consequences', *International Journal of China Studies*, 1(2): 461–85.

Yang Min (2008) 'Kauguo hunyin pinchuan lihun shouchang' [Intercultural Marriages Keep Ending in Divorce], *Guangzhou ribao*, 19 January.

Yang Tian (2008) 'Shewai hunyin de Shanghai suoying' [Chinese–Foreign Marriage in Shanghai], *Liaowang dongfang zhoukan*, 20 November. Online. Available at http://lwdf.net/oriental/cover_story/20081120142433639.htm (accessed 3 November 2009).

Yang, Wen-Shan and Lu, Melody Chia-Wen (eds) (2010) *Asian Cross-border Marriage Migration: Demographic Patterns and Social Issues*, Amsterdam: Amsterdam University Press.

Yang Xiaobing (1988) 'Hainan Province – China's Largest SEZ', *Beijing Review.com.cn*, 18 May. Online. Available at www.bjreview.com.cn/Cover_Story_Series_2010/2010-02/03/content_244683.htm (accessed 19 May 2010).

Yang Ying (2008) 'Guge "yi" chu yiduan kuaguo lianqing – Ying'guo shangren aishang dagongmei, Deqing ban "hui guniang" gushi dongrenxinxian' [Google 'Translates' Cross-Cultural Love, British Business Man Falls for Migrant Worker, 'Cinderella' Story in Deqing], *Jinri zaobao*, 1 June.

Ye Huiyuan (2004) '270 wei Wenzhou xiaohuo qunian xiqu yang xifu' [270 Wenzhou Men Married Foreign Women Last Year], *Wenzhou dushibao*, 9 February.

Ye Huiyuan (2005) 'Shewai hunyin zaoyu "7 nian zhiyang" – Wenzhou qunian yiyou 104 dui fenli' [Chinese–Foreign Marriage Encounters 'Seven-Year-Itch' – Wenzhou Registered 104 Chinese Foreign Divorces last year], *Zhejiang ribao*, 23 February.

Ye Xiaonan (2006) 'Xiyoucanban kan shewai hunyin' [The Pros and Cons of Intercultural Marriage], *Renmin ribao*, 15 July, 2nd edn.

Yi Wen (2004) 'Zhongguo dianshi tanhua jiemu fazhan 10 nian huigu' [The Development of Chinese Television Talk Shows over the Last Decade], *Xinwen zhishi*, 8: 39–41.

Ye Wenzhen and Lin Qingguo (1996) 'Fujian sheng shewai hunyin zhuangkuang yanjiu' [Analysis of Chinese–Foreign Marriage in Fujian Province], *Population and Economics*, 2(95): 21–9.

Yeh Yu-Ching (2010) 'Foreign Spouses' Acculturation in Taiwan: A Comparison of Their Countries of Origin, Gender and Education Degrees', in Lu, M. and Yang Wen-Shan (eds) *Asian Cross-border Marriage Migration: Demographic Patterns and Social Issues*, Amsterdam: Amsterdam University Press, pp. 201–20.

Yi Yuhan (2009) 'Yule hua langchao xia zongyi tanhua jiemu de zouxiang' [The Entertainment Trend and Future Orientation of Chinese Variety Television Talk Shows] *Wenjia ziliao*, 13: 31–3.

'You nü yu yuanjia' [Women Who Aspire to Marry Overseas] (1993) *Hangzhou ribao*, 22 July, 6th edn.

Yow Cheun Hoe (2005) 'Weakening Ties with the Ancestral Homeland in China: The Case Studies of Contemporary Singapore and Malaysian Chinese', *Modern Asian Studies*, Cambridge: Cambridge University Press, pp. 559–97.

Yu Liangxin (2005) 'Shouci pilu lihun neiqing: Wei Wei shengming ceng zao weixie' [The Inside Divorce Story Revealed For the First Time: Wei Wei's Life Threatened], *Hainan ribao*, 30 August.

Yu Xiaoyang and Du Zhanfan (2008) 'Qingdao yinian 360 li shewai hunyin waiguoren cheng zai Qing hen shufu' [Qingdao Registers 360 Chinese–Foreign Marriages Each Year, Foreigners Enjoy Living in Qingdao], *Qingdao chenbao*, 20 December.

Yu Zeyuan (2011) 'Zhongguo guaimai Dongnanya funü'an zengduo' [Trafficking of Southeast Asian Women Increases in China], *Lianhe zaobao wang*, 4 December. Online. Available at www.afinance.cn/new/yzsd/201112/403031.html (accessed 2 May 2012).

Yu, L. (1997) 'Travel between Politically Divided China and Taiwan', *Asia Pacific Journal of Tourism Research*, 2(1): 19–30.

Yuan Lanhua and Du Zhanfan (2005) 'Qianshou shijie de yinyuan – Daocheng shewai hunyin pandian' [Love Connects the World – Intercultural Marriage in Qingdao], *Zhongguo shehuibao*, 25 May, 2nd edn.

Yuan Ye (1995) 'Shen Danping he tade Ri'erman xiansheng' [Shen Danping and Her German Husband], *Renmin tiaojie*, 3: 24–5.

Yuan Zhonghai and Sun Xianglan (2007) 'Jiadao Dalu de Taiwan xin'niang' [Taiwanese Brides Living on the Mainland], *Huanqiu shibao*, 9 March.

'Yuandu chongyang qu zhao ai, mingxing kuaguo lian de beixi ju' [Looking For Love Overseas – The Tragicomedy of Celebrity Intercultural Relationships] (2009) *Shenzhen wanbao*, 7 July.

'Yuanfen lanmu jieshao' [Introduction of *Yuanfen* Program] (2008) *CCTV.com*. Online. Available at www.cctv.com/program/yf/05/index.shtml (accessed 22 June 2011).

Yuanjia Riben [Marrying Far Away in Japan] 2001, television series, CCTV-8, Beijing, no information available about date of broadcast.

'Yujing lüshi jieshou Beijing qingnian bao qingnian zhoukan *jinri Beijing* jizhe caifang' [Lawyer Yu Jing Has an Interview with a Reporter from the Beijing Youth Weekly's *Beijing Today*] (2010) *Zhongguo falü menhu wang*, 20 July. Online. Available at www.lawyeryu.net/?a=view&p=27&r=228 (accessed 20 October 2010).

'Zai gaige kaifang zhong qianjin' [Advancing the Economic Reforms and Open Door Policy] (2011) *Zhongguo Hangzhou*. Online. Available at www.hangzhou.gov.cn/dsyjs/dszz2/hz/T290619.shtml (accessed 27 October 2011).

Zeng Wanyu (2011) 'Zouru pingjingqi de Dianshi tanhua jiemu' [Chinese Television Talk Shows Enter a 'Bottleneck' Period], *Xinwen tiandi*, 5: 227.

Zeng Yang (1998) 'Shen Danping tan jiating he yang zhangfu' [Shen Danping Talks about Her Family and Foreign Husband], *Dangdai dianshi*, 12: 14–15.

Zhang, H., Pine, R. and Lam, T. (2005) *Tourism and Hotel Development in China*, New York: The Haworth Hospitality Press.

Zhang, L. (2008) 'The Forgotten "Star": Li Shuang', *Artzinechina.com*. Online. Available at www.artzinechina.com/display_vol_aid421_en.html (accessed 1 January 8, 2010).

Zhang Guangrui (2003) 'China's Tourism Since 1978: Policies, Experiences and Lessons Learned', in Lew, A., Yu, L., Ap, J. and Zhang Guangrui (eds) *Tourism in China*, New York: The Haworth Press, pp. 13–33.

Zhang Guannian (2007) 'Haiwai "weicheng": Xiang shuo aini bu rongyi' [Intercultural Marriage: 'I love you' Easier Said Than Done], *Nanning ribao*, 19 September.

Zhang Guoxiong (1997) '90 niandai Guangdong Wuyi qiaoxiang xin yimin de shewai hunyin guang' [New Immigrants' Perception toward Chinese–Foreign Marriage in 1990s' Wuyi (Hometown of Overseas Chinese) Region, Guangdong Province], Vol. 2, *South China Population*, pp. 37–42.

Zhang Keguo (2005) 'Shewai hunyin yuanhe zhunian jiangwen' [Why Is Chinese–Foreign Marriage Decreasing Yearly?], *Weihai ribao*, 23 September, 5th edn.

Zhang Kexuan (2004) 'Tuokou xiu: Zhuchiren wenhua de chaoyue' [Talk Show: Going Beyond the Host's Culture (sic)], *Huanghe keji daxue xuebao*, 6(4): 118–21.

Zhang Lei (2011) 'Li Yang jiabao'an kaiting qian weibo zhiqian, cheng ziji shi bucuo de fuqin' [Before His Domestic Violence Case is Heard in Court, Li Yang Apologizes on His Microblog and Says He is a Good Father], *Beijing wanbao*, 15 December.

Zhang Lisha (2008) 'Nüzi "jie jiaren" chuguo bei huyou – fayuan yishen panjue zhongjie fanhuan 8 wan hunjiefei'[Woman Cheated by Marriage Introduction Agency – Court Rules For the First Time That the Agency Must Return 80,000 Yuan], *Qingdao caijing ribao*, 29 August.

Zhang Qi (2010) 'Invisible Western Women', *China Daily*, 9 April. Online. Available at www.chinadaily.com.cn/life/2010-04/09/content_9707047.htm (accessed 3 October 2010).

Zhang Shanke (1988) *Taiwen wenti dashiji 1945.8–1987.12* [Historical Records of the Taiwan Issue 1945.8–1987.12], Beijing: Huawen chubanshe.

'Zhang Tielin Bolan ji qianqi baoguang, cengjing de yiguo jianxin aiqing' [Zhang Tielin Exposes Polish Ex-wife and Hardships of Intercultural Love] (2009) *Xinlang nüxing*, 26 October. Online. Available at http://eladies.sina.com.cn/qg/2009/1026/0953926708.shtml (accessed 27 August 2010).

'Zhang Tielin chuyan Mao Zedong, wangyou bu jieshou waiguoren shiyan Mao Zedong' [Zhang Tielin as Mao Zedong: Netizens Reject Foreigner to Act in Mao Zedong Role] (2010) *Huamei wang*, 19 October. Online. Available at http://news.bangkaow.com/news/20101019/65080.html (accessed 24 December 2010).

'Zhang Tielin hunxue nü'er baoguang, Zhongwen zhi huishuo "Kekou kele"' [Zhang Tielin's Mixed-Race Daughter Exposed, 'Coca-Cola' (*kekou kele*) Is All She Can Say in Chinese]

(2008) *Sichuan zaixian*, 18 September. Online. Available at http://hi.people.com.cn/2008/09/18/402249.html (accessed 2 May 2011).

'Zhang Tielin jieshi weihe jiaru Ying'guo guoji: rang shijie liaojie Zhongguo' [Zhang Tielin Explains Why He Acquired British Nationality: To Make the World Better Understand China] (2008) *Dongfang zaobao*, 6 January. Online. Available at http://yule.sohu.com/20080106/n254485278.shtml (accessed 21 December 2010).

Zhang Weiguo (2000) 'Dynamics of Marriage Change in Chinese Rural Society in Transition: A Study of a northern Chinese Village', *Population Studies*, 54(1): 57–69.

Zhang Xiamin (2010) 'Hunyin jiating zhidu yu hexie shehui de jiangou' [Marriage and Family System and the Construction of Harmonious Society], *Keji xinxi*, p. 454.

Zhang Xiaohong (2003) 'Gender in Post-Mao China', *European Review*, 11(2): 209–24.

Zhang Yan (2011) 'More Women Kidnapped for Brides', *China Daily*, 3 December. Online Available at http://usa.chinadaily.com.cn/china/2011-12/03/content_14206487.htm (accessed 5 December 2011).

Zhang Yan and Wildemuth, M. B. (2009) 'Qualitative Analysis of Content', in Wildemuth, M. B. (ed.) *Applications of Social Research Methods to Questions in Information and Library*, Westport, CT: Libraries Unlimited, pp. 308–19.

Zhang Yingjin (2010) *Cinema, Space and Polylocality in a Globalizing China*, Hawaii: University of Hawaii Press.

Zhang Yiye (2010) 'Nongmingong zai Yuenan bian dakuan, yu qu yang xifu huijia' [Rural Migrant Workers Are "Rich Men" in Vietnam, They Want to Take Their Foreign Brides Back to Their Hometowns in China], *Chongqing wanbao*, 25 January.

Zhang Yong (2008) 'Jianli huxin, Gezhi zhengyi, qiutong cunyi, gongchuang shuangying' [Building Mutual Trust, Laying Aside Differences, Seeking Consensus While Shelving Differences and Creating a Win-Win Situation], *Shenzhen guangdian jituan wang*, 30 April. Online. Available at www.sztv.com.cn/szmg_news/index.do?i=39545&m=0301&a=detail (accessed 24 September 2011).

Zhang Zhiqiang (2008a) 'Guangzhou Yiguanglian dongshizhang zixu yuelao' [Chair of the Guangzhou Yiguanglian Agency Brags That He Is an International Matchmaker], *Chengshi wanbao*, 19 March.

Zhang Zhiqiang (2008b) 'Jilin jinbai nüzi weijia waiguolang zao piancai pianse' [Nearly 100 Jilin Woman Cheated Out of Love and Money] *Fushun wanbao*, 6 March.

Zhao Baosheng (2000a) 'Bie jizhe jiadao Taiwan qu' [Don't Rush Into Marriage to Go to Taiwan], *Huanqiu shibao*, 15 August.

Zhao Baosheng (2000b) 'Hunyinfa jujue bao er'nai' [Marriage Law Outlaws Bans on 'Second Wife' Phenomenon], *Huanqiu shibao*, 31 October. Online. Available at www.people.com.cn/GB/channel1/11/20001102/296795.html (accessed 13 October 2010).

Zhao Dingxin (1996) 'Foreign Study as a Safety-Valve: The Experience of China's University Students Going Abroad in the Eighties', *Higher Education*, 31(145): 145–63.

Zhao Junhui (2007) '380 yu Chongqingren jinnian jie yanghun' [Over 380 Chongqingese Entered into an Intercultural Marriage This Year], *Chongqing chenbao*, 4 December.

Zhao Lei, Tao Duanfang and Cui Xiangsheng (2009) 'Tansangniya nüzi xiang jia dangdi huaren' [Tanzanian Women Want to Marry Local Chinese Men in Tanzania], *Huanqiu shibao*, 14 October, 4th edn.

Zhao Xin (1998) 'Rendanruju de Shen Danping' [Shen Danping: A Quiet Chrysanthemum], *Zhongguo fushi bao*, 31 July.

Zhao Yajuan, Liao Jinfeng and Cao Kanglin (1999) 'Ao'men yu zhujiang sanjiaozhou de jingji hezuo guanxi' [The Economic Relation between Macau and the Pearl River Delta], *Jiangji dili*, 19(5): 40–43.

230   References

Zhao Yang (2012) 'Gong'anbu xiangjie xinban Gang Ao Jumin laiwang neidi tongxingzheng' [Ministry of Public Security Elaborates New Version of Mainland Travel Permit for Hong Kong and Macau Residents], *Fazhi ribao*.

Zhao Yuanyuan (2007) 'Ningxia she GangAoTai ji shewai hunyin 8 nian ban le 333 dui nü zi yuanjia zhan 9 chen' [333 Chinese–Foreign Marriages in Ningxia over Eight Years, More Than 90 Per Cent of the Women Married Overseas], *Yinchuan wanbao*, 22 November.

Zhao Yuezhi (1998) *Media, Market and Democracy in China: Between the Party Line and the Bottom Line*, Urbana: Illinois University Press.

Zhao Yuezhi (2002) 'The Rich, The Laid-off and the Criminal in Tabloid Tales: Read All About It!', in Link, P., Madsen, R. and Pickowicz, P. (eds) *Popular China: Unofficial Culture in a Globalizing Society*, Lanham, MD: Rowman and Littlefield, pp. 111–36.

Zhejiang Provincial Government (2006) 'Brief Introduction of Jinhua'. Online. Available at www.zhejiang.gov.cn/zjforeign/english/node493/node499/userobject1ai5840.html (accessed 18 March 2010).

Zhen Xing (2009) 'Siqin Gaowa: qingxing you yige zhileng zhire de zhangfu' [Siqin Gaowa is Thankful to Have A Considerate Husband], *Happiness*. Online. Available at www.happy-2000.com.cn/Marriage/ShowInfo.asp?InfoID=52 (accessed 12 December 14, 2010).

Zheng Na (2007) 'Chinese Green Card System Continues to Evolve', *Zhongguo wang*, 22 August. Online. Available at www.china.org.cn/english/LivinginChina/221738.htm (accessed 16 July 2010).

'Zhenqing shilu' [True Stories] (2008) *Shanghai xinwen*. Online. Available at http://sh.eastday.com/hzlzt/node16913/index.html (accessed 9 July 2011).

Zhong Qing (1989) 'Aiqing wu guojie Dalu pinzeng shewai hunyin' [Love Crosses National Borders; Mainland Sees Frequent Occurrence of Chinese–Foreign Marriages], *Renmin ribao*, 12 March.

'Zhong Tai ban: Dalu jiang caiqu san xiang cuoshi fangbian Taiwan jumin ruchu jing' [Taiwan Work Office of the CPC Central Committee: Mainland to Adopt Three Measures to Facilitate Taiwan Residents' Entry and Exit to the Mainland] (2005) *Zhongguo xinwen wang*. Online. Available at http://news.sohu.com/20050513/n225544362.shtml (accessed 5 March 2013).

'Zhonggong zhongyang guanyu zhiding guomin jingji he shehui fazhan di 11 ge 5 nian guihua de jianyi' [CCP Central Committee's Proposal for Formulating the 11th Five-Year Program for China's Economic and Social Development (2006–2010)] (2005) *Xinhua wang*, 18 October. Online. Available at http://news.xinhuanet.com/politics/2005-10/18/content_3640318.htm (accessed 3 October 2011).

'Zhongguo "Tuokou xiu" jiemu de xingqi' [Rising Popularity of Chinese Talk Shows] (2003) Online. Available at http://news.xinhuanet.com/newsmedia/2003-05/13/content_867614.htm (accessed 20 May 2011).

Zhongguo gongmin tong waiguoren banli jiehun dengji de jixiang guiding [The Provisions for the Registration of Marriage between Chinese Citizens and Foreigners] (1983) *Ministry of Civil Affairs*, 26 August. Online. Available at http://202.123.110.5/fwxx/bw/wjb/content_374537.htm (accessed 10 August 2009).

Zhongguo gongmin wanglai Taiwan diqu guanli banfa [Measures for the Control of Chinese Citizens Travelling to or from the Region of Taiwan] (1992) *The State Council*, 1 May. Online. Available at www.chinalawedu.com/news/23223/23228/24138.htm (accessed 22 September 2011).

'Zhongguo liyi nü zaihun xuan shewai hunyin dongfang buliang xifang liang' [Divorced Chinese Women Choose Intercultural Marriage and Are Favoured by Foreign Men] (2007), *Chutian dushibao*, 16 August.

'Zhongguo maiyinnü xianzhuang fenxi' [Analysis of Female Prostitutes in Present-day China] (2009) *Xibu yixue wang*. Online. Available at www.wmed.cn/article/2009/0222/article_9160.html (accessed 13 October 2010).

'Zhongguo mingren kuaguo hunyin da souji' [Big Survey of Chinese Celebrities in Intercultural Marriages] (2006) *Soufang wang*, 4 April. Online. Available at http://news.km.soufun.com/2006-04-04/678159.htm (accessed 26 August 2010).

'Zhongguo nan zai Feizhou qu meinü' [Chinese Men Marry Beauties in Africa] (2011) *Xinhua wang*, 10 July. Online. Available at http://news.xinhuanet.com/photo/2011-07/10/c_121646876.htm (accessed 5 October 2011).

'Zhongguo nanren weishenme beishou waiguo nüren de qinglai' [Why Do Foreign Women Favour Chinese Men] (2011) *Jiankang wang*, 18 June. Online. Available at www.nihaobd.com/man/nxxl/248.html (accessed 5 October 2011).

'Zhongguo titan kuaguo hunyin lihun'an' [Chinese–Foreign Marriages and Divorces in the Sports Realm] (2008) *Anhui shichang bao*, 20 January.

'Zhongguo xin'niang zai ha Ri hunyin li tongku jian'ao' [Chinese Brides Suffer in Chinese–Japanese Marriages] (2008) *Zhongguo funübao*, 26 February.

Zhonghua quanguo funü lianhedi funü yanjiusuo, Shaanxi sheng funü lianhehui yanjiushi [The Research Institute of the All-China Women's Federation and the Research Department of the Shaanxi Women's Federation] (1991) '1986–1988 nian guonei nüxing gongmin tong waiguoren ji huaqiao, Gang Ao Tai tongbao dengji jiehun renshu' [Number of Marriages Registered between Female Citizens of the PRC and Foreign Nationals, Overseas Chinese and Compatriots from Hong Kong, Macau and Taiwan 1986–1988], *Zhongguo funü tongji ziliao 1949–1989* [Statistics on Chinese Women 1949–1989], Beijing: Zhongguo tongji chubanshe, p. 344.

Zhonghua renmin gongheguo gongmin chujing rujing guanli fa [Law of The People's Republic of China on the Control of the Entry and Exit of Citizens] (1986) Standing *Committee of the National People's Congress*, 1 February. Online. Available at www.fmcoprc.gov.hk/chn/lsfw/flzn/t9772.htm (accessed 12 August 2009).

Zhonghua renmin gongheguo guiqiao qiaojuan quanyi baohu fa [Law of the People's Republic of China on the Protection of the Rights and Interests of Returned Overseas Chinese and the Family Members of Overseas Chinese] (1990) *Standing Committee of the National People's Congress*, 7 September. Online. Available at www.gqb.gov.cn/node2/node3/node5/node9/userobject7ai1272.html (accessed 6 August 2008).

Zhonghua renmin gongheguo guoji fa [National Law of the People's Republic of China] (1980) *The Chairman of the Standing Committee of the National People's Congress*, 10 September. Online. Available at www.lawinfochina.com/law/display.asp?id=10 (accessed 12 August 2009).

Zhonghua renmin gongheguo hunyin fa [Marriage Law of the People's Republic of China] (1950) Promulgated on 30 April 1950 by the Central Government of the People's Republic of China and enacted on 1 May 1950. Online. Available at http://zhidao.baidu.com/question/3757923 (accessed 18 March 2012).

Zhonghua renmin gongheguo hunyin fa [Marriage Law of the People's Republic of China] (1980) *National People's Congress*, 10 September. Online. Available at www.mca.gov.cn/article/zwgk/fvfg/shsw/200707/20070700001363.shtml (accessed 10 August 2009).

Zhonghua renmin gongheguo hunyin fa [Marriage Law of the People's Republic of China] (2001) Adopted at the Third Session of the Fifth National People's Congress on 10

September 1980 and amended in accordance with the 'Decision Regarding the Amendment (of Marriage Law of the People's Republic of China)' passed at the Twenty-first Session of the Standing Committee of the Ninth National People's Congress on 28 April 2001. Online. Available at www.people.com.cn/GB/shehui/43/20010429/455250.html (accessed 18 March 2012).

Zhonghua renmin gongheguo waiguoren rujing chujing guanli fa [Law of the People's Republic of China on the Control of the Entry and Exit of Aliens] (1986) *Standing Committee of the National People's Congress*, 1 February. Online. Available at www.mfa.gov.cn/chn/gxh/tyb/bszn/dafw/t267621.htm (accessed 12 August 2009).

'Zhongyang xinwen jilu dianying zhipianchang' [China Central Newsreel and Documentary Film Studio] (2007) *Guojia guangbo dianying dianshi zongju*, 1 June. Online. Available at www.chinasarft.gov.cn/articles/2007/06/01/20070904104418530381.html (accessed 21 June 2011).

Zhou Huimin (2009) 'Laojie yi jinru fengzhucan'nian? Haikou "chengshi mingpian" chengdai baohu' [Old Declining Neigbourhood Requires Protection of Haikou City Name], *Xinhua News Agency*, 10 July. Online. Available at www.haikou.gov.cn/zlhk/ShowArticle.asp?ArticleID=67187 (accessed 2 March 2010).

Zhou Jianchang (2009) 'Xueyuan guanxi yu Min Tai hunyin' [Blood Ties: Fujian–Taiwan Marriages], *Xiamen shangbao*, 6 November.

Zhou Min (2009) 'Shantou jinnian yiban shewai hunyin 113 dui – nannü shuangfang nianling chaju suoxiao, nüxing waijia bili gaoda 88%' [Shantou Registered 113 Chinese–Foreign Marriages This Year – Age Gap Narrows, 88 Per Cent of Women Married Overseas], *Shantou tequ wanbao*, 13 December.

Zhou Qijun (2007) 'Shewai hunyin bing buru kanshangqu mei' [Intercultural Marriage – Not as Beautiful as It Appears], *Wenhui ribao*, 22 March.

Zhou Yun: suishu shi Jiang Wen de yiban, liangren 2005 nian jiu mimi jiehun' [Zhou Yun Is Half the Age of Jiang Wen, They Married Secretly in 2005] (2007) *Zhonghua wang*, 10 September. Online. Available at http://ent.china.com/zh_cn/star/news/11052670/20070910/14331696.html (accessed 20 May 2011).

'Zhu Chen Muhanmude' [Zhu Chen and Mohammed] (2009) *Xin wanbao*, 4 April.

'Zhu Chen: Weinai, huan niaobu ye shi hen xingfu de shi!' [Zhu Chen: Breast Feeding and Nappy Changing Are Great Too!] (2008) *Baoding wanbao*, 17 December.

Zhu Minghong and Che Shijun (2003) 'Jieqi nongjianü hong gaitou' [Lift the Red Marriage Veil from a Country Girl], *Zhongguo minzubao*, 11 February.

Zhuanfang Li Yang Jiabao [Interview with Li Yang on Domestic Violence] (2011) Kanjian, CCTV-1, Beijing, 25 September.

Zong He (2008) 'Ning Jing yu shenmi nan yuehui, bei yi jian weilai gongpo' [Ning Jing Seen on Date with Mystery Man, Speculation That She Has Already Met the in-Laws], *Chongqng shibao*, 7 May.

Zouwei and Fuqing (2012) 'Gong'anbu qiyong xinban Gang Ao jumin laiwang neidi tongxingzheng', [Ministry of Public Security Launches New Version of Mainland Travel Permit for Hong Kong and Macau Residents], *Xinhuawang*. Online. Available at http://news.qq.com/a/20121228/001113.htm (accessed 5 March 2013).

Zuo Hanying (2009) 'Woguo dianshi tanhua jiemu gailan' [An Overview of the Chinese Television Talk Shows], *Shoushi Zhongguo*, July. Online. Available at www.csm.com.cn/index.php/knowledge/showArticle/kaid/322 (accessed 5 October 2011).

Zweig, D. and Rosen, S. (2003) 'How China Trained a New Generation Abroad', *The Science and Development Network*, 22 May. Online. Available at www.scidev.net/en/features/how-china-trained-a-new-generation-abroad.html (accessed 19 May 2010).

Index

1950 Marriage Law: new marriage and family system 35
1980 Marriage Law: one-child family policy 35
1980 Marriage Registration Procedures 36
1986 Law of the PRC on the Control of the Entry and Exit of Aliens 140
1986 Law of the PRC on the Control of the Exit and Entry of Citizens 140
1986 Marriage Registration Procedures 36
1988 Notice on Issues Relating to Marriage Registration between Taiwan Compatriots and Mainland Citizens: categories of Taiwan compatriots 38–9; clarification of local government departmental procedures 38; marriages between citizens of mainland China and Taiwan 36
1990 Law of the People's Republic of China 3–4
1992 Measures for the Control of Chinese Citizens Travelling To and From the Region of Taiwan 140
1992 Statute Governing Relations Between People of the Taiwan Area and Mainland Area 141
1994 Marriage Registration Management Regulations 39
1994 Notice: prohibition of international marriage agencies 84
2001 Marriage Law: conditions for obtaining a divorce 35
2003 Marriage Registration Regulations: procedures for registering divorce 40; simplification of procedures 39–40
2003 Regulations on Marriage Registration 69
2004 Measures: standardized system of permanent residents for foreigners in China 41

2004 Measures for the Administration of Examinations and Approval of Foreigners' Permanent Residence in China 140
2010 Residence Permits for Foreigners 140

Abramovich, Roman 117
adultery 73
advertising, media 14
Ahn Jae-hyung 95
airplane tickets (marriage) 10
ai wu guojie 52
Akhavan-Majid, R.: framing theory 15
All-China Federation of Trade Unions 83
All-China Women's Federation (*Zhonghua quanguo funü lianhehui*) 77, 83
alliance portfolios: celebrity and entertainment 161
Al-Modiahki, Mohammed Ahmed 106
Anqing Wanbao (*Anqing Evening News*) 58, 126
aphorisms 80
arranged marriages 91–2
Article 1, 1988 Notice 38
Article 2, 1988 Notice 38–9
Article 4, 1988 Notice 39
Article 5, 1988 Notice 39
Asian brides: negative stereotypes 8
August 1983 Rules: categories of foreign applicants for marriage registration 37–8; documentation required by foreign nationals 38; intercultural marriage 36; preclusion of foreign nationals marrying on security grounds 38
Australia: Australian–Chinese marriages 32, 179; marriages with Chinese spouses 32; marriage to Chinese citizens 27

234 Index

autonomy, female 125–9

Baoding Wanbao (Baoding Evening News) 108
bao ernai 73–4
baorong 52
Barnes, Dexter 106, 107, 166
Basic Law of the Hong Kong Special Administrative Region of the PRC (1997) 37
Basic Law of the Macau Special Administrative Region of the PRC 37
Bei Aiqing Yiwang de Jiaoluo (*A Love-Forsaken Corner*) see *A Love-Forsaken Corner*
Beijing: marriage registrations 30
Beijing TV-1 14
Beijing TV-3 14
Beijing Film Academy 91
Beijing Film Institute 103
Beijing Impressions (*Beijing Yinxiang*): marriage between Chinese man and Dutch woman 137; summary 137
Beijing Jishi (Beijing Documentary) 107
Beijing Yinxiang (*Beijing Impressions*): summary 137; see also *Beijing Impressions*
Bellefroid, Emmanuel 23–4
bigamy 2; newspaper coverage, Chinese–foreign divorce 73–4
birth control policy 109n2
black–white relationships: studies 7
brain drain 55–6, 102
British Film Institute 103
Butian 92
bu xunjiu 13

Cai Xiaohau 150
Cambodia: women's marriage to Chinese men 12
Canada: divorce rates 71; marriage to Chinese citizens 27
Cao Cao 96
CCP (Chinese Communist Party): control of the media 13; curtailment of labour mobility 21; marriage introduction services 83; political supremacy of Chinese communism 23; state allocation of work and resources 21; Third Plenary Session of the Eleventh Central Committee 91; see also Maoist era
celebrity Chinese–foreign divorce: amicable divorces and exemplary fatherhood 110, 120–4; blame on male foreign marrying partners 115; career women 126; celebrity divorcées 120; celebrity gossip 116; cruelty and sexual abuse 115; devoted fathers 122, 123; emotive headlines in media reports 111; extra-marital affairs 114–15; female autonomy and exemplary motherhood 125–9; female-initiated divorce 125, 126; gendered reporting 116; high rates of 111–16; inevitability of 110, 112; infatuation of Chinese female celebrities with foreign men 113; Intimacy between the reader and celebrity 117; irreconcilable cultural differences 113–14; long-term separation 114; newspaper coverage of 110; parallelism in media reports 112; reasons for 112–13; speculation and hearsay 116–20
celebrity Chinese–foreign marriage: during the 1990s 96–102; during the 2000s 102–8; celebrity as a branded commodity 108; 'Chinese son-in-law' 105; concerns 108–9; criticism of 95, 96; ending of Ning Jing's career 97; fairy-tale marriages 95–6, 98–9; female celebrities living overseas 97, 101–2; feminization of men 106; focus on professional achievements 95; gendered reportage 96; greater exposure 102–3; growth of magazines as medium 94; ideal of romantic love and monogamous heterosexual marriage 100, 102; intercultural marriages 95; inverted gender roles 106; male celebrities 96; marriages of love 99; notion of contemporary ideal Chinese womanhood 100; patriotism 103–6; positive image of Chinese public figures 101, 102; positive stories by celebrities 101; powerful status of Chinese female celebrities 107; professional achievements of Shen Danping 94; property of the PRC 98; public gossip about marriage of Shen Danping 93–4; reverse migration of celebrities 103–5; visual imagery of inverted gender roles 106–7; 'wannabe ordinary women' 108; see also Shen Danping
celebrity gossip 110, 116
centralized planning: Maoist era 21
Chao, Emily: escape from local systems of patriarchal marriage 53

Index 235

Characteristics and Trends of Cross-Nation Marriage in Modern Shanghai 9
Chen Chong 95, 100, 121, 127
chengshu 63
Chenguang 151
Chenivisse, Sandrine 95, 113, 114, 117–18, 121–2
Chen Liangsheng 95, 103
Chen Lu 'ice butterfly' 104, 106
Chen Luyu 115, 126
Chen Shiqu 185
Chen Yan 153, 154
Chen Yin 135
Chiang Kai-shek 138
China *see* PRC (People's Republic of China)
China Central Newsreel and Documentary Film Studio (*Zhongyang xinwen jilu dianying zhipianchang*) 133
China Central Television (CCTV-4) 14
China Civil Affairs Statistical Yearbook 24
China Daily: positive assertion of female autonomy 125; public gossip about marriage of Shen Danping 93–4
China Society News (*Zhongguo Shehuibao*): 'Standardizing and Institutionalizing Chinese–foreign Marriage Services' 52; *see also Zhongguo Shehuibao*
China Women's News (*Zhongguo Funü bao*): 'Chinese Brides Suffer in Chinese–Japanese Marriages' 81–2; domestic violence 79; 'Loving Chinese–foreign Couples' 52; *see also Zhongguo Funü bao*
Chinese citizens: dominant group among foreign spouses 2
Chinese Civil War 138
Chinese Communist Party (CCP) *see* CCP (Chinese Communist Party)
Chinese–foreign divorce: celebrity *see* celebrity Chinese–foreign divorce; deception, adultery, bigamy and divorce 71–6; domestic violence 76–83; newspaper coverage *see* newspaper coverage, Chinese–foreign divorce; rates of 179; rise of 33–4; rising trend 68–71
'Chinese–Foreign Marriage Encounters "Seven-Year-Itch"': intercultural marriages in Shanghai 47; *see also Wenhui News*
Chinese–foreign marriage (*shewai hunyin*): defining and counting 176–9; definition 2–6; documentaries *see* documentaries; initial obstacles 21–4; key features of 137–8; marriage for love 57; migration 52–4; negative accounts of 10; newspaper coverage *see* newspaper coverage; positive accounts of 10–11; reform-era phenomenon 35; registration procedures 37; removal of barriers of communication 57; socio-demographic characteristics 178–9; statistics 24–35; television talk shows *see* television talk shows; *see also* intercultural marriage; statistics (Chinese–foreign marriage)
Chinese men: attractive marriage partners to foreign women 13; devoted fathers 122, 123; difficulties of rural workers finding domestic partners 12; low incidence of Chinese–foreign marriages 12; marriage to women from poorer countries 12; portrayal as ideal marriage partners 75–6; qualities of 13
Chinese women: career women 126; competent business partners 147–8; depiction as victims in newspapers 63–4, 75; disillusionment with Chinese men 63; domestic violence *see* domestic violence; educational qualifications 57; female autonomy and exemplary motherhood 125–9; hiding domestic violence from family and friends 80; independence and modernization 59; intercultural marriage to enter the USA 53; man's private property 80; middle-aged women in competitive job market 61; middle-aged women seeking foreign partners 63; motivation for marrying foreign men 10; second wives 73–4
Chinese Women and the Cyberspace 11
Chongqing Chenbao (*Chongqing Morning Post*) 105; *see also Chongqing Morning Post*
Chongqing Evening News (*Chongqing Wanbao*): blame on male foreign marrying partners 115; Chinese men with foreign nationality 72; visual images of inverted gender roles 106; *see also Chongqing Wanbao*
Chongqing Morning Post (*Chongqing Chenbao*): marriages of Chen Chong 127; *see also Chongqing Chenbao*
Chongqing Shangbao (*Chongqing*

Commercial News): marriage of Wei Wei and Michael Joseph Smith 126–7
Chongqing Shibao (*Chongqing Daily*): Ning Jing relationship 119
Chongqing Wanbao (*Chongqing Evening News*): on marriage between Gan Lin and Mark Roswell 105; *see also Chongqing Evening News*
chongyang meiwai 55
Chuangyezhe (*Entrepreneur*) 96–7
Chuanqi Gushi (*Legendary Stories*): summary 136; *see also Legendary Stories*
chuanwen cheng (hearsay) 116–20
chuguore 52–4
chunjie zhencheng de aiqing 58
Chutian Dushibao (*Chutian Metropolian News*): middle-aged Chinese women's search for intercultural marriage 62
Cinderella stories 59
Clark, Constance: social mobility 9
Common Ground (*Guoji Shuangxingxian*) 164, 171; format 158, 159; non-celebrity Chinese–foreign marriage 159; *see also Guoji Shuangxingxian*
Communist Youth League of China 83
Constable, Nicole: global hypergamy 7; marriage to American spouses 53
Crazy English 82
Cross-Border Marriages: Gender and Mobility in Transnational Asia 53
cross-cultural/intercultural marriage (*kua wenhua hunyin*): definition 16
cross-Strait marriage (*liang'an hunyin*): 16-character guideline for cross-Strait relations 147; bilateral trade agreement 139–40; definition 5; equal partnership between mainland brides and Taiwanese husbands 147, 148; improved cross-Strait relations 145–6; love and understanding 146, 147; marriage introduction agencies 142; in the media 143–8; Nationalist Party veterans 139; negative depictions of mainland brides 143; negative press coverage 144; numbers of registrations 140–1; origins of term 138; restrictions on migration 141; Taiwanese spouses 141–2; Taiwan legalizes business investment with the PRC 139–40
cross-Strait relations 138
cross-talk (*Xiangsheng*) 175n2
CSM Media Research 159
Cui Yongyuan 157

Cultural Revolution 91, 92

Dahe Bao (*Dahe News*) 106; 'Henan Girl Marries Polish Presidential Candidate, She Will Bring Him to Her Native Home' 59
Dalu jumin yu Taiwanjumin hunyin dengji guanli zanxing banfa 1998 39
Dan, Anchun 121
Dangdai Shenghuo Bao (*Modern Life*) 104
danwei (socialist work unit): urban Chinese people 21
Daqing Ribao (Daqing Daily): celebrity divorces 111–12
Da Shan 96, 101
A Date with the Countryside (*Xiang Yue*) 160, 165, 168–9
dazhe denglong nanzhao de baobei 63
deception: foreign men 73; marriage introduction services 85–6; newspaper coverage, Chinese–foreign divorce 71–3, 74–5; swindlers 72; women stereotyped as vulnerable group 75
Deng Xiaoping 65n1, 91, 139
Deng Zhonggang 152, 154, 165, 168–9
Ding Guangquan 162
Ding Jinhong: growth of Chinese–foreign marriage in Shanghai 9–10
divorce: 2001 Marriage Law 35; 2003 Marriage Registration Regulations 40; female divorcees 10; *see also* Chinese–foreign divorce
documentaries: 'American Wife in Our Village' 151; background information 137; *Beijing Impressions* (*Beijing Yinxiang*) 137; commercialization 133; cross-Strait marriage 138–43; definition 132; exotic foreign spouses 151; 'Foreign Son-in-law Comes to Our Village' 153; 'A Foreign Wife's Urban Dream' 151–2, 153; grassroots-up perspective 133; intercultural marriage 133, 134–8; key features of intercultural marriage 137–8; *Legendary Stories* (*Chuanqi Gushi*) 136, 153; new documentary and Chinese–foreign marriage 132–8; new documentary movement 133; *Predestined Love* (*Yuanfen*) 133, 133–6, 145–6, 147, 148, 151; rural Chinese and foreign nationals 149–55; rural communities excited by foreigners 150; social and economic superiority of foreign spouses 151;

special topics 133; *Stories* (*Jiangshu*) 153–4; 'Story of a Foreign-Son-in-Law's Marriage Proposal' 153–4; traditional approach 132; *True Stories* (*Zhenqing Shilu*) 136, 151, 152
domestic violence: abuse hidden from family and friends 80; Chinese brides abroad 78; Chinese women's experience of 77; couples living overseas 79–80; definition 77; divorce 2; implied notions of victim participation 79; legislation 77; link between hypergamy and male dominance 78; male victims of 82; migrant women 80; physically stronger men against physically weaker women 78; public debate about 77; toleration of by Chinese women 80–1; widespread reporting in Chinese media 77; women fighting violence with violence 81
Dongfang mei 60
Dongfang Tiyu Ribao (*Oriental Sports Daily*): marriage of Li Donghua 121
Dongfang Zaobao (*Oriental Morning Post*) 103; 'Single Life Enables Wei Wei to Regain Confidence' 127
Dongfang Zhiboshi (*Oriental Live Studio*): format 157; see also Oriental Live Studio

economic abuse 77
Eleventh Five-Year Plan 150
entertainment, media 14
Entman, Robert: framing theory 15
Esperanza, Friedli 95, 96, 98, 110, 112, 121
extra-marital affairs 2, 114–15
Extraordinary Husband and Wife (*Feichang Fuqi*): format 161, 162–3

Family Television Studio (*Jiating Yanboshi*) 163, 168, 171–2; format 160
Fang Qin 152
Farrer, James 182; growth of Chinese–foreign marriage in Shanghai 9; intercultural marriage migration 53; marriage between mainland Chinese citizens and Western expatriates 10; positive accounts of Chinese–foreign marriage 10–11
Fazhi Chenbao (*Legal Morning Post*): Chinese women's murder of Japanese husbands 81
Fazhi Wanbao (*Legal Evening News*): intercultural marriages in the PRC 48; see also Legal Evening News
Fazhi Zaobao (*Legal Morning Post*): complications from different cultural values and practices 70; 'Striking at the Heart of Chinese–foreign Marriages' 55
Fei Bin 171
Feichang Fuqi (*Extraordinary Husband and Wife*) 14; format 161; see also Extraordinary Husband and Wife
Feichang Jing Juli (*Talking With Li Jing*) 161
Fenghuang Zaoban Che (*Good Morning China*) 126
first-time marriages 29
foreign Chinese 161–5
foreign-country pumpkins 165–9
foreign nationals (*laowai/waiguoren*): definition 3; marriage to mainland China citizens 26, 177; (*waiguoren*): documentation required for marriage registration 37, 38, 40; intimate relationships with Chinese citizens 23; mainland China and foreign nationals 26; marriages with *guonei gongmin* 36; preclusion of marriage to certain groups of Chinese citizens 38; regulations restricting physical space in Maoist era 23
Fortune Time (*Caifu Rensheng*) 87
Fourth World Conference on Women (United Nations) 77
Four Tigers (Asia) 139
France: marriage to Chinese citizens 27
Fujian: marriage registrations 30
Fu Shuangye 135, 145
Fushun Wanbao (*Fushun Evening News*): deception 74–5

gaibian mingyun 63
Gang of Four 91, 92, 109n1
gan jiawu 13
Gan Lin 96, 101, 104, 105
Gansu: marriage registrations 30
Gao Wei 168
Germany: Chinese–German marriages 27
global hypergamy: definition 7
Global Times (*Huanqiu Shibao*): interview with Chen Chong 100; positive coverage of cross-Strait marriage 144; secret of successful marriage 100–1; Wei Wei's divorce 128; see also Huanqiu Shibao

238 Index

gold diggers 143
Grierson, John 132
Guangdong: marriage registrations 30
Guangdong Province: organized tours of citizens to Hong Kong and Macau 46
Guangzhou Daily (*Guangzhou Ribao*): marriage of Rupert Murdoch and Wendi Deng 117
Guangzhou Ribao (Guangzhou Daily): divorce of Li Donghua 112
Guanyu Taiwan tongbao yu Dalu gongmin zhijian banli jiehun dengji youguan wenti de tongzhi 1988 *see* 1988 Notice
gujia 13
Guo Ba Yin (*Have a Good Time*) 104
Guo Fangfang 112
guoji hunyin (international marriage) 16
Guoji Shuangxingxian (*Common Ground*) 14; format 158; *see also* Common Ground
Guo Li 134
guonei gongmin: marriages with foreign nationals 36; marriages with *huaqiao* 36; marriages with *tongbao* 36; marriages with *waiguoren* 36
Guo Zhenzhong 135, 145–6

Haikou: newspaper coverage of Chinese–foreign marriage 44; seaboard region 43
Haili 151
Hainan Daily (*Hainan Ribao*): 1999 report 45; marriage between citizens of the PRC and Taiwan 45; *see also* Hainan Ribao
Hainan Province: newspaper coverage of Chinese–foreign marriage 44; Special Economic Zone 44
Hainan Ribao (*Hainan Daily*): 1999 report 44; on Mark Roswell's marriage 101; *see also* Hainan Daily
Hangzhou: newspaper coverage of Chinese–foreign marriage 44, 44–5; seaboard region 43
Hangzhou Ribao (*Hangzhou Daily*) 51; Shen Danping 94
Haonan Haonü (*Good Men, Good Women*) 158
Happy Evening Roll Call (*Xingfu Wandianming*) 160, 168
Haubensack, Esther 96, 162, 165
Hayes, James 170
hearsay (*you chuanwen cheng*) 116–20
Heilongjiang: marriage registrations 30
Heilongjiang Ribao (Heilongjiang Daily): separation of Zhang Tielin 121
hei zhongjie 83
He Zhili 95
Home Return Permit 40
Hong Kong: businessmen taking mainland wives 46; categories of marriages 25–6; colonial occupation 3; cultural differences with China 6; documentation required for marriage registration 37, 40; ethnic Chinese 5–6; expansion of trade with the PRC 30; intercultural marriages 2; mainland wives 2; marriages to citizens of the PRC 3, 25, 26, 45, 176, 177; policing of border with the PRC 45–6; second wife phenomenon 73–4; single men marrying women from mainland China 46; spouses 26; tours of citizens from Guangdong Province 46
Hong Yi 148
household registration regulations: Chinese rural men 23; foreign nationals 23
household registration system (*hukou*): urban Chinese and rural agricultural producers 21–2
Hua Jiade 135
Huanqiu Shibao (*Global Times*): marriage of Li Donghua 98; *see also* Global Times
huaqiao (overseas Chinese): definition 3–4; marriage with *Zhongguo gongmin* 3–4; *see also* overseas Chinese
huaqiao (*overseas Chinese*): marriages with *guonei gongmin* 36
Huaqiao tong guonei gongmin, Gang Ao tongbao tong neidi gongmin zhijian banli jiehun dengji de jixiang guiding 1983 *see* March 1983 Rules
huaren: definition 4
Huashang Chenbao (*China Business Morning Post*): marriage of Jiang Wen 121–2
Hui, Peter 95, 100
Hu Jintao, President 124, 146; 16-character guideline for cross-Strait relations 147
hukou (household registration system): urban Chinese and rural agricultural producers 21–2
human interest stories, media 14
Hunxue Haizi de Shijie (World of the Mixed Blood Children) 94

Hunyin dengji tiaoli 2003 39
hunyin jieshaosuo (marriage introduction agencies) 9; *see also* marriage introduction agencies
hypergamy: cautionary tales of tragedy and personal disappointment 54–5; Chinese women 54–5; concept 7; definition 54; disadvantages of middle-aged Chinese women 61–4; link with male dominance 78; marrying up 63; middle-aged women seeking foreign partners 62, 63; motivation 56–7; newspaper coverage 64; warnings about 'blind worship of everything foreign' 55

Ichikawa, Tetsu: definition of terms *huaqiao* and *huaren* 4
Indonesia: women's marriage to Chinese men 12
intercultural (*kua wenhua*): definition 5, 6; *see also kua wenhua*
intercultural marriage: definition 2–6; individual agency 8; Internet dating 11; mail-order brides 7–8; negative stereotypes 8; *see also* Chinese–foreign marriage
intercultural marriage mobility: global hypergamy 7
interethnic: definition 5
Interim Measures for Managing the Registration of Marriages between Mainland Residents and Taiwan Residents 39
international marriage introduction agencies (*shewai hunyin jieshao*) 83
Internet: intercultural marriage and 11; online dating 11; users in the PRC 11
interracial: definition 5
interracial/interethnic marriage (*kua zhongzu hunyin*): definition 16
intracultural marriage: Chinese men/women in Australia 32
intracultural (*wenhua jian*): definition 5, 6

Japan: Chinese brides 31–2; divorce rates 70–1; educational level of female immigrants from China 31; expansion of trade with the PRC 30; intercultural marriages 2; marriage to Chinese citizens 26, 178–9
jiang aiqing jinxing daodi 59
Jiangshu (*Stories*): foreign brides 150; *see also Stories*

Jiang Wen 95, 113, 114, 117–18, 120, 121–2, 122–3, 124
Jiang Xiaoyu 136
Jiangxi Television (JXTV) 136
Jiang Yilang 123, 124
Jiang Zhenliang 134
jianqiang 63
Jiao Zhimin 95, 100–1
jiating baoli see domestic violence
Jiating Yanboshi (*Family Television Studio*): format 160; *see also* Family Television Studio
Jiating Zhoumobao (*Family Weekly*): 'Blindspots of Chinese–foreign Marriage' 86; complications from different cultural values and practices 70
Jilin: marriage registrations 30
Jinhua city: newspaper coverage of intercultural marriage 47
Jinhua Ribao (*Jinhua Daily*): intercultural marriages 47–8
Jinri Wanbao (*Today Evening News*): 'The Reasons for Divorce' 112–13
Ji Zenghe 145
jumin jia 23

Kersey, Paul 97, 104, 113, 114, 118–19, 125–6, 128
Khulpateea, Veda: definition of terms interracial and interethnic 5
Kim, Doo-Sub: cross-border marriage in Korea 32
Kim Lee 82
Kim Seung-hwan 112
Kon, Braby 173–4
Könitzer, Christian 104, 106
Korea *see* Republic of Korea
Kos-Read, Jonathan 96, 104, 105, 170–1
Kraeuter, Uwe 169, 172; marriage to Shen Danping 91, 93, 107
kua wenhua hunyin (cross-cultural/intercultural marriage): definition 16
kua wenhua (intercultural): definition 5, 6; *see also* intercultural
kua zhongzu hunyin (interracial/interethnic marriage): definition 16

Lang, Graeme: bigamy 74
laodong jiaoyang (reeducation through labour) 23, 42n1
laofu shaoqi 54
laowai (foreign nationals): definition 6;

see also foreign nationals
Lau, Jimmy 95, 121, 127
Law of the People's Republic of China on Control of the Entry and Exit of Aliens 22
Law of the People's Republic of China on Control of the Exit and Entry of Citizens 22
Law on Domestic Violence Prevention and Control (*Jiating baoli fangzhi fa*) 77
Legal Evening News (*Fazhi Wanbao*): marriage between Dexter Barnes and Zhang Shan 107; *see also Fazhi Wanbao*
Legendary Stories (*Chuanqi Gushi*): 'Foreign Son-in-law Comes to Our Village' 153; summary 136
Lei Feng 164
liang'an hunyin (cross-Strait marriage) *see* cross-Strait marriage
Lian Na 164
Li Donghua 95, 96, 98, 110, 112, 121
Li Lingyu 95, 110, 125, 128
Li Lisan 164
Li Mei 136
Lin Xia 134
Li Qiaofang 135
Li Qinqin 114, 115, 126
Li Sha 164
Li Shuang 23–4
Liucun Chakan 92
Liu Hong: intercultural marriage to enter the USA 53; Internet and intercultural marriage 11–12
Liu Jia 167
Liu Lihui: intercultural marriage to enter the USA 53; Internet and intercultural marriage 11–12
Liu Qing (Jimmy Lau) 121
Liu Ruoying 145
Liu Xuan 164
lixing: intercultural marriages in the PRC 48, 48–9
Li Yang 82
Li Yingnan 164
Li Yinhe: on Chinese–foreign marriage 52
lizhi: intercultural marriages in the PRC 48, 48–9
Li Zhiyin 96, 105, 170–1
long-term separation 114
A Love-Forsaken Corner (*Bei Aiqing Yiwang de Jiaoluo*) 91, 92
Lu, Melody 142
Luo Yuehua 135

Lü Xinyu 133
Lu Yu You Yue (*A Date with [host] Lu Yu*) 159–60, 161, 166–7

Macau: categories of marriages 25–6; cultural differences with China 6; documentation required for marriage registration 37, 40; ethnic Chinese 5–6; expansion of trade with the PRC 30; marriages to citizens of the PRC 3, 25, 26, 45, 176; second wife phenomenon 73–4; sovereignty of the PRC 3; spouses 26; tools of citizens from Guangdong Province 46
mail-order brides 7–8
maimai hunyin (mercenary marriage) 81
mainland sisters (*dalumei*) 143
mainland wives: Hong Kong businessmen taking mainland wives from China 46
Making News: A Study in the Construction of Reality 15
Malandina, Irina Vyacheslavovna 117
Maoist era: Chinese citizen cohabitation with foreign national 23–4; closed nature of Chinese society 22–3; intimate relationships between Chinese citizens and foreign nationals 22–3; rarity of Chinese–foreign marriages 21; restricted physical space for Chinese citizens 23; restrictions on population mobility 22; *see also* CCP
Mao Zedong, Chairman 13
March 1983 Rules: Article 2 37; categories of foreign applicants for marriage registration 37–8; intercultural marriage 36
marital conflict 169–74
marriage: conventional 1–2; registration outside mainland China 2
marriage introduction agencies (*hunyin jieshaosuo*) 9; illegal 14; *see also hunyin jieshaosuo*
marriage introduction services: 1994 Notice 84; affiliation with the CCP 83; bans 85; complaints 88; cross-Strait marriage 142; deception 87, 87–8; demand for services 84; employers and employees 86–7; establishment in the PRC 83; expansion of agencies 84, 84–5; fees 86–7; flouting of government rulings 85; international agencies 83–4; interpretation of guidelines 84–5; management of 84; newspaper coverage of deception 85–6;

police closures of 87; profitability of 84; profiteering 83; street flyers 85
Marriage Law (2001) 77, 81
Marriage Law of the People's Republic of China 35
marriage registration: categories for foreign applicants 37–8; documentation required 36–7
Marriage Registration Management Regulations 36
marriage-related mobility: hypergamy 7; individual agency 8
Marrying Far Away in Japan (*Yuanjia Riben*): subject matter 131; *see also Yuanjia Riben*
Ma Yashu 170
Ma Ying-jeou, President: 16-character guideline for cross-Strait relations 147
McCombs, M.: framing theory 15
Measures for the Administration of Examination and Approval of Aliens' Permanent Residence in China (2004) *see* 2004 Measures
media: coverage of Chinese–foreign marriage 14–15; emphasis on entertainment and advertising 14; human interest stories 14; mouthpiece of the Chinese Communist Party (CCP) 13; relaxation of control 13–14; revenue from private subscriptions 14; *see also* documentaries; newspaper coverage; television talk shows
media framing theory 15
Meigui Zhi Yue (*Red Rose Date*): format 158
Meiguo Laide Qizi (*My Wife from America*) 10, 76
Meiji huaren 49
Meiri Xinbao (*Daily News*): relationship between Jiang Wen and daughter 122–3
Meng Guangmei 145
mercenary marriage (*maimai hunyin*) 81
migrant women: domestic violence 80
migration, marriage 52–4, 103–5; greater exposure 103
Mingyun de Chengnue (The Promise of Life) 92–3
Ministry of Civil Affairs: disaggregation of Chinese–foreign divorce statistics 34–5; international marriage introduction agencies 83–4; lack of socio-demographic statistics 30; marital status of brides and grooms 29; Notice on Issues Concerning the Rigorous Implementation of the State Council's 1994 Notice on Strengthening the Management of International Marriage Introduction Agencies 84; statistics 1; survey on intercultural marriage 53
Ministry of Public Security: permanent residence cards 41; updating of Home Return Permit 40
Modern Family (*Modeng Jiating*): subject matter 131
Modern Life 119
Modern Television (*Dangdai Dianshi*) 94
More Talk Makes for Happiness (*Yue Ce Yue Kaixin*) 160, 164, 165, 167
Mosuo ethnic group 130n1
motherhood: female autonomy and exemplary motherhood 125–9
Murdoch, Rupert 108, 117

Namu 114; amicable divorce 120–1; *see also* Yang Erche Namu
Nanguo Dushibao (*South China Metropolitan Daily*) 113
Nanguo Jinbao (*Southern China News*): Chinese–foreign marriage introduction agencies 86
Nanjing: newspaper coverage of intercultural marriage 47
Nanjing Daily (*Nanjing Ribao*): 2006 report 47; Chinese–foreign divorce 68–9; Chinese men with foreign nationality 72
Nanning Ribao (*Nanning Morning Post*): 'Intercultural Marriage: "I Love You" Easier Said Than Done' 78–9
Nationalist Party (Taiwan) 46
nationalization: industry during Maoist era 21
National Law of the PRC 37
national marriage registration system 36
Nelson, E.T.: framing theory 15
Network Research Centre for Combating Domestic Violence of the China Law Society (*Zhongguo faxuehui fan jiabao wangluo*) 77
newspaper coverage: attraction of Chinese people to foreigners 59; campaigns against negative Western influences 56; celebrity divorce 110, 111–15; changing numerical trends 43–9; Chinese Cinderella stories 59; Chinese–foreign divorce *see* newspaper coverage, Chinese–foreign divorce; cross-Strait marriage 143–8; depiction

of Chinese women as victims 63–4; disillusionment with Chinese men 63; economic development of the PRC 52; focus on foreign nationals 180–1; gendered reporting of celebrity divorce 116; hearsay and speculation 116–20; hypergamous motivations for intercultural marriages 56–7; hypergamy 54–7, 61–4, 179; independence and modernization of Chinese women 59; intercultural marriage 14; intercultural marriage for love 57, 59, 180; intercultural marriages for middle-aged women 61–2; love in the 2000's 58–61; love of China 60–1; marriage partners from different countries of origin 49–54, 180; marrying up 63; mate selection 59–60; motivations for reporting on intercultural marriage 64; new form of hypergamy 63; people from wealthy industrial countries 53; portrayal of gendered stereotypes of women 63; reasons for failure of celebrity marriages 113; romantic fairy-tales 179–80

newspaper coverage, Chinese–foreign divorce: abuse by male citizens of the PRC 82; complications from different cultural values and practices 70–1; couples residing overseas 70–1; deception, adultery, bigamy and divorce 71–6; deception by Chinese men and women 76; domestic violence and divorce 76–83; focus on foreign nationals 73–4; foreign male marrying partner 71; illegality of marriage introduction agencies 85; limited coverage of men from Hong Kong, Macao and Taiwan 73–4; long-term separation of couples 71; marriage introduction services 83–8; portrayal of Chinese men as ideal marriage partners 75–6; rising trend 68–71; simplified divorce registration process 69

Nichols, Bill 132
Ning Jing 97, 103, 104, 112, 113, 114, 118–19, 120, 125, 125–6, 128
Ningxia: marriage registrations 30
Notice on Issues Concerning the Rigorous Implementation of the State Council's 1994 Notice on Strengthening the Management of International Marriage Introduction Agencies 84

Notice On 'Strengthening the Management of International Marriage Introduction Agencies *see* 1994 Notice
Nu Nei 152, 153, 154, 165, 168–9

OK! Xintiandi (OK! New World) 14
Open Door Policy: marriages after 48
Oriental Live Studio (*Dongfang Zhiboshi*): format 157; popularity 157
overseas Chinese (*huaqiao*) 3–4; documentation required for marriage registration 40; marriages to mainland China spouses 177; *see also huaqiao*

passports (marriage) 10
People's Court of Shunyi 125
People's Daily (*Renmin Ribao*): 2003 report on Shanghai foreign marriages 49; deception leading to divorce 71; integration of foreigners into Chinese family structures 52; love of Chinese culture 60–1; marriages after Open Door Policy 48; *see also Renmin Ribao* (*People's Daily*)
People's Republic of China (PRC) *see* PRC (People's Republic of China)
permanent residence: foreign spouses 41
Petrov, Denis Alekseyevich 104, 106
Philippines: negative stereotypes of brides 8; women's marriage to Chinese men 12
Phoenix TV 103
physical abuse 77
physical conflict 172–3, 174
population mobility: restrictions 1, 19, 22
PRC (People's Republic of China): 16-character guideline for cross-Strait relations 147; average annual income of citizens 23; birth control policy 109n2; brain drain 55–6, 102; citizens' entry and exit 22, 140; claims to political sovereignty 5; divorce rate 34; expansion of trade 30; facilitation of travel for people from Hong Kong, Macau and Taiwan 40; founding of 3; Four Exchanges 139; government support towards intimate and broader intercultural relations 40; harmonious society policy 124; Internet users 11; legal and administrative reforms 140; marriage mobility 9; nationality status of citizens 37; new socialist Chinese countryside 150; one-child family policy 35; passport-on-demand policy

22; peaceful reunification with Taiwan 139; permanent residence for foreign spouses 41; policing of border with Hong Kong 45–6; press coverage of cross-Strait marriage 144; revision to marriage laws and regulations 34; simplified administrative procedures for Taiwanese citizens in China 40–1; socialist development 139; strained relationship with Taiwan 3, 139; Three Links 139; total number of marriages 24; tourism with Taiwan 140

Predestined Love (*Yuanfen*): cross-Strait relations 135, 145–6, 147; equal partnership between mainland brides and Taiwanese husbands 147; foreign brides 151; intercultural marriage 134–6; summary 133; *see also Yuanfen*

Protection of the Rights and Interests of Returned Overseas Chinese and the Family Members of Overseas Chinese 3–4

psychological abuse 77

qinfen kekao 13
Qingdao: openness 51
Qing dynasty 3
Qinghai: marriage registrations 30
Qingxi Xixili (*Love in Sicily*) 131
qinshi nanan 58
Qi Yaomin 87–8

Ramaprasad, J.: framing theory 15
rational (*lizhi*, *lixing*): intercultural marriages in the PRC 48, 48–9
re'ai Zhongguo de erzi 105
Red Rose Date (*Meigui Zhi Yue*): format 158
reeducation through labour (*laodong jiaoyang*) 23, 42n1
reform era: governing marriage 35–41; phenomenon of Chinese–foreign marriage 35; *see also* statistics (Chinese–foreign marriage)
remarriages 29; Chinese–Korean marriages 29–30
Renmin Ribao (*People's Daily*): 1993 report on Chinese–foreign marriages 44; *see also People's Daily*
Renmin Tiaojie (*People's Mediators*) 94
Report on Major Results of the Third Wave Survey on the Social Status of Women in China 77
Republic of China (ROC) *see* ROC

Republic of Korea: Chinese–Korean marriages 29–30, 179; Chinese male husbands 32; diplomatic relations and expansion of economic ties with the PRC 32; increase of Chinese–Korean marriages 32; intercultural marriages 2
ROC (Republic of China) 3, 138; adoption of market-based economic policies 139; controlled immigration from the PRC 141; rejection of PRC's overtures 139; *see also* PRC (People's Republic of China); Taiwan
Roswell, Mark 96, 101, 104, 105
Rui En 153–4, 154
Rules on Marriage Registration between Chinese Citizens and Foreigners *see* August 1983 Rules
Rules on Marriage Registration between Chinese Citizens and Overseas Chinese and Hong Kong and Macau Compatriots *see* March 1983 Rules
rural population: corrupt officials 149; documentaries 149–55; household registration status for men 22; liberated marriages 154–5; marriage of women for social advancement 22; migration to towns and cities 149; modern Chinese masculinity and femininity 152; positive media accounts of rural migrant workers 149–50; second-class citizens 22; stereotypical media accounts 149

Sanba Xian shang de Nübing 92
Scheufele, Dietram 15; framing theory 15
Seventeenth National Congress of the Chinese Communist Party 146
sexual abuse 77
Shan Gen 115
Shanghai: categories of Chinese–foreign marriages 10; marriage registrations 30; motivation of Chinese women for marrying foreign men 10; newspaper coverage of Chinese–foreign marriage 44, 47; perceived failure of Chinese men 10; seaboard region 43; significant growth of Chinese–foreign marriages 9–10; social progress and renewed confidence 51
Shanghai Civil Affairs Bureau 9–10
Shanghai Dongfang Dianshitai (*Shanghai Oriental Television*) 157
Shanghai Dragon Television 136
Shanghai Fazhibao (*Shanghai Legal*

Daily): 1988 report on Chinese–foreign marriages 44, 45, 51; *see also* Shanghai Legal Daily
Shanghai Film Studio (*Shanghai dianying zhipianchang*) 131
Shanghai Legal Daily (*Shanghai Fazhibao*): 1988 report on Chinese–foreign marriages 45, 51; Chinese–foreign divorce 67; marriages to partners from different foreign countries 51
Shanghai Marriage Registration Office 44
Shanghai Morning Post: complications from different cultural values and practices 70
Shanghai Television 14
Shantou: Special Economic Zone 44
Shashou Qing (Killer's Love) 104
she Gang Ao Tai hunyin (Hong Kong, Macau, Taiwan-related marriage): definition 4–5, 16
shehui zhuyi jingshen wenming jianshe 65n2
Shen Danping 169, 172; biography 94; film roles 92; friends/work opposition to marriage to Uwe Kraeuter 93; interview with China Fashion Weekly 99; magazine articles 94; marriage to Uwe Kraeuter 91, 93, 107; public gossip about marriage to Uwe Kraeuter 94; role in *A Love-Forsaken Corner* 92; television appearances 92–3
Shen Hengde 135
Shen, Hsiu-hua: male entrepreneurs in Taiwan 74
Shenzhen: marriage introduction agencies 9; Special Economic Zone 44
Shenzhen Wanbao (Shenzhen Evening News): relationships of Chinese celebrities 112
sheqiao hunyin: definition 5
shewai hunyin (Chinese–foreign marriage): definition 4, 16; *see also* Chinese–foreign marriage
Shidai Xinbao (*Times News*): 'Middle-Aged Women in Pursuit of Intercultural Marriage Study Harder to English to Please Foreigners' 61–2; *see also* Times News
Shi Dantong 114
Shihua Shishuo (*Tell It Like It Is*): format 157
Shi Ke 104, 106
Shi Ke Drama Studio 106

Shui Rang Ni Xindong (Who Moves Your Heart) 158
Sinification 161–5
Sino-foreign marriage (*Zhongwai hunyin*): definition 4, 16
Siqin Gaowa 95, 99, 103
Smart, Josephine: bigamy 74
Smith, Michael Joseph 95, 99, 105, 106, 113, 126–7, 128
socialist centralized planning: Maoist era 21
Socialist Spiritual Civilization 52, 65–6n2
socialist work unit (*danwei*): urban Chinese people 21
social mobility: motivation for marriage 9
Special Administrative Regions (SAR): Hong Kong and Macau 3, 65n1
Special Economic Zones: definition 44; establishment of 44
speculation 116–20
Standing Committee of the National People's Congress 77
State Council 42n1, 84
statistics (Chinese–foreign marriage): Australian–Chinese citizens 32; average age of couples 30; Chinese–foreign divorce 1, 33–5; citizens from developed countries 26–7; citizens from Hong Kong, Macau and Taiwan 25, 26; in economically developed areas 30; in economically undeveloped areas 30; educational levels 30–1; first-time marriages 29; foreign nationals from neighbouring countries 27; involving mainland spouses from China 26; Korean–Chinese citizens 32; lack of demographic statistics 30; mainland China and foreign nationals 26, 31; overseas Chinese and mainland China citizens 27; percentage of total marriages in China 24; PRC females entering intercultural marriages 27–9; PRC males entering intercultural marriages 27–9; registrations outside the PRC 31–2; remarriages 29; rise and fall in numbers of marriages 24; younger PRC mainland women and older foreign males 30
Stories (*Jiangshu*): foreign brides 150; 'Story of a Foreign-Son-in-Law's Marriage Proposal 153–4
street flyers 85
swindlers 72

Taiwan: 16-character guideline for cross-Strait relations 147; 1988 Notice 36, 38–9; 1998 Measures 39; allows business investment with the PRC 139–40; bilateral trade agreement 139–40; categories of compatriots 38–9; categories of marriages 25–6; Civil Code 141; cross-Strait marriage 138–43; cultural differences with China 6; documentation required for marriage registration 38–9, 39, 40; economic powerhouse 143; ethnic Chinese 5–6; expansion of trade with the PRC 30; history 3; intercultural marriages 2; mainland wives 2; marriages to citizens of the PRC 3, 25, 26, 45, 46, 176–7; Martial Law 138–9; negative depictions of mainland brides 143; negative portrayal of Taiwanese men marrying mainland brides 143–4; political and economic autonomy 139; second wife phenomenon 73–4; simplified administrative procedures for Taiwanese citizens in China 41; spouses 26; strained relationship with the PRC 3; tourism with the PRC 140; travel permits to mainland China 139; *see also* ROC (Republic of China)

Taiwan Compatriots Certificates 41

Taizhou Evening News (*Taizhou Wanbao*): economic development of Wenzhou 48

Taizhou Wanbao (*Taizhou Evening News*): decreasing Chinese–foreign marriages 47

Talking With Li Jing (*Feichang Jing Juli*) 161, 170

Tang Ying 76

television: competition and independence 14

television talk shows: celebrity and entertainment 158, 161; celebrity Chinese–foreign marriages 160–1; Chinese–foreign marriage 159, 181; *Common Ground* (*Guoji Shuangxingxian*) 158, 164, 171; *A Date with the Countryside* 160, 165, 168–9; *Extraordinary Husband and Wife* (*Feichang Fuqi*) 161, 162–3, 165, 166, 169, 170–1, 172–3, 173–4; *Family Television Studio* (*Jiating Yanboshi*) 160, 163, 168, 171–2; fluency in Chinese dialects 165; foreign Chinese 161–5; foreign-country pumpkins 165–9, 182; foreign spouses lacking Chinese language skills 166–7; foreign spouses unfamiliar with everyday Chinese culture 167–8; foreign spouses unfamiliar with everyday Chinese life 168–9; format 156; framing foreign spouses 167; *Good Men, Good Women* 158; *Happy Evening Roll Call* 160, 168; love and marriage 158; *Lu Yu You Yue* (*A Date with [host] Lu Yu*) 159–60, 161, 166–7; making marital conflict fun 169–74; *A Match Made in Heaven* 158; *More Talk Makes for Happiness* (*Yue Ce Yue Kaixin*) 160, 164, 165, 167; non-celebrity Chinese–foreign marriages 159, 160; *Oriental Live Studio* (*Dongfang Zhiboshi*) 157; physical conflict 172–3, 174; popularity 157; in the PRC 156–61; proliferation 158–9; *Red Rose State* 158; *Shanghai Dongfang Dianshitai* (*Shanghai Oriental Television*) 157; stereotype of 'fierce' Chinese woman 173; *Talking With Li Jing* 161, 170; *Tell It Like It Is* (*Shihua Shishuo*) 157; *Wenhua Shidian* (*Cultural View*) 157; western format adopted in China 157; *Who Moves Your Heart* 158; *Yingshi Tongqisheng* (*Movie Express*) 157; *Youhua Dajiashuo* (*Let Us Talk*) 157

Tell It Like It Is (*Shihua Shishuo*): format 157

Tewksbury, David: framing theory 15

Thiagarajan, Monica: definition of terms interracial and interethnic 5

Tiananmen Square 55–6, 102

tianmi er langman 58

Tian Weili 153–4, 154

tiaoban 54

Tibet Autonomous Region 30

Times News (*Shidai Xinbao*): couples residing overseas 70–1; *see also Shidai Xinbao*

tongbao: marriages with *guonei gongmin* 36

Torv, Anna 117

traditionalism 9

trafficking 185

transnational marriage (*kuaguo hunyin*): definition 4, 16

transnational migration 103–5

Treaty of Nanjing 3

True Stories (*Zhenqing Shilu*): 'Coded Love Letter' 152; 'A Foreign Wife's

Urban Dream' 151–2, 153; summary 136
Tuchman, G.: frame analysis concept news reporting 15
Turner, Graeme 116; definition of celebrity 90
Tyminski, Stanislaw 106

UNICEF: definition of domestic violence 77
United Kingdom: marriage to Chinese citizens 27
United States of America (USA): marriage to Chinese citizens 26–7

Vietnam: women's marriage to Chinese men 12

waiguoren (foreign nationals): divorce rate 34–5; marriages with *guonei gongmin* 36; marriage to mainland China citizens 26; see also foreign nationals
waiguoren (foreign nationals): definition 3
Wang Hongye 96, 162, 165
Wang Jiali 54–5
Wang Xiaofei 145
wanyan quanzu 38
Weihai: newspaper coverage of intercultural marriage 47
Weihai Daily (*Weihai Ribao*): rationality of decreasing intercultural marriages 48
Weihai Ribao (*Weihai Daily*): decreasing Chinese–foreign marriage 47
Wei Wei 95, 99, 99–100, 105, 106, 112, 113, 125, 126–7, 128
'Wei Wei: A Journey to Love and Happiness' (*Wei Wei: xingfu yougui*) 99
Wendi Deng 108, 117
wenhua jian (intracultural): definition 5, 6
Wenhua Shidian (Cultural View) 157
Wenhui News: hypergamy 56; marriages to partners from different foreign countries 51, 56; seven-year-itch 68; see also 'Chinese–foreign marriage Encounters "Seven-Year-Itch"'
Wenzhou: newspaper coverage of intercultural marriage 47
Wenzhou Dushibao (*Wenzhou Metropolitan News*) 57
Williams, Lucy: domestic violence 80
World Ice Arena 104, 106
Wu Di 134
Wuhan Chenbao (*Wuhan Morning Post*) 122

Wuhan Morning Post (*Wuhan Chenbao*): life of Ning Jing 125–6
Wuhan Ribao (*Wuhan Daily*) 104
Wujin Ribao (*Wujin Daily*) 58–9
Wu Mulan 106
Wu Wei see Kraeuter, Uwe
wuxian aiyi 58

Xiamen: Special Economic Zone 44
Xiangsheng (cross-talk) 175n2
Xiang Yue (*A Date with the Countryside*) 160
Xiao Fan 135
Xiaoshan Yingzhi 95, 112, 114, 115
Xiaoshan Zhili 110, 112, 114–15, 115
Xingfu Wandianming (*Happy Evening Roll Call*) 160
xin jilupian yundong 133
Xintai Television Station 151
Xinwen Lianbo (*China Central News Daily*) 157
xiongjin 52
Xu Liang 171–2
Xu Xiyuan 145

Yangcheng Wanbao (*Yangcheng Evening News*): Chinese–foreign divorce 69
Yang Erche Namu 112, 113, 114; see also Namu
Yang'guangxia de Piaobo:Wo de Yishu yu Hunlian (Life in the Sun: My Art, Love and Marriage) 94
Yang Haili see Haili 136
Yang Jingying 136, 151
Yaogun Qingnian (Rock Kids) 104
Ye Shanghai 92
Yi Aiqing de Mingyi (In the Name of Love) 93
Yi Guanglian 87–8
yiguo yuanyang 52
yijian rugu 58
Yingshi Tongqisheng (Movie Express) 157
Yi Nian You Yi Nian (Year after Year) 92
Yin Li 151
Yinyue Tiandi 99
you aixin 63
Youhua Dajiashuo (Let Us Talk) 157
You Liya 171–2
Yow Cheun Hoe: overseas Chinese (*huaqiao*) 4
Yuanfen (*Predestined Love*) 14, 17; summary 133; see also Predestined Love

Yuanfen Tiankong (*A Match Made in Heaven*) 158
Yuanjia Riben (*Marrying Far Away in Japan*): subject matter 131
Yue Ce Yue Kaixin (*More Talk Makes for Happiness*) 160; see also More Talk Makes for Happiness
Yueliang Moon 122
Yu Mei-Kuei: domestic violence 80
Yu Ziru 171

Zhang Menghan 135
Zhang Mi 112
Zhang Shan 104, 106, 107, 166
Zhang Tielin 103–4, 121, 122
Zhang Wenjie 168
Zhang Wenting 173–4
Zhang Xiaoying 87
Zhang Xin 117
Zhanzheng Ziwuxian 92
Zhejiang: marriage registrations 30
Zhejiang Daily (*Zhejiang Ribao*): 'Dreams Ends in Baghdad' 72; seven-year-itch 68
Zhejiang Ribao (*Zhejiang Daily*): 'Dreams Ends in Baghdad' 54–5
zhencheng 13
Zhenqing Shilu (*True Stories*): summary 136; see also True Stories
Zhiyao Ni Guode Bi Wo Hao (*Wishing You a Better Life Than Me*) 92, 94
Zhongguo faxuehui fan jiabao wangluo (Network Research Centre for Combating Domestic Violence of the China Law Society) 77
Zhongguo Funü bao (*China Women's News*): intercultural marriages in the PRC 48; see also China Women's News
Zhongguo Fushi Bao (*China Fashion Weekly*) 99
Zhongguo gongmin: marriage with *huaqiao* 3–4
Zhongguo gongmin tong waiguoren banli jiehun dengji de jixiang guiding 1983 see August 1983 Rules
Zhongguo Jiankang Yuekan (China Health Monthly) 94
Zhongguo nanren 105
Zhongguo nüxu 105
Zhongguo Shehuibao (*China Society News*): 'Love Connects the World–Intercultural Marriage in Qingdao' 51; see also China Society News
Zhonghua quanguo funü lianhehui (All-China Women's Federation) 77
Zhongmei hunyin jieshaosuo 49
Zhong Shi 145
Zhongwai hunyin (Sino-foreign marriage): definition 4, 16
Zhou Xia 135, 145–6
Zhou Yun 118
Zhu Chen 106, 108
Zhuhai: Special Economic Zone 44

eBooks
from Taylor & Francis

Helping you to choose the right eBooks for your Library

Add to your library's digital collection today with Taylor & Francis eBooks. We have over 50,000 eBooks in the Humanities, Social Sciences, Behavioural Sciences, Built Environment and Law, from leading imprints, including Routledge, Focal Press and Psychology Press.

Choose from a range of subject packages or create your own!

Benefits for you
- Free MARC records
- COUNTER-compliant usage statistics
- Flexible purchase and pricing options
- 70% approx of our eBooks are now DRM-free.

Benefits for your user
- Off-site, anytime access via Athens or referring URL
- Print or copy pages or chapters
- Full content search
- Bookmark, highlight and annotate text
- Access to thousands of pages of quality research at the click of a button.

Free Trials Available

We offer free trials to qualifying academic, corporate and government customers.

eCollections

Choose from 20 different subject eCollections, including:

- Asian Studies
- Economics
- Health Studies
- Law
- Middle East Studies

eFocus

We have 16 cutting-edge interdisciplinary collections, including:

- Development Studies
- The Environment
- Islam
- Korea
- Urban Studies

For more information, pricing enquiries or to order a free trial, please contact your local sales team:

UK/Rest of World: **online.sales@tandf.co.uk**
USA/Canada/Latin America: **e-reference@taylorandfrancis.com**
East/Southeast Asia: **martin.jack@tandf.com.sg**
India: **journalsales@tandfindia.com**

www.tandfebooks.com